T0204807

HAITI –
TODAY AND
TOMORROW

An Interdisciplinary
Study

Edited by

Charles R. Foster
Albert Valdman

**UNIVERSITY
PRESS OF
AMERICA**

LANHAM • NEW YORK • LONDON

CONTRIBUTORS

ERNEST H. PREEG, a career Foreign Service Officer, served as American Ambassador to Haiti from 1981 to 1983. He is the author of two books on trade policy and a monograph on Peruvial-American relations published by the National Planning Association in 1981. He is currently a visiting fellow at the Overseas Development Council.

IRA P. LOWENTHAL is an anthropologist completing his doctorate at The Johns Hopkins University. His dissertation, on which his contribution to this volume is based, is entitled *Culture, Conjugality and Domestic Organization in Rural Haiti.* Over the past six years, he has worked as a consultant on peasant social organization and agriculture for a variety of development agencies operating in Haiti.

GLENN R. SMUCKER is a consultant on economic development currently residing in Haiti.

LEON-FRANÇOIS HOFFMANN is Professor of French at Princeton University. His areas of specialization are French Romantic Literature and Haitian Literature and Culture. He is the author of *Romantique Espagne, La Peste à Barcelone, Répertoire géographique de "La Comédie humaine", Le Nègre romantique, Le Roman haïtien,* and *Essays on Haitian Literature.*

ALBERT VALDMAN is Professor of Linguistics and French & Italian at Indiana University. His areas of specialization include descriptive aspects of Haitian Creole and related educational issues. He is the author of *Basic Course in Haitian Creole, Le Créole: Structure, statut et origine,* and *Haitian Creole-English-French Dictionary.*

ULRICH FLEISCHMANN is Professor of Cultural Science at the Freie Universität Berlin (Federal Republic of Germany). His main areas of specialization are sociology of language and sociology of literature with particular respect to developing societies in West Africa and Latin America (mainly Mexico, Brazil and the Caribbean area). He has done research on Haiti since 1965 and published several books on the literature, on language problems, and on the social development of this country.

JACOMINA P. DE REGT, a rural sociologist with the World Bank, is currently the project officer responsible for operations in the education sector in Haiti. She has worked in the fields of integrated rural development, social impacts of tourism development and planning for forced resettlement due to hydro-electric development.

GERALD F. MURRAY is an Associate Professor of Anthropology at the University of Massachusetts in Boston and a Research Associate at Harvard University's Center for Population Studies. He has done fieldwork in Haiti, the Dominican Republic, and several Central American countries. He was for two years Director of the Agroforestry Project described in this paper.

ROBERT MAGUIRE has worked as Representative to Haiti of the Inter-American Foundation (IAF) since 1979. He is the author of the monograph "Bottom-Up Development in Haiti."

CHRISTIAN A. GIRAULT, a graduate of McGill University, is full-time research fellow at the Centre National de la Recherche Scientifique unit on the campus of Bordeaux-Talence (France). His area of specialization is the economic geography of the Caribbean with particular emphasis on Haiti and the Dominican Republic. He is the author of *Le Commerce du café en Haïti* and is currently preparing the edition of *Atlas d'Haïti*.

MATS LUNDAHL is Associate Professor of Economics at the University of Lund, Sweden. He is a specialist in development economics. His publications include *Peasants and Poverty: A Study of Haiti* and *The Haitian Economy: Man, Land and Markets*.

JAMES L. WALKER is the Program Economist for the U.S. Agency for International Development in Haiti. He is on leave from the University of Nevada-Reno, where he is Associate Professor of Economics and Director of the Bureau of Business and Economic Research. His areas of specialization include economic development, labor economics, and regional development.

JOSEPH GRUNWALD has recently been appointed consultant in Latin American affairs to the Inter-American Institute of San Diego, California. Previously he was Senior Economist of The Brookings Institute.

LESLIE DELATOUR, formerly an economic consultant to the AID commission in Port-au-Prince, is a staff member of the World Bank.

KARL VOLTAIRE is a staff member of the World Bank.

DAVID NICHOLLS is Vicar of Littlemore Vicarage in Oxford, England. He is the author of the standard history of Haiti, *From Dessalines to Duvalier.*

PATRICK BELLEGARDE-SMITH is Associate Professor of International Studies at Bradley University. His areas of research include Caribbean political economy. He is the author of *In the Shadow of Powers: Dantès Bellegarde in Haitian Social Thought.*

MICHAEL S. HOOPER is an attorney and executive director of the New York-based National Coalition for Haitian Refugees.

YVES DAUDET is Professor of Law at the University of Aix-Marseille III (France) and Director of the Institut d'Etudes Politiques. He is also head of the Center for Research on Central America and the Caribbean. Most of his publications deal with the juridical aspects of development.

FRANÇOIS BLANC was professor at INAGHEI of Port-au-Prince in 1982. Master in Law (University of Law and Politics, Aix-en-Provence, France), his thesis (1983) dealt with Administrative Reform in Haiti.

AARON SEGAL is an associate professor of Political Science at University of Texas-El Paso. He is co-author with Brian Weinstein of a handbook on Haiti.

ULI LOCHER is Associate Professor of Sociology at McGill University, specializing in the sociology of migration. His publications deal with the migrations of Haitians, anglophone West Indians and Montreal anglophones. Two recent volumes focus on French-English relations in Quebec. He has been a consultant to various governments and international agencies on questions of migration and development.

ALEX STEPICK is an associate professor of Sociology at Florida International University in Miami. He has written extensively on the rights of Haitian refugees.

CAROLE BEROTTE JOSEPH is a Lecturer in Bilingual Education at the City College of New York. Her areas of specialization include socio-linguistics and related educational issues, curriculum development, and multicultural education. She has lectured extensively throughout the country on the education of Haitian youngsters and needs of parents. Currently, she is Director of the Bilingual English-Haitian Creole Teacher and Parent Training Project at City College.

CHARLES R. FOSTER is adjunct professor of Political Science at George Mason University and formerly held the post of acting chief of Bilingual Education in Higher Education of the United States Department of Education. He is co-author with Albert Valdman of *International Issues in Bilingual Education*.

ACKNOWLEDGEMENTS

Both authors became interested in Haiti many years ago and have made numerous visits to the island. In examining the literature on Haiti over the years we were struck by the lack of interdisicplinary approaches to Haitian studies and by the relative isolation of scholars in various fields.

The essays in this book are by different authors located in various parts of North America and Europe. Many of them were first presented in a meeting of twenty-five specialists in Racine, Wisconsin, co-sponsored by the Indiana University Foundation and the Johnson Foundation. We are grateful to Rita Goodman and Kay Maurer of the Foundation for their hospitality and support. We are also grateful for the encouragement of Sidney Mintz who read the manuscript in whole or in part.

It is difficult to take a number of papers, no matter how excellent, and to make a book out of them. Fortunately, our task has been eased by the willingness of the authors to make extensive revisions of the articles. We have thus been able to provide a design that divides up the book into separate sections.

Editorial assistance was provided by David Slayden, Annette Fromm, and Loretta Wawrzyniak. We also wish to thank Helga Keller for preparation of the index, Helen Hudson of the University Press of America for her ready counsel, and Jeff Puryear of the Ford Foundation which partially underwrote the costs of publication. Without them this volume would not have been produced.

CONTENTS

CONTENTS

INTRODUCTION

ERNEST H. PREEG

Business leaders in Port-au-Prince are fond of referring to Haiti as the best kept secret in the Caribbean. They are alluding principally to the very favorable economic conditions that exist for assembly industry. Over two hundred companies have set up plants in Haiti during the past ten to fifteen years, creating up to 60,000 jobs and placing dollar earnings from industrial sector exports well above those from coffee, the principal traditional export commodity. This favorable and dynamic development contrasts sharply, however, with most reports by the media and the general perceptions of Haiti abroad, which tend to emphasize massive poverty, widespread corruption, political repression, and a feeling of hopelessness about this mountainous, overpopulated country of five to six million people.

The fact is that Haiti is a land of sharp contrasts, and one of the most poorly understood and isolated of societies. Widespread rural poverty coexists with a modern business/banking sector; recently built highways and port facilities are juxtaposed with mountain villages accessible only by foot or donkey; and the immobility of the peasant farmer contrasts with several daily flights between Port-au-Prince and the United States, fully booked in both directions, mostly by Haitians. Haiti has been a pariah among nations throughout most of its existence since winning a bloody independence from France in 1804, initially as a successful slave revolt during a period of colonialism, later as a poverty-stricken nation best known for Voodoo practices and self-serving political leaders. The United States did not official recognize Haiti until 1862, after the southern states had seceded, and the U.S. marine occupation from 1915 to 1934 was

1

justified as a humanitarian mission to bring to the nation order and progress out of chaos and bloodshed. During the past quarter century, the name Duvalier has evoked highly charged and varied emotions, ranging from bitter hatred to adulation, obscuring in the process important differences between the father and son as national leaders.

Haiti is also of considerable importance to the United States. Its location on the eastern shore of the Windward Passage, only forty miles from Cuba, gives it prominence for U.S. security interests in the Caribbean region. U.S. economic interests in Haiti are substantial and should grow steadily. The motivation for Haitians to migrate illegally to the United States in large numbers will continue for years to come even under the most favorable projection for economic and social development within Haiti. The widespread poverty and human suffering which exist in such a close neighbor—and the oldest black republic—have to evoke deep humanitarian concerns in the United States, particularly in the American black community.

President Reagan's Caribbean Basin Initiative (CBI), launched in January 1982, presented an unprecedented opportunity for Haiti to break out of its vicious cycle of economic distress and political isolation. Consequently, the past three years have been the most active period of relations between our two countries in a generation. Discussion of the CBI in the United States, however, has tended to neglect the role of Haiti and has focused rather on the more appealing democratic experiences in Jamaica and the Dominican Republic and, by necessity, on the convulsive problems of Central America. Haiti remains one of the best kept secrets of the Caribbean.

For all these reasons, this volume, consisting of papers given at the Wingspread Conference in Racine, Wisconsin, in September 1982, is most welcome. Little serious research on current conditions in Haiti has appeared in recent years and, as far as I am aware, this was the first international conference on Haiti in at least a decade. The papers provide up-to-date appraisals of a number of key aspects of Haitian society. I might add in passing that the conference itself was a unique opportunity for experts on Haiti from several countries to get together and exchange views, in formal sessions and in private conversation, on virtually all aspects of Haiti and its place in the international community. I was particularly struck by the tendency of participants from such diverse backgrounds to lapse into Haitian Creole during their discussions. The Creole language is a deep cultural bond among all Haitians and students of Haiti.

The volume is appropriately subtitled "interdisciplinary perspectives" and is not intended to provide a comprehensive or definitive assessment of contemporary Haiti. It is rather an important first step in understanding better what the underlying political, economic, and cultural issues are, and a basis for follow-up study and analysis, as pointed out in the final remarks by Foster. For all readers, the papers provide a solid introduction to a wide range of issues affecting Haiti and its future development. We also hope it will kindle a lasting interest in this beguiling country and its people.

As background for the papers that follow, this introductory chapter is divided into three parts: a very brief look at the history and culture of Haiti through the end of the 1970s; a more detailed account of what has been happening within Haiti and in Haitian-American relations during the period 1980-83; and some comments on what might lie ahead.

I

The long Haitian struggle for independence from 1791 to 1804 had a truly heroic dimension, and the oustanding leadership of the revolt—Toussaint-L'Ouverture, Dessalines, Pétion, Christophe—is a continuing source of national pride and identity. After achieving independence, however, the nation's history has been characterized by disappointment and tragedy. Internal turmoil and rebellion were frequent. Governments tended to be autocratic, venal, and transitory. External debts were contracted and repaid at great cost to the country, often within sight of foreign gunboats. Meanwhile, economic development was neglected and the large majority of the population eked out a bare subsistence under harsh conditions. The particularly disruptive period beginning in 1911 set the stage for the landing of U.S. marines in 1915. While the occupation provided relative political tranquility and built up the country's economic infrastructure, it was viewed by most Haitians as a national humiliation. In the face of mounting protest, the marines left peacefully in 1934.

The course of Haitian history is also marked by the political division based on color between the so-called mulatto elite and the large majority of predominantly lower class and peasant blacks. The war for independence was in many respects a three-way struggle between the French, the semi-enfranchised mulattoes, and the black slaves. The color line was never absolute and unity among all Haitians against the French was ultimately achieved. However, the suspicions engendered and the cruelties perpetrated between the two indigenous groups left their lasting mark. During the first century of independence the country was mostly dominated by the mulatto elite, at times by manipulating a pliable black president, but rivalry between the factions continued and, if anything, intensified over time.

This historic class rivalry led to a significant political development during the 1920s and 30s, the emergence of a black nationalist movement stressing

Haiti's African roots and unique cultural identity. Unlike almost all previous leaders of whatever color, these *noiristes* rejected the superiority of European culture and values and viewed the nation's history as a struggle between the European-oriented mulatto elite and the majority of authentic black Haitians. The nationalist movement had its roots in an emerging black middle class of teachers, lawyers, and doctors, many trained in reform programs sponsored by the American occupation. One of the more active, early members was a young medical doctor named François Duvalier.

The mulatto elite, generally supported by the military, nevertheless continued to be in basic control through the mid-1950s, despite attempts by the populist President Dumarsais Estime (1946-50) to change the political balance. Then on September 22, 1957, after ten months of turbulence and violence, François "Papa Doc" Duvalier was elected president, beginning the black populist "Duvalier Revolution" now in its twenty-seventh year.

The fourteen-year rule of Papa Doc has been highly criticized, and there is no question that the nation suffered through a period of brutal political repression and major regression in its economic development. The professional classes fled the country, development projects were neglected or frought with corruption, and a xenophobic nationalism characterized Haitian foreign policy. The United States closed down its economic assistance mission in 1962 and thus, ironically, during the years of the Alliance for Progress, when the United States was making its greatest resource commitment ever to the hemisphere, the poorest country in the region received almost nothing.

But there is another side to the François Duvalier era, namely the major political transformation in the country that he carried out against considerable odds. His objective was to supplant the traditional elite power structure with a black, basically middle class leadership, and he largely succeeded. The military officer corps was one target, and with good reason, based on the numerous plots against him. Duvalier's decisive if brutal suppression of these plots resulted in the creation of a new officer class. The members of the then existing corps, whose senior ranks were filled mainly from elite families, were almost all killed, exiled, or sent into retirement. The corps today is drawn predominantly from middle-class black families who are loyal to the populist objectives of the Duvalier regime. Similarly, Duvalier's longstanding opposition to the influence of the French dominated Catholic church led to confrontation, including temporary excommunication of Duvalier himself, and later reconciliation and victory. The church leadership was indigenized for the first time, its role in the educational system reduced, and its political influence quashed. As for the elite families in the private sector, the record is not so clear. They no longer played a major role in government and were the target of much of the initial violence and extortion by the regime. Many individuals fled the country, but most of the business community stayed and made their peace with the government in the traditional Haitian way of paying appropriate tribute. Duvalier, moreover, needed the support of the business community and in the last years of his presidency encouraged new investment and pursued policies favorable to the private sector.

But whereas François Duvalier brought about a major and probably lasting change in the power structure of the country—the old elite families will never again, so to speak, rule the roost as they had in the past—this change would have served little positive purpose if it were not accompanied by the economic and social reforms proclaimed in the rhetoric of the regime. Opponents were quick to point out that the Papa Doc years simply replaced one corrupt, self-serving elite with another which was even worse. The task of carrying out the economic objectives of the Duvalier Revolution were in fact left to the son, Jean–Claude Duvalier, who was proclaimed president-for-life upon the death of his father in April 1971.

The Jean-Claude presidency, now in its thirteenth year, is not well-known or understood outside of Haiti, in part because the record is mixed and more elusive than that of the father, in part because comparatively little serious study has been devoted to it. Jean–Claude Duvalier is himself a difficult subject to assess. Few observers, in 1971, expected the shy teenager to last out the year, but he has established himself, at a minimum, as an astute political survivor in a country known for its Byzantine power politics. (The Nicholls paper sheds light on factors which play a role in this process.) Unlike his father, Jean-Claude is a private person who shows little outward emotion. He proceeds cautiously in making decisions and is personally alien to the violence that characterized the François Duvalier era. His record in dealing with the country's overwhelming economic and political problems is controversial, although more clear cut in the economic field.

During the 1970s, Jean-Claude Duvalier placed principal emphasis in economic policy on building up the country's infrastructure, with the help of substantial foreign assistance, and on fostering labor intensive manufacturing industry. (This objective met with considerable success as described in the Grunwald paper.) Other areas of the economy, however, registered smaller or no progress. The provision of basic services, such as health and education to the rural poor, which start from an extremely low base, showed only modest gains, and the agricultural sector stagnated. (The mixed record with respect to foreign assistance is elaborated upon in the Walker paper; the papers in Section II address the education sector and several others deal with the problems of the agricultural sector.)

The political situation showed marked improvement during the 1970s compared with that in the Papa Doc era. The security forces were restrained, particularly with respect to acts of violence, and by 1978 all known political prisoners had been released. A number of able, younger technocrats were brought into the government and efforts were made toward conciliation with the mulatto business community. Toward the end of the decade, fledgling opposition parties were permitted to form and restrictions on the media were relaxed.

Overall, in fact, there was widespread hope in early 1980 that both the economic and political climates were improving under Jean–Claude Duvalier and that this trend would continue. The economy had been growing at a 4 to 5 percent rate per year since the mid-1970s and political liberalization was helping the regime's international image. 1980 turned out, however, to be a year of setbacks and disappointment. The national economy suffered from two external shocks: the second oil crisis and Hurricane Allen which devastated the coffee crop. The government, meanwhile, instead of tightening its fiscal control, went on a spending spree, which included several ill-advised investment projects and a rise in the unbudgeted palace accounts, with the predictable result of a serious financial crisis. Projects financed by foreign aid also fared poorly, and the USAID program in Haiti came under severe congressional fire. Finally, political liberalization came to an abrupt halt in November with a government crackdown that resulted in over fifty people being arrested and another twenty exiled.

Under other circumstances, such disappointing developments might have induced the international community, and the United States in particular, to withdraw somewhat and keep at arms length from a Duvalier regime that has never been popular abroad. Ignoring Haiti has always been politically convenient in Washington. 1981 was different, however, for two reasons. The first was the "boat people" phenomenon, in which large numbers of poor, mostly illiterate, Haitians migrated illegally to southern Florida via boat. The plight of the boat people not only catapulted Haiti's agonizing poverty to the front page and the evening TV screens but also created a major domestic problem in Florida with respect to job displacement and higher costs for social programs to care for the Haitians. The second was President Reagan's Caribbean Basin Initiative which placed top priority on improved economic performance in the entire region. Although Haiti was not a motivating factor for the initiative, it was, perforce, as the poorest and one of the most populous countries in the region, to be an important participant. And so the problems of Haiti and the interests of the United States coincided and a period of unusually active and, in many respects, productive collaboration between the two countries ensued.

Before proceeding to the most recent period, two comments are in order with respect to Haitian national culture which impose limitations on the possibilities for economic, social, and political change. The first is that Haiti remains a predominantly rural, peasant society. Over seventy percent of the people still live in the countryside, mostly on small farms. Their traditional culture provides for social stability and engenders admirable personal qualities. The culture is rich in terms of language, religion, and art forms. But this can also present formidable barriers to change and modernization. The tendency in approaching Haiti is to think that one must deal with a relatively few government officials who wield political power and a growing, but still small, business community, almost all of whom reside in Port-au-Prince. Coming to grips with Haitian poverty, however, really means dealing with three to four million peasants who live in thousands of hamlets, usually situated in rugged terrain, and who are deeply committed to continuing life as it has been lived for generations. (Several of the papers in Section I and elsewhere deal with various aspects of this theme.)

The second and related comment is that this dominant traditional culture is in the process of weakening and in some respects perhaps breaking down. Whereas the urban population was less than ten percent of the total a generation ago, it is now almost thirty percent and will continue to grow with the steady rural/urban migration. Roads and schools built in the countryside bring mobility and exposure to modern life. The peasant, once arrived in the city and if fortunate enough to find a job, rapidly adjusts to the discipline of the time clock and the gratification of the weekly pay check. The drive to educate children so that they may move up the economic and social ladder is especially strong among the urban lower-middle class and poor. While the rural peasant will likely remain basically apolitical, the same may not hold true for the urban factory worker, not to mention the growing number of clerks, technicians, teachers, and other professionals.

One of the most difficult questions in regard to Haiti concerns the political attitudes of the peasants and the urban poor after a quarter century of Duvalier government. They remain cynical, are wary of any government, and expect little good from it. This has always been the case in Haiti and not much has changed under the current regime. However, twenty-six years of official black nationalist rhetoric and ceremony extolling the peasant and his role in society has had its inevitable impact. As one missionary who has lived four decades in Haiti explained: "Before Duvalier, the peasant felt himself a piece of property; now he considers himself a citizen." This change in attitude is undoubtedly being reinforced by the process of modernization within the country. The mass of poor Haitians, in the cities as well as in the countryside, is a gradually waking force with which any future government will have to contend.

II

In early 1981, concern about developments in Haiti were expressed in the U.S. Congress through an amendment to the Foreign Assistance Act, sponsored by Congressman Dan Mica of Florida. A product of consultation between the Congressional Black Caucus and the Florida delegation, the Mica amendment stipulated that all aid to Haiti was conditional on the full cooperation of the Government of Haiti to stop illegal migration, improved aid project performance and a satisfactory record on human rights. If these conditions were met, it was the sense of the Congress that economic aid to Haiti should be increased by up to $5 million above the existing annual level of about $30 million.

The content of the Mica amendment was very much in keeping with the general approach of the new Reagan administration to the Duvalier government. The emerging CBI would offer increased benefits for Haiti, but only if the serious problems that had developed during 1980 were dealt with effectively. President Duvalier, in turn, was receptive; he needed the support of the United States, especially under the difficult prevailing circumstances, and understood the opportunity presented by the new administration in Washington. The period 1981-1983 thus became directed toward resolving the immediate problems and building a stronger framework for cooperation over the longer term. There were four principal, interrelated areas of concern: illegal migration, financial stabilization, improved aid project performance, and human rights/liberalization.

Illegal migration. Although Haitian migration to various parts of the Caribbean basin had been going on for decades, the large exodus by boat to Florida only became prominent in the later 1970s. After early successful amateur voyages, professional traffickers moved in, charging up to $2,000 per head. It was a dangerous trip and we will never know how many died at sea, but by mid-1981, some 1,500 Haitians per month were landing on the south Florida beaches. Although the vast majority were seeking a better economic life, our judicial system was at an impasse as to whether these Haitians qualified as political refugees with a right to remain in the country, and so any Haitian, once arrived, was pretty sure of staying indefinitely.

In keeping with the Reagan policy of bringing illegal migration under control, negotiations began with the Haitian government that resulted in the so-called interdiction agreement of September 1981. The agreement permits the U.S. Coast Guard in international waters to board suspect vessels and return to Haiti those aboard believed to be intending illegal migrants. The Haitian government undertook not to persecute or harass such migrants returned, and subsequent interviews by embassy officers confirmed that this commitment was being honored. The small patrol craft of the Haitian navy carried out coordinated coastal and harbor surveillance.

The interdiction program has been almost entirely successful in stopping the boat people trafficking. The deterrent effect of the Coast Guard presence caused traffickers to shut down or switch to other, non-human cargo. The total number of Haitians apprehended entering Florida illegally dropped from 8,069 in 1981 to 134 in 1982. The immediate objective of stopping illegal migration had thus been accomplished.

This does not mean, however, that the pressures to migrate from Haiti or legal and adjustment problems in the United States have waned. (The papers in Section V treat some of these issues.) The detention of almost 2,000 Haitians already in the United States in late 1981-82 was a highly charged issue domestically as well as in our bilateral relations until the courts ordered their release in late 1982. The Coast Guard is still stationed in the Windward Passage with no end to their mission in sight. Shutting down the boat people trade resulted in a doubling of the number of Haitians seeking a tourist visa at the American consulate in Port-au-Prince. Some 300 line up each morning, many with fraudulent documents or other illegal intent.

The fundamental motivation for migration, recognized by both governments, is to seek a better life than the one which now exists in Haiti. The longer-term solution is to work together to improve the economic, social, and political conditions in Haiti.

Financial stabilization. By mid-1981, the financial situation in Haiti was precarious and the government was losing credibility in its management of public finance. International reserves were exhausted, the budget deficit was up to six percent of GDP, inflation rose above ten percent, and the national currency, the gourde, which had been stable at 5:1 with the dollar since 1919, was being discounted at 10 to 15 percent. A forceful financial stabilization program was called for, and in a speech on August 8, 1981, President Duvalier announced such a program that included fiscal reforms, budget cuts, and a new standby agreement with the IMF. The program got off to a slow start, however, and it was not until February 1982, with the appointment of a new economic team headed by the distinguished World Bank economist Marc Bazin as financial minister, that the implementation really got underway. A tough IMF agreement was negotiated in April 1982 which was to run through September 1983. It included a 20 percent cut in government spending, increased revenues from customs, a new value-added tax, and more credit for the private sector. The IMF would, in turn, provide $38 million of credit to pay for essential imports. Performance during the first months was promising.

Bazin, however, pressed ahead on the reform program with unaccustomed vigor, stepping on political toes, and his personal popularity made him a political threat in the eyes of some supporters of the government. Bazin was replaced in early July, raising widespread skepticism in the international community that the stabilization program would, in fact, not be pursued. Bazin's successor as finance minister, Franz Merceron, with the backing of the president, nevertheless did follow through, and all IMF targets were met or exceeded during the seventeen-month program. By late 1983, the budget deficit was down to one percent of GDP, the discount on the gourde was five percent or less, inflation had abated, more credit was available to the private sector, and progress had been made on longer-term fiscal reforms.

In the summer of 1983, a new two-year agreement with the IMF was negotiated and adopted by the IMF Board in November. It calls for continued austerity and further steps at fiscal reform. Much skepticism remains as to whether the Haitian government will continue the fiscal reform process which runs counter to national tradition, wherein public finance is run like a family store for the benefit of the occupants and friends of the palace. But Haiti currently is in the good graces of the IMF and is one of the few countries in Latin America not burdened by large budget deficits, an excessive foreign debt, and runaway inflation.

Improved aid performance. The USAID program in Haiti, resumed in the mid-70s, ran into problems of weak counterpart support from the government, traditional practices of favoritism and corruption, and overambitious project design. This led to some very frank "development dialogue" in 1981 with the Haitian government on how to improve performance and gain support for an expanded program. The results were, overall, encouraging.

Half of our aid program in Haiti is through private voluntary organizations (PVOs) and other non-governmental entities. Some 300,000 children, or one half those in school in Haiti, receive a daily lunch—thanks to the PL-480 Title II food aid program administered by various PVOs. Many other projects are underway and increased emphasis has been given to the non-governmental sector since 1981. A highly successful new initiative is a reforestation project to stem soil erosion for peasant farmers. (See the Murray paper; a smaller, people-to-people project is recounted in the Maguire paper.) A noteworthy private sector initiative was the creation of a medium-term investment bank, the Development Finance Corporation, for which members of the business community put up one million dollars of equity capital in order to gain five million dollars of AID support. A Peace Corps program was established for the first time in Haiti in 1982, providing sorely needed people-to-people technical support, particularly in rural areas.

Aid projects with the Haitian government are generally more complicated to operate and receive the closest scrutiny. A couple of small non-performers were shut down in 1981. Of the three large USAID projects, two—a secondary roads project using labor intensive construction methods and the creation of a rural health delivery system—were basically sound and their implementation was strengthened further. The third, in agriculture, was not producing intended results and was scaled back considerably. The agriculture ministry, in fact, has long been the most difficult to deal with, and painstaking consultation led to a new start which could result in a multi-year program in the agricultural sector under PL-480 Title III, whereby the Haitian government would undertake policy changes to improve incentives for private farmers and would provide increased resources and qualified personnel for field projects. The opening of talks on a Title III agreement was announced during a visit to Haiti by Assistant Secretary of State Thomas Enders in January 1983, and negotiations are well advanced as of early 1984.

The fact that aid programs in Haiti have improved and are showing credible results gradually has been getting through to the donor community. U.S. aid increased from about $30 million in FY 81 to some $45 million in FY 84. While substantial, this is still considerably less than the doubling to tripling of aid levels that has resulted in other countries in the Caribbean basin. The World Bank has also been stepping up its program in Haiti.

Human rights/liberalization. This is the most highly charged and controversial area of Haiti's relations with the United States. The Haitian government has made efforts to reduce human rights violations and to implement a program of gradual "democratization," but critics are far from satisfied with the results thus far. All those arrested in November 1980 were released by September 1982, but the most outspoken oppositionist, Sylvio Claude, was subsequently harassed and rearrested for two months in late 1983. Relatively few people are in prison on political charges, the number ranging from about ten to forty over the past few years, and prison conditions were considered reasonably satisfactory during inspections by the International Red Cross and the U.N. Human Rights Commission. Justice is still often arbitrary, however, illegal detention for weeks or months without formal charges is frequent, and beatings by police occur. An underlying problem is the absence of visible or effective checks on the activities of security and law enforcement officials.

The democratization process, abruptly halted in November 1980, was resumed in 1983 with the holding of the first municipal elections in more than twenty-five years. Although there were many charges of voting irregularities, the elections were largely open contests between competing candidates, with almost no violence. Independent slates of candidates were elected in a number of places, including the second and third largest cities after Port-au-Prince. Followers of Sylvio Claude were not, however, permitted to contest in the capital, and several were arrested. More important National Assembly elections were held in February 1984, with an outcome similar to that of the municipal elections. A large number of candidates competed openly and the majority of incumbents were defeated, but the censure of strongly independent or oppositionist candidates was more pronounced; the few clearly identified as such were harassed or not permitted to win.

The overall political situation in Haiti is thus mixed. The government remains authoritarian and no oppositionist political forces currently operate in the country. At the same time, there is a relatively low frequency of violence and politically motivated arrests, and modest steps toward greater participation in the political process have been taken. The government has indicated that further progress will be made, particularly with respect to judicial process and media liberalization, but it is not yet clear how extensive such changes will be. In this context, the Hooper paper on the human rights situation in Haiti needs to be read in perspective. Michael Hooper is an unyielding advocate for human rights, and, in my view, his paper constitutes strong advocacy rather than a balanced presentation. I suggest it be read together with the annual human rights reports on Haiti released by the State Department in recent years.

III

What are the future prospects for Haiti? There are two central, interrelated questions: one economic, the other political. The economic question is whether Haiti, despite its poverty and lack of natural resources, can aspire to a development path of high, sustained growth which, in the process, will modernize the economic structure of the country. Subject to two important caveats, I believe that such an outcome is clearly feasible. Jean–Claude Duvalier showed foresight in emphasizing the economic infrastructure program in the mid-1970s and is now in position, thanks to CBI trade preferences and recovery in the American economy, to capitalize on new export opportunities through rapid expansion of labor intensive manufactured exports. Haiti has a dynamic, sophisticated business community and a hardworking, easily trained and low wage labor force. The agricultural sector is far more problematic, but sharply increased yields for most crops are technically feasible and the export potential for agroindustry is vast.

The caveats on the economic side are, first, that the government of Haiti follow through on its intended fiscal and other reforms and, second, that the international community, in response, provide the requisite assistance over the next several years. The fiscal reform program is essential, not only to generate needed financial resources for development programs, but to build public confidence in government, to convince the taxpayer that, contrary to tradition, public revenues are collected in a more equitable way and serve the public good rather than the private interests of the powers that be. Other reforms concern changes in policy, principally with respect to agriculture and trade, and basic administrative reform, as contained in a new law of 1983, which would create a career civil service for the first time in Haiti.

If such reforms move ahead at a reasonable pace, it is incumbent upon the international community to be responsive with needed financial resources and technical assistance in order for Haiti to make the transition from a "least developed" to a "newly industrialized" country. Haiti, in this respect, could epitomize the development model envisaged in the CBI. But successful implementation of the current IMF program will squeeze available government resources and require substantial cutback in projected programs. Under these circumstances, a good case can be made for an increased commitment by the international community during the next few critical years.

The political question is whether Haiti can make a peaceful and non-disruptive transition from the pattern of autocratic rule and exploitation that has prevailed since independence and develop into a more open, just, and democratic society. Views vary widely not only with respect to the whether but to the how of this question. President Jean-Claude Duvalier has reduced human rights violations in recent years and has taken a few modest steps in his process of "gradual democratization." Others, including the United States government, are pressing a faster pace of political change within Haiti and, at Congressional initiative, an amendment to the aid legislation, signed into law in December 1983, made all economic assistance from the United States subject to the condition that the government of Haiti "is making a concerted and significant effort to improve the human rights situation in Haiti by implementing the political reforms which are essential to the development of democracy in Haiti, including the establishment of political parties, free elections, and freedom of the press."[1]

The economic and political prospects are of course related: political oppression tends to stultify economic initiative while the forces of economic modernization, already well underway in certain sectors of Haitian society, will inevitably clash with the traditional autocratic ways of government. Indeed, it is quite likely that Haiti is entering one of the most unsettling periods of political, social, and economic change in its history.

The United States and Haiti have been friends and neighbors since we emerged as the first two independent nations in the Western hemisphere.

The relationship has not always been an easy one. It seldom is between close neighbors, particularly when there are such great differences in national culture, historical experience, and political institutions. Haiti is now going through a difficult period of change and we, as the large and richly endowed neighbor, need to be responsive as a good neighbor. The question is how best to respond. As explicit in the Garcia amendment, we are currently involved in the political process within Haiti, using economic aid as potent leverage. Under such circumstances, we need maximum understanding and communication at all levels, between governments and peoples. I always considered this to be a central purpose of my tour in Port-au-Prince. The papers assembled here, expressing a wide range of views on a number of key aspects of Haiti and its relationship with the United States, should further this process of mutual understanding.

NOTE

[1]This revision of the earlier Mica amendment was introduced by Congressman Robert Garcia of New York. Since no aid authorization bill was passed for FY 1983, this amendment was included in another piece of legislation. The other conditions of the Mica amendment dealing with illegal migration and aid project implementation were retained.

LABOR, SEXUALITY AND THE
CONJUGAL CONTRACT IN RURAL HAITI[1]

IRA P. LOWENTHAL

One of the most striking features of Caribbean domestic organization generally is the apparent variety of arrangements through which mating, parenting, and householding are accomplished. This diversity is not simply a matter of class differentiation or regional variation. A full range of organizational alternatives seems to exist within almost every community, even though each alternative may be practiced in different proportions from one community to the next in correlation with such variables as class and occupational structure, local religious influence, or demographic factors. Further complicating the picture is the fact that any individual's choices among these alternative modes of organizing their lives with respect to mating, parenting, and householding are not necessarily either exclusive or permanently binding.

In rural Haiti, for example, men may simultaneously marry, maintain a consensual wife in a second household, and conduct one or more relatively stable extra-residential affairs. Women, although formally enjoined to monogamy, may nonetheless enter several different kinds of union in succession, either with the same mate, or with a number of different partners. Children, in their turn, may thus be born to a married couple, to a married man by another woman, to a couple in a consensual union, to a mother not in union with any man, and so forth, with potential implications for their civil and social status. They may reside with both parents, with either parent alone, with either parent together with a step-parent, with maternal or paternal relatives or, in a significant number of cases, with no blood relatives at all.

15

Rural Haitian households themselves are not fixed units, either in terms of their personnel or their internal organization. Adults as well as children change residential affiliation with relative frequency, and are able to activate at least temporary residential rights along a number of different lines of relationship. Households may be headed by either men or women, and female-headed households are not at all necessarily characterized by the absence of a male mate.

Faced with this kind of intra-community diversity, much thinking about Caribbean domestic life has been dominated by efforts to typologize and to order this apparent confusion—to develop or to elicit models that "make sense" of this proliferation of mating alternatives, child-rearing arrangements and household forms, and their seemingly endless possible permutations.[2]

For the Haitian case, some of the organizational and formal distinctions that have received considerable attention include, for example, those that differentiate between *maryaj* (religiously sanctioned marriage recognized by the State) and *plasaj* (consensual union), or between monogamy and polygyny, or between male- and female-headed households or, finally, between independent, nuclear-family residential units and the patriarchal *lakou* (compound).[3] A more recent typology of *sexual* union types in Haiti is even more ambitious, with no fewer than five kinds of union identified and defined (Allman 1980).[4]

Such typological exercises undeniably have some significant role to play in any analysis of Haitian peasant domestic organization. When imposed on an unruly reality by the researcher, they at least lend some analytic order to what would otherwise be undecipherable data. When derived from people's own systems of categorization and terminology, they are themselves one kind of data concerning the organization of domestic life. Unfortunately, such formal typologies, whatever their source, tend to overwhelm subsequent analysis and are often taken to have substantive implications as well. That is, once typologies have been established, analysis proceeds *from* them, precluding interpretive approaches that might be based upon the *content,* as opposed to the *form* of central social relationships, such as those between a husband and a wife, or a parent and a child, or between two household members.

*   *   *   *   *

A Haitian adolescent refers to his father, who never lived with his mother, let alone with him, and whom he has not seen for more than a decade, as "a better father than most." An older man, in two long-standing and fruitful unions with two women, is said to be "a better husband" to his *plase* (consensual) wife than to his church-wedded wife. Another man contends that "marriage is the union between a man and a woman ... without union, marriage is nothing." This sentiment is echoed and enhanced in the common peasant aphorism, often cited by *both* men and women alike, which holds that "a good *plasaj* is better than a bad marriage."

All of this, from the mouths of peasants themselves, is telling us something. The message, I think, is that there is something more basic going on here—something that typologies based on formal or organizational criteria may fail to capture. Of course, different modes of publicly marking union formation, or different ways of organizing parenthood with respect to residence, may be more or less desirable under particular individual circumstances. Moreover, some single form of union, or some specific residential arrangement, may carry greater prestige in the eyes of one's fellows. Yet there are potentially many more—perhaps non-formal—criteria available for the classification of these primary relationships by those who participate in them, and for the public evaluation of the ways in which they are carried out by others, particularly in small, face-to-face community settings. Indeed, the very extent to which the specifically formal features of relationships are taken to be central to the relationship's character and successful fulfillment is likely to vary, not only from individual to individual, but between communities within a single society and, finally, cross-culturally.

Without denying the importance of such distinctions as that between *maryaj* and *plasaj,* particularly from the point of view of the peasants' own prestige system, I want to suggest that what we need to be looking at first, *before* we begin classifying things according to their different forms, are the most basic features of primary relationships, such as those between spouses, or between parents and children. Is it not possible that in Haitian rural society, at least, the normative system pertaining to primary social relationships may have more to do with the substance of the relationship itself than with the form in which it is realized?

*   *   *   *   *

The remainder of this paper focuses briefly on male/female relationships in rural Haiti,[5] and tries to characterize Haitian peasant conjugality, or the relationship system between spouses, in substantive rather than in formal terms. It takes as its starting point some of the peasants' own fundamental conceptions concerning such matters as maleness, femaleness, labor and sexuality—all of which provide the backdrop against which conjugality, a *particular* kind of relationship between a man and a woman, takes on its characteristic shape and significance.

The two most important domains, broadly conceived, within which all rural Haitian men and women confront each other as men and women—relating to each other in ways essentially *determined,* in terms of their own cultural understandings, by the fact of their maleness and femaleness—are (1) the gender-based division of labor, and (2) sexuality itself. While both of these domains presuppose some kind of relationship for their enactment, any number of kinds of relationship will do. I understand Haitian peasant conjugality to be one quite specific way of realizing and integrating the more general possibilities of male/female complementarity inherent in these culturally-ordered domains.[6] In devoting a considerable amount of attention to the general features of these two domains, therefore, I hope to set the stage of a substantive understanding of rural Haitian conjugality.

THE GENDER-BASED DIVISION OF LABOR

Perhaps the most well-known and certainly one of the most frequently cited "facts" about the differences between men and women in rural Haiti is that men are primarily involved in agriculture, while women are almost exclusively charged with marketing. Like most broad generalizations, this one begins with a grain of truth but runs the risk of oversimplifying a complex situation.

Agriculture is definitely *seen* as a male domain by peasants themselves. When the labor of adolescent or adult men is available, either within the household or on the basis of extra-household ties, it is men who "make gardens." Moreover, agricultural knowledge and decision-making are, for the most part, also seen to be in the hands of men whenever a competent man is an active member of the household productive unit. In spite of important contributions made by both women and children in terms of specialized labor at particular points in the agricultural cycle of the majority of basic food crops (both sowing and harvesting depend heavily on female and child labor), food production is conceived of by peasants themselves as quintessentially a male activity. Thus, *"gason fè jaden"* (men make gardens).[7]

By and large, however, men make gardens for someone and that someone is invariably a woman. Most commonly, though not exclusively, she is a socially recognized spouse of the man. The control of produce, then, as opposed to production itself, falls to women—as men's gardens mature. Piecemeal domestic consumption from standing gardens is usually controlled and determined by women. In the case of major grain and bean crops, however, produce is finally harvested, bulked and stored. At this point, staple crops cease to be simply "food." Measured and in hand, they also represent a calculable cash equivalent at prevailing internal market prices. There is a certain ambiguity in control of the crop at this stage, but a man who "lives well" (*viv byen*) with the women in his life will generally leave the details of the disposition of the harvest to this mate.

The autonomy of women in this connection is more apparent than real since they are generally charged with meeting the bulk of domestic expenditures from the cash fund generated by the sale of produce. This is where the role of women as marketers is both most obvious and most widespread. Virtually all rural women responsible for the running of a household must engage in economic transactions of the following type on a regular basis: they sell household produce and purchase household necessities—they *fè provizyon*. They manage, on a day-to-day basis, the entire domestic economy.[8]

This universal provision marketing on the part of rural women, however, should not be confused with profit-oriented commercial involvement in the internal marketing system or related trade networks. While most women in the area I studies have had some experience in commercial marketing activities of one kind or another, and many among them periodically enter the commercial sector to take advantage of opportunities as they arise, relatively few support a functioning household economy entirely through marketing (IICA 1974). This does not at all undercut the fact that almost all women do have the requisite basic skills, if not the capital or time, to be *potentially* successful in commercial activities—right to the point of economic independence. Thus, while it is hardly true that all women are commercial marketwomen, virtually all women do market, and any woman may become a marketwoman when necessity requires or opportunity allows. This potential independence in the economic sphere significantly shapes both male and female conceptions of womanhood in rural Haiti. The mere possibility of autonomy for women, in precisely that sphere where they are most commonly dependent upon men—economics—greatly enhances a woman's maneuverability in the conduct of her conjugal career.[9]

By way of contrast, the essential *dependence* of men on women's domestic labor is an obvious, if infrequently stressed, aspect of labor complementarity. There are a whole range of tasks that adult men simply should not perform (*gason pa fèt pou fè yo*), but upon whose performance the successful maintenance of any household—and the satisfaction of any individual's personal needs—depends.[10] It is not so much that men must not, or cannot, perform women's work (*travay fanm*), but that to do so compromises their dignity as men. It is something to be ashamed of (*ou do ront sa*), and it invites ridicule from others, both women and men (*y'ap pase-ou nan betiz pou sa*). In the day-to-day course of things, then, domestic labor is overwhelmingly the responsibility of women and, through them, may be delegated in part to children of either sex. When men cry out, as they sometimes do—especially when actually faced with the unsavory prospect—that they "can't live without a woman" (*m pa ka viv san fanm*), it is to these basic domestic services provided by women that they primarily refer.

Indeed, over and above her actual participation in terms of agricultural labor, a woman is understood to help a man to work (*li ede l travay*), and even to work together with him (*yo travay ansanm*)—precisely in terms of her domestic contributions to their common household and/or to his personal comforts. While men, at least, do not widely tout their dependence on women in this sense, the economic value of women's domestic labor is formally recognized and codified in customary local principles of conjugal property rights.[11] Nonetheless, when separation of a couple and the subsequent separation of their common property are *not* at issue—that is, in the normal course of everyday life—there is another domain of male-female complementarity whose organization and ideology, in effect, both skews and overshadows the process of material cooperation *per se*. This domain is that of sexuality itself.

SEXUALITY

Like the gender-based division of labor, sexuality is a realm of activity that is far broader, in some very real sense, than conjugality, but whose practice and code provide a ground against which the particular relationship between spouses may be more clearly perceived. There are also some significant differences between these two domains of gender complementarity.

Labor cooperation between men and women is not strictly limited to the conjugal pair. Similar arrangements may exist between brother and sister, mother and son, and even father and daughter, and these may become important under particular individual circumstances. These other arrangements, however, are somehow *ad hoc* and ephemeral, based on the good graces and availability of close kinsmen willing and able to help out. The satisfactory management of cross-sex labor cooperation, in fact, appears to be integrally related to the existence of an on-going and at least prospectively long-term relationship, explicitly built around this kind of complementarity.

On the other hand, the satisfactory transaction of *sexual* relations as such does not necessarily implicate the partners in an enduring relationship. The norms of reciprocity governing sexual interaction *per se* allow for the relatively immediate gratification of both parties and do not depend for their fulfillment either on long-term processes such as the maturation of crops, or on a series of on-going prestations such as the daily provision of domestic comforts. Sexual relations can be short-lived affairs and may be accomplished quite adequately by single men and women. Indeed, it is the mated individual who is likely to face difficulties in this sphere, restricted by both circumstance and convention from casting the net of sexual involvement as widely as might sometimes be desired.[12] The peasants' basic notions concerning sexual interaction, then, seem to be grounded outside of conjugality, and connubial bliss is itself but one variant within a much broader range of potentially satisfying encounters.

Furthermore, whereas people's ideas about the gender-based division of labor are fairly straightforward and are operative in almost any social context, sexuality and sexual relations are interpreted by people according to two quite distinct and competing sets of propositions. In the area I studied, there is what might best be called a "public" ideology of sexuality, and this is counterposed to a "private" ideology. Men and women agree on the fundamentals of both but, in cross-sex interactions, generally proceed on the basis of the public ideology. The private ideology of sexuality, on the other hand, rarely forms the basis of any kind of cross-sex interaction and is revealed primarily in contexts that are gender-homogenous.

Public and private ideology differ in the way they portray female sexuality. Public ideology is based on a core fiction about women's sexuality. This fiction is consciously and conscientiously maintained, *by women themselves,* for strategic purposes. By publicly projecting an image of their own sexuality that is at variance with their actual experience and attitudes women establish the basic ground rules for sexual interaction. Just why they should be concerned to do so will become clear shortly.

Unlike female sexuality, male sexuality is unambiguously portrayed in both public and private spheres: *Gson se chen* (Men are dogs), a popular aphorism avers and, like dogs, men are held by both men and women alike to be willing to drop almost anything for the sake of an agreeable sexual partner. The case is, of course, overstated here in the form of a simple cliche, yet the fact remains that men openly evince a strong and relatively constant desire for sex. Moreover, men plainly enjoy sex. It is both a "pleasure" (*plezi*) and a "party" (*banbòch*) for them. Finally, men are held to *need* sex, if not quite as frequently as they seem to desire it.

For women, as they themselves tell it, having sex is a lot of work and is sometimes referred to as such. Each sexual act is tiring and fraught with minor physical dangers, such as a sore lower back (*tay fè mal*), or the more serious chronic lower back and internal disorder (*tay ouvè*). Public ideology, then, has it that women neither enjoy nor desire sex as such and, as noted above, it is women themselves who support and maintain this image of their own sexuality.

Men's suspicions that women simply "don't want to *show* that they like it" are confirmed by women themselves, when they can be persuaded to talk about their intimate behavior and experiences. Women among themselves attest eloquently to their own desires and describe the actual experience of intercourse in glowing terms.[13] They generally refuse to share this perception openly with men, for to do so would be both "a waste" (*yon gaspiyay*) and an act of "frivolity" (*pa serye*).

Another aphorism solves the riddle of what they mean by this: *Chak fanm fèt ak yon kawo tè—nan mitan janm-ni* (Every woman is born with a *kawo* of land—between her legs). Female sexuality is here revealed to be a woman's most important *economic* resource, comparable in terms of its value to a relatively large tract of land. Indeed, when discussing their relations with men, adult women are likely to refer to their own genitals as *interè-m* (my assets), *lajan-m* (my money), or *manmanlajan-m* (my capital), in addition to *tè-m* (my land). The underlying notion here is of a resource that can be made to work to produce wealth, like land or capital, or that can be exchanged for desired goods and services, like money.

In any event, female sexuality is indeed exchanged—directly and explicitly—for the things men can provide, including gifts of cash or produce and, in a longer term relationship, labor. Under *no* circumstances is sexual gratification in itself considered just recompense to a woman for her sexual services. After all, sex is work for women, not fun. Even the suggestion of an exchange of *dous pou dous,* or sweetness for sweetness—though sometimes made by a plucky yet obviously desperate man—is laughable.

It is in this sense that the public ideology of female sexuality may best be thought of as a codified bargaining position or strategy, knowingly recreated, sustained, and manipulated by women themselves.[14] Having what men want and claiming not to want what men have, at least sexually, puts women at a distinct advantage. Men know this, as I have stressed, but are unable to do much about it, for women are essentially unyielding on this point and it is they who must be approached for satisfaction in these matters.

Thus, sexual encounters are never "simply" sexual—or at least never *should* be. Rather, they are appropriately and quite explicitly linked with the productive activities of men. Each individual woman manages her own sexuality in these terms, and understands sexual relations generally as one important arena in which any woman's material interests may be legitimately and successfully pursued.[15]

Men are not simply passive in relation to a system of sexual reciprocity whose basic terms are, in effect, dictated by women. The rules of the game once established, play may proceed along a number of different lines.

Men's strategies aim at decreasing the actual material cost of their sexual liaisons and/or increasing their potential access to a wide number of partners.

Although limitations of space make it impossible to describe either male or female sexual strategies in any great detail, it should be clear that sexuality in rural Haiti is a field of real competition between men and women. In this way it differs quite sharply from the field of labor complementarity which is characterized, as we have seen, by cooperation and consensus. Moreover, the fundamental logic of sexuality, at least in the area I studied, centers on the particular form of competition and reciprocity that has been outlined here, explicitly linking female sexuality to male economic prestations. When a peasant woman grasps her genitals in both hands—in a gesture not uncommon in public disputes with a man—and asks defiantly *"Pouki sa m gen sa?"* (Why do I have this?), men and women know precisely why she has "this." Their shared understanding colors much of the interaction between men and women in all spheres, including that of conjugality proper, to whose consideration we now turn.

THE CONJUGAL CONTRACT

Haitian peasant conjugality both proceeds from and transcends these two most basic modes of interconnection between men and women. The conjugal relationship in rural Haiti—and by this I mean any conjugal relationship—may best be understood as an effective contractual arrangement between a man and a woman that pertains directly and quite explicitly to both their sexual and their labor relations. This conjugal contract simultaneously transforms the tenor of their sexual relations and initiates the full range of their labor relations, vis-a-vis each other. The remainder of this paper will be devoted to demonstrating that these contentions are not simply heuristic, but that they correspond directly to people's own fundamental conceptions concerning the nature of union.

The salience of the idea that conjugality is both contractual and an exchange is most clearly demonstrated in the way that people talk about and actually accomplish union formation—that point in a relationship when the conjugal bargain is actually struck. "To be in union" is *fè afè* (lit.: to make an arrangement/to make a deal), and this term applies equally well to both conjugal alternatives, *maryaj* and *plasaj*. Moreover, *fè afè*, along with both *fè kondisyon* (to set conditions) and *antann-yo* (to come to an understanding) all refer more specifically to the act of forming a union. When union formation is referred to, then, it is invariably described in terms that evoke an arrangement, an agreement or a deal between the two parties involved. Indeed, while the use of *fè afè* is limited to conjugality, both *fè kondisyon* and *antann-yo* refer more generally to the satisfactory agreement of *any* two parties, to *any* kind of a deal.

The use of these terms to refer to both the process of union formation and the state of being in union is not simply metaphorical. Union formation, except in those increasingly rare instances where highly formalized marriages are arranged exclusively by a couple's families (and here, of course, the transacting parties are simply different), is always accompanied by one or more private discussions between the two prospective partners, during which the terms of their proposed conjugal relationship are fixed, more or less precisely. These sessions, properly referred to as *fè kondisyon,* are reported to comprise an explicit discussion of the rights, duties, capacities and expectations of each party, vis-a-vis the other, in the context of the proposed union. Here demands and needs are specified and promises are made concerning the future conduct of conjugal relations and the fulfillment of the partner's needs. Thus, while a union may be made public and may be ratified in a variety of ways, that which is being made public or being ratified has, in its substance, already been established between the two concerned parties through discussion of, and agreement upon, their respective roles as conjugal partners.

Union formation in any particular instance, of course, creates a highly specific, personal understanding and bond between two people, predicated on the mutual satisfaction of the particular individuals concerned. At the same time, conjugality is contracted in accordance with a unified body of community norms governing unions generally. While each conjugal contract may reflect in its details the particular circumstances and personal preferences of the individuals involved, the general terms and the transactional character of the contract are culturally determined and specified *a priori.* As indicated at the outset of this section, the basic categories or fields of relationship covered by the conjugal contract are sexuality and the organization of labor.

Transforming Sexuality

Most commonly, couples entering union will have had some experience in sexual relations with each other prior to union formation. The tenor of these relations will have followed the basic paradigm described above, characterized by competitive negotiations concerning the terms of the sexual exchange. Even where sexual relations are not a part of pre-union interaction, the potential framework for the courting couple's sexuality would have been limited by the conventions of competitions and quid-pro-quo reciprocity governing such relations. The conjugal contract, in either case, is explicitly predicated on a mutually agreeable transformation of the field of sexuality for both partners. It is not just that a couple's sexual relations undergo a change in virtue of their being in union. Rather, entering into union is precisely *about* effecting such a change.

Two terms easily elicited in any listing of the polite terms for intercourse and sexual relationships point clearly to the difference between sexual relations in, and out of, union. The two terms are *byen avèk* (lit.: well with) and *nan dezod* (lit.: in mischief/in disorder). *Byen avèk* denotes the existence of regular sexual contact between the two parties whose relationship it is used to describe but is most emphatically limited in its usage to couples who are *not* in union. To use *byen avèk* to describe any relationship that might suitably be glossed with *fè afè* is to insult the parties to that relationship grievously and to imply that their union is a sham. Indeed, so clear is this distinction that the usage of *byen avek* has undergone a kind of hyper-restriction—it is only rarely used to refer to the sexual relationship between a man and a woman who are even so much as intending to enter into union at some later date and is habitually restricted to those relationships where there is clearly no such intent.

The usage of *nan dezòd* parallels that of *byin avèk* but refers more specifically to the act of intercourse itself. To *fè yon ti dezòd,* or to *al nan dezòd,* is to have sex with a partner with whom one is decidedly *not* in union and, again, to use *nan dezòd* to describe the sexuality of a couple in union is to seriously impeach the actual character of their relationship.

The substance of this distinction between *byin avèk* sexuality and the sexuality of those who have *fè afè* is prefigured in the wider semantic field of *dezòd,* whose meanings in everyday parlance include considerably more than its sexual referent. In its most general sense, *dezòd* refers to mischievous or disorderly conduct and is used as an adjective to describe persons who have a tendency to behave badly in this sense. Its most common usage is in reference to young children who misbehave and do not mind their elders, or to adolescents who are acting "too big for their britches."

What is mischievous about *dezòd* sexuality, informants made clear, is that it implies no explicit or enduring responsibility on the part of the male partner toward the woman involved. Put quite simply: *"Ou mèt byen avèk yon fanm san ou pa gen devwa avè l menm."* (You can be *byen avèk* a woman without having any responsibilities toward her at all.) What is disorderly about a *byen avèk* relationship is less easily elicited, but the disorderliness characteristic of *byen avèk* sexuality has to do with the attribution of paternity. In a *byen avèk* relationship, this is always open to question. Because *byen avèk* sexuality relieves the male partner of any enduring material responsibility, it also leaves the woman free to entertain relationships with more than one partner simultaneously. Consequently, paternity may be openly contested by any number of parties with a variety of different motives. One potential father may claim paternity, while another heartily denies the possibility, or all potential fathers may deny responsibility as genitor of the child. Meanwhile, the mother may have her own ideas concerning who is—and who might best be—the father of her child. Of course, Haitians themselves point out, one cannot quite be sure at this juncture. This *is* disorder—of a most disturbing kind—for all concerned.[16]

Union takes both the mischief and the disorder out of *byen avèk* sexuality, by radically transforming the terms of sexual interaction, for both parties. The man, for his part, assumes his *devwa* (duties) vis-a-vis the woman. What might once have been an "appreciation" (*apresyasyon*), a "gift' (*kado*), or some "help" (*konkou*) proffered in exchange for sexual relations, now becomes a generalized, diffuse and enduring responsibility for the male partner. This distinction is as clear to Haitians as it is in the English renderings of these terms, as one man's remark concerning his former paramour reveals: *M te konn ede l, men m pa t janm rèskonsab li.''* (I used to help her, but I was never responsible for her.)

Generally these newly assumed male responsibilities are characterized simply as *"okipasyon fi-a''* (support for the woman), or *"teni fi-a sa-l bezwen''* (providing the woman what she needs). The particular details of any specific conjugal contract, of course, vary with respect to the man's capacity, the woman's demands, and her current situation. Over and above these details, however, what the man actually proffers at this stage is a primary lien on his overall future productivity, some significant portion of which (depending upon his own prior commitments to children, former mates, current mates, or parents) will henceforth be devoted to the satisfaction of the woman's needs (including meeting *her* prior commitments, primarily to dependent children and parents) and to the support of their prospective offspring together.

In her turn, the woman agrees to give the man his "due" or his "right" (*dwa*). Her sexuality is here proffered for an extended—prospectively limitless—period of time and made available to her mate essentially on demand, subject only to customary restrictions related to menstrual and post-partum taboos. Moreover, the *exclusivity* of the man's sexual access to his mate is promised and assured, and his unquestioned paternity of her offspring thereby guaranteed, at least in principle.

The conjugal sexual relationship, then, while firmly grounded in the wider field of sexual relations, also represents a significant and recognized departure from the norms governing sexuality generally. On the one hand, the basic categories of exchange here remain the same—to wit, male productivity and female sexuality. Furthermore, the conjugal sexual agreement is still fundamentally contingent, with a woman's sexual compliance and her fidelity in particular, conditional upon her husband's continued and adequate support and vice versa. On the other hand, there are clearly some essential differences between the actual terms of the conjugal arrangement and the conventions of competitive, quid-pro-quo reciprocity characteristic of sexuality out of union. By contrast, sexual reciprocity in union is both generalized and extended, from the point of view of the man, and exclusive, from the point of view of the woman. In consequence, as we have seen, sexuality in union is both serious and orderly in ways that sexuality out of union can never be.[17] This transformation of sexuality—through the regularization of its exercise and the routinization of the economic relations that underlie it—invariably constitutes the first and primary clause of the conjugal contract.

Initiating Labor Relations

The conjugal contract also invariably affects the second major field of relationship organized around gender distinction—the division of labor. Labor relations between the new spouses, however, are not so much a transformation or reorientation of the more general system of division of labor by gender; rather, they represent the realization of actual labor cooperation based upon that cultural system. Nonetheless, labor cooperation between the partners is always a major theme in their newly planned relationship as spouses. Indeed, such cooperation is a culturally logical consequence of their new sexual relationship itself, since the successful fulfillment of this latter necessarily entails the institution of full-blown, gender-specific labor relations between them. With respect to the male partner, whose profferral of a primary lien on his productivity is already explicit in the conjugal sexual contract, this connection is clear. As for the female partner, her complementary *labor* contribution is an equally necessary, if less obvious, concomitant of her new status as one of the primary recipients of her partner's productive effort and its fruits. A closer look at the emergent situation of the new spouses reveals why this must be so.

The new husband, regardless of his prior circumstances and obligations, must undertake the cultivation of at least one garden plot for his new spouse and provide cash resources sufficient to satisfy her immediate needs for daily consumption. A husband unencumbered by prior claims against his productivity may throw the bulk of his productive energies and resources into his new task and, indeed, ought to do precisely that. A man already committed to others—particularly if these are other spouses—must, on the other hand, carefully manage the apportionment of his effort and goods under these new circumstances. If he fails to do so he will be subject to criticism from virtually every quarter. Finally, of course, the actual extent of his personal resources, in terms of cash, skills, land, etc., will in either case determine the absolute amount of support received by his new spouse. What is most important for our present purposes, however, is the fact that as he accedes to the status of spouse to a particular woman, he accepts the responsibilities of primary provider to her and her dependents. Subsequently, a clearly identifiable measure of his overall productive effort is re-directed to the fulfillment of these new responsibilities.

Precisely because his new responsibilities, and the energy and resources diverted to fulfill them, are so extensive and hence so salient to others, the new husband can hardly appeal to any other woman, regardless of her status vis-a-vis him, to aid him in the task of supporting his new spouse. Rather, he must look to his new spouse herself to perform all of those complementary productive and domestic chores that fall within the purview of *travay fanm* and which, in their sum, "enable him to work"—for her, of course.[18]

Kinds of Unions, Kinds of Spouses

While the view of Haitian conjugality presented here is not "known" in any articulable sense by peasants themselves, the analysis has been guided by a number of conceptions and perceptions that are, in fact, the peasants' own. Among these, the notion of the conjugal contract, its appropriate scope and its specified content, has perhaps been the most trenchant for my purposes.

Given the demonstrably central role that the idea of conjugality *as* contract plays in the peasants' own understanding of union, it should not be at all surprising that particular unions are evaluated, categorized, and typologized by people themselves, precisely in terms of whether the parties to them successfully meet their conjugal obligations to each other. Moreover—and perhaps no less predictably—this local typology completely cross-cuts the legal and prestige-related distinctions between *maryaj* (church or civil marriage) and *plasaj* (consensual union). Indeed essentially formal considerations such as these latter, concerning how a union is publicly established and marked, are ultimately superseded by higher-order community evaluations based on the actual conduct of spouses in any on-going union.

On a day-to-day basis, such public judgements concerning other peoples' unions remain highly particularistic and, for the most part, guarded. They are linked to the currency of gossip about known individuals and are discussed within the confines of specific gossip networks. When conflict erupts, however, either between two spouses or between one spouse and a third party, the outlines of a more fully articulated and quite generalizable system of evaluation sometimes emerge. In direct elicitation, guided by enquiries concerning such events, as well as in quest of explanations for such common aphorisms as *"Yon bon plasaj pi bon pase yon mov maryaj"* (A good *plasaj* is better than a bad marriage), the details of a consistent evaluative system were revealed.

The categories and criteria of this evaluative system are unambiguous and may be applied to any union although, as in all such matters, the assignment of any particular union to a particular class is often negotiable. The fundamental distinction drawn in connection with the evaluation of unions is between two types: "honest" unions (*maryaj* or *plasaj onèt*) and "dishonest" or "vagabond" unions (*maryaj* or *plasaj malonèt,* or *vakabon*). These may also be referred to simply as "good" or "bad" unions, respectively (*yon bon maryaj* or *plasaj* versus *yon move maryaj* or *plasaj*).

An honest union, whether *maryaj* or *plasaj,* meets four distinct criteria or conditions, no partial combination of which are sufficient for the relationship to qualify as truly "honest" or "good." Of these, three pertain directly to specific conjugal responsibilities of the husband, while only one has to do with the wife's obligations. An honest union requires of the man that he (1) *okipe fanm-nan jan li kapab* (take care of the woman in the manner that he can), (2) *rete ak fanm-nan* (stay with the woman), in the sense of establishing some regular pattern of co-residence with her, even if only partial, and (3) *mete l nan yon kay* (put her in a house). Of the woman, an honest union makes a unique demand: sexual fidelity (*ke li pa tronpe msye li;* literally: that she not fool her husband).

Individuals, too, are evaluated with respect to their very suitability for union, and these evaluations mirror the structure of concern implicit in the *onèt/malonèt* distinction. Whether a man is willing or able to marry or whether a woman will settle for nothing less than a church wedding remain peripheral considerations at the level of community judgement I am describing. Rather, the irreversibly flawed husband is the *gason kourèd* (stingy man; literally: stiff-necked man) or the *gason chich* (cheap man). The unredeemably tainted wife is, of course, the *bouzen* (loose woman; literally: prostitute). Their opposite numbers, the *bon gason* (simply the "good man") and the *fanm serye* (serious woman) are, conversely, lauded as potentially excellent mates.[19]

The *gason kourèd* and the *bouzen,* along with their positive counterparts, allow us to view—from yet another vantage point—the substance of Haitian conjugality: that contractual relationship between a man and a woman which links their sexuality and their productivity in what may be, if only in virtue of its explicitness, a peculiarly Haitian innovation in the world of male/female relationships.

CONCLUSION

This paper has attempted to treat issues that are more often than not wholly ignored or dealt with only superficially in discussions of the rural Haitian mating system. It has established what might best be thought of as the basic substantive features of the conjugal relationship in rural Haiti and described how these are understood by Haitian peasants themselves.

Peasant conjugality here emerges as a unitary sociocultural phenomenon, regardless of the formal characteristics of its enactment in any particular instance—that is, regardless of whether the relationship in question has been marked by a marriage ceremony or not. The peasants' own normative system appears to be much less concerned with formal considerations of this kind than is commonly thought to be the case and much more focused on the fulfillment of conjugal duties and the actual substance of the relationship between spouses than the available ethnography seems to indicate. While there is no doubt that "form of union" is an important issue in peasant life, it is an issue that can only be approached fruitfully on the basis of a clear understanding of what conjugality itself *is*—and what it means—in Haitian rural life.

NOTES

[1]Fieldwork upon which this paper is based was carried out between September 1976 and August 1980, supported jointly by the Organization of American States, the National Science Foundation, and the Danforth Foundation. The paper is actually a much abridged version of a chapter from my forthcoming dissertation: *Culture, Conjugality and Domestic Organization in Rural Haiti*. Support during the writing of the dissertation has been provided by the Carter G. Woodson Institute for African and Afro-American Studies, University of Virginia, where I am currently a Research Fellow.

Thanks are due to Alexis Gardella, Léon-François Hoffmann, Gerald F. Murray and Richard and Sally Price, all of whom offered thoughtful criticisms of earlier drafts of this manuscript. I am particularly indebted to Eugene K. Galbraith, a colleague whose own work in northeast Brazil raises theoretical issues that closely parallel those that concern me here. Finally, although my profound personal and intellectual debt to the members of the community where my research was conducted cannot be repaid in the form of an acknowledgment, it is perhaps worth noting that their hospitality and cooperation are the foundations upon which whatever understanding I have achieved ultimately rests.

[2]The literature on Caribbean domestic and family organization is extensive, particularly for the British and formerly British West Indies, and no attempt to review it in detail will be made here. Price (1971) provides a useful summary of the major issues and problems raised by this corpus, the bulk of which appeared in the 50's and 60's. More recently, some of the theoretical and ethnographic shortcomings of this literature have been discussed by Manyoni (1977), Rubenstein (1980) and Smith (1978).

[3]There is, unfortunately, precious little material available that deals specifically with peasant domestic organization in Haiti. The most important single work (Bastien 1951) has never been translated from the original Spanish, although a long article based on this work appeared in English (Bastien 1961). In addition, only a handful of articles on selected themes have been published, including Simpson (1942), Comhaire-Sylvain (1958 and 1961), Louis (1968), Legerman (1975), Williams, et al. (1975), Laguerre (1977) and Larose (1977?). When these go beyond descriptive ethnography, analysis focuses primarily on formal and organizational variation, rather than on the substantive features of relevant primary relationships, as I will advocate here.

[4]Allman (1980), primarily concerned with fertility, is at pains to name and to classify any relationship that includes regular sexual activity. His five "union types" thus include courtship (renmen), engagement (fiyansaj) and casual sexual relationships (viv avèk) as distinct types, in addition to plasaj and maryaj. His use of the term "union" to refer to all these relationships is unfortunate, since that term generally is restricted to conjugal relationships—those between socially-recognized spouses. True spouses in rural Haiti are united either through maryaj or plasaj, exclusively. As we will see, when it is social, rather than sexual union that is at issue, it is precisely the ways in which these publicly-acknowledged unions differ in kind from mere sexual relationships that hold the key to the cultural significance of peasant conjugality.

[5]The generalizations that follow only apply, strictly speaking, to a small area in the middle of Haiti's southern peninsula, north of the market town of Fond-des-Nègres, where the bulk of my field research was conducted. On the basis of much shorter stays in several other parts of the country, however, I suspect that at least some of what I have to say may be applicable to a much larger segment of Haiti's peasantry.

[6]"Parenting"—the bearing and rearing of children—is excluded here, both because of space limitations and because the relationship between co-parents is, in fact, quite independent, in terms of local cultural understandings, of that between spouses. Like the conjugal relationship with which it often, though not necessarily, overlaps, it is another quite particular way of realizing the potentialities of male/female complementarity that this paper attempts to characterize.

[7]In general, the heavy physical tasks of clearing, cultivating, and certain kinds of weeding, accomplished with tools such as the machete, axe, pick and hoe, are almost always performed by men. Indeed, when a woman must "handle a hoe" (manyen wou), this is remarked upon as an unfortunate circumstance, precipitated by a combination of poverty (the inability to hire wage labor or to compensate exchange labor) and solitude (the lack of a capable man, in any appropriate status, to do the job).

Interestingly enough, a woman who knows how to handle a hoe, but need not actually do so, is complimented by both men and women: she is a potential asset to her household when male labor is temporarily unavailable and potentially self-sufficient when necessary or desired. This is in marked contrast to the shame and ridicule most often associated with the male performance of women's work, to be described below.

[8]The sale of most produce (with the exception of export crops marketed directly to licensed speculators) and the purchase of most necessities for everyday use is women's work and is seen as such—to the extent that a single male will almost never publicly engage in the sale of such produce, or in the purchase of household provisions, and will seek out a trusted female relative or friend to do his weekly marketing for him.

The implications of this particular division of labor in accordance with gender should not be underestimated. It has been suggested, for example, that the widespread participation of women in marketing and the marketplace, in conjunction with the widespread exclusion of men from this sphere, may lead to marked differences in personality orientation, skills distribution, and social attitudes between the sexes (Mintz 1971).

[9]This is another topic that, unfortunately, cannot be pursued at length here, but it should be noted that a significant minority of women in their thirties and forties deliberately opt out of the conjugal system that this paper describes, either temporarily or entirely. They depend upon

the labor of their adolescent sons, or upon wage labor, for the pursuit of limited agricultural production and devote their own time to commercial marketing activities. They are quite explicit in their assertions of economic independence and openly declare their satisfaction at being able to escape the aggravations (*traka*) of conjugality. They forego the kinds of reciprocity that conjugality entails in favor of personal independence and, when successful, are usually lauded by most other women for their achievement.

[10]Generally agreed upon as tasks an adult man should never do are the following, listed here in descending order of aversion, according to a group of male informants: provision marketing, emptying and cleaning chamberpots, sweeping, doing laundry, ironing and cooking. A number of other tasks, apparently too insignificant (to men, at least) to appear in an elicited task of this kind, but nonetheless never performed by men, include making beds, cleaning the houseyard, washing dishes and scrubbing pots, pounding and winnowing grains for home consumption, etc. Simplifying somewhat, four major kinds of tasks appear to be the exclusive domain of women: marketing (*fè mache*), housekeeping (*fè menaj*), food preparation (*fè manje*) and laundry (*fè lèsiv*).

The one major, recurrent household chore that falls by convention to men is the gathering and cutting of heavy wood to be used for cooking. While women and children may scavenge for kindling and smaller branches, wood that requires cutting before it can be used is carried home and prepared by men. Significantly and consciously *excluded* from this gender-linked division of domestic labor is the care of children (*swaye pitit*). Men are apt to point out that caring for one's children is not just the duty (*devwa*) but also the right (*dwa*) of men as well as women. This is not to say that either the least desirable or the most egregious chores involved in raising children, particularly those associated with infants, do not fall in large measure to women. Rather, men are proud to *claim* at least that they participate fully in childcare, while loath to even consider the possibility of doing the women's work described above.

[11]In the simplest of contexts adequate for illustrative purposes here—the co-residential monogamous union—all wealth produced through agriculture, or ultimately traceable to agriculture, or to other productive activity of the man during the course of the union, is considered to be common property, to be divided equally between the partners or their respective heirs when the union is dissolved or terminated by death. The explicit rationale for this notion of common property which, incidentally, does not vary with "type" of union, points to the woman's continuous domestic service as the basis for her rights. In marked contrast is the parallel principle pertaining to wealth produced through female commercial activity. These proceeds, regardless of the source of the original capital for commercial investment, which often comes from the spouse, remain the sole property of the woman herself and subsequently pass to her heirs exclusively.

[12]The present discussion of sexuality excludes a number of important issues, including all those aspects of restricted sexuality that apply to a particular social status or relationship: e.g., chastity (young women), fidelity (mated women) and incest (kinsmen). I am attempting to explore more fundamental notions of heterosexuality here and, indeed, considerations having to do with the kind of reciprocity to be described often override—and are used to justify transgressions against—sexual restrictions of all kinds, save those barring incest within the nuclear family.

[13]My direct access to information of this kind, as a male ethnographer, might justifiably be greeted with some skepticism. I suspect that it was the sheer length of my field stay, abetted by the fact that I was hardly seen as an eligible "man" by most women, that allowed me to elicit such descriptions successfully. The unabashedly explicit treatment of sexuality in general, in the course of everyday life, was of course the precondition to any success at all in these matters.

[14]I am grateful to Gerald F. Murray for pointing out that it is not at all necessary to assume that women "invented" this view of their own sexuality. On the contrary, similar conceptions of female sexuality have been quite widely reported, especially in Latin America. What makes the Haitian case particularly interesting, and perhaps unique, is the way in which women themselves have co-opted this misrepresentation of their sexual response and turned it to their own advantage in negotiating the terms of sexual interactions.

[15] There are, of course, both legitimate or respectable, *and* illegitimate or contemptible, ways for women to pursue material advantage within this system. A peasant woman is as likely to be criticized for being *overly* concerned with the economic aspects of her sexuality (she is a *fanm visyèz*) as she is for ignoring her "natural" gifts and their exchange value entirely (she is *pa serye*). In addition, the professional prostitute (*bouzen*) is locally characterized as falling entirely outside the bounds of this system of sexual reciprocity. Women, in particular, point out that the prostitute effectively *relinquishes* control over her sexuality, for she has both given up the privilege to exercise personal discretion in her choice of partners and degraded the value of her sexual services by fixing a cash equivalent for them and being openly available to anyone who meets her minimal terms. While any woman's motives may be more or less instrumental in the initiation and pursuit of a sexual relationship, she is engaged in a personal, social interaction with her partner, not a strictly economic transaction, and makes choices concerning her potential paramours with respect to important non-material criteria, such as physical attractiveness, personality, and so forth. An "honest woman's" (*fanm onèt*) affections are emphatically *not* for sale, in spite of the fact that they may generally not be had nor held without appropriate "appreciation" (*apresyasyon*).

[16] The importance of paternity to the Haitian male—both its accurate attribution and the subsequent fulfillment of its responsibilites—cannot be overstressed. In this connection, the reluctance of some men to legally marry, which is often attributed to their lack of commitment to norms of familial responsibility, might be better understood as the obverse of their strong commitment to paternal obligations: by law and custom, a married man's subsequent children with other women cannot become his heirs. Recognizing the possibility, at least, of fathering one or more outside children (*pitit deyò*) after marriage, the realistic and responsible man is understandably reluctant to prospectively "disinherit" his future offspring.

[17] It is perhaps worth noting at this point that with that seriousness and order comes the possibility, at least, of enhanced sexual satisfaction for both partners. In consequence of the reorientation of the *terms* of sexual interaction, the overall *tenor* of sexual relations between the partners may be transformed as well. Taking place in the context of reasonably assured fidelity and extended reciprocity, sexual relations within a mutually satisfactory union reportedly surpass all others as an arena for personal relaxation and pleasure—particularly, women aver, for them.

[18] A wife, finally, is *entitled* to material support from her mate in virtue of her sexuality, rather than in direct exchange for her own domestic and productive labor contributions to the conjugal unit. These latter are logically consequent to the terms of their sexual relationship and appear as "given" rather than contingent aspects of their life together. Notwithstanding the fact that the significance of her material contributions are unambiguously recognized in customary law, as noted previously, it is thus understandable that the salient everyday conception of what conjugality is all about—both what it means at its best and what can go most wrong with it at its worst—is phrased consistently in terms of the sexual exchange and not with reference to the organization of labor *per se*. Thus, accurate perceptions of the extent and value of women's labor contributions to the conjugal unit are systematically undercut by an acute emphasis on women's sexual functions and fidelity as the source of their entitlement within that unit. This clearly has important implications, which cannot be pursued here, for the status and relative power of Haitian peasant women within the conjugal unit and in society at large.

[19] A host of additional considerations do come into play secondarily, of course, both in the public evaluations of already mated individuals and in the personal selection of potential mates for oneself. Some such considerations are practical, pertaining to skills, resources, family ties, etc.; others may be simply aesthetic or idiosyncratic, pertaining to personal appearance, personality and comportment. Moreover, outside the specific context of union, there are even greater flaws that may blemish the reputation of any man or woman—the praedial larcenist (*volè[z]*: thief), for example, is the most despised of all characters in this agricultural milieu.

THE SOCIAL CHARACTER OF RELIGION IN RURAL HAITI

GLENN R. SMUCKER

A knowledge of traditional religion is central to understanding Haitian social realities, values, and notions of human nature. Certainly Catholic and Protestant Christianity in Haiti cannot be fully understood without reference to the cult of ancestors and the belief in magic, but the social character of Haitian religion also sheds light on social change as well as outside efforts to organize peasant communities. The pivotal issues involved are the ideologies of Haitian social life, class, the relationship between politics and religion, and the transactional character of relations with fellow human beings and with the world of spirits. Despite weak⁺ governmental structures, rural Haiti is integrated into the national culture in certain ways which are reflected in peasant ideologies of religion and politics. The present analysis thus proposes a model or ideal type for understanding the ideological structure of Haitian voodoo which will be useful for comparative studies and for futher explorations of Haitian religion.

This paper seeks to synthesize religious practices and premises with special attention to social context, turning from the all too common focus on the lurid and spectacular. My observations suggest that Haitian spirits are archetypal personalities whose characteristics give entrée to a fuller understanding of Haitian values and the tissue of human relations. Close attention to charges of witchcraft reveals distinctive patterns of social conflict and behavioral sanctions. There is both a symbiotic relationship and a religious dissonance between institutional Christianity and Voodoo cosmology. At the same time, strong parallels exist between institutional Christianity and the secular assumptions of community development.

Haitian ritual life is made up of the Roman Catholic Church and various Protestant churches, as well as the public and private observances pertaining to the cult of dead ancestors and other ancestral spirits and the use of magic and witchcraft. The population of Haiti is predominantly Catholic, and the Catholic Church is a state church. The Catholic character of the country reflects the French colonial heritage of the 18th century. Since the reforms of Vatican II the Catholic mass is sung in Creole and the new hymns have a Protestant ring to them. The new liturgical music is more popular with young people, but rural wakes and prayers for the dead still feature the old Gregorian tunes sung in falsetto voice, robust chest tones, wails, and field hollers. Between 15 and 25% of the population, however, is Protestant.[1] The Protestant presence in Haiti dates to the early years of independence, but the rapid growth of Protestantism in rural areas is a phenomenon of recent origin, primarily of the last quarter century. Despite the importance of institutional forms of Christianity, few Haitians of any class would deny the existence of influence of ancestral spirits. Furthermore, most Haitians acknowledge the role of magic and witchcraft in interpersonal relations. Because witchcraft is a realm of religious practice distinct from the cult of ancestral spirits, most servitors of family spirits are quick to denounce its practice. It is important to distinguish the question of belief from active religious practice as not all believers in spirits are active servitors of spirits.

Syncretism and Ambiguity

A common source of confusion in discussing Voodoo[2] is the syncretistic character of Haitian religion. The servitor of spirits does not distinguish Catholicism from spirit worship as two discrete religions. On the other hand, he or she does make distinctions in terms of religious practice and social context. For the servitors of family spirits there is no inherent conflict between spirit worship and Christianity; to be Catholic is to serve family spirits because the saints of the church and the inherited family saints are all God's creations. Outwardly, servitors of family spirits observe formal Catholic obligations in keeping with church practice and clerical authority. Servitors also carry out ritual prayers and offerings to ancestral spirits. This is done privately in the home and publicly at pilgrimage sites and patron saint festivals. In Voodoo ceremonials, Catholic prayers, saints, and symbols are incorporated without the approval or participation of Catholic priests. The "syncretism" in Haitian religion emerges as an uneasy co-existence of Haitian rites and universal Catholic rites. Nevertheless, there is a distinct social compartmentalization between formal Catholic observance and the cult of family spirits.

The social compartmentalization of religion takes several forms. There is a social class distinction between peasant parishioners and the clergy. Religious practices between peasants and upper-class Haitians also differ in keeping with the relative social status of Afro-Haitian, as opposed to Franco-Haitian, cultural traditions. Furthermore, some peasants do not keep up the traditions of the ancestor cult. Finally, the unified system of formal Catholic rites plus domestic Voodoo rites entails a social segregation in terms of place.

As a belief system, the Voodoo religion crosses class boundaries; it is truly a national religion. In terms of ritual practice, Voodoo is largely a folk religion of the peasantry and the urban poor. Middle- and upper-class families also participate, but rarely in public settings. Upwardly mobile families and the traditional upper classes tend to identify strongly with the Euro-Haitian cultural heritage. As a result, they avoid public affiliation with traditional Voodoo practice due to the social stigma imposed on Afro-Haitian cultural traits and the lower classes.

This religious syncretism illustrates a general pattern in Haitian culture: a large capacity to integrate new forms into traditional culture. These new forms may be accompanied by new meanings, but their uses and meanings are much more likely to be transmuted, retaining outward shapes but imbued with inner meanings in keeping with Haitian views of the world. Saint-Jacques, for example, is celebrated as the patron saint of a parish church, but at the caves of La Porte, Saint-Jacques is served with animal sacrifice. In effect, the Catholic clergy fulfills vital roles in a cultural symbiosis with the cult of ancestors. Priests may unwittingly play a key role in Voodoo practice even while speaking out against the Voodoo religion. Consequently, a religious dissonance is embedded within Haitian religion; Voodoo views itself as compatible with Catholicism but the reverse does not hold.

This ambiguity is sustained by clerical control over the church sacraments in formal Catholic settings (church, school, burial sites), but by lack of control over domestic practices which incorporate Catholic prayers and symbols into Voodoo ceremonials. The very words of the priest may be taken to mean something other than what is intended. In Creole the word "saint" is a generic term which refers to saints of the church as well as inherited family *mistè* (mysteries or spirits). Devotees of family spirits wholeheartedly agree with priestly admonitions against "superstition" and "Satanic practices" for these are understood as references to the traffic in *zombi* (dead souls), magic, and witchcraft—a matter which in no way casts aspersion upon the inheritance of saints or the cult of ancestors. For a servitor, church baptism is a precondition for the baptism of family spirits who "possess" family members. The family spirits may well demand that parents prepare children to take communion, or they may suggest that adults go to confession and take communion as a remedy for illness or protection from witchcraft. In short, official Catholic rites of the mass, baptism, communion, marriage, and burial are significant in Voodoo cosmology. These rites boost one's life force, provide healing from illness, and enhance social status.

The dissonance in Haitian religion is indicated by the contrast between Catholics who also serve family spirits and others known as *katolik fran* ("frank" Catholics) who do not serve family spirits. The stance of *katolik fran* implies the rejection of traditional ancestral rites and the use of magic. The *katolik fran* is a Catholic counterpart to the Protestant notion of conversion, or *konvèti,* whereby acceptance of Protestant belief and communion requires the rejection of Voodoo practice. It is worthy of note that in neither case does rejection of Voodoo practice suggest the suspension of belief in Voodoo, i.e. the world of spirits, magic, and the cult of ancestors. Rather, the Protestant *konvèti* and the Catholic *fran* both find themselves under special protection from magic and the considerable risks of not properly serving ancestral spirits. Inherited family spirits may well demand Protestant conversion as a protection against insidious forms of supernatural illness.

Métraux (1972) makes mention of "domestic" and "public" forms of Voodoo but focuses primarily on elaborate public forms, the temple cults of Port-au-Prince. Temple Voodoo is a subject of great interest in its own right. Rituals of the region of Port-au-Prince and the nearby plains of Léogane and the Cul-de-Sac are especially elaborate and contrast strikingly with the rites of the northern mountains. The urban and lowland village settings for these forms demonstrate the adaptability of Haitian religion to a variety of social milieux. It not only adapts but thrives in the most densely populated quarters of the capital; the importance of regional variations is thrown into sharp relief, however, by the limited focus of Métraux's work. Unlike Herskovits (1937), Métraux deals relatively little with the domestic Voodoo more characteristic of northern mountain people and other rural dwellers. The Voodoo temple societies described by Metraux do not exist universally; however, *houngan* religious specialists are present as seers and curers in most rural areas.[3]

The most important elements of rural Haitian religion have little or nothing to do with the priests or temples but rather with the family cult of the *lakou* (residential compound). In rural Haiti domestic Voodoo is tied to the social organization of peasant life and the economy of the household. It is linked to inheritance rights and is economically significant in terms of the cost of ceremonies and the traffic in land. There are ceremonials with a public character but these are festive family affairs with many family friends, neighbors, and distant relatives in attendance. These more public ceremonials are manifestations of traditional family rites of the *lakou* and have no connection to a temple. Other public rituals include pilgrimages to holy places and patron saint festivals where crowds gather for rites of supplication and sacrifice. There are also processional societies such as the *rara,* Judas bands of Holy Week, and nocturnal secret societies, e.g., the *champwèl* and *bizango.*

In general it is not fair to say, as Métraux suggests, that domestic Voodoo is losing importance in favor of temple Voodoo. This may be true of more densely settled areas, especially in cities, where ex-peasants and wage laborers are often cut off from the land and traditional family rituals. What is certain is that rites and practices do vary from one region to another. There is also evidence of change in the rituals over time, but domestic Voodoo is still widely practiced in rural Haiti thirty years after Métraux's fieldwork.

Voodoo—Assumptions, Values and Goals

Given the diverse manifestations of Voodoo, it is useful to take note of the assumptions, values and goals which are common to the religion. The social context of Voodoo includes the household, the *lakou,* the temple, the parish church, the cemetery, spirit *kapital* (spirit repositories), pilgrimage sites and public thoroughfares where processional societies dance along the paths and crossroads. The beliefs and practices of Voodoo also permeate almost every aspect of daily life among peasants, from the household to the field garden and marketplace. This reflects the pragmatic and personalistic character of the religion and suggests its importance as a unifying cosmology.

In the Voodoo cosmos there is an animist quality which underlies the whole nature. This is evidenced in the butcher's custom of smearing blood in the eyes of a dying animal to blind its *nanm* (soul) and prevent it from returning to haunt its killer. Sweet basil may be planted in the yard for herbal and ritual usage, but these plants are deemed "jealous." They recognize and prefer their master; they may die if another tries to care for them or touch them. Snakes are generally thought to be malevolent. They may curse the ground where they die and cause a tree to grow deformed and barren. On ritual occasions in the family *lakou,* food is prepared and offered to spirits. Most of it is consumed by the human celebrants and only a small portion is actually left for the spirits. Food offered to spirits and eaten by humans, however, is not filling, for its *nanm* has been consumed by the spirits to whom it was offered.

Spirits animate the things of nature. Old trees in the yard or near a spring are spiritual *kapital,* repositories of spirits which cannot be cut on threat of misfortune and dishonor to guardian spirits. Caves, cliffs, shady ravines, and quixotic natural formations have a *nanm,* housing spirits. They often become pilgrimage spots known far and wide. The mud basins of La Plaine du Nord attract thousands of pilgrims during the annual patron saint festival. The parish festival of Ville Bonheur is known throughout Haiti due to the popularity of the saint housed in the waters of Saut d'Eau.

Plants and animals in Haiti have specific names but there is a marked preference for using generic names—even with reference to a creature in the garden. A bird may be called a *bèt* (animal) rather than *zwazo* (bird) or a more specific name such as *fowizi* (owl). Names are not lightly invoked, and references to people in the third person are often by pronoun, title, or general terms such as "the man" or "the other person." This quality of indirection is a reluctance to name names in public, for naming has magical or political overtone; things are not always what they seem to be. Plants are jealous, and a creature in the garden at night may be a lost soul, a witch, a human being in altered form.

God, however, is distinct from the rest of nature. God is desirous of having his name called, and people constantly invoke the name of God in everyday speech. Plans are made for the morrow "if the Lord wills." Even in the midst of tragedy, "God is good." God is the source and creator, the animating force of all nature. God sends the rain, children, spirits, and the food which grows. He is the *gran mèt,* the great master, a distant figure far removed from the quarrelsome personal relations among men, women, and spirits. He is a less capricious figure than his human and spiritual creations. Life's miseries are tied up with relations among human beings and spirits. It is people who quarrel and make each other ill. As a consequence, "Blow for blow God laughs," for God is good and humans err. There is a quality of negativity in mortal doings unlike the positive life forces of God. God always sends the rains; even drought does not last forever. Men and women use magic to tie off the rain, but there is no magic to make rain fall, only God can make it rain. There is also irony in God's cosmic rule, for babies are born in times of drought when there is no food. Ambivalence is found in the very act of giving life. Nevertheless, acts of God are accepted philosophically as in the natural order of things. The saints may be cursed but God is praised.

The Cult of Ancestors

The heart of folk religion in Haiti is a family cult of ancestral spirits, of which there are three distinct categories: the dead, the saints or spirits, and the twins. All ancestral spirits go hand in hand with kinship and the land. The tripartite division of family spirits appears to be universal throughout the country, but there are many local variants in Haitian language and religion including different names for similar categories of spirits.[4]

The traditions of the ancestor cult are fundamentally local. They are tied to the household, the *lakou,* and the *natif natal* (birthplace). In keeping with the pattern of spiritual inheritance and earthly kinship, the dead and other spirits are quintessentially local spirits. These spirits are inherited individually though they may reflect generalized archetypes which may be recognizable throughout different regions of the country. There are spirits, however, whose names are unknown outside a particular community.

The most significant contrast to be drawn in the world of Haitian spirits is a marked distinction between "inherited" family spirits and "purchased" spirits. In general terms the inherited are beneficent *ginen* (Guinea spirits) whereas purchased spirits are malevolent, tied to dead souls. This view of protective versus maligning spirits cannot simply be likened to the Euro-Christian dualism of angels and evils as pure embodiments of good and evil. Haitian spirits are ambivalent and capricious, capable of both good and evil. Inherited spirits may serve protective functions, but they are jealous and must be fed or they withhold protection and cause illness. Purchased spirits are associated with untoward human ambition, greed and sorcery, but they may be useful, perhaps essential, for protective magic in the face of human enmity and witchcraft. Nevertheless, they too must be controlled properly for they are "hardened" and demanding. If their appetites are not duly appeased, their usefulness may backfire on the purchaser and his or her family.

The world of spirits also has a transformative character. In the Haitian cosmology, both human beings and spirits are able to shift quite easily back and forth between ordinary and extraordinary levels of being. In a very literal sense, all visible and invisible beings are capable of taking both physical and spiritual forms. Most such transformations are under the instrumental control of human beings. As a consequence, reality is multi-layered and complex; appearances are deceiving. In this world of sudden transformations, spirits are invoked in face-to-face encounters. Through spirit possession the personality of a man and woman is jerked away, displaced for a time by a spirit who talks, dances, eats, drinks, and interacts with possessed and unpossessed alike.

Church saints and family spirits have different names. Church saints do not generally possess their devotees; however, some servitors are possessed by a purchased spirit called Lucifer. Others serve the Vierge Noire (Black Virgin) from Our Lady of Czestochowa, Patron Saint of Poland. Yet another servitor takes Saint Philomene as his wife in a rite of mystical marriage. As a rule saints of the church are accompanied by Haitian spirits in a system of parallelisms. Historical figures are sometimes transformed into spirits as in the case of La Reine Sanite, a freedom fighter from the revolutionary period. Sanite was married to General Charles Belair, the nephew of Toussaint Louverture. Today La Reine Sanite is resident of the caves of La Porte. Saints of the church, spirits of twinship, inherited and purchased spirits all manifest themselves in the dream life of their devotees. In Haitian transformations, human beings are capable of turning into non-human forms at will through witchcraft. Even death is not free of further transformation for the dead are buried but never truly gone. Spirits of the dead may be purchased in the cemetery for use as *zombi,* which take physical or spiritual forms. Dead ancestors are consulted for advice or favors. They may also appear uninvited in dreams.

Relationships with spirits are fundamentally reciprocal and transactional. The inheritance of spirits is tied to ritual obligations on the part of family members. In the relational quality of these ties, servitors appease the appetites of the spirits in order to buy protection from their bothersome ways. Spirits may withhold protection from stingy followers. They may actively cause illness and misfortune within the family. Performing ceremonials when they are long overdue is tantamount to making good on an old debt. Rather than paying off this debt or continuing to serve unresponsive or stingy spirits, devotees may also choose to perform ceremonies which send away the spirits and break off ties of obligation. This is a risky venture, for the spirits may well be needed in the future. In the Haitian scheme of things it is advisable to hedge one's bets and protect relationships rather than cut them off. The existence of family spirits cannot be ignored. Relationships with these spirits are not always rewarding but they are always negotiable.

The reciprocal premise in spirit worship goes beyond the appeasement, rewarding, or sending away of hungry spirits. The ancestral dead and other family spirits are guardians who protect faithful servitors from witchcraft, sickness, and misfortune. A servitor once described spirits as the doctors and nurses left by Jesus to care for the faithful in times of need. Spirits also serve as oracles who offer advice. Answers are given through dreams or possession. Such replies may require further interpretation, for communications often take symbolic form. Spirits offer warnings and predictions with regard to the future. Dreams in general are predictive manifestations of the *ginin* family spirits.

Faithful servitors also make demands of spirits, enlisting their support to gain health and success in economic endeavors. This takes the form of cajoling, making deals, and promising ritual favors in return for support in meeting personal or family needs. The requests made of spirits are often very specific, expressing needs for articles of clothing, a particular sum of money for a child's baptism, a winning number on the lottery, child support from an errant father, success in love, access to a job, healing from persistent illness. In return for his or her help, a saint may be promised a pilgrimage, a mass for the dead, acts of charity to the poor, the wearing of a *rechangn* (ritual clothing) in honor of the saint, an elaborate dinner or *gombo* (service) for the spirit, all on condition that the spirit is able to make good on the deal.

Recalcitrant spirits who are slow to respond to their servant's requests may be cursed, threatened and accused of theft or treachery. Threats are made to cut off ties or to convert to *levanjil* (the gospel), a reference to evangelical Protestantism. Conversion is simply one of several alternatives for dealing with the spirit world. Protestant conversion is a legitimate means of escaping ritual indebtedness to spirits when they turn a deaf ear or withhold pity in hard times. The threat of conversion is a serious threat to the spirits, for a saint without followers loses prestige and is forgotten.

The quirks and appetites of spirits are notably human but greatly exaggerated and unsocialized like those of children. They are ambivalent and capricious beings, hardly to be trusted, subject to ruse, trickery, bouts of jealousy, unbridled appetites, and a flair for the dramatic. Ritual possessions give full vent to cultural and social reversals which spoof and caricature local values and mores. Spirits are allowed to violate normal codes of polite behavior to the great amusement of those present. On festive ritual occasions they mock their hosts, make disparaging remarks and tell off-color jokes at the expense and amusement of everyone present. They in turn are targets of bantering humor on the part of others and engage in numerous spontaneous interactions. In general, the dramatic element is a fundamental aspect of Haitian religious experience. Improvisational drama and performance are essential to ritual possession at family celebrations honoring the spirits.

The Social Character of Witchcraft

Voodoo may aptly be described as a cult of sickness and healing. It explains the genesis of illness and misfortune. It is pragmatic and personal in its instrumental use. A knowledge of sorcery enables any human being to cause illness or misfortune to another. It is incorrect to define Voodoo in terms of witchcraft, but it is impossible to understand the ancestor cult without reference to the magical causation of illness. Family spirits are guardian spirits able to protect family members from illness and misfortune caused by witchcraft and other spiritual forces. The devotees of inherited family spirits are quick to denounce the practice of maligning magic, the purchase of *lwa* and the traffic in *zombi*.

Despite the rift between magic and the cult of ancestors, witchcraft and charges of witchcraft are part and parcel of everyday life in L'Artichaut. The world of spirits, witchcraft and subtle manipulation is expressed in proverbs which describe Haitian society:

Ti peyi gran nasyon.	Tiny country, great nation.
Afè nèg pa janm piti.	Haitian matters are never small (simple).
Dēyē mòn gen mòn.	Behind mountains are mountains.

Peasant society is "great" in the sense of complicated, being composed of unseen realities, hidden mountains. There is a general preoccupation with the manipulation of power, both spiritual and political. One should never trust appearances for Haitians are persons of spirit, magic, and power which remain unrevealed in the polite etiquette of everyday encounter.

In the literature on Voodoo the term *lougawou* is generally translated as "werewolf" in keeping with its European etymology. A more accurate translation in the Haitian context would be "witch." Witches are human beings who employ magical power against human enemies, or who protect themselves, their property, and special relationships from abuse by those who would do them harm. Everyone is born with the capacity to be a witch, or rather, to learn the witch's craft.

Illness has various causes, but the basic distinction made in determining treatment is to discern whether the illness is from "natural" or "supernatural" causes. It is commonly assumed that people make each other sick, but the reason why is not always clear: "For everyone who dies there is always a cause." Jealousy, hatred and quarrels result in charges of witchcraft. The spector of witchcraft in human relations, especially illness and death, is permeated with a sense of indirection, the unknown, and the unverified. If a supernatural cause is determined, the question of who did it remains. In the Haitian aesthetic, indirection and cunning are more highly valued than direct confrontation. Magic is often preferred over brute force as an instrument of human expression. This results in an atmosphere which approaches paranoia if left unmitigated by protective measures and compensating relationships. In this light, the close link between magic and mental illness is not surprising.

The expression of mental illness in provincial Haiti is culturally mediated, i.e. there are culturally appropriate forms of madness. The behavior of crazy people is not random. It takes specific and standardized forms such as the refusal to eat, drink, or talk, a complete lack of interest in childcare or nursing on the part of postpartum mothers, an unwillingness to wear clothing or to observe traditional standards of modesty and cleanliness, a propensity for contrary behavior and trickster humor. The dramatic expression of madness gathers crowds who are willing to give a coin in return for an amusing performance such as scandalous stories, curses, gossip, impolite language, and comic impressions. People afflicted with madness sometimes live from begging and collecting the castoffs from streets and garbage dumps. There is a great latitude for deviant forms of behavior among those recognized as afflicted with madness.

Madness is a form of social deviance which lends legitimacy to the escape from normal social obligations and personal responsibilities. It is generally diagnosed as caused by witchcraft in which a person's *bonanj* (innate intelligence and personality) is displaced by *zombi*. Uncouth language in the mouths of crazy people is interpreted as the unregulated speech of troubled spirits. Even Protestant pastors may cast out demons in a ritual parallel to Voodoo practice. Voodoo rites of *èkspédisyon* (a form of exorcism) appear to have considerable merit in treatment of mental illness, but difficult cases give ample opportunity for the financial abuse of clients by traditional curers and sorcerers.

Magic is not simply an aggressive act. The most common forms are by nature protective. Protective magic is used to safeguard against illness and to protect gardens from blight or theft caused by human enemies. It is also useful in garnering good luck in sex, marital relations, gaining a job, gambling or farming. Furthermore, magic is tied to reciprocity in relationships. Witchcraft is recognized as an expression of concrete social relations between people.

Byen mennen byen,	Good brings good,
mal mennen mal.	evil brings evil.
Fe koupe fe.	It takes iron to cut iron.
Inosan dwoge.	Innocence is its own protection.

Injury by witchcraft is a matter of avoiding abusive relationships and quarrels with others. Shoddy treatment of others engenders a similar response; magic begets magic. The purchase of a magic charm is no assurance of protection in the face of unwise behavior. Discretion is the higher value in social relations:

Bōkō ba ou pwen	The sorcerer gives you a charm,
li pa di ou dōmi nan kafou.	he doesn't suggest sleeping in crossroads.
Konplo pi fō pase owanga.	A conspiracy is stronger than magic charms.

The use of magic does not give one immunity from indiscretions or the abuse of others. A magic charm is no true protection from enmity.

There is a quality of negativity in the practice and ideology of witchcraft. A garden may be protected by the use of magic charms, but magic does not make the garden grow. Magic does not supplant empirical effort nor can it replace the natural growth forces of life and the natural world. It can tie off or intervene but it cannot create life. A woman may be pregnant for years with a static fetus which fails to grow; it does not die nor does it thrive, for it is "tied" by magical or other supernatural forces.

The negativity in magic reflects the underlying ambivalence of human nature in Haitian cosmology. "There are no good Haitians" is a common saying. It expresses the social devaluation of what is Haitian as opposed to what is foreign or European, but there is more here than meets the eye. The Haitian moral code recognizes the full range of human propensities. One person cannot trust another outside the bonds of reciprocity which tie them together, as Haitian morality is conditional and relative, based on reciprocity. Relationships are transactional; they are subject to a give and take among human beings and between human and spirit.

In the realm of morality there is a religious dissonance which pits the assumptions of Voodoo cosmology against those of Christian missionaries. In rural Haiti the key moral issues are not based on internalized codes of good and evil sanctioned by feelings of guilt and the fear of deferred punishment in the hereafter. Protestant missionaries say that new converts must be taught a new sense of sin and new feelings of guilt. A Catholic priest notes that his parishioners may choose not to confess everything— either for reasons of embarrassment or because confession and communion have other meanings in keeping with the demands of family spirits. In the moral universe of Voodoo, the social controls of prestige and shame, honor and dishonor, and ties of obligation are more important than unmediated abstractions and internalized guilt.

In this context, witchcraft is linked to concrete violations of social mores. It serves as a social leveler, is protective of personal and property rights. Those who own land generally have stronger magic to protect their property than those desiring to take it away. Charges of witchcraft in L'Artichaut go hand in hand with sexual competition, mother-in-law conflicts, brother-in-law conflicts, competition for jobs, and the acquisition of sudden wealth. For every charge of witchcraft in L'Artichaut there is independent evidence of quarrels and social conflict. Suspicion of those people with whom the victim does not get along accompanies every illness attributed to witchcraft. Those who seek untoward power through witchcraft are accused of ambition.

In rural Haiti there is a decided respect for power, magical or political, while the abuse of power is severely criticized and actively sabotaged. Witches are thus socially acceptable people, esteemed for their knowledge of witchcraft. Witches need not be feared generally unless one has personal quarrels with them. In most cases, the suspicion of having caused magical illness or death goes unpunished by the authorities. That a particular misfortune has been caused by a particular person cannot be proved. It can only be suspected, attributed to another, or divined by seers who read candles, shells, cards or ash. Even then, the seer does not usually discern the offender's identity, but rather confirms the unnatural (magical) character of the illness.

Apart from a lucrative traffic in illness and misfortune, Voodoo tends to be economically conservative. People spend large sums of money on ceremonial obligations rather than investing in economic ventures or acquiring land. The ritual requirements of peasant life result in the turnover of resources on a large scale. A death in the family, for example, usually results in the dissipation of wealth. Specific plots are designated by their owners to cover the cost of a decent burial. In some cases, however, obligations have the effect of re-distributing wealth on the part of the more well-do-do.

The realm of magic and witchcraft strongly reflects ambivalent aspects of Haitian cultural life. In keeping with other elements of Haitian religion, witchcraft has an inherently dramatic character sustained by the reality of creatures abroad in the night and the role of magic as an instrument of social conflict and control. A Haitian cultural norm of studied ambiguity is expressed in the realities of spirits, magic, and witchcraft resulting in a kind of normal paranoia in social relations. This need not imply that Haitians relate to the world in a pathological manner. Rather, the religious and social world of rural Haiti is complex and multi-leveled. A cultural norm of "socialized ambivalence" (Herskovits 1937) is outwardly camouflaged by a propensity for storytelling, good humor, and subtle use of language. On the surface, this gregarious joking behavior may seem to be at odds with the "normal paranoia" engendered by witchcraft. Yet, the very intensity of verbal repartee reflects a level of heightened consciousness in Haitian social life which flows from the world of magic, fear of the unknown and a marked sensitivity to the social significance of symbol in everyday life.

The Catholic Church

Peasant participation in Catholic rites is formal and public, a link with peasant society that aptly illustrates Refield's sense of an interaction between great and little traditions, or "hierarchic and lay culture." As far as most peasants are concerned no real distinction exists between Catholic belief and the practice of folk religion. Yet the Catholic Church has periodically mounted unsuccessful anti-superstition campaigns in an attempt to obliterate Voodoo practice. The most recent such campaign dates to the 1940's under President Lescot. Given the tight integration of Catholic rites into Voodoo cosmology, the actions of the church suggest a pattern of cultural integration which is embedded in social contradiction.

Rural folk religion is closely tied into a whole social structure which the Catholic Church tends rather to maintain than to destroy. Anti-superstition campaigns simply renew the imposition of hierarchic culture over a socially degraded lay culture. These campaigns never served to mediate peasant political or religious interests. On the contrary, they had the effect of exacerbating the ancient rift between Euro-Haitian and Afro-Haitian cultures, intensifying a sense of class antagonism, and fostering old patterns of anti-clericalism among both peasants and intellectuals.

Since the 1940's the Catholic Church in Haiti has changed as a result of local politics and the reforms of Vatican II. Significant numbers of the clergy showed renewed interest in issues of social justice and economic development. Some priests took the initiative in the community development movement, inventing the term "Christian community development." Others incorporated traditional worship forms such as the Voodoo drum into the church liturgy. Nevertheless, the church still promotes integration into the established hierarchies of society, especially the apparatus of the state.

Haitian peasants tend to view the office of priest in a fashion similar to political office—a position of power and authority which lends itself to financial reward. The parish church is the dominant physical structure in most rural communes. This prominence is consistent with the social character of the clergy. The clergy is strongly hierarchical, based largely in towns and cities, and strongly influenced by foreigners who play a key role in the propagation of Euro-Haitian culture. On one occasion I overheard a discussion between representatives of the northern bishop and local farmers of L'Artichaut. The question was asked, "Who makes up the Church?" The catechism provides a standard reply, but these farmers answered according to their perceptions of the matter: "It is the bishop and the state, God and the state, who make up the Church."

Historically, the Haitian Catholic Church has served as an extension of the state to a greater degree than many other national churches. This relation is due in large part to the slave revolt of 1791 that led to independence in 1804 which in turn resulted in a schism with Rome ending 56 years later in the Concordat of 1860 (Comhaire 1956). During this time the state maintained its own clergy outside the bounds of Vatican jurisdiction. The state promulgated a law assigning to the president the right to appoint all parish priests. The consequences for church and state in Haiti are stated succinctly by Msgr. Jan (1959: 427, my translation), a former bishop of the Cap-Haitien diocese:

During the period of the schism, that is from 1804 to the Concordat of 1860, the different Haitian heads of state usurped the ecclesiastical jurisdiction, naming and dismissing parish priests, verifying or disapproving letters of ordination, fixing the limits in which they must exercise their ministry.... The Church is a branch of public service over which the state exercises its control as over all other administrations.

This tradition of state control over the church continues to be an issue in Haitian politics.

The Catholic Church is a force to be reckoned with in establishing and maintaining a government in power. During the post-Concordat period as a missionary church, the foreign clergy, with many Breton priests, tended to support the cultural aspirations and political views of the European-oriented Haitian elite (Nicholls 1970). Nevertheless, there is an old tradition of anti-clericalism among Haitian intellectuals with ties to Protestantism, e.g., Louis Joseph Janvier (1886). There is also a significant anti-clerical tradition among town burghers attracted to Free-Masonry. The Masonic Lodge continues to be an important institution in Haiti's towns and cities. In this connection, a respected *notaire* once remarked, "Voodoo is the peasant superstition, and the Masonic Lodge is the superstition of the bourgeois." Members of the Lodge are nominally Catholic, supporting neither Protestantism nor Voodoo practice.

Following the American Occupation (1915-1934), a resurgent Haitian nationalism was strongly critical of the foreign clergy. When President François Duvalier came to power in 1957, all five Catholic bishops were foreigners. A church-state struggle culminated with the expulsion of the archbishop and, in turn, the excommunication of the Haitian president by the Vatican. When official relationships were reestablished in 1966, Haitian bishops were appointed following their nomination by the Haitian president. The political implications of this resolution favored tradition. The historical preponderance of the Haitian state was re-affirmed, brooking no opposition from the clerical hierarchy—especially from the foreign clergy.[5]

The accession of an indigenous national clergy has not resolved the issue of social relations between priest and parishioner in local communities. The efficacy of church ritual is taken for granted as beneficial and essential, melding smoothly into the peasant view of life, yet there is social conflict. The ritual role of the priest is highly respected, but the personal character of the priest is subject to gossip and criticism. The priest is perceived as a professional entrepreneur who derives prestige and remuneration at the expense of others. There is criticism of the inevitable cost of devotional cards, baptism, first communion, marriage, and funerals. On the basis of the ability to pay, the celebration of masses and prayers for the dead are the cause of invidious social distinctions.

Protestantism

Pressoir (1945) traces the origins of Haitian Protestantism to Great Britain and the United States. He points to the influence of early 19th century English traders, abolitionists, educators, and missionaries; the immigration of Afro-Americans from the United States, bringing the Baptist and African Methodist Episcopal Churches to Haiti; the immigration of Protestant Jamaicans following the emancipation of slaves (1830's) and the failure of the sugar economy (1848); and the arrival of American Baptist missionaries in 1845.

No overarching hierarchy unites all Protestant groups. In keeping with old traditions of the separation of church and state, Protestant churches and missions do not lend themselves to state control. In general, they are disparate in character, subject to church splits and the formation of independent conferences. To a certain extent this reflects the schismatic fundamentalist heritage of American evangelicals whose missionaries are most numerous in the missions to Haiti. It is not difficult for independent Haitian Baptist congregations to find a mission sponsor among American independent Baptist missions. In effect two schismatic institutional traditions encounter each other to mutual benefit. Haitian Protestant churches actively seek out the material and social benefits of foreign mission sponsorship. Ironically, this situation actively promotes growing levels of dependence on foreign donors during a post-colonial era of Protestant missions in other parts of the world.

Government policy has generally favored Protestant missionization and foreign missionaries despite national policies directed against the Catholic clergy. Comhaire (1955) notes that Protestants were not appointed to the rural police force prior to the American Occupation. In 1942, Protestants were appointed on the assumption that they are less subject to local pressures and more accountable to the central state. This coincides with the era of anti-superstition campaigns under President Lescot (1941-1946). During a period of economic stagnation in the 1960's, Protestant missions flourished under a government laissez-faire policy which appeared to treat mission efforts as a useful type of foreign aid. Protestant missions have made a conspicuous contribution to the debate over literacy, favoring Creole over French. They have built schools, medical facilities, orphanages, and churches and operate a broad range of programs in education, agriculture, and handicrafts.

Though not a state church, the Protestant church exists and flourishes by the good graces of the state apparatus. A number of Protestant politicians and pastors have achieved prominence since the 1957 election of President François Duvalier. In 1969, he gave a well-publicized private audience to Oral Roberts, a Methodist evangelist from the United States. The key issue in state-church relations seems to be one of power maintenance. So long as Protestant churches are supportive, or at least politically neutral, their activities are generally tolerated and even welcomed. For the people of rural Haiti, the issue is more than one of simple neutrality. The presence of any foreign program bespeaks a position of tacit political support. The general perception is that no program exists unless it is "sent" by the president.

Given the political controversy over a foreign Catholic clergy, the government's toleration of foreign Protestant clerics is ironic. The Protestant clergy still has a strong complement of foreigners, chiefly Americans, despite trends toward indigenization. There is some effort to replace foreign mission personnel with American-trained Haitians who operate programs linked to American funds and policies. However, Haitian clergy and laity provide little support for several local ties to foreign Protestant missions and missionaries. The explanation for the government's lenient Protestant policy seems to lie in a dual strategy. The underlying political issue is not based on a consistent nationalist policy of de-colonizing the clergy; rather, the primary issue is one of eliminating sources of clerical opposition, and otherwise using the churches to promote support for the president. A secondary concern is the fostering of certain forms of economic development and "public services" in health and education.

At the level of ideology is a long-standing intellectual tradition which perceives Protestant religion as suited to modernization of the great masses of people. This is linked to a tendency among Haitian elites to favor an infusion of foreign culture, either American, French, or German models, as a solution to "backwardness" and underdevelopment. These attitudes also reflect the historical interests of France, Great Britain, Germany and the United States in the Caribbean. Haiti's elites have always tended to look outward for education and cultural models. This attitude came under heavy criticism by nationalist ideologies emerging out of the U.S. Occupation period. At present, American missionaries and other foreigners are commonly perceived as the bearers of civilization.

Protestantism and Anglo-Saxon cultural models went in and out of vogue with the Haitian state throughout the 19th century. Janvier (1886) suggested that Emperor Soulouque and President Geffrard should have "Protestantized" rather than "clericalized" the nation. He noted that a Haitian Protestantism would be more national in character, and less dangerous to Haitian independence, than a Catholic Church with a foreign clergy. Certain themes have cropped up repeatedly in the politics of Haitian religion: nationalist sentiment against a foreign clergy and support for Protestantism; support for Voodoo combined with criticism of the Catholic clergy; support for the Catholic clergy in tandem with sentiment against Voodoo and Protestantism.

Beidelman (1974) observes that missionary notions of religious conversion constitute a theory of social change. In addition, the process of missionizing clearly serves to introduce unintended values and attitudes. Protestantism in rural Haiti is a movement of considerable interest because of its modernizing ideological character. For example, Baptist church membership is based on rational adult decision-making as an assertion of personal convictions. To the degree this is sustained, its character is highly individualistic. Membership is not based on ancestral heritage or infant baptism but on a personal decision that may go against the preferences of family and community. Church membership is also contingent upon the agreement of a congregation of people who are not neighbors and kinfolk. There is a strong impulse toward literacy in Haitian Protestantism due to the conservative free church tradition which emphasizes Biblical literalism and the importance of Bible study. Membership in the Baptist Church entails a public rejection of the Catholic Church and the ancestral spirits. All in all, Protestant conversion constitutes a serious commitment to cultural change.

The Catholic Church has periodically had its anti-superstition campaigns; nevertheless, it has somehow managed to maintain an uneasy symbiosis with the Voodoo currents in Haitian religion. It teaches the catechism while benignly tolerating the folk traditions. Among Protestants, the Episcopal Church has taken pains to be familiar with Voodoo theology and symbols as a means of making Christianity relevant. Folk elements have been incorporated into Haitian Pentecostalism, including the use of drums, ecstatic religion, and spirit possession. In contrast, the Baptist mainstream takes a forceful stance against Voodoo practice and belief in every form. Baptists combine the evangelical fervor of an anti-Catholic heritage with the crusade against pagan rites. Voodoo is uncompromisingly denounced as demon worship.

In practice, the ideal thrust of Baptist evangelism does not always work out as intended. Conversion accounts reveal much about the periodic crises in peasant families and the role of Protestantism as a response to social and economic stress. While conversion is highly individualized, in practice it often serves as a collective family response to hardship. Conversion accounts also stress the Protestant way as yet another treatment for illnesses with supernatural causes since traditional curing rites are often very expensive. Most conversion accounts show practical considerations to be more significant than a crisis in conscience. According to one missionary pastor, the realities of conversion and changing economic aspirations are addressed in an implicit message to new converts and prospective church leaders: "Hook up with us and there's really no reason to go to Miami."

Protestant conversion thus tends to be pragmatic. It does not deny the reality of traditional Haitian religion but serves as a clear-cut alternative for dealing with traditional explanations of illness and economic hardship. In the process of doing so, new notions of being and value are introduced. Protestantism is also subject to the Haitian propensity for religious syncretism. There is a degree of ambivalence, however, in conversion. New converts sometimes leave the church in response to the demands of ancestral spirits. New elements in the Haitian experience tend to be successful only as they verify and provide continuity to the old. Protestantism vociferously denounces the "Satanic worship" of the Voodoo cosmology, but it also incorporates the reality of Voodoo as a means of propagating its own gospel of deliverance.

Baptist ideologies stress personal and individual membership by rational choice, legal admission standards, abstract principles of community, bureaucratic procedure, and collective planning for the future. This contrasts in key ways with traditional values in Haitian peasant cosmology which tend toward kinship ties and patron-client relationships rather than equal and individualized membership in groups. Peasant codes of honesty and personal responsibility are relativistic and subject to transaction and reciprocity. Strangers and non-kin are treated differently than those with special ties of obligation. These traditional values tend to undermine the functioning of Baptist institutions and other new organizational forms such as the secular community councils.[6] The stress on literacy in church and council tends to favor the young, sabotaging values of respect for age superiors and the aged. The sanctions for Haitian moral codes tend to stress external social controls such as threats of witchcraft, honor and dishonor, prestige and embarrassment, social status, and ties of obligation. In practice, these values are incorporated into the functioning of church and council, but these organizations outwardly stress personal responsibility to an impersonal group based less on personal ties than common commitment to an abstract ideology. Haitian codes of behavior are oriented more to expedience and pragmatism than to the moral abstractions of institutional Christianity.

Thus we find two ideal types, two distinct and contrasting sets of values co-existing at the same time. Both Voodoo cosmology and Baptist theology are composed of abstract values and beliefs, but Haitian values are explicitly relational, transactional, and sanctioned by external social controls. Traditional views of the world are focused on the here and now, on managing one's relationships to other beings, mortal and spiritual, properly, and on the pragmatic instrumental role of religion in the material world.

The Politics of Voodoo

What are the political implications of Haitian religion? The ancestor cult appears to be fundamentally apolitical. It is conservative as a guardian of peasant traditions and an expression of traditional values. As a religion of the poor it tends to compensate for economic hardship and mediates expressions of physical and spiritual needs. As a religion of peasant society, the cult of ancestors is closely tied to the land and the family economy of the *lakou*. Haitian Voodoo, as a religion of the oppressed, appears to channel social conflict away from political expression into the realm of the supernatural. Furthermore, the symbols of Voodoo are used as an ideological justification for political control by the governing elite. Historically, Voodoo has not served as an obstacle to revolt as is evident in the legendary ceremony of Bois Caiman leading to the uprising of the slaves during the revolutionary period. In later times, the *caco* guerrillas of the 19th and 20th centuries used protective charms and assaultive magic directed against the enemy in battle.

In terms of the politics of Voodoo, it is important to distinguish between domestic Voodoo and temple Voodoo. The elaboration of temple societies and religious specialists is a phenomenon of densely settled lowland areas and cities. Such areas have their own distinct local traditions, but they are also subject to an influx of people who are strangers to the area, cut off from traditional ties to land and kin. To some extent, a temple society under the control of a Voodoo priest or priestess plays the role of a surrogate family. The kinship motif is incorporated as the dominant metaphor of temple organization. Nevertheless, membership in a temple is more individualized, more of a personal choice than membership by birth in the cult of family spirits. There is a clearer parallel here to the traditional distinction between spectators and ritual performers than in the family cult where virtually everyone participates. Temple Voodoo there tends toward greater hierarchy and an elaborated division of labor.

Temples are also more subject to political influence. The temple leaders of Port-au-Prince, Leogane, and the Cul-de-Sac evidence a high degree of association with politicians and members of the civil militia. When François Duvalier gained control of the presidency in 1957, temple Voodoo was legitimized in new ways, contributing to a flowering of urban temple Voodoo. Voodoo continues to flourish in Port-au-Prince and has also been quite successful in accompanying the Haitian diaspora overseas. In view of the fierce Protestant assault on Voodoo practice during the last quarter century, perhaps the most remarkable feature of this religion is its persistence and adaptation to new social environments.

The rise of a new political elite since the 1940's has fostered the use of Voodoo as symbol. Haitian politicians are masters of the art of symbol and ceremony. No politician has been more successful than François Duvalier in the use of Voodoo signs, colors, mystical numbers, and portraits devoted to enhancing presidential power by identification with the popular religion. At this time there are numerous *houngan* in the region of the capital who give strong public support to government. State authorities at the highest level lend their patronage to Voodoo temples and priests. Well-established priests often carry a pistol, an important badge of political authority and power. Despite this convergence of mystical and political authority, temple Voodoo does not have a central hierarchy. New temples represent the entrepreneurial efforts of new *houngan,* priests who claim ritual kinship to other established priests through personal networks, *kanzo* initiation, and apprenticeship. In the end, temple Voodoo retains the local decentralized impulse which characterizes much of Haitian religion. Temple Voodoo is not a denial of the agrarian roots of the cult of ancestors served in the family compound, but rather an adaptation to a new and urbanizing social context. In this setting it tends more in the direction of congregationalism— groupings based on the re-definition of social relations in terms of fictional kinship among strangers, i.e., non-kin. Despite the absence of a clerical hierarchy, temple Voodoo represents a new opportunity for political influence from above mediated through personal ties between temple leaders and government authorities.

The social contradictions in folk religion illustrate the general character of peasant ties to the broader society. Voodoo does not lend itself to political manipulation, but its pervasive character is used in various ways by churchmen, politicians, and businessmen. It serves as a justification for institutional Christianity and missionary efforts and is invoked politically to rally nationalist sentiment, assure political support and build a tourist industry which feeds off tourist Voodoo. The foreign press is still prone to cite Voodoo as exotic evidence of Haitian backwardness. Voodoo first came to be of special interest to Haitian intellectuals during the American Occupation. Nationalist political interest in peasant religion and culture attained fruition in the postwar governments of Durmarsais Estimé (1946-1950) and François Duvalier (1957-1971) who was succeeded by his son Jean-Claude in 1971. The idea of Voodoo was rehabilitated by a new political elite. It is no small irony that the peasant majority which openly practices the religion is still generally excluded from political and economic power.

NOTES

[1] Romain's estimate (1970) of 15 percent is likely too low at the present time given the continued expansion of Protestant adherents, especially Pentecostals, during the past decade.

[2] The word "voodoo" is an outsider's term, a Euro-American word of Dahomean origin. It derives from the Fon word for "god" or "spirit." The Haitian word *vaudoun* refers specifically to a dance, never a religion. Dancing the *vaudoun* is traditionally linked to ritual although it may also be danced on secular occasions. The idiomatic Creole term for the cult of ancestral spirits is best translated as "serving the spirits." Despite the problems in using the word "voodoo" to refer to Haitian religion, it is a convenient term for outsiders, both foreigners and Haitian intellectuals, who wish to discuss Haitian folk religion and distinguish it from institutional Christianity.

[3] The term *houngan* is usually translated as "Voodoo priest." It may also be translated as curer, diviner or sorcerer. In practice, the term refers to two distinct ritual roles: (1) a Voodoo temple leader, (2) a curer or diviner without links to a temple or congregation. In the Cul-de-Sac, the term *houngan kanzo* refers to acquisition of ritual power by purchase and formal initiation, whereas *houngan makout* refers to ritual knowledge and skills based on inheritance. In L'Artichaut there are no temples but a similar distinction is made between purchased versus inherited ritual powers.

[4] E.g., northern Creole speakers refer to inherited family spirits as *jangn* and purchased spirits as *lwa*. Port-au-Prince servitors use *lwa* as a general reference to all spirits while making the same distinction between purchased spirits (*lwa achté*) and inherited spirits (*lwa rasi-n*, literally "root spirits"). Northerners use the word *jimo* for spirits of twinship whereas Port-au-Prince speakers generally use the term *marasa*.

[5] For further discussion of church and state in Haiti see Cabon (1933), Pressoir (1945), Jan (1958, 1959), Bastien (1966), Duvalier (1969), Nicholls (1970, 1974, 1979) and Paré (1972). For discussion of religion and politics, see also Brown (1972), Martinez (1972) and Bebel-Gisler and Hurbon (1976).

[6] The term "council" has reference to a state policy of establishing *konsèy kominotè* (community councils) in rural areas by means of extensive subsidy through foreign aid. See Smucker (1982) for a history of the community council movement and a detailed case study of one such council.

FRANCOPHILIA AND CULTURAL NATIONALISM IN HAITI

LEON-FRANÇOIS HOFFMANN

After Haiti gained its independence from France in 1804, the Haitians retained French as their official language and established strong sentimental bonds with the former metropole. They emulated French cultural models and tried to adapt French political, social, and legal institutions to Haitian needs. In their eyes, no other country had developed a more admirable code of social behavior or a richer intellectual heritage. At the same time, Haitians have always felt compelled to define and cultivate their unique national culture. Francophilia and cultural nationalism have thus coexisted throughout Haitian history, if sometimes uneasily. Of course, this uneasy coexistence remains almost exclusively the concern of that small minority of the population (about 10%) who, by virtue of their literacy, share in varying degrees the "French" component of the Haitian collective personality. For the illiterate peasant and proletarian masses, "Haitian-ness" is not a concern: in their own coherent and elaborate *Weltanschauung,* the French model is not relevant, let alone problematic. Further, since the entire structure of Haitian society has been undergoing profound changes for the last two or three decades, generalizations about Francophilia and cultural nationalism need adjustment and refinement if they are to be applied to the Haiti of the 1980's.

Before examining the French heritage, several preliminary observations should be made:

1. The relations between France and her former colonies have been and remain quite different from those between other European powers and their

respective former colonies in the New World. The United States, several countries of Hispanic America, and Brazil have by now equalled or surpassed their metropole in population, standard of living, economic development, and intellectual achievement. For former French possessions (with the possible and very recent exception of Quebec) this is not the case. Haiti, along with the newly-independent nations of France's erstwhile African empire, are conscious of their relative weakness in relation to the metropolitan "Hexagon." They are still trying to define and adjust the modalities of their participation in the Francophone cultural context, to which they often feel peripheral. Paris is the undisputed center of Francophony; the equivalent cannot be said of London, Madrid, or Lisbon.

2. Haiti and other former French colonies which have retained French are constrained by the rigidly prescriptive nature of the French language, which demands conformity with Parisian linguistic norms in social and intellectual discourse. Standard Parisian French is intolerant of regional lexical, syntactic, and even phonetic variations. Speakers of French in the former French colonies thus feel that they play little or no part in the elaboration and development of the language they use. While Parisian slang or neologisms enrich "Haitian French," no creolism or Haitian regional expression is expected to enrich metropolitan French. The situation is different in other New World ex-colonies: no one would seriously argue that American, Mexican, or Brazilian linguistic expressions or intonations are "inferior" or "incorrect," and that those of Great Britain, Spain, or Portugal provide the only acceptable norm. In fact, the British, Spanish, and Portuguese do not hesitate to adopt linguistic regionalisms from overseas.

3. When decolonization came to the New World, either the majority of the population (as in the United States and Canada) or the vast majority of the ruling class (as in Latin America) was of the same ethnic stock as the former metropole, except in Haiti, where all the French settlers and their White descendents emigrated or were eliminated. Further, while the rest of the continent continued to receive significant numbers of European immigrants after independence, Haiti did not. For all intents and purposes, all Haitians are totally or partially of African descent. The feelings of identification, kinship and racial solidarity which bind so many citizens of the Americas to their European cousins are absent in Haiti.

*   *   *   *   *

Francophilia

Once independence was achieved and the French eliminated, the new ruling class faced two main tasks: the organization of a nation that, after twelve years of savage war, was left with an economy in shambles and practically no administrators and technicians, and the consolidation of a precarious independence through diplomatic recognition abroad. Only by emulating Western organizational and technical models—more precisely, French models, with which the new leadership was better acquainted— could Haiti hope to achieve these goals. Thus the Haitians adopted French forms of government and public administration, as well as the French legal and educational systems. King Henri-Christophe, who ruled the northern part of Haiti between 1806 and 1820, did appeal to the British for technical aid and military assistance against a threatened invasion by the French, but, at his death, the country was reunited under the republican, French-oriented régime founded by Alexandre Pétion, whose successor, Jean-Pierre Boyer, successfully negotiated diplomatic recognition by Paris in 1825.

The links to France were not simply a matter of necessity but also one of choice. Many Mulattos, who formed the majority of the new ruling class, had French fathers or grandfathers. Some, as Presidents Pétion and Boyer, had been educated in France. Most were fluent in French and considered themselves more capable of leading the country towards development and "civilization" than the Créole-speaking and sometimes illiterate Black army officers with whom they shared power. Culturally, at least, the educated Mulatto class, which in colonial times had come to own approximately one third of the plantations and one fourth of the slaves, had more in common with French planters and administrators than with the illiterate mass of the *nouveaux libres,* as the former slaves were called. As for the Black members of the new elite, they were anxious to establish their superiority to the masses and their equality with their Mulatto partners. Familiarity with the French language and with the French way of life were obvious factors of differentiation; Francophilia was the expression of class self-interest.

It may seem peculiar that the newly independent Haitians modeled themselves on their former oppressors. Haitians were conscious of this paradox and attempted to resolve it by asserting that they had been oppressed in colonial times not by the French but by the *colons,* a disreputable minority of adventurers recruited from the dregs of French society. The *colons,* not the French, were held exclusively responsible for the horrors of the colonial system. Their lobby, not the people of France, was responsible for the misguided efforts of Bonaparte to reconquer the country and for Louis XVIII's reluctance to recognize Haitian independence. The *colons* were accused, not entirely without justification, of having been French in name only; Haitians pointed out repeatedly that they had not hesitated to appeal to the Spanish and the English when their interests were endangered, and that it was Toussaint Louverture, Brigadier-General in the French army whose native regiments fought under the revolutionary tricolor, who expelled the Spanish and British troops they had called in. In the eyes of the Haitians, the true French had promulgated the Rights of Man and extended them to the slaves that they, decades before any other nation, had emancipated. The fact that emancipation, rescinded by Bonaparte, had been honored mostly in the breach and that Martinique, Guadeloupe, and French Guiana remained slave colonies until 1848 was glossed over as an unfortunate detail. It was more important both for the country and for its ruling class that, as Louis-Joseph Janvier put it:

> The French should know how attached the Haitian nation is to the country who was the first to abolish slavery. (*La République d'Haïti et ses visiteurs (1840-1882)*, 2 vol. Paris, Marpon & Flammarion, 1883, II, 615).

This attachment was in large part a matter of national and especially of ruling-class self-interest, to be sure. Nevertheless, it long remained genuinely sincere; still today, the French revolutionary motto: *Liberté, Egalité, Fraternité* appears on the facade of Haitian governmental buildings.

During the nineteenth century, the Francophilia of the Haitian elite did not abate. Indeed, the opposite occurred. In 1825, twenty years after the fact, the government of Charles X recognized the independence of Haiti. The resentment of unrequited admiration and the latent fear of an attempt at reconquest were dispelled; France could henceforth be regarded as a diplomatic ally as well as a cultural model; the unsympathetic stepmother was now a benevolent older sister. The Haitian elite sent its sons to study in French lycées and universities. To have spent some time in the Latin Quarter was a source of social prestige and, naturally enough, those who had had this opportunity came back singing the praises of *la Ville-lumière* and *la Belle France*. The Haitian government and Haitian private schools contracted French teachers to come educate and, so to speak, gallicize Haitian students. Nineteenth-century Port-au-Prince newspapers often printed advertisements offering the services of visiting French men and women as tutors in music, painting, and deportment.

Once the Concordat was signed with the Vatican in 1860, French priests and missionaries, specially trained at Saint Jacques Seminary near Quimper, arrived in droves. Until François Duvalier's regime, the Haitian church was led by Breton monsignors. The French teacher and the French priest were exemplary figures. Monsieur Hodelin, in Frédéric Marcelin's novel *Thémistocle-Epaminondas Labasterre* (Paris: Olendorff, 1901), for example, is a Frenchman, a teacher at the local lycée who came to Haiti as a young man, a lay saint who dedicates his life to teaching the youth of a country he deeply loves. But he is much more than a pedagogue, never hesitating to criticize the selfishness and venality of the ruling class, preaching national regeneration through honesty, hard work, and dedication to the common people. Through the French teacher, the Haitian novelist holds up French wisdom, efficiency, and respect for human dignity as models and inspiration. Another example is Fernand Hibbert's *Séna* (Port-au-Prince: Imp. de l'Abeille, 1905): the eponymous hero is a corrupt Haitian senator who finally realizes his ambition to visit Paris. There he attends lectures at the Collège de France and meets French intellectuals by whom he is tutored in civic responsibility and political morality. The protagonist returns home determined to mend his ways and work for reform. In vain, as it turns out: he is imprisoned and later murdered by the clique in power.

The Francophilia of the Haitian elite is perhaps best expressed in Demesvar Delorme's *Les Théoriciens au pouvoir* (Paris: n.ed., 1870): the essayist affirms it, justifies it, and proposes the imitation of France as a national goal for Haiti:

> Our country waged a long war against France, and yet the country we like best is still France ... France speaks the language of human rights and of the generous impulses of the soul. ... Our young nation will be the founder of a new French civilization in the New World (I: 182-3).

During the nineteenth century, foreign merchants carved out the lion's share of Haitian commerce. They derived huge profits from the exploitation of the local economy and didn't hesitate to intervene in the political life of the country. The many revolutions and coups d'état which punctuate Haitian history up to the American occupation were often subsidized by the foreign merchants acting directly or through their embassies. Diplomatic pressure and even the dispatching of warships to enforce the demands of foreign merchants were common. This was, naturally enough, deeply resented by the Haitians. As late as 1940, H. Terlonge wrote in the 3 April issue of *Le Temps*:

> From the very day of Independence, a crafty, subtle, insidious and treacherous undertaking was set in motion. The foreigners came and called the tune. Thanks to their sinister manoeuvers we have succumbed to ruin and sordid poverty. Finally came what we know: the occupation and its manifold evils.

Significantly, German, American, and especially Syrian merchants were singled out for censure; not so their French counterparts. The German merchants were accused of Teutonic brutality, the Americans of Anglo-Saxon insensitivity, the Syrians of Near Eastern shiftiness. The French illustrated no unfavorable characteristic that could be imputed to their national origin.

To a considerable extent, the financial difficulties which made Haitian stability and progress impossible were directly traceable to the French. In exchange for the recognition of Haitian independence, President Jean-Pierre Boyer granted France a fifty percent tariff preference and pledged the enormous sum of one hundred and fifty million francs as reparations. In order to pay this "indemnity," Haiti was forced to borrow from French money lenders; and repeated re-negotiations of the original loan remained a major drain on the country's finances well into the twentieth century. Yet Haitian writers and the Haitian press seldom expressed resentment against the French for this scandalous exploitation.

There is more: several French travellers and journalists published extremely derogatory accounts of Haiti in which the country was held up to ridicule in most unfair and clearly racist ways: Granier de Cassagnac in 1844, Gustave d'Alaux in 1856, Paul Dhormoys in 1859, Victor Meignan in 1878, Edgard La Selve and Victor Cochinat in 1881, C. Texier in 1891 and Eugène Aubin in 1910, to name the most reprehensible.[1] Haitian writers never failed to protest against these defamatory attacks. Louis-Joseph Janvier, for example, in his two volume rebuttal *La République d'Haïti et ses visiteurs (1840-1882)* (Paris, Marpon & Flammarion 1883) systematically corrects lies and exaggerations, tirelessly explains and justifies what French hacks had chosen to deride and condemn. Yet France and the French are not implicated: "France is the capital of nations. Haiti is the Black France," writes Janvier (I, 57). Haitians insist on considering their French detractors as malicious, self-serving individuals, just as unworthy of belonging to "the capital of nations" as were the *colons* of yore.

The systematic celebration of France and the unwillingness to recognize actions prejudicial to Haitian interests taken by her government or by some of her citizens are of course not gratuitous. As we have seen, a fundamental preoccupation of the elites was to establish clearly their superiority to those they ruled. Further, the different strata of the ruling classes were engaged in a constant struggle among themselves, a struggle in which mastery of French, familiarity with things French and at least theoretical acceptance by the French on an equal footing were powerful weapons. The solution to Haiti's problems was proclaimed to be the acquisition and spread of Western culture and technology. Since it was agreed that France, among all the nations, was the most worthy of emulation, she was idealized, while criticism of the West was deflected onto other possible models. Moreover, the Haitians' knowledge of foreign countries was overwhelmingly derived from French books and from the French press, and Haitian public opinion was thereby influenced by French chauvinism. Pastor Mark Bird, a Protestant missionary who spent forty years in Haiti, complains in *The Black Man, or Haytian Independence* (New York, the author 1869, 323), that:

> The civilization and institutions of Europe and the United States are all viewed by means of the French press, and consequently with French hues and tints.

Besides, the French educational system had been imported by Haiti lock, stock and barrel. French religious orders ran the most prestigious schools and conscientiously fulfilled the task of Frenchification entrusted to them. So that as late as 1950, Mme Fortuna Guéry remembers in her *Témoignages* (Port-au-Prince, Deschamps, 1950, 72-73) that, when she was a girl:

> We learned that 'France was our country.' We knew the Marseillaise better than the Dessalinienne (*Haitian national anthem*). The 14th of July was celebrated with lavish ceremonies and the 1st of January (*Haitian Independence Day*) was only the day of New Year presents and best wishes.

Francophilia, however, was not only a function of class egoism and Gallic brainwashing. Since it was taken for granted that a model was needed, where else could the Haitians turn? The obvious alternative was the United States, whose status as a major and growing power and success in matters of organization and development were evident. But so was the imperialistic nature of its foreign policy, especially towards the Caribbean; as early as 1868, President Andrew Johnson had proposed to Congress the simple annexation of Hispaniola. Haitian political independence was no longer in danger from the French, while American intervention was fast becoming more than a remote possibility. Slavery was not abolished in the United States until 1863, and Jim Crow laws and other forms of racial discrimination remained the norm. Demesvar Delorme, in his *Réflexions diverses sur Haïti* (Paris, E. Dentu, 1873, 123, 133), warns his countrymen of the American peril:

> Haitians, if ever, may God forbid it, you were to lose your nationality, you would not have the right to speak as men in your own country. You would be reduced to bowing your heads before foreigners

(. . .) You would be despised and mistreated in the way men of our race are despised and mistreated in the United States. This danger is no longer remote (. . .) it is here, present, pressing, in our island, at our doors.

The fear of American intervention, the revulsion from American racism, and the distaste of Urbane Haitian aristocrats for plebeian American vulgarity reinforced the elite's Francophilia, which became even stronger under the American occupation of 1915-1934.

Admiral Caperton's Marines landed practically unopposed, and many Haitians welcomed them, not with enthusiasm, but in the hope they would put an end to the anarchy which had raged in Haiti during the preceding decades. However, when it became obvious that the occupation was going to last and that the U.S. Marines had no respect for Haitians, treating them as backward natives, anti-Americanism, along with Francophilia, increased.

The "ugly American" now becomes a stock figure in Haitian writings, and is more often than not contrasted with the admirable Frenchman.[2] The French are tolerant, Americans are racists; the French dislike violence, Americans exercise it blindly; the French are cultured and well-mannered, Americans are ignorant and boorish; French women are elegant and charming, their American sisters are vulgar and materialistic. In fact, emphasizing the French qualities of Haitian culture allowed the Haitians to affirm their superiority to the "Anglo-Saxon barbarians" under whose domination they suffered. Francophilia became a form of patriotism.

The Haitian ruling classes had neither the means nor the determination to take arms against the American soldiers. They could, however, resist what they perceived as the American attempts to replace France as a cultural model and to reduce Haitians to second-class dependents. Even before the occupation, Georges Sylvain had warned:

What would become of us, lost in the mass of enslaved New World Blacks? A pinch of Anglo-Saxon dust! . . . The more we hold on to our French culture, the more likely we are to keep our Haitian personality (quoted in Magloire 1908: 187).

The Americans tried to encourage the study of English to the detriment of French and to replace French academic programs, which stressed Greek, Latin, and French literature, with training in carpentry, typing, animal husbandry, and other "useful" trades. This effort the Haitians resisted vigorously. The constitution of 1918 was drafted in Washington and imposed on the Haitian government, which at least managed to stipulate, in article 24, that "French is the official language. Its use is mandatory in administrative and judicial matters" (Dejean 1975: 56). In the seven previous constitutions of Haiti, French had not required the protection of legal status. Dantès Bellegarde, who served as Minister of Education from 1918 to 1921, wrote in an article significantly entitled "The Island of Haiti is the Little France of the New World" (*Les Nouvelles,* January 22, 1923):

Nothing can deprive France of the place she occupies in our hearts. We are linked to her by blood and by language; this forms a sweet and solid link that we have neither the wish nor the power to break.

One could of course point out that, while Bellegarde, a distinguished Mulatto intellectual and diplomat, enjoyed a world-wide renown for eloquence, the Créole-speaking Black peasant guerillas who faced American machine guns with machetes and old hunting rifles were linked to France neither by blood nor by language. Be that as it may, an anonymous journalist, reviewing W. B. Seabrook's sensationalistic and derisive *Magic Island* (New York, The Literary Guild of America, 1929) affirmed in the July 1st 1930 issue of *La Petite Revue*:

By her legislation, by her customs, by her education, Haiti has a civilization, French, to be sure, but perhaps superior to whatever the U.S. could offer her.

Indeed, many Haitians have attributed to its French culture the country's successful resistance to assimilation by the Americans. G.L., in an article published in *Le Temps* on June 12th, 1937, for example:

It is said that Haiti imitates France. That is how it should be. (. . .) Hence that strong personality which impressed the occupiers. Without that suit of armor, without all those French traits that are inborn in us or that we have assimilated, we would have remained primitive Africans, and the U.S. would have swallowed us up in one gulp.

More recently, Jean Fouchard remembers, in *Trois discours* (Port-au-Prince, Impr. de l'Etat, 1962, 64):

To organize the Resistance, we used as barricades our origins and our language (. . .) and the road to Enlightenment that, for so many generations, French educators had mapped out in the hearts of our youth.

But, as we shall see, while the French heritage was reaffirmed during the American occupation, a more vigorous pursuit of the national identity was undertaken.

Cultural Nationalism

It is seldom easy to define precisely what is meant by cultural nationalism in the ideology of a social group. The goals and strategies of each cultural nationalism are determined by the specific context which nurtures it and, of course, no two such contexts are exactly alike. We might, for the sake of clarity, distinguish two types of cultural nationalism:

The first type emerges when a social group feels dominated by a more powerful group, perceived as alien, which attempts to impose upon it its language, laws, customs or values. The social group feels "colonized." Such cultural nationalistic currents are generally linked to a desire for increased political autonomy, in Third World regions placed under the tutelage of a foreign country, Quebec and parts of the former Austro-Hungarian Empire, for example—but not in Haiti.

The Haitian revolutionaries did not at first strive for independence, but for emancipation and the attainment of human rights. Only when it became obvious that the former could not be achieved without the latter did the two become inextricably linked. Once Saint Domingue became Haiti, the Haitians never considered any form of political union or association with France. Having attained their political goal, they felt that when asserting and celebrating their French heritage they were affirming an integral aspect of their national personality.

The other type of cultural nationalism may arise when members of a society come to feel that its autochthonous traditional culture is threatened by the march of history, that its collective personality is being altered in favor of a lifestyle perceived as superimposed upon it rather than organically evolving in harmony with national specificity. Such cultural nationalisms tend to be conservative or even reactionary: they preach a return to tradition, to "the way things used to be." Such, for example, are Gandhi's rejection of Western technology along with British domination, or the Ayatollah Khomeini's call for an unadulterated Islam purged of modernist infections introduced by lackeys of the West. In other cases, cultural nationalism can be limited to the celebration of an autochthonous ethos, to be rediscovered and promoted for the sake of a stronger sense of national identity: the recent exaltation by Mexico and Peru of their Amerindian past, the Nazi revival of Germanic mythology, or the more modest regionalist cultural movements in today's France are possible examples.

Cultural nationalism in Haiti is not of that type either, since the autochthonous culture of Hispaniola had disappeared with the elimination of the native Arawaks before the French and African ancestors of the Haitians reached the island.[3] The roots of "Haitianity" are found in West Africa and in France and—to pursue the metaphor—its trunk is nurtured by both, with its elite branches drawing most of their sustenance from the first, and its popular branches from the second.

Haitian cultural nationalism does not dismiss or downgrade the French components of the nation's originality. Rather, it argues for the affirmation of those factors which differentiate Haiti from its former metropole and make it something other than "a little Black corner of France." Aspects of Haitian cultural nationalism can, it seems to me, be grouped under the general headings of "Racial Pride," "Linguistic and Cultural Authenticity" and "The Popular Ideology."

Racial Pride

Haitians have always proclaimed themselves to be descendants of Africans and citizens of the Black Republic. Legend has it that, when the time came to design the national flag, Dessalines adopted the French tricolor after ripping out its white band, as a symbolic refusal of white colonialism under any form. The first Haitian Constitution gives the automatic right of residency and great facilities for the acquisition of citizenship to any person of African descent.[4] The African origins of all true Haitians are proudly affirmed even by light-skinned Mulattos. Insofar as the affirmation of differences from the French manifests a nationalist current in Haitian ideology, Black pride is one of its fundamental components.

Haitian Black pride is more than platonic; the Haitians have always protested mistreatment of their brothers, whether in or out of Africa. Particular indignation has been expressed at the persecution of Blacks in the United States, at abuses perpetrated in the African colonies, at Mussolini's rape of Ethiopia, and at apartheid. In the League of Nations, the U.N. and other international agencies, the Haitian delegation has strongly supported Black interests. The Créole word for "man" is nèg; all foreigners, whatever their phenotype, are called blan.

This does not mean that Haitians look to Africa for cultural models. Until very recently, next to nothing was known of Black African religion, social organization, philosophy, or aesthetic expression. To speak of Black African civilization long seemed a contradiction in terms.

The anthropological study of the cultural links between Haiti and West Africa, in matters of agricultural technology, market organization, religion, performing arts, etc., remains rudimentary at best. However, interest in

Black Africa on the part of Haitian intellectuals has been growing steadily in the last few decades. Numerous Haitian teachers and technicians are working today in Francophone Africa, and an *Institut d'études africaines* has recently been organized in Port-au-Prince.

But these are recent developments. Until African countries gained their independence, Haitians saw themselves as spokesmen for Blacks everywhere, not because their country might represent a flowering of African civilization in the New World, but because their independence and successful integration into Western culture refuted the racist contention that Blacks were congenital primitives incapable of self-government and "progress." In 1838, an anonymous editorialist had written in the September 27th issue of *L'Union*:

> Haiti has regenerated the African race and its descendants. The result . . . has been the rehabilitation here of the race which elsewhere is kept in infamy.

Camille Borno would reassert, in *La Feuille du Commerce* for June 22nd 1861:

> Our origins make it our duty to prove, by incontrovertible acts, that Blacks, just like Whites, have been created intelligent. (. . .) The vindication of the Black race is the challenge we have taken up; is it not worthy of Haitian society?

Conversely, Haitians feel that when their country flounders the whole Black race is disgraced. As *L'Opinion Nationale* put it on February 4th 1893, at a time when Haiti was in the throes of anarchy:

> What must foreigners think of our Republic? If they know what is going on within our borders, don't you think that the friends of our race are shrugging their shoulders and sighing in desperation?

Haitian cultural nationalism has always manifested itself in the affirmation that not only Haitians but all Blacks are as intellectually and temperamentally capable as Whites to succeed in Western artistic and scientific endeavors. Now that African traditions are being recognized, the exploration of Haiti's cultural ties to the African "Homeland" will no doubt be pursued.

Linguistic and Cultural Authenticity

The Haitians, as we have seen, tend to have an almost fetichistic attitude toward the French language. In 1909, Dr. Nemours Auguste wrote that, beside national pride, "one of the most perfect tools for the regeneration of our society" was French:

> (...) the clearest, best balanced of languages, the most supple and intelligent servant of thought known to Mankind since the days of Greece (Pompilus 1961).

In the July 1927 presentation of a new journal, significantly entitled *Revue indigène* (which was to play an important part in Haitian intellectual history), Noumil Sylvain pointed out that

> In this Spanish and English-speaking America, our glorious destiny is, along with Canada and the French West Indies, to maintain the French language and French traditions. . . .

But the very fact that attachment to the French language seems to need constant reaffirmation indicates a certain uneasiness. Many Haitians point out that to call their country "French-speaking" when the overwhelming majority of the citizenry neither speaks nor understands French is wishful thinking at best and hypocrisy at worst. They further point out that even for the educated minority it is seldom considered the mother tongue but rather a painfully acquired one. As early as 6 November 1837, Emile Nau wrote in *L'Union*:

> In our writings and our conversations, French always sounds as an acquired language; one of the benefits of civilization would be to naturalize it among us. (...) It will, however, have to be modified and adapted to our needs (...) and perhaps France will not read with displeasure her language thus bronzed under the tropical sun.

Frédéric Marcelin humorously describes the Haitians' relations to their official language in *Thémistocle-Epaminondas Labasterre* (Paris, Olendorff, 1901, 203):

> What anxieties we suffer because of this devilish French language! The concentration it demands makes us sweat where we already sweat enough because of the climate.

And the poet and novelist Philippe Thoby Marcelin, in an article entitled "The Language Problem" (*La Relève,* avril 1938, 18), concurs:

> We take it for granted that we speak pure, elegant, refined, stylish French (. . .) this is one more proof of our propensity to see ourselves different from what we actually are. (. . .) For us, French is an acquired language (. . .) and, right from the time we utter our first words, a thing foreign and almost inimical.

As far as language is concerned, cultural nationalism will argue for acceptance of "Haitian French" (i.e. the regional semantic and lexical variations peculiar to the French spoken in Haiti) and of creolisms as a legitimate means to enrich Haitian French.[5] It can go further, proclaiming Créole to be the national language of all Haitians and demanding its recognition on a par with the official language. Thus T. Carrié in "A Castle in Spain" (1889) argued:

> Even though Haiti is independent, we are still supposed to be ruled by the Académie française, which has no jurisdiction over certain turns of phrase, certain expressions which are our own, which express our climate, our way of life, our African origins? Oh, come now!

Twenty-five years later, the novelist Fernand Hibbert points out in *Les Simulacres* (1914) that:

> The French we speak and write is no more the French of France than American English is the English of the British Isles. And let me add that nothing is more ridiculous than a Haitian purist (1923: 66).

The Haitian attitude towards French has always been a mixture of pride and uneasiness: pride in being part of Francophony, uneasiness at the obstacles this appurtenance poses to the development and expression of the national identity, uneasiness, bordering on resentment, at remaining not a political but a cultural dependency of France.

In matters linguistic, the defense and celebration of Créole is the most obvious manifestation of cultural nationalism. This is still an ongoing process. Créole was first regarded as a bastardized, degraded form of French, fit only for communication with peasants and servants. Little by little, it came to be considered as a dialect, charming in its bucolic naïvety; poets even condescended to use it for occasional love poems or humorous pieces, transcribing this oral language as best they could with French phonemes. Following the example of French dialectologists, amateur linguists began to study its syntax and to propose etymologies for its lexicon.

With time Créole gained broader acceptance, both among intellectuals and in social use. More and more poets wrote in Créole. Morisseau-Leroy's 1953 play *Antigone en créole* inspired other playwrights. Novelists began by including occasional Créole words in their works; whole dialogue passages in St.-Aude's *Parias* (1949) are in Créole; Frankétienne's remarkable *Dezafi* (1975) is the first Haitian novel written entirely in Créole. Créole periodicals have a wide circulation both in Haiti (*Bòn Nouvèl*) and among exiles (*Sèl*, published in Brooklyn since 1972). In 1979, prescriptive rules for the transcription of Créole according to strict phonetic principles were adopted. Once reserved by French-speaking Haitians for informal conversation with close friends and relatives, Créole is now accepted in an ever-increasing variety of social situations. Article 35 of the 1964 Constitution reaffirms the status of French as the official language, but adds:

> Nevertheless, the Law determines in what cases and under which circumstances the use of Créole is allowed and even recommended to safeguard the material and moral interests of those citizens who have insufficient knowledge of the French language (Mathelier 1976: 360).

The growing pervasiveness of Créole in Haitian life is still bitterly resisted by many, and parity with French is still to be won. Yet there is no doubt that, in the area of language, the cultural nationalist ideology is gaining ever-increasing support.

Cultural nationalism manifests itself in education as well. The French system originally adopted in Haiti has been increasingly criticized. The more so because it has remained "frozen": the necessary adaptations continually made in the metropole were imperfectly carried out in Haiti, if at all. Haitian critics have always protested against the fact that the French educational system is ill-suited to the real needs of the country. Some argued that elements of the more pragmatic Anglo-Saxon system should be incorporated, and that it was scandalous to produce graduates knowledgeable about French literature, history, and geography, yet ignorant of Haitian realities, and even (especially after completing their education in Paris) alienated from their own country.

While some progress has been made in improving teaching materials, much remains to be done. Haitian literature, for example, is, for all intents and purposes, not yet part of the curriculum. As far as education is concerned, cultural nationalism still manifests itself by vigorous protest rather than concrete reform. If and when it will achieve the indispensable overhaul of Haitian education remains to be seen.

As the demands for Haitianization of education became more vigorous, the feeling grew that French teachers—and especially those who ran the prestigious congregational schools—were an obstacle to needed reforms. This disillusionment was exacerbated by the "Anti-superstition Crusade" that the French clergy conducted in the early 1940's with the reluctant assistance of President Elie Lescot. Anti-*vodùn* sermons were preached, peasants were encouraged or pressured into publicly renouncing their ancestral gods, and processions were organized to destroy sanctuaries and ritual objects. Not that most elite Haitians favored *vodùn,* to be sure, but many saw the "Crusade" as intolerable meddling in the internal affairs of the country, all the more so since France and things French had by then lost some of their prestige, and Haitian intellectuals were engaged in a vigorous reappraisal of what constituted the national identity. This reappraisal was, to a considerable extent, motivated by Populist ideology, as we shall see.

The Populist Ideology

Cultural nationalism is a constant factor in Haitian intellectual history. Throughout nearly two centuries of national existence, it has become increasingly articulate and pervasive. Once again, it should be stressed that it is complementary to the French heritage; in other words, its spokesmen do not argue that the French heritage is simply an alien component of the collective personality, the symbol of authenticity, the pathological sequel of colonization. What they do see as alien, inauthentic, and pathological are the elite's refusal to acknowledge the African dimension of its own personality and its refusal to recognize that the untutored masses, whose share of the French heritage is minimal at best, are the depositories of cultural traits which are nothing if not Haitian.

Haitian intellectuals have long lamented the abyss that separates the urban, literate, French-speaking, Christian, Western-oriented "haves" from the rural, illiterate, Créole-speaking, *vodùnist* "have-nots." Windsor Bellegarde put it most graphically when he wrote, in "Psychologie de l'éducation haïtienne" (*Haïti littéraire et scientifique,* January 20th, 1912):

> Haitian society appears to the sociologist's eye under the form of two distinct organisms, of two superposed social strata, differing one from the other as much by their structure as by the whole of their respective inclinations.

The populist dimension of cultural nationalism was at first socio-political rather than cultural. It inspired protests against the elite's oppression and exploitation of the masses and denunciations of its failure to exercise its responsibility of raising the masses' standard of living, education, and political participation. "Our ruling class," wrote Rodolphe Charmant (1946: 292):

> has always failed in its duty to lead, direct and organize. It has instead made use of the country ... , believed itself to be of superior lineage, even of a different race, striven to distance and isolate itself from the common people, claimed the privileges of an oligarchist caste, and grossly exploited public goods and revenues.

But, for a long time, the self-appointed spokesmen of the downtrodden proposed measures that took no account of the peasants' culture. Their solution was simply to bring the benefits of Western type development to the masses, to integrate them into the French-oriented upper-class way of life. How? Antoine Innocent explains:

> Education: That is the whole secret.
> Let us then build schools in the countryside and libraries and lecture halls wherever needed ... Let us establish theaters in our towns, let us offer the masses concerts, let us, in a word, do all the things liable to initiate them to a feel for beauty (1906: 167).

What Innocent proposed, in fact, is to teach the destitute, who have no "feel for beauty," Greek, Latin, and French; to offer them plays by Racine and Corneille, as well as Berlioz symphonies and Bizet operas. This, paradoxically, is a typically colonialist attitude. The Haitian elite's duty, like the White man's burden, is to extend its own culture to its charges, totally disregarding their own "native" cultural heritage.

At the same time as the French heritage was reaffirmed during the American occupation, Haitian intellectuals embarked upon a systematic critical reappraisal of the values which had led Haiti to such sorry straits. Their conclusions were formulated by Jean Price-Mars in the important book *Thus Spake the Elder* (1928). He argued for the reassessment and acceptance of the Haitian collective personality, reminding his elite countrymen that 90% of the Haitians were practitioners of *vodùn* and speakers of Créole, that theirs was a rich, complex, and valuable culture, and that is was in fact the most authentically Haitian contribution to the cultural treasure of mankind. Price-Mars and his school went further; according to them, elite Haitians refused to face the fact that their mentality and attitudes were only partially traceable to the French and that their sensitivity was also influenced by their African heritage. The country's difficulties, it was argued, were partly due to the insistence on behaving like "Black Frenchmen" and seeing Haitian reality simply as a tropical variant of French reality to be treated according to the French norms.

Price-Mars' conclusions were considered revolutionary and are, still today, far from being universally accepted. But they gave powerful support to cultural nationalism. Peasant life, until then practically ignored, was investigated and illustrated by novelists and poets. The Bureau d'Ethnologie, with a mandate to study the language, religion, and traditions of the masses, was founded in 1941. In 1944, the Centre d'Art was opened, to assist and promote "naive" Haitian painters of humble origins. Choirs began to include Créole peasant songs in their repertoire, and dance companies did the same with folk-dances. The idea that Créole was a respectable, full-fledged language and *vodùn* more than a hodge-podge of primitive superstitions gained progressively wider acceptance.

Despite its strong populist component, cultural nationalism has not yet inspired significant concrete measures to improve the lot of the downtrodden, whose standard of living remains as abysmal as ever and whose level of participation in the political and intellectual life of the country is still minimal. But, at least theoretically, the contribution of the masses to the Haitian cultural originality is now generally acknowledged. So long as it does not endanger its privileged status, the Haitian elite is now willing to recognize that the national collective personality is also rooted in the African tradition as it developed among the forgotten majority of rural citizens.

Conclusion

There is no doubt that Haitians no longer look to the French model as the only acceptable one in matters of social organization and personal behavior. This distancing from the French heritage can be attributed to a variety of causes: the failure of the French to prevent, or even to protest against, the American occupation; the eclipse of France as a major power during and immediately after World War II; the identification of the traditional elite as more French than Haitian by a new elite, recruited from the middle and lower strata of the *classes moyennes* (which feels, not without some justification, that it had been discriminated against by the "Gallicized" aristocracy); the growing number of Haitian professionals trained in American, Canadian, Latin American, and other non-French universities; the presence in the United States of hundreds of thousands of Haitians from all social classes and the hope of many more to join them. For this latter group of potential emigrants, knowledge of English is as essential to the attainment of a better life as fluency in French used to be. The presence in Haiti of large numbers of development technicians from all over the world and the broadened outlook of Haitian intellectuals who, for political and economic reasons, have been forced to settle abroad (seldom in France), have strengthened this trend.

The French heritage is becoming, it seems to me, a matter of historical interest rather than a living reality. As to cultural nationalism, it is difficult to assess its strength and to predict how it will manifest itself in the future. There are two main reasons for this uncertainty. First, many intellectuals are in exile and put all their energies into purely political activity; they consider the overthrow of the present regime to be their most urgent task. Precise proposals as to ideological lines for an eventual new government are generally regarded as premature and potentially divisive. All political groups (in the diaspora as well as in Haiti) claim to be populist, but no one would argue that a consensus exists as to linguistic (French vs. Creole) and educational policy, attitudes towards *vodùn,* modalities of mass participation in government, or foreign policy orientation.

The second reason is the spread of what I would call a *comprador* mentality among the Haitian "haves." Despair of ever finding an ideological basis for national progress and a reluctance even to speculate on the matter appear to be widespread. Concern is focused on personal and family financial success and on the technical feasibility of this or that punctual scheme for limited development. Most of the Haitian upper classes now have family and business ties abroad and, as a result, have the option of leaving the country with relatively little trauma. For them, the failure of Haiti is no longer as vital a concern as it used to be. Haitians, like many foreign merchants and entrepreneurs, are deeply appreciative of Haiti's beauty and charm. They are content to stay, as long as the political and economic situation allows it, but do not feel obligated to invest their energies in matters of national interest. This aloofness is an adaptation to the deep crisis the country is undergoing. Before this crisis is resolved, it will be very difficult to predict with any accuracy the modalities in which cultural nationalism will inform a renewed debate on the future of Haiti.

NOTES

Unless otherwise indicated, all translations of quotations are mine.

[1]Adolphe Granier de Cassagnac, *Voyage aux Antilles françaises,* 2 vols., Paris, *1842 and **1844; Gustave d'Alaux, *L'Empereur Soulouque et son Empire,* Paris, °1856; Paul Dhormoys, *Sous les Tropiques,* Paris, °°1864; Victor Meignan, *Aux Antilles,* †1878; Edgard La Selve, *Le Pays des Nègres,* Paris, ††1881; Victor Cochinat, articles in *La Petite Presse,* Sept.-Dec. 1881; C. Texier, *Au Pays des généraux,* Paris, ‡1891; Eugène Aubin, *En Haïti,* Paris, ‡‡1910. On the relations of Haiti with foreign countries and on the activities of foreign nationals in Haiti, see Hénock Trouillot, "La République d'Haïti entre la francophonie et l'américanisme, XIXe siècle et début du XXe", *Revista de historia de América* (México) 80, julio-diciembre de 1975, 87-145.

*Fontains	°Michel Lévy	†Plon	‡C. Lévy
**Les Imprimeurs Unis	°°Librairie Centrale	††Hachette	‡‡A. Colin

[2] See Gindine 1974 and Hoffmann 1980.

[3] In point of fact, some Haitian writers have made a timid attempt at co-opting the Arawaks as "ancestors." Jean-Joseph Vilaire (1881-1967) wrote a series of *Sonnets indiens*; Frédéric Burr-Reynaud (1884-1946) wrote poems in honor of Queen Anacaona, whom Alcibiade Fleury-Battier (1841-1883) had chosen as the heroine of his verse drama *Anacaona*; Henri Chauvet composed a five-act drama entitled *La Fille du Kacik* and, more recently, Jacques-Stéphen Alexis enlisted the shades of the Arawaks in the cause of his pan-Caribbeanism. But to claim that this Indianism is significant in the context of Haitian nationalism would, I think, be an exaggeration.

[4] On Haitian attitudes towards race and color, see Nicholls 1979.

[5] On the characteristics of Haitian French, see Pompilus 1961.

THE LINGUISTIC SITUATION OF HAITI

ALBERT VALDMAN

The low level of educational development in Haiti has been attributed, in part, to the complex relationship between French and Haitian Creole (Creole). This erroneous assumption conveniently divorces educational underdevelopment from the economic, political, and social inequities that feed it, and it obscures the fact that there is no complex linguistic problem in Haiti. What does in fact exist is the effort, successful so far, of some segments of the population to maintain a linguistic differentiation that helps to perpetuate their economic, social, and political privileges.

Compared to that of most Third and Fourth World countries, the linguistic situation of Haiti stands out by its extreme simplicity. The Black Republic is neither bilingual nor diglossic; it is in essence a monolingual country where only a small proportion of the population (no doubt not exceeding five percent) may be considered composed of balanced bilinguals —that is, persons able to use fluently the community's main languages. All Haitians, from the landless peasant to the affluent and socially prominent dweller of Pétionville, share in the everyday use of Creole; 90 percent of the population communicate and express themselves only by means of that tongue.

During the spring of 1982 a fierce verbal war was waged in the press of the Republic of Port-au-Prince. At issue were the relative merits of the educational reform conducted vigorously by the former minister of education, Joseph C. Bernard. The debate centered in fact on a single issue: the introduction of Creole as the main classroom vehicle for the first four years of primary schools. One of the arguments opponents of the change

77

put forward was that cutting off rural children's contact with French would effectively deny them opportunities for economic and social advancement and isolate them in a linguistic ghetto. Proponents of the reform program advanced that, in addition to the fact that the use of Creole would insure more effective learning of school subjects, the teaching of French as a foreign language would lead to the acquisition on the part of rural children to a functional mastery of the country's official language not generally imparted by present pedagogical practices.

Although the choice of classroom language may not be the determining factor in accounting for Haiti's educational underdevelopment, the issue must be tackled seriously in any restructuring of the educational system. High priority should be given to a thorough analysis of the nature of communicative networks in Haiti and to the precise functioning of the country's two languages. It is this analysis that I will attempt to sketch out here. In particular, I will deal with the notions of bilingualism and diglossia as they apply to the Haitian situation, and I will discuss such issues as the standardization and modernization of Creole, touching upon the oft-debated issue of the "bridge to French" (*le passage au français*).

Bilingualism and Diglossia in Haiti

The term bilingualism is inappropriate to refer to the linguistic situation of Haiti on at least two counts. First, Haiti, unlike Canada for example, is not officially bilingual. The 1918 constitution written under the aegis of American overseers during the occupation ironically proclaimed "French is the official language. Its use is required in public services."[1] That status was confirmed by the 1964 Constitution which, however, adds the following qualification (Article 35 *in fine*):

The law determines the cases and conditions in which the use of Creole is permitted and even recommended for the safeguard of the material and moral interests of those citizens who do not have a sufficient knowledge of the French language.

No complementary documents were drafted to specify the circumstances when the use of Creole was permitted or tolerated, except the decree of December 18, 1979, relative to the educational reform, promulgated by the Legislative Chamber. That decree specified that "in order to make education accessible to all" and "in order to safeguard cultural unity":

The use of Creole, as a language spoken by 90 percent of the Haitian population, is allowed in the schools as classroom vehicle (*langue-instrument*) and subject of instruction (*objet d'enseignement*).

By careless drafting, the authors of this text perpetuated the erroneous notion that in Haiti some proportion of the population does not use Creole as its means of everyday communication. The text should have read: "as a language used exclusively by 90 percent of the population."

The latest constitution of Haiti (1983) declares both French and Creole to be national languages of the state (Art. 62). Although French is still recognized as the official language, the drafters of the article fudge by stating that it "serves" as the official language. While this phrasing represents some accommodation to the wishes of the groups in Haitian society promoting the vernacular, the 1983 constitution falls quite short of officialization.

Second, the proportion of Haitians who possess a high level of communicative ability in French and for whom the official language could serve all linguistic needs does not exceed five percent. Few Haitians are balanced bilinguals and, by the most sanguine estimates, ten to fifteen percent at most are able to demonstrate some level of communicative ability in the official language.

In his seminal article on diglossia, Charles A. Ferguson (1959) characterized the relationship between French and Creole in Haiti as one of four prototypical diglossic cases. According to Ferguson's classical definition, diglossia describes the strictly complementary use by a linguistic community of two highly differentiated *varieties* of the same language. In addition a dominance relationship exists between the two varieties: the High (H) variety enjoys social prestige in the community and is assigned administrative, educational, and belletristic functions, the Low (L) variety is relegated to vernacular functions.

Haiti fails as a case of strict diglossia on several counts:

1. French and Creole are two distinct languages, not two varieties of the same language as are, for instance, High German and Swiss German in German-speaking Switzerland. Indeed, French and Creole are not even genetically related in the way that French and Latin are, for example.

2. In a diglossic situation the L language is acquired at home but the H language is learned by more formal processes such as schooling. Bilingual Haitians acquire both languages at home and, as is the case for children in all francophone countries, perfect their control of the official language at school.

3. True functional complementation no longer obtains between French and Creole. On the one hand, for the bilingual elite, French serves all vernacular functions. On the other hand, no domain of use and no communicative situation is exempt from the encroachment of Creole. In rural Haiti and among the urban masses, all intellectual, psychological, and social needs are served by Creole. The vernacular tongue has gained entry to

all spheres of rural and lower class urban life and culture, the religious domain, local administrative matters, radio and television, and even in schools as transitional language. In addition, as Dejean (1978) perceptively observes:

One can hardly state that Creole is excluded from various sophisticated domains of use to which an illiterate population has in fact no access.

Haiti is best characterized as a nation composed of two linguistic communities: the bilingual elite and the monolingual rural and urban masses (see Figure 1).[2] The two-community model reveals two important

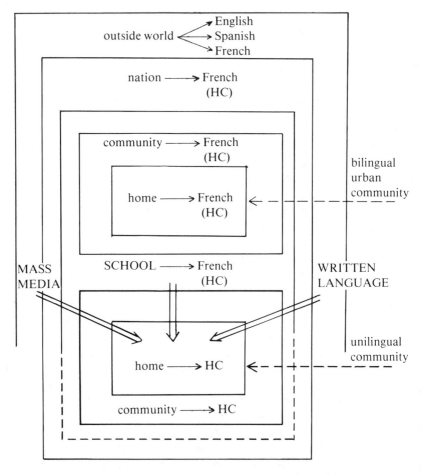

Figure 1. Communication Networks in Haiti

aspects about the linguistic situation of Haiti. First, there is little linguistic interaction between the two communities. Second, the rural folk and the urban lumpen proletariat have few opportunities to use or even hear French because the schools constitute the main vector for the transmission of the official language.

An analysis of the linguistic situation of Haiti must include an inventory of the functions played by the various languages known by diverse segments of Haitian society. The following account makes use of a five-way differentiation of linguistic functions adapted from a model proposed by Gobard (1974). Gobard identifies vernacular, vehicular, referential, and magico-religious functions which may be performed by different varieties of a single language, by different languages, or by a combination of both. The vernacular function refers to everyday communicative and expressive needs in interactions with intimates and within the in-group; the vehicular function refers to communication with out-groups, either within or outside of the community; the referential function describes the transmission of the cultural heritage of a society; and the magico-religious function involves attempts to seek mediation of supernatural forces.

Language Functions	Monolingual Community	Bilingual Community
Vernacular	Creole	Creole/French
Vehicular		
within Haiti	Creole	Creole/French
outside Haiti	(Spanish, English)	English/Spanish/ French
Referential	French, (Creole)	French (English, Latin)
Symbolization of power	French	French

Table 1. Model of Language Functioning for Haiti

Gobard's model fails to provide for another important function of language: the indication of a speaker's membership in various social groups and the symbolization of power relationships within the community or the polity. In Haiti, French symbolizes membership in the social elite and in the groups that hold economic and political power. Bentolila and Ganni (1982) also see in that language an instrument for the acquisition of privileged status and "a vector for the importation of educational models alien to the socio-cultural realities of the country." Those not proficient in French perceive it as a means of escaping poverty and depreciated status while those who do possess proficiency use it as a means of excluding the masses from the political process and denying them economic opportunities. As Lundhal has observed (1979), French serves as an effective filtering device that keeps the rural masses in their place. That French functions more as a social marker than as a means of communication is clearly perceived by monolingual speakers. Table 2 presents the results of a language attitude survey and in-depth interview conducted among a group of parents of school children in the Les Cayes area. Most of the respondents were peasants with little or no schooling.[3]

The responses to the questionnaire reflect the alienation the Haitian peasant feels toward French. For him the official language plays no major role in his daily life; he does not need it to solve day-to-day problems or to cope with his immediate environment, and, surprisingly, he believes that his native tongue is appropriate for many of his interactions with the world outside. Rural parents do not appear to oppose the introduction of Creole in the classroom provided however that the acquisition of certain competence in French remains the primary objective of the schools. At the same time, they realize that the acquisition of any useful level of competence in the official language requires an extended period of schooling, in the opinion of most of our respondents, several years of secondary level instruction. In commenting about his own deficient proficiency in French, one of the parents remarked apologetically:

M pa pale li klè paske se nan sètifika m rive / (I don't speak it—French —any clearer because I only got as far as the last primary school grade).

Indeed, since in psycholinguistic studies the term acquisition connotes the learning of a language under natural conditions according to a program determined in large part by inner mechanisms, it is inappropriate to describe the process by which Haitian children develop a mastery of French. Several parents employed a term widely used in Haiti to refer to loas that are not part of one's family legacy, achte "bought," to characterize French:

Franse se pa lang pa-n, se lang achte ... Ti moun fet pou konnen kreyòl paske se lang-ni, li pa achte / (French is not our language it's a "bought" tongue ... Children learn Creole naturally because it's their language; they haven't 'bought' it).

	French	Creole	Both French & Creole	English	Spanish	NR
What is the language of Haiti?	1	23				
Which language is most beautiful?	8	16	2	2	1	2
In which language are a trade or skills best imparted?	9	25				
In which language can you say anything you wish?	0	28				
Which language is most useful for children?	7	8	10	9	1	1
Which language is most appropriate for the following situations:						
to get a job	20	17				
in an administrative office	18	11				
to make speeches	17	12				
with educated people	16	9				

	At school	Elsewhere	
Where does one learn French?	23	1	

	Most widely spoken language	To get work	Reflects good breeding and social standing	Others
Why is it important to learn French?	12	10	5	10

	Yes	No	NR
Should Creole be used in schools?	18	6	4

	Insufficient schooling	Lack of intelligence	Lack of practice
Why do some school children not acquire fluency in French?	17	4	4

	To learn French	To learn good health habits	To acquire literacy	Others
What are the most important objectives of schools?	14	13	14	10

Table 2. Results of Language Attitude Questionnaire

(N = 28; for some of the questions several answers were possible.)

What was most impressive in the respondents' extended statements about their perception of French and Creole during the interviews was their keen perception of the use of French by compatriots to signify their superior social standing:

Gen moun ki pale franse se pa ogèy, 1 ap eseye ba yon lòt moun baryè ... Lè yon enjenyè pale fransè avè ou, se pou dekonsidere ou ... Lè ou pale ak yon moun an krèyol li gade ou kòm yon moun san enstriksyon. (There are people who use French to show off, they try to set up barriers between themselves and others. When an agricultural agent speaks French with you, it's to put you down. When you speak Creole with some people, they consider you uneducated.)

Finally, there is no doubt that for the Haitian peasant, Creole is the national language and French is the relic of an externally imposed social order:

Aprann franse itil. Pou devlope lespri-ou plis epi sitou paske ann Ayiti apre lendependans se franse ki gen premye plas ... Franse twòp dwa. Nou poko pran independans-nou paske apre independans-nou se krèyol pou nou te li ekri a. Nou pa te dwe sèvi ak lang blan. (To learn French is useful to broaden your mind but especially because of her independence it was French that was given the first place ... French is too rigid. We still haven't gained our independence because after Independence we should have used Creole as a written language. We shouldn't have used the foreigner's language.)

Language Planning in Haiti

Notwithstanding the fact that Creole is the only language shared by all Haitians, there is no inherent principle of language planning that compels its use as the primary school vehicle or as the official language. Nor, contra the celebrated UNESCO article of faith (1951), has it been convincingly demonstrated that in a multilingual country, in all situations, literacy is most effectively imparted in a child's mother tongue.

In a rigorously designed and controlled method-comparison study conducted in the Philippines, the exclusive use of English as classroom language during the first six years of schooling proved to be more effective in the acquisition of English, of the written form of the native language, Tagalog, and of school subjects, than two bilingual approaches—one introducing English after two years of initial instruction in Tagalog and the other after four years (Davis 1967). The educational success of immersion-type bilingual education has been well-documented (Lambert and Tucker 1972; Swain 1981). Whether the vernacular or some other language used in the community should serve as official language or as language of instruction depends on a variety of sociolinguistic, economic, social, and political factors. The latter evolve from the power relationship among the various linguistic groups of the polity; in Haiti any promotion of Creole cannot but result in a diminution of the privileges of the bilingual elites. Since recent discussions about language policy in Haiti have resurrected the alleged inadequacy of Creole, I will focus my discussion on three linguistic factors: (1) the relative uniformity and invariance of the vernacular; (2) the level of standardization and modernization the vernacular has attained; (3) the relative utility of the available language varieties in international communicative networks.

Variation in Creole

The relative uniformity of Creole underscores the simplicity of the linguistic situation of Haiti. The Haitian vernacular shows little geographically or socially determined variation. Dialect variants manifest themselves only at the lexical and phonological levels; the grammatical structure of Creole remains remarkably constant. The only documented difference involves the possessive construction which is expressed by simple juxtaposition of the noun and postposed personal pronouns in southern and central Haiti, but by the use of a linking element *a* in the North: "my father" *papa-mwen/papa-m* versus *papa a mwen/papa a m.*

There are no available thorough descriptions of linguistic variation in Haiti based on current theories and methodological practices; the few available studies (Hyppolite 1946, 1951; Orjala 1961; Etienne 1974) start from the erroneous premise that regional or social variants are clearly demarcated, a given feature identifying a particular speech variety. In fact, as is the case elsewhere, linguistic differences are often variable rather than categorical. Individual speakers alternate between competing alternants, and usually it is the proportion of use of one as versus the other of the alternants rather than the presence or absence of a particular alternant that is significant. For instance, the use of *pe* or *ape* instead of *ap* to express the progressive aspect represents one of the stereotypical features of the South. In an extensive corpus of material (twenty hours of recording) gathered among predominantly rural speakers from the Les Cayes region, the use of *ap* outstrips that of *pe,* the proportion of retention of the local feature no doubt reflecting social and other differences among the speakers. Any adequate study of dialect variation in Haiti therefore must contain a quantitative dimension and must also rigorously control the social characteristics of the subjects consulted as well as the sociolinguistic circumstances of the speech acts observed.

Current discussions about variation in Creole recognize three broad geographical dialect zones: South, North, and Central (Port-au-Prince):

	North	Central (Port-au-Prince)	South
"peanut"	amizman	pistach	
"basket"	dyakout	makout	
"cauldron"	kaderik	bòm	
"candle"	chandèl	bouji	
"pot"	kanistè	mamit	
"progressive"		ap	pe/ape
"to banter"		jwe	badinen

Geographical dialect variants are marked by two traits. First, lexical variants that set off the North and South are localized relic forms being pushed out by competing forms emanating from the central areas. Second, the forms that impose themselves as less localized or socially deviant are in most cases closer to the French cognate (in the case of forms matched by French cognates):

	French	Central	Peripheral
"thirst"	soif	swaf	swèf/swaf
"pepper"	poivre	pwav	pwèv/pwav
"already"	déjà	deja	dija/deja
"to forget"	oublier	bliye	bilye, blilye/blie
"well behaved"	sage	saj	say, chay, chaz/saj
"garlic"	aïl	lay	laj/lay
"clothing"	habits	rad	had/rad
"eight"	huit	uit	wit/uit

In view of the economic, social, and political power that French symbolizes it comes as no surprise that generally variants closer to French cognates, real or imagined, enjoy higher prestige. The most salient differences between sociolects occur at the phonological level: more urban speech, reflecting higher socio-economic-cultural standing, shows a higher proportion of front rounded vowels, postvocalic *r,* non-nasalized vowels in the contact of nasal consonants, and final unassimilated voiced stops:

	French	Urban	Rural
"rice"	riz	duri	diri
"two"	deux	dø	de
"sister"	sœur	sœ	sè
"brother"	frère	frèr	frè
"story"	histoire	istwar	istwa
"Saturday"	samedi	samdi	sanmdi
"family"	famille	famiy	fanmiy
"leg"	jambe	janb	janm
"meat"	viande	vyand	vyann
"tongue"	langue	lang [lãg]	lang [lãŋ]

Variant features in fact connote several indexical marks: geographical location, urban vs. rural, educated and polished vs. illiterate and uncouth, lower or higher socio-economic level. For instance, it cannot be claimed that *pe* signals only a speaker's southern origin, for many residents of the Cayes of Jérémie regions might not on some occasions evidence any realizations of that feature. In each of these regions, the greater the proportion of *pe* as opposed to *ap,* the more likely is the speaker to be a rural rather than urban dweller and the lower his socio-economic and educational level.

It is interesting to note that speakers will often interpret more highly valued variants as instances of French. Several of a group of 75 school pupils, ranging in age from nine to eighteen years, assigned the more central variant of the progressive aspect marker *pe* to French:

lè ou pale franse ou pa di *tep, m pe;* ou gen dwa di *tap, m ap.* . . . An franse ou di *m ap manje,* an kreyòl ou di *m pe manje.* (When you speak French, you don't say *tep, m pe;* you should say *tap, m ap.* . . . In French you say *m ap manje,* in Creole you say *m pe manje.*)

The socio-economico-cultural connotations of most linguistic variants, particularly the front rounded vowels and post-vocalic *r,* lead to widespread hypercorrection and stereotyping. Lower-class and rural speakers identify the vowels / y ø œ / as marks of urban, high-class, and educated speech. Their imperfect knowledge of the class membership of words with variable pronunciation, e.g., *jezi/jezu* "Jesus", *ze/zø* "egg", *sè/sœ* "sister", will lead them to generalize this variable behavior to any Creole words ending in a front unrounded vowel. Two anecdotes will exemplify this behavior. A Port-au-Prince driver who was transporting me from Duvalier Airport to my hotel commented in the course of a discussion about language use in Haiti:

Wi, men sa se lelut (l'élite) de la capitale. (Yes, but that's the capital elite.)

He was treating *l'élite,* which contains the invariable segment /i/, as if it were a member of the class of words marked by the alternation between /i/ and /y/, as for example, "juice": *ji* or *ju.*

On another occasion in the town of Tomazeau, several colleagues and I, including the American anthropologist Gerald Murray and a Haitian education specialist, were conversing with a group of children returning from school. I turned toward a small girl and asked her how she called the thing she wore on her hair; I wanted to know whether she used the term *papiyon, kokad* or *ne/nø* to refer to a ribbon. After she answered *Sa son no,* I asked her the word for "nose." Not unexpectedly she generalized the rounding to the invariable word *nen* and replied: *Sa son nø* instead of *Sa son nen.*

STANDARDIZATION

Rural or Urban Norm

Standardization is used in the sociolinguistic literature to refer to a formal, conscious process of language uniformization usually undertaken by official organisms, although several individual endeavors rank among the more celebrated cases of standardization.[4] But standardization often takes the form of an informal, gradual process which reflects speaker attitudes toward the various levels of linguistic alternants exhibited by vernacular speech, themselves the manifestations of the socio-economic and cultural distinctions symbolized by linguistic options. In Haiti language planners, that is to say those individuals who have striven to endow Creole with a stable written form, rapidly came to an agreement on the variety of the vernacular that should be reduced to writing. A consensus rapidly formed around the central (Port-au-Prince) variety; few highly marked local features, such as *pe* for *ap* and *gan* for *gen* "to have" (South) or *kin a m* for *pa m* "mine" and *i di* for *li di* "he/she said" (North), occur in the abundant pedagogical and religious writings in Creole. Only recently within the frame of reference of the educational reform, have teachers from the Cape Haitian region suggested that materials destined for the early grades should contain local variants.

But a topic that has provoked much discussion is that of a choice among forms ordered along the gradients reflecting socio-economico-cultural differences and rural vs. urban provenance. As was pointed out in Section 4 above, such a choice necessarily implies reference to French cognates. More specifically, the issue centers on whether the standardized written form of Creole should reflect the potential use of front rounded vowels for such words as *jezi, ze, sè*, or whether it should instead be based on the habitual pronunciation of monolingual rural speakers? In opting for a rural norm Dejean (1981) ascribes the observation of front rounded vowels among peasants and lower-class city dwellers to lack of familiarity with folk speech on the part of foreign linguists and of Haitian observers prejudiced by the speech habits of their own milieu. He backs up his claims with reference to an impressive list of rural communities in which he served as a missionary priest for a total period of nine years, even indicating the exact date of observations. Nonetheless, even carefully noted anecdotal observations do not a reliable corpus make. In our own Les Cayes corpus, we have noted the use of front rounded vowels by unschooled peasants. (Surprisingly our corpus is relatively free of hypercorrections.) The issue of a rural instead of an urban-targeted norm was at the heart of the controversy that opposed members of the Haitian intelligentsia favorable to the Indigenist movement (particularly the journalist Charles-Fernand Pressoir) to the proponents of the McConnell-Laubach orthography. Pressoir (1947) also invoked his superior familiarity with folk speech and ascribed to the foreign expert lack of knowledge about folk usage:

> ... not sufficiently familiar with our language to perceive fine variations (McConnell) only attempts to represent the vowels of "rough" Creole ("gros créole") without taking into account for the alternants used, not only in the speech of cultivated Haitians but also in the language of a considerable number of proletarians who are in contact with the mass of "rough Creole" speakers.

The Spelling Issue

From the polemics that grace the columns of the Port-au-Prince press, the observer could not guess that Creole has been endowed with a nearly ideal autonomous spelling for nearly five decades. In the early forties, the Northern Irish methodist pastor, Ormonde McConnell, assisted by the American literacy specialist, Frank Laubach, devised a phonologically-based system that provided a suitable representation for the language from a linguistic point of view. Subsequent attempts to modify that spelling have been inspired by socio-political rather than linguistic or pedagogical considerations. The counter-proposal put forward by C.-F. Pressoir was rooted in the illusion that the McConnell-Laubach orthography, by its use of so-called English-based scriptural conventions, constituted a Trojan horse planted by Anglo-Saxon imperialists who wished to complement their political domination of Haiti with control of its culture. The effect of the

Pressoir counter-proposal was to render the representation of Creole more abstract and, potentially, more difficult to acquire on the part of monolingual speakers. More recently a team of linguists from the University of Paris-V (René Descartes) devised yet another phonologically-based autonomous notation which, while preserving some of the French-based conventions of the Pressoir spelling (e.g., the use of digraphs vowel plus *n* for the representation of nasal vowels), reintroduced some of the "Anglo-Saxon" conventions of McConnell-Laubach. A comparison of the three autonomous phonologically-based notations for Creole (Table 3) shows that they differ only with regard to a few details.

Both the Pressoir and University René Descartes (IPN) spellings constitute adequate notation for Creole. The elaboration of competing phonologically-based autonomous proposals has had the unfortunate result of keeping alive a pseudo-problem. Now that the IPN notation has been declared semi-official by the Haitian government, perhaps language planners will move on to the more urgent modernization tasks (Valdman 1982).

From the perspective of language planning it is instructive to attempt to discern why there have been continuous attempts to make the elaboration of an orthography for Creole a central issue. At the core of the spelling issue is the simplistic notion of "the bridge to French" (*le passage au français*). McConnell himself did not consider the acquisition of literacy in Creole as a sufficient self-contained objective. He made certain concessions to French spelling conventions: the use of *é* and *è* for /e/ and /ɛ/, respectively, or *ch* for /š/ in order to facilitate the acquisition of French orthography during a second-stage program and in order to motivate the target adult population for whom, in McConnell's view, literacy in Creole represented only a transitional skill. The Pressoir proposal was simply another effort to strengthen the bridge between Creole and French. Of course, the purest form of the *passage au français* delusion is the etymological spelling that still draws support from the more benighted segments of the francophile intelligentsia.

As Dejean accurately remarks (1971), accepting the notion of the *passage au français* entails an oversimplistic view of the relationship between language and spelling. The inclusion of several very specific common notational conventions between Creole and French has no significant effect on facilitating the acquisition of any sort of functional proficiency in French, be it overall linguistic competence or the mere ability to decipher written texts. The *passage au français* is a mirage that distracts language planners' attention from the more complex problems posed by a transitional-type bilingual education program requiring a carefully orchestrated transition between the Haitian vernacular and the country's official language.

IPA	McConnell-Laubach	Pressoir (ONAAC)	IPN (Rene Descartes)
Nasal vowels			
ẽ	ê	in	en
ã	â	an	an
õ	ô	on	on
ẽn	én	inn	enn
ãn	ân	ann	ann
õn	ôn	onn	onn
ũn	ûn	oun	oun
ĩn	în	i-n	in
Oral vowel & N			
in	in	i-n	in
òn	òn	òn	òn
an	an	a-n	àn
un	un	oun	oun
Mid vowels			
e	è	è	è
	e	é	e
o	o	o	o
ɔ	ò	ò	ò
Semivowels			
j	y/i	y (initial, final intervocalic)	y
		i (pre-vocalic)	
w	w	w (initial and intervocalic)	w
		u (pre-vocalic)	
R before rounded vowels			
w	r	r	w

Table 3. Letter correspondences between three spelling
systems for Haitian Creole

NORMALIZATION

The devising of a systematic set of correspondences between written signs and the phonemes of a language constitutes only one aspect of the elaboration of an orthography. Additional conventions must be formulated for the representation of variable forms and the ordering of discourse. All notations devised for Creole aim at the representation of isolated forms of words, so that, for example, the allegro fused forms *son* or *avòw* are noted *se yon* "it is a" and *avè ou* "with you," respectively. Such universal agreement does not exist, however, for the representation of the elided forms versus the full forms of pronouns, the variant forms of determiners, or truncatable verbs (see Table 4 for illustrative samples of the scriptural practice of followers of the Pressoir spelling).

In Creole all five personal pronouns occur in a long or in a short (or elided) form. The alternation is partly determined by the syntactic or phonological context and partly free. The long form always occurs following a consonant, for example in (i) only *li* but not *l* may occur after *douèt* (dwèt).[5] After the preposition *pou* the elided form is also excluded. Except for these two cases, both the full form *li* and the elided form *l* may occur freely. Similarly, in (ii), except for the obligatory use of the short form *n* before the verb marker *ap,* either of the two first person plural forms *n* or *nou* may occur. In using the Faublas-Pressoir notation the four authors seem to have opted for partial normalization involving preference for full forms in cases where the two variants are acceptable. The rules they have used are, however, far from obvious. For example, in what appears to be similar phonological and syntactic contexts, the long and the short forms of the third person singular pronoun are present: (i) *sa-l touché* versus (iv) *m-ap kite-li désann*. The above samples extracted from texts that typify current scriptural practice, show that authors of creative, religious, and didactic materials are not yet prepared to adopt an invariable representation for each word or grammatical form in the language.

Some language planners advocate the adoption of strict normalization rules (Vernet 1980: 130ff.). With the introduction of Creole at the primary level, some degree of normalization is desirable in published texts. On the part of new literates, however, normalization entails the learning of abstract and highly specific encoding rules which constitute violations of the bi-unique phoneme-to-grapheme correspondences acquired as a first step. It may be preferable to allow new literates considerable leeway in written expression. In early stages, one might tolerate non-normalized production; it should suffice that they adhere to the phoneme-to-grapheme correspondences. Thus, although one might wish to consistently write the

i. **Bòn Nouvèl**

Lè yo poté méni-a ba msié, li touché ak douèt li.
'When they brought the menu to the man, he pointed with his finger.'

Malè pou li, sa-l touché, sété mayi moulin.
'Unfortunately it was corn meal that he pointed to.'

Msié vi-n ront.
'The man became embarrassed.'

Pou-l pasé ront la, li di li pral mandé yon lòt bagay.
'In order not to be embarrassed any more, he said that he wanted to order another thing.'

ii. **Korijé tè nou**

Lè n-ap mété pirin nan jadin nou, nou doué mélanjé-l ak dlo anvan nou mété-l nan tè-a.
'Before we spread liquid manure on our land, we must mix it with water before we put it on the earth.'

M-konnin anpil moun ap di yo pap fè sa.
'I know a lot of people who say they don't do that.'

iii. **M'-komansé li kounię-á!**

Bonjou méda-m yo, kouman nou yé?
'Good day, ladies. How are you?'

Jak ba-l manjé épi li vi-n fè yon gro zouazo.
'Jack gave it food and it became a big bird.'

Manman, ti chanté-a bèl. Chanté-l ankò, tanpri.
'Mother, this little song is beautiful. Sing it again, please.'

iv. **Pélin Tèt**

Sa ki di-ou sa? Mwin djès fin palé, trin-an èstòp rayt dévan (douvan) pyé-mwin. Ou wè, mwin té di-ou. . .
'Who told you that? I've just told you, the train stopped right in front of my feet. You see, I've told you. . .'

M-ap kité-li désann anvan mwin alé.
'I let her go before I left.'

Table 4. Normalization practices in several texts using the Pressoir spelling

full isolated forms of pronouns: *Li ale avè ou;* one would allow learners to write allegro, truncated, and fused forms: *L ale avòw.*

It is not irrelevant to note that French models manifest themselves subtly in this area. In French words with variable pronunciation, that is, those involving liaison and unstable *e* loss or retention are provided with an invariant spelling (e.g., *nous allons* vs. *nous lavons;* cela, *le regard, ne me le redites pas*). In contrast, English spelling allows for individual variation in the representation of contractable forms: *should not* or *shouldn't, I am* or *I'm.*

Modernization

The most important tasks in the modernization of Creole are lexical enrichment, the elaboration of rhetorical devices appropriate for the new and used domains that the vernacular is acquiring, and the expansion and diversification of the types of materials available to new literates. I have treated the first topic at length elsewhere (Valdman 1978, 1982), and a group of French Antillean linguists and writers (GEREC 1976, Colat-Jolivière 1976, Bernabé 1978) have made interesting proposals for the lexical enrichment of Guadeloupean and Martinican Creole hinging on the effort to maintain maximal differentiation between the vernacular tongue and French. In the stylistic domain, the Creole writings of Franketienne, notably his novel *Dézafi* (1975), illustrate skillful navigation between the Scylla of frenchification and the Charybdis of mere transcription of the spoken idiom and the exploitation of synchronic and diachronic strata of Creole to enrich its lexicon and diversify its styles. Here again the issue of the individuality of Creole as opposed to subordination to French rises to the fore.

French as the Window on the Outside World

In a recent article on the relationship between language and educational problems in Haiti, two French consultants to the Institut Pédagogique National, Bentolila and Ganni (1981b), recognize that, squeezed between the expansion of English as regional vehicular and the extension of the domains of use of Creole, French is being relegated to a symbolic role as a language of power and dominance, and as the vehicle of a culture alien to the Haitian populace. They ask:

Squeezed between Creole, the language of daily communication, and English, carried by American power, can French come out of its ghetto and, as a constituent of the Haitian cultural heritage, can it find a multi-functional dynamism it has never had in Haiti?

I would be inclined to answer in the negative. It is unlikely that the economic, social, and political forces that fuel the expansion of English or the extension of Creole will abate in the foreseeable future, or that countervailing forces will endow French with a newly found dynamic multi-functionality. True, in the light of the current migratory, commercial, and cultural currents in the Caribbean, the dominance of English can only increase, but a new diglossic situation pairing English and Creole is difficult to imagine.

Bentolila and Ganni (1981a) claim, without adducing any documentary evidence, that there exists an explicit American policy aimed at reducing the role of French in Haiti as a first step toward, precisely, the institution of a Creole-English diglossic situation. This policy is supposedly being implemented in various devious ways, notably by research and development activities in linguistic spheres conducted by American universities. This is simply a new variant of the famous Trojan Horse theory invoked in the 1940's by the Haitian educated elite to combat the McConnell-Laubach phonologically-based orthography. In this instance, this myth is being resuscitated to bolster a French-inspired attempt to maintain French in Haiti by making it a veritable instrument of communication. In terms of the five-function model of language functioning presented in Section 3 above, this involves adding the internal and external vehicular functions to the referential and symbolic functions French already fulfills. To claim the existence of an explicit American linguistic plan for Haiti whose ultimate goal is the replacement of French by English is to show ignorance of the subtle forces that determine language shifts since time immemorial. There is no need for any explicit American policy for the spread of English since, as a result of economic and political trends that began at the turn of this century, communicative networks have been spun which are turning English into the primary vehicular language of Haiti. As is always the case in language shift, the primary vectors for the spread of English are not Americans but those segments of the Haitian population that derive economic, social, or political advantage from using the language. Whatever direct benefits that would accrue to Americans by the spread of English loom insignificant compared to the economic and political influence they already wield in Haiti. Indeed, insofar as the maintenance of the status quo characterizes the United States policy toward Haiti, if anything, that country has a vested interest in the maintenance of the Creole-French diglossia that conforts the present dominant groups.

To claim that French could become Haiti's window to the outside world —its primary external vehicular language—is to ignore profoundly the nature of the cultural and economic currents in the Caribbean. Not only is most trade involving Haiti transacted in English, but that language is being carried to Haiti by two relatively new channels. First, a growing number of members of the American diaspora return to their homeland, some on a permanent basis. To describe their American experience they resort to massive borrowing and calquing from English. Indeed, English affects core areas of the vocabulary in speech samples that show code switching and code mixing; witness the previously cited sentence from Franketienne's *Pélin Tèt,* a play set in Brooklyn:

Mwin *djès* fi-n pale, trin-an *èstòp rayt* dévan pyé-mwin.

Second, Haitian viewers' marked preference for American television fare has led the privately owned cable service to offer its subscribers up to three different programs at prime view in time slots. These programs are pirated by the cable service from satellite transmissions and broadcast with the original sound track.

CONCLUSION

Two strategies present themselves to language planners in Haiti: (1) the vernacularization of French by means of massive programs in adult and primary education or (2) the recognition of Creole as the country's primary language and the extension of its use to the official and referential functions reserved for French. Viewed from the perspective of these two strategies, the educational reform program described in J. de Regt's contribution to this volume does not loom as revolutionary. It is simply one tactical approach to the vernacularization of French. It entails the use of Creole as transitional classroom language and the imparting of oral proficiency in French in order to lay the ground for the establishment of French as an effective instructional medium in the second primary cycle. A noteworthy by-product of this approach resides in the acquisition of literacy skills in the vernacular on the part of those children who are forced to abandon their studies.

However, my sketch of the linguistic situation of Haiti has identified several factors that would raise doubts about the cost-effectiveness of this solution. We have seen that French is excluded from communicative networks in rural areas and among the urban lower classes and that its primary vector of transmission is the school. The severe deficiencies of the Haitian educational system (nonexistent administrative infrastructure, lack of trained teachers, low pay scales, inadequate facilities, inappropriate pedagogical models, etc.) render it incapable of mounting a massive program in the teaching of French as a near-foreign spoken language. The traditional approach, despite its numerous shortcomings, sets the more limited and attainable goal of imparting the ability to read French and to acquire subject content by means of it. These considerations lead Lofficial (1979:71) to advocate greater emphasis on the written language. While he supports imparting initial literacy by the intermediary of Creole, Lofficial (1979:71) advocates greater emphasis on the ability to read French. He argues that mastering that skill requires less specialized materials than the acquisition of a spoken competence in the language and that imparting it requires less training on the part of traditionally trained teachers.

The other alternative, the officialization and promotion of Creole, appears to be more cost effective. The vernacular has achieved a level of standardization and modernization sufficient for its use as a medium of instruction at the primary school level and for vocational training: it shows remarkable uniformity, thus obviating the politically divisive problem of choice of standard norm; it is endowed with an efficient orthography; it possesses a respectable though insufficient body of writings. To be implemented successfully this strategy for educational development requires the proclamation of Creole as an official language endowed with the same juridical prerogatives as French. It would appear in street signs, in legal documents, and its use would be extended to all official acts and events. Agencies of the government would promote its development as a codified norm and its extension to all vehicular functions.

The officialization of Creole does not imply the devalorization of French. Examples abound of the recognition by states of more than one official language or of more than one standard variety: Swedish and Finnish in Finland, English, Hindu, and local languages in India, or different varieties of Norwegian in Norway. The officialization and promotion of Creole does imply, however, that it be considered as a speech variety in its own right, not as some inferior, modified version of French.

Such a reversal of attitudes is not likely to be easily effected given the monolingual speakers' perception of the relationship between Creole and French. Various facts about linguistic variation in Creole reflect tendencies that would militate against its valorization. For example, we have seen that in all parameters of variation—dialectal, sociolectal, or stylistic—the more highly valued variant is the one less distant from French. It is also noteworthy that even for alternants that do not correspond to a French cognate (*pe* or *ap* "progressive aspect," *bichèt* or *laye*—French, *van*—"winnowing basket") the more highly valued alternant, i.e. the one perceived as less uncouth, rural or local, may be labelled as French. There is strong opposition in many quarters to a written representation of the vernacular that does not confort the illusion that Creole is a deviant variety of French. Certain approaches to lexical enrichment and stylistic diversification tend to create mesolect, intermediate forms that cannot be assigned unambiguously to one or the other of the two codes.

Official promotion and recognition of Creole cannot by itself readily eradicate or modify deeply ingrained depreciative attitudes toward the vernacular held by monolingual speakers as well as the bilingual elite. It must be accompanied by profound social transformations and a political evolution that will change the factors that have spawned these attitudes in the first place. The rural monolingual masses can no more be expected to profoundly modify their attitudes toward Creole and French than they can be expected to initiate major social and political changes. On the other hand, to apply the French sociologist P. Bourdieu's model of linguistic exchanges, the Haitian power elites who oppose the introduction of Creole in the schools are defending a threatened capital. They are condemned to oppose the full development of Creole, that is to refuse its officialization, for the *value* of their competence in French can only be preserved if the *market* is protected. The linguistic market consists of the complex network of social and political conditions of speech production and use (Bourdieu 1982: 45-46). But, as Nicholls argues in his contribution to this volume, the Haitian elites are composed of a variety of groups with different, sometimes antagonistic interests. To gain a fuller understanding of the linguistic situation of Haiti, one needs to identify which segments of the bilingual power elites can hope to derive advantage from an extension of the role of Creole. How much of the value of French are these segments of Haitian society prepared to surrender? These considerations set the limits on the development of Creole and manifest themselves in the positions taken by various groups on the technical linguistic issues discussed here: the elaboration of an orthography, normalization, standardization, and modernization.

NOTES

[1]Opinions differ as to the reasons that motivated the American Occupation Administration to officialize the status of French. No doubt, some members of the Administration were sensitive to the deep attachment of the Haitian elite to French cultural values. Perhaps this move represented grateful acknowledgement of French acquiescence to the American occupation. It might also have served to allay the élite's opposition to the repeal of the law forbidding foreign ownership of land. In any case, this episode underscores the élite's ambivalent loyalty to two cultural and linguistic traditions: the French colonial and the African.

[2]The two-linguistic community model I am proposing corresponds to the two-country model postulated by Weinstein and Segal (1984). They state (1984:1):

Haiti is two countries in one ... Haiti's political history has been characterized by the division of the country into two clearly separate populations. One is the rural masses from whom have emerged an original and vibrant culture, the wellspring of Haitian identity. The other is composed of urban-based elites who have saddled the land with an immobile political order unwilling to tackle the enormous economic and social problems the country has faced from independence the morning of January 1, 1804, to the present.

[3]The data presented in this paper were collected as part of an observational study of traditional schools in the Les Cayes area and a language attitude survey conducted under the terms of a research contract with USAID (AID-521-C-142). I would like to acknowledge the contributions of Yves Joseph (Institut Pédagogique National d'Haïti), research associate, and Felicia Roberts (University of Wisconsin), research assistant. The study could not have been undertaken without the able collaboration of our field interviewers, Mme Yvon Clothaire, Mme Myrtha Laurent, Mlle Rose-Laure Roméla and, of course, the many school pupils and parents who participated graciously and welcomed us into their homes, and the school administrators and school teachers who allowed us to observe classes at Colette, Laborde, and La Ruche primary schools. However, I am solely responsible for the analysis and interpretation of the data and the opinions expressed in this paper.

[4]In 1853, Ivar Aasen began to develop a new written norm, landsmål, based on Norwegian folk speech as an alternative to the Dano-Norwegian standard then in usage in Norway.

[5]To convert the Faublas-Pressoir notation to the semi-official IPN system and to International Phonetics Association alphabet values, see Table 3.

LANGUAGE, LITERACY, AND
UNDERDEVELOPMENT

ULRICH FLEISCHMANN

A Non-diglossic Speech Community and a Diglossic Language Setting

Part of the paradox of the language situation in Haiti is that it escapes most of the terms and models used to describe and classify the linguistic basis of "new nations" (Fishman 1971). Haitian Creole is neither a "Language of Wider Communication" nor a "Language of Great Tradition" (at least as Fishman conceived of them). It is simply the mother tongue of all Haitians and would easily qualify as a "national language," not only because of its relative homogeneity within the entire Haitian territory but also due to its relative maturity. A basic normalization and an acceptable orthography has been acquired in Haitian Creole and a process of "cultivation" through the creation of an autonomous Creole literature and the translation of literacy and other texts into Creole has begun after forty years of continuous national effort (Fleischmann 1981).

Seen from this point of view, the Haitian language situation would not (or would no longer) qualify as diglossic, as Valdman (this volume) correctly points out. Nevertheless, if one compares the Haitian use of language to Ferguson's (1959) list of variation distributions within diglossic situations, it can still be safely stated that at least Creole monolinguals expect the use of an H-variation for most public situations (occasional exception taken for political speeches and news broadcasts). For example, Ferguson's first item (1959:329), "Sermon in church," is still a problem for clergymen of all religious denominations who support the use of the vernacular during church services. Their rural clientele, however, see the efficiency and legitimacy of religious functions connected to the use of an

H-variation and would consider a Creole sermon as inappropriate, because "it lacks power."

It is surprising to note that particularly Creole monolinguals, who are not diglossically competent, behave as if they were. This paradox can be compared to more recent developments in the definition and description of "diglossia." Fishman (1967), in his well-known attempt at redefining the concepts of diglossia and bilingualism, sees the former mainly as it functions within a certain social context. In a recent article, Lafont (1982) places the definition of diglossia entirely at the level of attitudes of the "diglossic" speaker. In the absence of true competence in one of the variations, *un fantasme* of diglossia, which performs certain social functions, is maintained as part of the subject's ideas on language and society. Though Lafont's case, based on the Occitan-speaking minority in southern France,[1] does not seem to be immediately related to the Haitian situation, his explanations offer some important clues to its understanding. According to his theory, diglossia is primarily a superstructural feature, a part of the subject's metalinguistic concepts. Whether the subject is able to transfer this concept to his linguistic reality would be a secondary (though still very important) issue, depending on a number of variables of a socio-economic order. According to this concept of language and linguistic competence the former Occitan speaker has *preparé historiquement l'effectif passage à la francophonie* (Lafont 1982:236). He says *effectif* because the social and economic development of the central French national state has put the means to take this linguistic leap at the individual's disposition. In this sense, the monolingual Haitian Creole speaker may be considered "diglossic" as well, though his linguistic situation presents exactly opposite features. He, too, has been ideologically prepared to aspire to competence in French ever since the time of slavery. But since the monolingual rural dweller has never been offered a real chance at linguistic and social integration at the preconceived national level, due to the unique Haitian development process, francophonia, just like occitanophonia, remains *un fantasme du sujet diglossique* for him.

This explanation of diglossia helps one to comprehend the Haitian linguistic tragedy at both the individual and overall national levels. Since the linguistic functions of the different variations remain, the non-diglossic subject in a diglossic society has to use a number of devices in order to compensate for the lack of the H-variation. These devices are well known in Haitian society and are similar to those used by the incompetent Occitan speaker in situations where the use of that language would be required (Lafont 1982:235). Monolingual Haitians in "public situations" would either resort to a seemingly ridiculous "hyper-correct" imitation of French[2] or else use certain quasi-ritual "French" formulas in their Creole speech that would eventually be considered socially as "French." Effective communication on this quasi-H-level, however, is sharply reduced and depends to a great extent on the conversational partner's good will because these subterfuges mainly allow for only emphatical communication. Therefore, monolingual Haitians would, whenever possible, avoid situations which, by requiring the H-variation, might cause embarrassment. Thus, at the national level, at least 80 percent of the population live socially and economically in an entirely marginal linguistic position.

This adaptation of the term "diglossia" to the Haitian situation should not be seen as an attempt at maintaining an unnecessary definition for its own sake. It has a number of implications for the understanding of the Haitian language situation and its links to the country's socio-economic problems. The Haitian upper class have traditionally been ill at ease at concisely describing the linguistic situation of their country. With the growing awareness of the role of Creole as the country's language, the former fiction of a linguistic *France noire*[3] was replaced by labelling the country "bilingual."[4] This label conveys the idea of a national bilingualism like Canada's, which is linked to a notion deliberately used by Haitians as well as foreign scholars in order to describe the cleavages between the "French" town and the creole countryside: that there are "two Haitis," i.e., two linguistically and culturally different societies. Though this image might be useful in order to characterize the polarization and geographical distribution of the two cultural settings of the country, it may, however, become erroneous when it conveys the notion of two societies which are independent from each other and relatively equal in providing for the material and social needs of their members. In reality, "French" and creole society and culture are far from being distinctive entities, neither on the social nor on the geographical level. Individuals or social groups, wherever they may be located, may, irrespective of their real competence, try to orient their actual cultural and linguistic behavior according to what they conceive as "French" or "Creole." Thus, they create a complex and multi-dimensional cluster of cultural and linguistic interactions which, in spite of their variability, are part of one overall cultural system. For specific purposes, we can certainly identify a separate Creole culture with a complete set of economic, social, and cultural institutions, but we should not forget that it is, and always has been, closely related to the dominant "French" culture in a way which is best characterized by the diglossic relation of the two languages.

The dominant H-variation constantly encroaches upon the L-variation[5] which, being unstable and little valued, offers little resistance to this pressure. In terms of linguistic as well as general development, the "low" or Creole variation has been deeply affected by the mere existence of the "high" French variation ever since the time of slavery, even though the monolingual and monocultural individual has no access to it. He cannot provide for the development of his own culture and language because he is constantly waiting for the historically prepared entry into the 'French life" (Lafont 1982) which, according to the predominant attitudes, is the stronghold of development and well-being. The mere existence of sectors considered as "French" or "modern," however, strangles the Creole culture not only through direct exploitation or administrative trespasses, but also by ideologically denying it any opportunity of autonomous development.

The homology between both linguistic and general development is by no means accidental. The short discussion above shows that the connections are multiple and can be found at all levels of social and cultural interaction. First, there is the simple fact that the rural monolingual is denied, or deliberately avoids, participation in the socio-economic or political activities at the national level and, thus, is excluded from the country's development. The fatal consequences of this became drastically obvious in the last decade when, until 1979, the national income showed a modest growth rate. In the monolingual agricultural sector, however, it stagnated or even decreased.

A second level of connections is more complex. The instability of the Creole language reflects and confirms the instability of social relations with the Creole culture. This is considered an undesirable burden as long as the hope of moving up into the French culture prevails.

A third type of connection is linked directly to the developmental potential of Creole culture. The limited use and degraded status of Creole within the diglossic situation immediately affects the production and distribution of collectively shared knowledge, which is necessary for the Creole communities to adapt to the changing conditions of survival. Here the linguistic limitation of Creole culture and the instability of Creole social structure, both part of the problematic situation of the non-diglossic individual in a diglossic world, come together and further the dramatic decay of the Haitian peasant's living conditions.

Rural Social Structure and Creole Literacy

In the discussion of this process of socio-cultural decay and its consequences that follows the possible role of the Creole language in different types of developmental situations will be demonstrated. Language use and development are still in relative equilibrium in a number of communities on the Plateau Central, which I visited in 1976. These communities are situated in an area that is relatively dry and sparsely populated (by Haitian standards), near the border of the Dominican

Republic. In the early 18th century it was a kind of no-man's land. Only after the final concession to Haiti around 1860 did it become more permanently inhabited and exploited by Haitian settlers. They were able to acquire some wealth through cattle-raising and cotton farming. This production of commercial goods and the relatively marginal position of the area in relation to both the Haitian and Dominican capitals allowed for a balanced development that depended on internal production as well as external trade relations. This period, still referred to as the "Golden Age" by older inhabitants of the area, lasted until the 1930's. It was followed by a number of setbacks due, in part, to plant diseases which destroyed the cotton plantations and to the population increase and subsequent reduction of free grazing land. A number of troublesome interferences by the central Haitian authorities were also negatively influential. It is important to note, however, that as the inhabitants succeeded in adjusting to the new circumstances there was always at least a partial recovery in this area. For instance, extensive cattle-raising was compensated for by corn and sugar cane farming, leading to the introduction of new agricultural techniques such as the use of the plow—which was borrowed from the Dominican peasants—in place of the hoe. Nevertheless, the area was deeply affected by the political and economic problems of the 1960's, upsetting the former balance between internal development and outside relations. The social structures of the communities have been endangered by an increasing withdrawal into a subsistence economy.

But compared to other parts of rural Haiti the area is still well off. A number of self-help projects suggested and introduced by development agencies have been taken up successfully by the inhabitants and help to maintain the area and its communities as functioning social and economic units. They include the constitution of cooperatives for the production and marketing of goods, community-based initiatives to reconstruct and maintain the road system with the help of road tolls, and the construction and use of a local sugar mill, among others.

It is obvious that beyond their immediate economic purpose, most of these projects aimed at the social reorganization of the communities, whose cohesion had been endangered by increasing poverty. The expansion of literacy in Creole played a notable part in this context. It would certainly be going too far to attribute overall success to the area's literacy programs, but to my knowledge this rural area is the only one in Haiti where the written use of Creole has begun to establish itself as a customary practice. There is a small-scale production of mimeographed newspapers as well as an increase in the exchange of messages written in Creole in this area. Reports and accounting within the projects are also kept in Creole. It should be noted, however, that the acquisition of literacy is a secondary activity linked to the development projects and the restructuring of rural society in a unique way. An example illustrates the function of the new literacy. At the founding session of an agricultural production cooperative in Bassin Bleu, a village in the area, it was surprising to observe the lengths to which the peasants went to formulate the group's regulations as accurately as possible, particularly concerning financial obligations and the distribution of benefits. There was also notable concern over the fact that only one member of the group was literate enough to keep the books and that no one else would be able to control him. On the monitor's suggestion most participants agreed to take part in a literacy program, thus enabling them to keep a watchful eye on the group's financial transactions.

This example points out not only the role of literacy as a new form of collective knowledge established *within* the area, but also shows that cultural change is felt as a necessity imposed by changing social relations within the group. Though the peasants of Bassin Bleu still form a relatively well-integrated community, the face-to-face relations are no longer sufficient to cope with increasing distrust and competition among Haitian rural folk.

Like all cultural change, however, the implantation of literacy requires a minimum of social consent and surplus production in order to be successful. If the oral culture itself is already deeply affected, literacy can take on an entirely different function. The events of Marbial in the late forties illustrate this point. At that time, most of the harvest was destroyed and part of the arable land devastated by a series of droughts and floods. These catastrophes hit a people who, unlike those of the Plateau Central, were already living at the bare survival level with a fragile social and cultural system. The extremely adverse conditions induced UNESCO to test a large-scale functional literacy program there for the first time. The teaching of Creole orthography was linked to the known measures of social and economic reorganization: the constitution of agricultural cooperatives, the teaching of new handicrafts, and the foundation of community-ruled development committees. Five years later the project was quietly abandoned. Final studies were not published and this unique opportunity to take advantage of the experiences of the Marbial failure for further literacy programs was lost. There is, however, an impressive collection of preliminary accounts, reports, and other documentation partially buried in the UNESCO archives (1953; A. Métraux 1951; R. Métraux 1951; Bastien 1961), which shows that the reasons for the Marbial failure are in some way related to the general literacy problem in Haiti.

Most of the responsibility for the failure was placed on political and organizational conflicts at the national level, where the instrumentalization of Creole was discredited as a measure to further the influence of

Protestantism and the United States.[6] Such conflicts were certainly of some importance, but from its beginning the project also had to face problems arising from the local community which continue to affect similar ventures to this day. The local people only participated to the extent that they could gain immediate personal advantages. The newly founded committees eventually met only when they had to display their organization to foreign visitors. Furthermore, the introduction of new agricultural techniques, even when simple and obviously useful, did not lead to lasting innovations.

Preliminary reports on the area (cf. A. Métraux 1951) admitted that there was some efficiency in the traditional agricultural of the valley. This efficiency, however, was linked to specific conditions such as the abundance of land and manpower (A. Métraux 1951) neither of which were still readily available. The lack of crop rotation, for example, had to be compensated for by clearing new land. Soil erosion and climatic changes were furthered by elements such as scarcity of cultivable land, deforestation and the cultivation of unprotected steep slopes and population increases. The dispersion and insufficient upkeep of commercial crops, such as coffee, resulted in difficult harvesting conditions.

Why did the Marbial peasants, unlike their fellows on the Plateau Central, not adapt themselves to these changing circumstances? Métraux and others found that changes in Marbial were impeded by two consequences of social disintegration in the daily life of the peasants, namely the lack of time and the lack of available knowledge. The gradual breakdown of social systems in Marbial manifests itself in a number of interdependent processes, one of which is the dissolution of the large rural families. Formerly the cohabitation of brothers and sisters and their families prevented the splitting up of land imposed by Haitian laws on inheritance. Both population increase and family members claiming their part of the family land after migration increased the number of land disputes, which, when taken to court, facilitated a fatal encroachment of town people on rural property. In addition, the disappearance of the traditional family exacerbated the degeneration of community institutions and festivities. Voodoo ceremonies, the traditional wakes and the *koumbit*-type of neighbor cooperation on which the community bonds among self-sufficient farmers rely, all depend on the traditional family and its hospitality. Pauperization and loss of community life reinforce each other and create a climate of boredom, fear, and mutual distrust, which encourages an unscrupulous fight for lots. Everybody is ready to join up with outside lawyers, land surveyors, or the police in order to obtain personal advantage even at his neighbor's expense (cf. Sylvain n.d.:11; Comhaire-Sylvain 1961:195; Moral 1961). Thus, time becomes a crucial factor in the introduction of innovation, since there is a disproportion between the peasants' physical strength and the amount of work connected to change.

Even more aggravating are problems with the social distribution of knowledge. This brings us more specifically to the problem of language and literacy. It has often been maintained that the Haitian peasant tends to withhold any information pertaining to his personal circumstances, his possessions, and his work (Larose 1976:46). His behavior is not only an attempt at preserving dignity or protecting himself against the greediness of others; it also results from the particular social function of oral knowledge, under which heading I, of course, include not only the so-called "rational" knowledge, but also knowledge that is considered "magic."

In oral cultures, knowledge is not freely available. It is bound to the social group which creates it and which controls its use. If this control disappears, as was the case in Marbial, a particular form of knowledge can be used by individuals in order to enhance their own position at the expense of others. In this case, for instance, religious practices, which originally were a social institution serving to explain and influence fate through common action, became a magical tool used by individuals against others. In fact, one can easily observe in Haiti that knowledge and abilities are considered "scarce commodities." They can be used for or against the community, according to its degree of social integration. The difference between the example of the Plateau Central and that of Marbial is that in the first case, additional knowledge could be integrated into the collective knowledge of a still well-functioning community. In Marbial, however, new knowledge increased social hierarchization and competitive behavior. Literacy, as a generalized condition of communication, became a necessity because it allowed the individual to dissociate the availability of knowledge from problematic interpersonal relations. Literacy, in this case, has to be in Creole for any knowledge bound to the French language will remain a "scarce commodity" for a long time.

The Instability of Creole Culture and Language

Before pursuing this discussion, I wish to examine another aspect of the further instrumentalization of the rural Creole language. Though the social conditions surrounding the introduction of literacy should be examined for each individual case, communities of the Marbial type are undoubtedly more representative of the Haitian rural culture than those of the Plateau Central. This is only partially due to the catastrophic pauperization of the rural areas. Such conditions only accentuate the inherent structural instability of creole cultures in general. They differ from other "native" cultures in that their existence is due to colonization and that each of their articulations in a given time, space, and situation designates a specific, yet varying, relationship with the dominant culture. Even if one allows for a certain idealization, communities based on creole culture cannot be considered as culturally integrated as, for example, a remote African village,[7] for each member is in some way aware that his culture seen from a socially more elevated position appears as a "lower variant" of the dominant culture. Only a relatively remote and closed community will really accept creole ways as the basis of the vital group solidarity. If the community has already been disturbed and/or if the individual member sees a chance to move into other socially more acceptable groups, he will gradually "de-creolize" his behavior and language. Creole culture is therefore based on an inherent ambivalence which serves to signal adaptation either to the local culture or to the dominant one. This generalization may be applied to other cultures, particularly those also in colonial situations. In creole cultures, in some way "pure" results of colonial situations, the importance of symbolic content by far exceeds the practical purpose. An excess of symbolism may confer special meanings on any cultural phenomenon which may be used to enhance status and power in disintegrating communities. This explains why the use of knowledge often appears as "irrational" when it is directed against others, even when nobody takes profit from the damage that is done.[8]

In this respect, language and language use in rural Haiti (whether referring to the "language" during ceremonies, the equally cryptic use of French, or different variations of Creole) have a particularly crucial role in demarcating the access to information and knowledge by various speech strategies. Oral Creole is a very creative language. Many still see it as a "non-language" characterized by the absence of "rules." On the semantic level this creativity means that, though a nationwide intelligible form of Creole speech exists, there is a continuous change and generation of meanings in the narrow local context. Therefore, Creole speech can take on double and even multiple meanings. The information it conveys can vary considerably according to the social context. The diligent use of contradictory explicit and implicit references, for instance, is a highly esteemed art which Haitians call *pale andaki*.[9]

In the integrated community these particular speech tactics have an important social function, for they create and confirm the solidarity of the community's members. It is characteristic of the ambivalence of creole cultures that such positive traits may have exactly opposite effects when the community disintegrates. Thus the ambiguity of the spoken word may become a serious handicap to a more formal regulating of social relations. Agreements in Creole are mostly vague enough to allow for a number of varying interpretations. For the moment, oral Creole is a perfect tool for Ti Mallice to cheat Bouqui wherever he can.[10]

It would be wrong, however, to understand this as a plea for further expansion of French, which in Haiti is often presented as a particularly clear and precise language. I do not have to insist on the fact that these qualities pertain primarily not to the language itself, but rather to its social function. Creole will lose its pronounced shifting tendency on the semantic level through the process of normalization and standardization of the language, which is bound to follow the written use of it. On the other hand, the use of French in rural areas may well serve to obscure the real issues even further. Indeed, the teaching of French literacy has had very adverse effects on the disintegrating rural communities. Since about 90% of the few children in rural classes never get beyond the preparatory classes, French is of no practical use within the rural community. This situation has led to a disproportionate increase in its symbolic value. Its effects on communication within the community are negative. The non-understanding of French, rather than the understanding of it, makes it such an important and powerful language.

One often hears the argument that rural folks themselves would rather have "French" schools than Creole literacy. This is certainly true, for in the disintegrating communities the knowledge of French is considered a mighty *pointe,* a charm with magical powers to be used against others and for one's own protection. The rudimentary acquisition of French does not help to overcome this "irrational" mentality. On the contrary it fortifies it.[11] Creole literacy programs, on the other hand, have a rather ambiguous status which is partially connected to the inconsistent language policy on the national level. Literacy programs usually get a good start, for in competitive communities where knowledge is a scarce commodity the individual grabs eagerly at everything which is offered free and might enhance his ability to improve. The initial enthusiasm, however, soon turns into disappointment when the pupil realizes that the additional knowledge offered is not functional either in the symbolic sense or in the practical sense. It does not confer attributes of the dominant culture, nor does it help to overcome the community's poverty.

The introduction of literacy into Haitian Creole culture may ensure its survival, however, if it helps restore the culture's capacity to produce its own and adapted collective knowledge. The present diglossic state of the country is such that any capacity for innovation seems to be magically bound to "French" culture and "French" ways. It would be an irresponsible romanticism not to admit that the Haitian oral culture is in a deplorable state. An inventory of the most frequently used proverbs in the countryside shows what a limited outlook on life this oral culture offers. There are hardly any proverbs or rules which give positive advice on agricultural matters, for instance. Most of them have a defensive implication: do your own thing; don't stick your neck out; don't trust anybody; don't help anybody.[12] There is no justice and no reward for ability and work, no way to change fate, for the rural world seems to be surrounded by unknown and irrational forces. *Tout sa ou pa konn pi gran pase ou,* says one proverb; "Everything you do not know is bigger than yourself," describes perfectly why creole culture, full of fears and competition, remains in its present state of inability to innovate.

Transition in Creole Literacy as a Social Process

The continuity of the absurd and dysfunctional role of French language and culture is usually attributed to the alienated elite of the country, which uses the linguistic cleavage of the country to preserve its social and material privileges. The attitudes towards this linguistic situation within the middle and upper classes, however, are rather ambivalent. This ambivalence reflects the social and economic reality of Haitian underdevelopment in many ways. On the one hand, the stagnation of the country prevents the increase of the number of social and economic positions within the upper level of society in proportion to social mobility. Since the days of independence, the majority of such positions are bound to commerce and administration, i.e., two unproductive sectors which can expand only in relation to productivity within other sectors. For this reason competition within the elite is considerable and the linguistic cleavage is a very effective means to limit the number of competitors and reduce the ever-present danger of total disruption of social order within the country. This explains why, in spite of all rhetorical exercises, there cannot be an increase in the efficiency of the educational system beyond a certain point without changing the economic structure of the country.

On the other hand, it is just as true that the present degree of normalization and instrumentalization of the Creole language described in Valdman (1975) and others is essentially the result of continuous, though highly debated, efforts by Haitian intellectuals during the past forty years. These efforts, however, have been confined to the upper classes. The monolingual part of the population is barely aware of the changing status of their mother tongue: we find the paradoxical situation of a small fraction acquiring a certain degree of bilingualism, while the larger monolingual sector continues to live within a diglossic situation.

The reasons for these ambitious efforts of Haitian intellectuals at raising the status of Creole have been more ideological than pragmatic. Based on its revolutionary origins and links to the French Revolution, Haiti has more of a traditional consciousness of nationhood than other Caribbean countries and even some Latin American countries. The Haitian Independence of 1804 was meant to guarantee the continuity of Jacobinian revolutionary ideals against the perverted Napoleonic policies of restoration. Linked directly to the modern nation-building process with its conceptual frame of egalitarianism, advancement of mobile middle classes, and an all-embracing national culture, but bound as well to socio-economic realities of a post-colonial plantation society, the attitudes of educated Haitians present a complex cluster of contradictions. As far as the language issue is concerned, the French language either appears as a symbol of dependent nationalism[13] and a link to international modernism, or as one of the major obstacles to the integration and identity on the national level and thus to the abolition of the enormous social cleavages inherited from the colonial past. This is, briefly, the background to apparently strange and contradictory evaluations of Creole. In an enquiry conducted in 1975 among 200 educated Haitians, only a minority (18.5%) would concede the quality of a language, including the existence of a grammar, to Creole (Fleischmann 1978). The majority of the same sample (82%), however, agreed that Creole is the national "language" (i.e. the one and only nationwide idiom). It would be difficult to understand these obviously incongruent opinions without making reference to the emotional value educated Haitians attach to their mother tongue. Critical attitudes towards that language "without grammar" and "without history" reflect perspectives adopted from outside. They do not affect the widely shared view that there is a particularly Haitian level of understanding and communication bound to the Creole language. *Pale kreyòl,* beyond its literal sense, has the connotation of reference to a specific Haitian culture and "logic" which is "national" insofar as it is considered independent from class and color lines. It excludes the foreigner who will perceive only the "official" but "non-Haitian" interpretation of an event or opinion (Valdman 1975:15).

Throughout Haitian history, particularly since the emergence of the Indigenist Doctrine, there were efforts to identify and revaluate this genuine Haitian perception. The attempt at developing and equipping the Creole language, from the first initiatives of Pétion (Brutus 1948) until the more continuous efforts since 1940, are part of this "nationalism." Whenever these efforts reached the stage of practical application, however, the dominant classes found ways to manipulate and confine their effects in order not to endanger their own social positions.

The main and most tangible battleground of these controversies was the public education sector, on the one hand, considered the main entryway into the privileged classes and thus conceived of as highly quality-oriented and elitist since the first sophisticated college was founded (Brutus 1948). On the other hand, reflected in the fact that legislation concerning obligatory formal education has existed since 1870, there is a truly

Republican concept of public education. These discrepancies between the proclaimed general right to enlightenment and practical interest of the elite to ensure their own social reproduction have led to a tendency to divide the Haitian educational system into two unequal halves: a relatively well-provided urban system, and an extremely poor rural system which was administered not by the Department of Education but by the Department of Agriculture. Though perceived very differently, both systems share an extreme selectivity, which reflects the double purpose of public education in providing a certain channel of social mobility. This philosophy corresponds to the "national" ideal while at the same time reducing and controlling mobility according to the upper classes' interests.

The main and fatal problem of the well-known deficiencies of the Haitian school system consists of the fact that it is bound to the prevailing reforms. As an instrument of a strictly confined social mobility, the Haitian school, to put it crudely, tends to make learning difficult and unsuccessful. It constitutes a waste of the already meager human and material resources of which the society disposes. This is characterized by the fact that only 1% of those who attend rural primary school finish successfully (OAS 1972); some 86% of secondary school students drop out (de Ronceray 1971). The problem is further illustrated by the fact that there are scarcely any alternative educational facilities for those who leave school prematurely. School is a very unmanageable ladder from the lowest to the highest rungs. Even those who finish primary school without continuing on the secondary level are considered socially as failures. In a very lucid report a UNESCO team reached the conclusion that even moderate reforms of Haitian schools would upset the entire financial system of the nation (UNESCO/BID 1974:44).

Change of Language and Change of Development Orientation

The entire raging controversy of the teaching of languages in Haiti in the future has to be understood within this context. The tedious learning and use of French within the school system is part of a "ritual" initiation into the upper classes. Its purpose is to make learning difficult and unsuccessful and thus to discourage and eliminate the majority of the aspirants. The French language is an integral part of a school system which is destined to produce a small number of highly qualified persons at enormous human and material expense (OAS 1972).

With such an emphasis upon predominantly social purposes, the Creole literacy campaigns of the past forty years were bound to fail. The peasants were perfectly aware that beyond all the good intentions, and in spite of all the positive feelings which upper-class Haitians expressed in favor of their native Creole, these campaigns were just another form of continuing and even strengthening the traditional division of the Haitian educational system. They understood this system for what it had always been: the only channel of upward social mobility, which would open some doors to a few of them or to their children. They wanted a "French" school and would not accept the "Creole" school, even as a substitute, as long as the ways of the town were "French" and as long as the Creole culture of their own environment was considered a lesser variation.

In addition to the cases studied above, these overall aspects of the Haitian language situation should demonstrate that, in spite of the simplicity of the mere linguistic facts, there are no simple solutions, for they invariably interfere with a complex and historically fragile social equilibrium. The present linguistic situation of the country is certainly more than ripe for decisive steps towards a further instrumentalization of Creole. But we should be aware that at the present the main impediments are not linguistic deficiencies of the Creole language which can be overcome by mere technical steps (Valdman 1975). The continuity of a diglossic situation, which as an historically cultivated mental disposition and social situation survives the linguistic realities and prevents instrumentalization through an excess of symbolic values and significance attached to the language.

In this respect one should not overlook the immediate consequences of a further officialization and instrumentalization of Creole, particularly within the educational sector. It will open up the congested school system, abolishing the linguistic advantage of the ruling urban class and pushing a considerably larger portion of low class students into institutions of higher learning. Further instrumentalization of Creole should be accompanied by a diversification of the educational system, giving access to a wider range of intermediate social and professional positions which potentially already exist. Haiti, like other polarized societies, is overflowing with unqualified labor and has more than a sufficient number of highly qualified professionals, but it lacks a qualified work force at the medium level (OAS 1972:292).

It seems that while the progress of Haitian social development has stagnated throughout the country's entire history, rapid changes have occurred in the social structure due, above all, to poverty. The traditional opposition of a "French" urban bourgeoisie and the Creole rural masses is breaking down under the impact of a massive rural migration towards the towns, mainly the capital. A "ruralization" of urban life is occurring at the same time as the emergence of new social groups which no longer fit into the polarized social system. It is not surprising that these migrants, through a gradual adaptation to a new and extremely difficult environment, develop more pragmatic approaches to culture and language. They would profit immediately from a change in linguistic policy.

In order to know more about possible changes in attitudes towards Creole culture and language 100 persons in a slum area of Port-au-Prince[15] were interviewed. This sample makes up most of the population of one block in Bel Air, a quarter of Port-au-Prince with a heterogeneous, though mostly poor, population of more or less recent migrants. The information obtained was condensed into four groups of variables: data on the former and present socio-economic status of the migrant and on the circumstances of migration; the degree of personal satisfaction the informant obtains from life in town; the degree of adaptation to the dominant culture in town and particularly the ability to use the French language; and attitudes towards Creole culture and Creole language.

The results obtained were at first surprising, but later fit into the general picture of the relations between French and Creole that have been outlined here. The informants were classified into two groups according to their personal data. In one group, group A, external conditions of socio-economic integration into town life were relatively unfavorable. Group A included women and unqualified or unskilled young people, recently removed from remote rural areas, who earned little money, mostly through odd jobs. The second group, group B, included all those who were fairly well-adapted: had been in town for some time, spoke French fairly well, had a steady income, etc. The surprise was that the less favored people, group A, were more satisfied with life in town. In spite of the fact that they were still dependent on the tools offered by the Creole culture and language they emphatically rejected, they particularly idealized the not-yet mastered French language. On the other hand, those of group B, who were better off economically, were less satisfied with life in town and were generally skeptical about the value of urban culture and the French language. This surprising opposition between the *real* conditions of the migrant and his attitude towards urban life and urban culture reproduces exactly the opposition between the symbolic value of the dominant culture and its practical meaning which has been discussed in the course of this essay.

The peasant who spends his entire life within his stagnating rural environment dreaming of a different life within a different culture will hardly realize that this opposition exists, but the migrant does. What happens may become more intelligible when condensed into a fictitious biography. A young person of Creole cultural background, living in a remote rural area, migrates to town one day. He soon realizes that life in town is hard, maybe even harder than at home. But he still believes in the opportunities he might have if he adapts to urban culture and language. His rejection of his Creole culture is a symbolic act by which he anticipates his social rise within the new environment, setting himself apart from the people he left at home. After some time, with considerable effort he has adapted to the ways of the town and speaks French fairly well. He realizes, however, that there is no social or material reward for this endeavor, that there is no practical use for this knowledge, that he still is a miserable migrant living in a run down room in Bel Air and probably will be for the rest of his life. At this point, like informants in group B, he will acknowledge that instead of learning French he should have used the linguistic tool he already had to acquire knowledge that could be useful for survival in a very competitive society. It is significant that nearly all informants put forward pragmatic reasons referring to their personal situation when asked why they would opt for a further instrumentalization of Creole. General considerations about the linguistic and cultural values of the respective languages which prevail in the academic discussions (both inside and outside the country) disappear when mere survival is at stake.

Researchers might be genuinely concerned about other questions, like whether Haiti does not need a language granting access to "universal culture," or whether the originality and creativity of Creole does not suffer from further instrumentalization. The overwhelming majority of Haitians, however, live in such circumstances that these general considerations become irrelevant. For the marginal, urban population, as well as for the rural communities, it is more important that the linguistic tool they manipulate be best adapted to their own social environment and to their own daily problems.

NOTES

[1] In fact, there are some relations between the two cases. In both cases the penetration of the French language is due to its ideological, i.e. Republican and Modernist, position, which goes back to the French Revolution and which ensures its centralist function (Gordon 1978:31-41).

[2] To my experience, at least sociolinguistically speaking, the so-called "hypercorrect forms" are to be considered as part of a consistent "pseudo" H-variation of Creole, which is ridiculous only when compared to the norm, i.e. in interaction between a speaker of French and a Creole monolingual. In interaction among Creole monolinguals it is considered a perfectly adequate code.

[3] This idea of an essentially French-speaking Haiti was quite common in the past. One of its defendants was the Haitian intellectual Dantès Bellegarde, who discusses the linguistic situation concluding, "le créole ... est plus proche du français que certains patois de France" (1934:12).

[4] This notion is implicitly present in the new Haitian constitution which permits the use of *both* languages.

[5] Fishman's assumption of a non-conflictive coexistence of the variations within diglossia (1967:32) has to be reconsidered as most of the participants of the Montpellier Colloquium on Diglossia agreed.

[6] For a more detailed discussion of these aspects see Fleischmann 1980:87-120.

[7] Cultural anthropologists see the Caribbean (creole) area generally characterized by the weakness of community structure. See, for example, Mintz 1971; Benoist 1971.

[8] A similar phenomenon is observed by Lévy (1976), who describes the competitive behavior of Martinican fishermen trying to prevent the success of other fishermen, "comme si ... le succès d'un pêcheur porterait préjudice à le réussite des autres" (1976:90).

[9] The Haitian writer Franketienne describes the "pale andaki" as follows: "Parler en daki, est dire une chose qui pour l'ennemi a un sens, mais qui pour les gens du même groupe a un sens différent, c'est-à-dire que la parole à ce moment-là est porteuse d'une certaine ambiguité, mais les gens qui vivent au sein du même groupe, les 'partenaires' faisant partie du même ensemble donné, spécifique, comprennent très bien, savant de quoi ils s'agit" (Fleischmann 1979:19).

[10] A French observer describes this situation as follows: "Le discours lui-même se doit de pallier l'absence de fixation par l'écrit: les redondances sont très nombreuses. On a l'impression de tourner en rond. Les images sont multiples. Les 'sagesses' paysannes donnent lieu à d'innombrables proverbes, véritables affiches de prévention. Toujours au niveau du discours, les éléments paralinguistiques prennent une importance que nous ne soupconnons pas en tant qu'étrangers à cette société. Le 'mn' du créole haïtien peut revêtir un nombre incalculable de sens. Le symbolisme des gestes, de la tenue même, est si poussé qu'un paysan peut, grâce à cela, délivrer des messages que nous sommes bien incapables de saisir. La cause et l'effet étant intimenent liés, nous avons affaire à use société étriquée, très peu ouverte sur le monde extérieur, très hiérarchisée, et où le verbe prend une place énorme, se substituant souvent à l'acte. La routine et le merveilleux sont à la base de tout explications des phénomènes naturels et le goût pour la légende et le conte ne font que renforcer ce pouvoir du parler" (Groupe de recherche 1976:3).

[11] These attitudes are very well described by Fanon (1952), particularly in the chapter "Le noir et le langage." Here, for instance, he describes the reaction of spectators when a woman faints during an election speech, "Français a té tellement chaud que la femme là tombé mal cadi" (p. 31).

[12] Some of these proverbs are:

"Nèg rayi nèg depi lan Ginen."	The negro hates the negro since (his arrival from) Guinea.
"Nèg toujou gen you koud nèg pou yo fè."	The negro always knows some tricks to use against others.
"Fè nèg dibyen, se Bondye ou bat."	Do good to somebody, then you beat God.
"Rann sèvis bay chagren."	To help somebody brings trouble.
"Ravèt pa gen rezon douvan poul."	The cockroach has no right in front of the chicken.
"Mèt kò veyé kò."	Each one for himself.

[13] The typical argument along this line is that French had been withheld from the slaves, such that the expansion of this language would later be "une conquête, un véritable butin arraché à l'ennemi sur le champs de bataille" (Derose 1956:5-6).

[14] A detailed description and analysis of this enquiry was published in Fleischmann 1982.

BASIC EDUCATION IN HAITI

JACOMINA P. DE REGT

ISSUES IN BASIC EDUCATION

Overview

The Haitian education system faces serious problems and constraints in its aim to provide basic education for its children. Not enough children complete their primary education, and even those who do are often inadequately trained. These problems, particularly acute in rural areas, stem from three sets of causes: (1) less than half of rural children attend school; (2) only about twenty percent of those who do attend school complete primary level schooling; (3) learning achievement among school leavers is comparatively low. It is important for national development that these problems be solved, but the government must first overcome formidable financial, human, and organizational shortcomings. Because of the magnitude of these problems, the lack of resources in the education sector is especially acute. This situation implies that the problems can be solved only in phases over the long run. The issues, the government plans, and the constraints, along with some of the consequences if good quality basic education cannot be provided, are discussed in sequence below.[1]

119

Low Enrollment Rates

An initial problem facing the Haitian education system is that less than half of the children attend school. Furthermore, the participation of those who attend is unequally distributed along the urban/rural continuum, by region and by sex. In 1980/81 some 620,000 children were enrolled in primary school. This represented a 70% gross enrollment rate and a 43% net enrollment rate of the 6-12 age group.[2] In rural areas, enrollment represented only a 30% net rate for the same age group. In contrast, some 509,300 of the 6-12 year olds, or 57% of the age group in 1980/81, were estimated not to be in school.

Disparities in participation follow the rural/urban continuum (30% of the relevant age group is enrolled in rural areas versus 72% in urban areas), and vary widely among the nine departments of the country, with net enrollment rates varying from 27% (Ouest) to 65% (Nord-Ouest). Rural representation indices range from 0.519 (Grand'Anse) to 1,847 (Artibonite) (Table 1). Girls are found to be enrolled less frequently than boys: 43% in rural areas and 46% nationally. Enrollments of girls, however, grew at about 1% per year faster than those of boys over the last five years.

The overall low and unequal rural primary enrollment rates by region are caused mainly by: (1) the lack of sufficient school places and the dispersed location of existing facilities; (2) the cost of education to the parents; and (3) other socioeconomic factors, such as the need for child labor in the fields and caring for siblings, and the poor health and nutrition of the children.

The disparity between the number of rural and urban schools and classrooms available in 1979/80 is shown in Table 2. Following this trend, for the 1981/82 school year only 12,700 classrooms are available while 13,500 are needed. The real deficit, however, is greater because at least 30% of public schools and 20% of private schools need to be replaced or repaired. The fact that 30% of public schools operate in rented, converted houses explains the high percentage of needed replacement for public schools. Most private schools are also in former residences. In addition, 22% of private schools operate in the open air, without buildings. Schools and settlements are usually widely dispersed, often compelling students to walk more than five kilometers one way. This trek serves as an obstacle for the physically weaker children to attend school regularly, particularly under rough weather conditions.

Secondly, the cost of education is a deterrent to enrollment. The annual cost to a family per child for public schools was G90, or $19 in 1979/80; this included school fees, uniforms, learning aids and books. The annual cost for private education is about the same in rural areas, but higher in urban areas. These costs frequently constitute an excessive burden for rural families. The average annual income per family in rural areas is about G765

(1980 estimate). The expense of the family for the education of one child thus represents 11% of the average income, and 22% with two children of primary school age. Two to four percent would be considered normal in most countries. There is an additional cost of sending children to school: even young children can make a substantial contribution to the operation of the household by caring for siblings, working in the fields or selling newspapers in the streets. Finally, 75% of school-age children suffer from protein-calorie deficiencies, as shown in a 1979/80 study. Of children enrolled in schools, 41% received only one meal at home, 38% two meals. The nutritional status of six-year-olds was 80% of the optimal, dropping to 60% for the seven-year-olds.

The economic development of a country is influenced by low participation in the education system, with its resulting low levels of literacy. Higher literacy rates are linked to better health status, higher life expectancy, lower child mortality and economic growth. An increase in literacy rates of 20% correlates with a GDP growth of 0.5%, according to worldwide comparative studies (Hicks, 1980). Worldwide correlations do not predict that the same would occur in Haiti, but improved rural literacy rates would enable the rural population to better understand instructions for improved production techniques which could result in higher productivity. For the individual, access to basic education opens an avenue to better jobs and higher earnings even if in the short run migration is necessary to find the opportunities.

The long-term solution to the problem of low enrollment rates is to increase enrollments quickly, especially in rural areas. However, the government cannot afford such dramatic steps, so the short-term solution should be to increase enrollment rates selectively by focusing the limited government resources on the most disadvantaged areas.

Low Efficiency

The second major problem facing the Haitian education system is that not enough children entering school complete the primary cycle. This means that the efficiency of the school system is low. For instance, the completion rate for the cohort entering school in 1978/79 would be, based on historical coefficients, 47% in urban areas, 20% in rural areas. Most children stay in the lowest grades due to high repetition and dropout rates. For example, in the rural areas some 59% of the students were in preschool[3] and first grade, compared to 43% in the first two grades in urban areas in 1980/81. The urban repetition rate and dropout rate is consistently lower per grade than the rural one (Table 3). Both rates are substantially higher for the lower grades. In fact, 59% of the urban students and 76% of the rural students drop out before they can be expected to have attained full literacy (i.e., after grade 4).[4]

Because of starting school at a late age, followed by frequent repetition, 39% of children enrolled are overage, i.e. more than a year older than the legal age corresponding to that grade. The legal primary school age is from 6 to 12 years. At present, 34.5% of the students in primary school are 12 years and older. Only 26% in the urban areas, in contrast to 13% in the rural areas, pass through primary school without repeating one grade; 22% urban and 39% rural repeated three years or more.

The inefficiency of the system has multiple causes, some of which overlap with those already discussed. The undernourishment and malnutrition caused by poverty is a major determinant of the dropout rate. Studies show that even mild to moderate malnutrition affects cognitive development independent of other conditioning variables. Added to poor health and malnutrition are the conditions in which the child receives his or her education; for instance, overcrowded classrooms (95 children per classroom is not uncommon in rural areas), and teachers instructing multiple grades per classroom without being adequately prepared for multi-grade teaching. Also, present curricula and teaching methods do not take into account the great number of overage students who have interests and learning abilities different from the regular age group students. All students follow the same program because teachers are not trained in the technique of grouping by age or ability level and providing distinct individualized or group programs. Compounding these constraints, students may enter school at any date during the year, making consistent progress difficult to plan. Lastly, students are taught in French and teachers determine the advancement of students to the next grade based to a large degree on their mastery of French, with which the children express their mastery of knowledge skills and concepts. This final factor by itself explains most of the crowding at the lower levels.

The consequences of low efficiency are, above all, represented by a waste of resources. Table 4 shows the human costs of inefficiency: 20 student-years to produce one graduate in the rural areas, 15 student-years in the urban public schools, but only 7 student-years in urban private schools. The urban private schools are about three times as efficient as the rural schools in producing graduates. The total financial resources wasted on the 1978/79 cohort are about $340,000, about $200,000 by the government and about $140,000 by the parents. The former could pay the salaries of an additional 167 teachers, or given an additional 8,000 children access to education. Another human consequence is the psychological conditioning towards failure that the children receive, resulting in both low self-esteem and low achievement motivation.

To improve efficiency, measures such as more discipline regarding school dates and number of days and hours, automatic promotion, grouping of students by age and an accelerated program for the overaged, as well as a better quality package for the normal student, could be introduced. Data from pre-school nutrition centers constructed by CARE (Cooperative for American Relief to Everyone) show that 87% of the children who participated in the one-year program were promoted from grade 1 to grade 2 versus 37% of the nonparticipants. This success may be due to better school readiness, as well as better nutritional status.

Low Quality

The third problem facing the Haitian education system is the low rate of cognitive achievements of students who complete primary education. Low learning levels are evident, but there are no reliable indicators of how much students learn. However, achievement can be measured and compared with other countries in an indirect way by measuring inputs. The low or inadequate inputs described below all indicate a low quality educational system, which cannot do anything but produce low results. The inputs reviewed are: funds spent per student, teacher qualifications, teacher supervision, relevance of the curriculum and of the language of instruction, and the availability of learning materials and physical facilities.

1. The *funds* spent per student are low compared with other countries, e.g., in 1979/80 the unit cost per primary student was $55, or 19% of the per capita GDP. Of this, the parents' contribution, $19, went to uniforms, tuition and textbooks. The government's expenditure (U.S. $36, or 13% of per capita GDP) was almost entirely spent on teacher salaries with little remaining for classroom supplies or teaching aids. Most classrooms do not have maps, paper, glue, scissors or even a blackboard with chalk. The government spends $.60 per student on these supplies and aids, despite the fact that from the entire tuition, $2.40 per student is officially earmarked for this purpose.

2. *Teachers.* In 1980/81 some 14,900 teachers taught primary school— 5,500 public; 9,400 private. About 27% of the teachers were considered qualified (graduates of teacher training colleges or equivalent) including 20% in the private sectors and about 40% in the public sector. An additional 19% completed secondary education—first cycle and could become qualified in equivalency courses. All other teachers need more extensive in-service training. In general, teachers are poorly prepared to teach in rural circumstances, with more than one grade per classroom, overage students and infrequent attendance of students.

Five years ago, only half of the teachers were unqualified, compared with three-fourths at present. This deterioration of the system results from high teacher attrition, estimated at 9-10% per year. Teachers leave their profession for higher-paying employment both abroad and in Haiti.

Salaries for public teachers were raised to $100 per month for all teachers in 1979, but are still lower than those received by drivers or secretaries in Port-au-Prince. Private sector teachers earn only $40 per month on average. Compounding the financial constraints, little incentive is given to recruit qualified teachers for the rural areas, as most teacher training colleges are in urban areas.

Supervision of teachers, providing them with pedagogical support, is poorly organized. Teachers deal with three levels of supervision: inspectors at the district or zonal level, pedagogical advisors attached to Regional Pedagogical Centers, and their directors in the schools (see Table 5). The three levels are neither integrated nor are tasks clearly delineated by level. Directors and inspectors have not received proper training to provide pedagogical support; they deal mostly with administrative and statistical matters. The inspectors' mobility is limited by lack of transport and travel budget. The National Pedagogical Institute (IPN) has a parallel structure of 19 Regional Pedagogical Centers with some 100 pedagogical advisors. Trained in a ten-month course in supervision, they form a corps of well-motivated and well-trained professionals. With curriculum experiments underway since 1978, the IPN has had little time to devote to regular pedagogical assistance. Until 1981/82, advisors spent about 50% of their time giving teacher in-service training courses and 50% supervising the introduction of the experimental curriculum. Since 1981/82, the teacher training colleges provide in-service teacher training, and IPN is experimenting with intensive supervision of fewer classrooms in the experimental curriculum. Generally, however, a rural school teacher receives little direct pedagogical supervision.

3. *Relevance of Curriculum and Language.* The present primary school curriculum copies the early twentieth-century French model, using the same textbooks and teaching techniques of one-way classical exposition by the teacher to passive students. Memorization is the key factor in both instruction and students' evaluation. This anachronistic curriculum is geared toward the children of the elite, who successfully fulfill the academic requirements to go on to secondary and university level education. The premise of academic progression and the materials presented based on French circumstances are alien to the Haitian world, especially in the rural areas. In Haiti, where few children have the means and opportunity to pursue academic careers, education needs to be presented in such a way as to be useful to children who may never have more than two to four years of schooling.

The use of language in the educational system is quite ambiguous. Creole and French are the national languages in Haiti, with French the official language. Virtually all the population speaks Creole. About 20% are able to speak and write French, but only 5% use French almost exclusively. All education has been presented in the French medium, imposing a learning and emotional barrier on the rural child. The gap between the classroom (Francophone environment) and the home (Creolophone environment) generates a duality in the early childhood experience which negatively affects intellectual and emotional development.

4. *Availability of Learning Materials.* Learning materials, including textbooks, notebooks and pencils, as already mentioned, are to be purchased by the parents. Because these costs often exceed the limited financial means of parents in rural areas, at present, only one in four rural students owns a textbook. The average cost is $1-2 per book, or $6-8 per grade per student. Textbooks produced and distributed by the private sector are mostly in French and have remained unchanged for years, thus reinforcing the disparity in communicative skills. On the other hand, missions and other private organizations have produced materials in Creole for use in their schools.

5. *Availability of Physical Facilities.* In most rural areas, schools are dilapidated and so poorly maintained that they interfere with teaching. For example, in 1976/77 about 60% of the students had no desks or chairs. Even in urban areas, in 1978 45% of public schools had no blackboards. Classrooms also tend to be overcrowded. The average number of children per classroom approaches 100 in public primary schools and 50 in private schools (1978/79). The rural student/teacher ratio in public schools in 10:1 vs. 37:1 for urban areas (1978/79).

The situation described above is especially discriminatory for rural poorer regions, thereby resulting in the loss of a great potential in human resources. As farming families, their limited—or lack of literacy hinders their ability to use information to improve their productivity or health. As entrants to the urban labor force, their incomplete basic education limits their ability to receive further instruction in vocational skills or pursue further education to enhance their upward mobility. Low efficiency and low quality in education now results in limiting rural youths' chances for upward mobility, for example in giving access to secondary schools in urban areas, because, with the exception of four agricultural (grades 7-9) schools, there are no opportunities for education beyond grade 6 in rural areas.

The solution to the problem of low and unequal participation lies in correcting the imbalances by concentrating government investments in the disadvantaged rural areas, especially in those with the lowest representation indices. Based on a school mapping exercise, facilities should be distributed to those areas which have the least access to schools. Any expansion of the system, however, should naturally be accompanied by improvements in efficiency and quality.

RECENT CHANGES IN BASIC EDUCATION

Overview

Over the last three years, formal education in Haiti has undergone a profound change. In 1978, the two autonomous primary education systems (urban and rural) merged into one under DEN (Department of National Education). National legislation established Creole as the main language of instruction. A review of the primary school curriculum was started to develop a curriculum responsive to the socioeconomic and cultural challenges of the Haitian society. In 1979 an Organic Law gave the basis for reorganization of DEN, which is gradually being implemented. A new education system consisting of ten years of basic education was established in March 1982. The five year period, 1982-86, is crucial for the consolidation and extension of the changes under way.

Five Year Development Plan and Constraints

The government plans formulated for the next five years are ambitious. During the third five-year development plan (1981/82-1985/86), three major undertakings are scheduled:

1. to *increase the gross enrollment* rate nationally from 70% to 83% by 1983, an increase in 168,500 student places, and to increase the gross enrollment rate in rural areas from 54% to 71% by 1987, or by 128,500 student places;

2. to implement gradually the *reform of the educational structure* starting in October 1982/83;

3. to *modernize education administration* through:
   (a) reorganization of the central structures of DEN; and
   (b) decentralization and regionalization of tasks, functions and responsibilities.

These three undertakings are important and necessary steps in the process of adapting the education system to the requirements of the present society. But difficult financial, human and managerial constraints may contribute to extending the projected timetable.

1. *Increase in Enrollments.* In order to introduce 10 years of basic education to all Haitian children by the year 2000, the government plans to increase enrollments by about 5% per year, or about 34,000 new students per year. This is higher than the target for the previous five years (22,300 students per year) and considerably higher than the actual achievement (about 13,600 students per year). It is clear in percentage annual growth that the shortfall was caused in the public sector performance with 1.7% annual growth rather than the 5.1% foreseen. In effect, the public sector lacked funds to construct additional urban schools and pay additional teacher

salaries. The private sector, however, increased its enrollments to about 9% per annum.

In view of the performance under the Second Development Plan, the targets for the Third Development Plan are unrealistically high. It is unlikely that the public sector can reach these targets, because the budgets, both development and recurrent, are likely to be lower than expected by DEN at the time of establishing these targets, and DEN is unlikely to have the capacity to implement the projected expansion. In addition, the growth of the private sector is unpredictable.

DEN's share of the public sector budget is likely to be lower than the one predicted at the time of writing the Development Plan. First, DEN expects 80% of its development budget of $100 million to come from foreign resources, not yet committed. If resources were assured, DEN's proposed allocation to primary education (60%) and to expansion of the system (80%) would ensure adequate availability of funds for expansion of the primary education system. Second, the recurrent budget, in the present economic situation, is not likely to grow and education's share in it may decrease. The rate of increase determines the number of new teachers that can be paid (teacher salaries form 95% of the budget), and this, in turn, determines the rate of enrollment increases. Given the difficult situation, certainly for the next three years, DEN's projected enrollment growth is unlikely to be reached.

Lastly, the performance of the private sector is unpredictable. In its projections, DEN assumes a private sector growth of 6.5%, lower than that in previous years (about 9%). It expects the private sector to construct about 3,700 new classrooms, mostly in urban areas. However, the urban private sector's growth responds to parents' demand, and in the present economic circumstances that may slacken. In rural areas, where many private schools are funded through foreign charitable or community sources, growth patterns are unpredictable. DEN, through its policy of treating rural private schools as public schools in the educational reform, may provide a stimulus to the rural private sector. No government incentive is expected for the urban sector.

2. *Education Reform.* The government plans to introduce the new educational structure gradually over a period of three years, starting with one-third or some 1,300 grade 1 classes in 1982/83. This educational reform was prepared during the last three years by DEN and IPN staff, the Curriculum Committee,[5] and UNESCO technical assistance. Experimentation with some of its features was financed under a World Bank Credit. The present educational reform grew out of the deliberations and experiments conducted over the last several years. However, from the outset it was not clear that it would lead to a major restructuring of the whole educational system.

The educational reform consists of the introduction of a new school *structure* comprising ten years of basic education in three cycles (4 + 3 + 3) followed by three years of secondary education. In addition to structural changes, the educational reform features the following points:

(a) new curricula and syllabi;
(b) new teaching methods;
(c) introduction of the "Teacher Charter";
(d) automatic promotion from grades 1 to 2 and 3 to 4; and
(e) improved school supervision and inspection.

The restructuring of the system and dividing the ten years of basic education into three cycles is an important step forward towards the goal of providing education for all. In this system, children who abandon school after four years will have finished a self-contained education package, and it is expected that they will be functionally literate (op. cit. Footnote 4). In addition, the reform features qualitative improvements.

New *curricula and syllabi* have been developed for grades 1 to 3 and are in various stages of being tested. Curriculum objectives and content for grades 1 to 4 have been agreed upon. Objectives for grades 5 to 7 will be established later. The new curriculum for grades 1-4 differs from the previous one in that it is taught in Creole, includes three months of school readiness skills in the first grade, and has only four subjects: reading, writing, mathematics and environmental sciences. The latter are geared toward learning through observation of the natural and social environment.

The new syllabi, textbooks, workbooks, teacher guides and teacher aids are to be developed by the government (IPN's Curriculum and Educational Materials Unit). Reviewed by the Curriculum Committee and DEN, these and some other existing materials consistent with the program objectives will be the only materials allowed for use in both public and private schools. The government wants to ensure that eventually all classrooms have teacher guides, teaching aids, texts and workbooks for the children. However, only public and rural private schools would be provided with the teacher guides and teaching aids. Urban private schools would have to purchase these materials themselves. Parents would have to purchase the texts and workbooks for their children from commercial outlets. At present, books are often too expensive for parents, as already discussed; therefore, the government wants to ensure that better and cheaper texts and workbooks are available, by both developing them and establishing maximum prices. Materials for grade 1 are currently on the market, and to ensure that the new programs would be taught this school year, all children have received their work- and textbooks free of charge.

The *teaching innovations* under the reform program would consist of:
(i) use of Creole as language of instruction in grades 1 to 4;
(ii) a teacher staying with a cohort for two years;
(iii) grouping children in classrooms according to levels and ability;
(iv) evaluating children by intermediate trimestral objectives and moving them accordingly among groups; and
(v) increasing participation of children, utilizing their individual experiences and capabilities, discovery learning rather than memorization.

All teachers are to be trained in these innovations and the curricula. Over the last few years several thousand teachers, public as well as private, have received instruction in various aspects of the new programs. This training was of varying length and quality, however. A systematic training program including radio programs is planned, allowing teachers to receive in-service training and gradually, within three years, acquire a teacher training college equivalency diploma. The in-service training courses are given by the staff of teacher training colleges and of Regional Pedagogical Centers (CPRs).

The efficiency of the system is supposed to be improved by introducing *automatic promotion* between grades 1 and 2 and between grades 3 and 4. During a period of two years, children would be able to move at their own pace in achieving the objectives set for grade 2 and grade 4. They will be grouped according to ability and the teacher will reorganize groups as necessary each trimester. DEN predicts an average of only 20% failure at the end of such a two-year period, compared with 63% in rural areas at present.

In the future, the supervision system would integrate both inspection and pedagogical functions of supervision. This would only be possible, however, when the education reform is fully implemented in 1993. The advisors could then turn to routine supervision instead of supervision of experimental programs. Meanwhile, inspectors and school directors are receiving training in pedagogical supervision techniques, and new inspectors follow the same pre-service training course as pedagogical advisors.

3. *Modernize Education Administration.* The government is creating regional departments in the process of carrying out an administrative reform consisting of a reorganization and decentralization of DEN. The reorganization of DEN, substantially carried out in the fall of 1981, is in accordance with the Organic Law of 1979. This law created a new Department of Education and describes the new functions of all departments and sections (see Chart 2). Under this structure, a Director General was appointed and five functional Departments were created (Planning, Inspection and Pedagogical Assistance, Education, Personnel and Administration). In the old structure, DEN lacked basic functions of a

modern administration, such as having an adequate data base on the
personnel of the sector, or educational planning. IPN, an autonomous
institution, was also reorganized at the same time. It consists of four
sections under the Study Directorate: training, evaluation, preparation of
curricula and education materials, and supervision. The formerly
independent Educational Radio and Teaching/Learning Materials Unit
have been incorporated into IPN. The reorganizations are taking place
in step-by-step fashion, as all participants attempt to reach agreement on
the many changes proposed. Although the Organic Law is clear on the
functions of each unit in DEN, the blueprint does not exactly fit the existing
situation or take into account, for instance, the changes caused by the
educational reform going forward simultaneously. Some of IPN's functions
in pedagogical supervision and in-service training, for example, would have
to be transferred to the Department of Inspection and Pedagogical
Assistance of DEN. A period of three years, starting October 1981, was
predicted for the introduction of the administrative reform.

Simultaneously, under the government's regionalization scheme, DEN
would decentralize and create nine regional departments with ten districts
each. These departments would become responsible for the day-to-day
functioning of the education system, while the DEN's central departments
would retain policy-making and normative functions. Regionalization is a
recent policy; two regional educational departments were created in
1981/82. Until the process is complete, in three to four years, a mixture of
old and new procedures will continue to be used; new and existing structures
will exist side by side (e.g., district inspectors and regional pedagogical
centers).

Constraints

In order to achieve these objectives (increase access, and carry out an
educational as well as administrative reform), the Haitian government faces
formidable constraints of a technical, human, political, financial and
managerial nature.

1. *Technical Constraints.* During the period 1978-1981, now called the
experimental phase, many aspects of the educational reform were tested:
different texts, different teacher training programs, different applications
of the use of Creole and French. During the 1981/82 school year the
conceptualization of the elements of educational reform crystallized. Due to
political pressures to introduce the reform on a nationwide scale by
September, 1982, however, no final experimentation with the total package
occurred. After a change in ministers in 1982, it was decided to introduce
the reform progressively. By January 1983, about one-third of the grade 1
classrooms used the new curriculum, the teachers were trained (or some

retrained in a crash course in December 1982), and the text- and workbooks were distributed to all classrooms. In practice, this school year is a transitional one; it is the year of experimentation on a large scale, of involving staff at all levels of the Ministry, the year to iron out the logistical and technical problems. It should also be the year in which incipient evaluation programs already developed will begin.

The technical problems with the reform are still numerous. A French evaluation report points towards problems with teachers. They will have to change their traditional teaching style, for instance, and become literate in written Creole rather than building on their oral Creole tradition in the classroom. The detailed and cumbersome teacher guides now produced by IPN (averaging 200 pages each) stifle the very initiative and innovative responsive classroom teaching style that the reform hopes to instill in teachers.[6] The work going on at IPN still is very much based on individual school subjects, rather than on an integrated concept of what it is that one wants to change in the classrooms. Consequently, the teacher training is geared towards guiding teachers in the use of new textbooks and teacher guides. Adult education methods of motivating subject-specific teachers to reflect on their behavior and attitudes tend not to be used (CEPI, 1982). Who evaluates what is not yet settled, although parts of the evaluation scheme have been experimented with for several years. The educational radio programs for teacher training do not yet exist; programs in school readiness skills, oral French and environment have been used for several years, but not all schools receive them. Whether parents will be able to afford the educational materials produced by IPN, or whether ways to produce cheaper materials will have to be found, have not been answered. In short, a multitude of technical problems still remain to be solved during the phase of the implementation/reform. The solution of these constraints hinges on the solutions found for the human, financial, political and managerial constraints.

2. *Human Constraints.* The human constraints are the most crucial ones. First is the school age population with low levels of health and nutrition. The cognitive development of the majority of these children has been impaired through reduced brain growth due to chronic malnourishment since infancy, and through increased susceptibility to disease. Malnourished school children typically have low attention spans, low levels of energy and frequent absences due to illness (World Bank, 1980). Any intervention in the education system has to take this into account.

The second constraint is the teachers, poorly qualified and poorly remunerated. Teaching as a profession is not an attractive one at the moment; it pays less than other professions (secretarial staff for instance) and there are no career incentives. To counter this a draft *Teacher Charter* spelling out a career path and salary levels differentiated by years of service and qualifications has been prepared. As a first step towards its implementation, a 1981 survey was made of all public teachers, identifying level of qualification, pedagogical experience, family size, etc. As a second step, the Administrative Committee on Civil Service approved the draft *Charter* in March, 1982. In September, 1982, a Civil Service Charter was established, including teachers as civil servants. The need for a special *Teacher Charter* was thereby removed; however, the proposals to modify the remuneration and grading are still valid. In view of government financial constraints, the salary proposals would probably have to be phased in over a five-year period. However, the establishment of a legal basis for the profession and even modest modifications of the salary structure are important steps forward in attracting new staff to teaching, improving the morale of existing staff and motivating them to undertake the changes so important to the successful implementation of the educational reform.

A third human constraint lies at the level of qualified staff to plan, supervise and manage the reforms. Government employment, with low civil service salaries and lack of career incentives, does not attract qualified staff in sufficient numbers. The total pool of qualified professional staff in Haiti thus is small. This lack of staff affects IPN, and its regional offices and DEN at all levels.

3. *Political Constraints.* Most opposition to the education reform in 1982 centered on the introduction of Creole as a teaching language. Direct instruction in the maternal language greatly aids children in comprehending the materials taught while reducing inefficiencies in the school system (Dutcher, 1982). The debate on the language issue in Haiti, however, greatly transcends this pedagogical level. Although not couched in these terms, it touches on fundamental development questions for the country: can Creole become the official language and if so, what are the implications for the present social and economic structure? That the use of Creole in teaching (with the right methods) will reduce inefficiencies in the education system can be subjected to empirical tests in Haiti. This type of research, however, will not provide answers to the latter questions and the debate is likely to continue. The outcome of this debate will affect the introduction of the educational reform packages as now conceived.

4. *Financial Constraints.* Financial constraints will most likely reduce the growth in creating new school places, but probably will also influence the outcome of the educational reform. The direct costs of the reform represent only 10% of the DEN development budget ($10.8 million) for the 1982-1987 period and should not cause any major problems. The problems are evident in the demands for a higher operational budget for items such as:

new teachers, better-paid teachers, more and better-paid supervisors, more teaching aids, and in-service training programs on a continuous basis. Similarly, the implementation of the administrative reform demands more and better-paid staff. The government will have to decide what the relative importance of basic education is in view of its priorities and the austere budget situation in the near future.

5. *Managerial Constraints.* The responsibilities for the successful implementation of the educational reform are divided and, from an efficiency point of view, quite unclear. DEN, specifically the Directorates of Planning and Primary Education, IPN, and the Curriculum Committee are all involved. IPN was responsible for the preparation of the reform. IPN continues to be responsible for the experimentation with new programs at higher grade levels, but it is also responsible for many of the implementation aspects, namely textbook production, training programs, pedagogical supervision, and educational radio. The Curriculum Committee is primarily responsible for setting the curriculum objectives, and for monitoring the experimental as well as implementation phase. The Directorate of Primary Education has direct line responsibility over the inspectors and teachers, while the Directorate of Planning is responsible for overall sector plans and financial allocations. Evaluation is done by IPN and by DEN, Department of Planning. No single person, other than the Minister of Education himself, has authority over all these organizational units. Coordination among these units is essential, and since early 1982 the then Minister created an informal "project-management" team consisting of heads of all these units who met with him and briefed him once a week. This approach proved to be successful, and was largely responsible for the progress made in early 1982. This team now meets occasionally and still functions rather well. The diffused lines of responsibility do, at times, create coordination problems and delays although it is also a way to ensure that all interested parties have an opportunity to be heard. Simultaneous reorganization of the Ministry and creation of regional directorates only exacerbates the confusion around responsibilities for reform implementation.

Another dimension of the managerial problems with the implementation of reforms is the fact that some 60% of primary education is carried out in private schools. DEN, at present, has no effective means of monitoring or controlling what goes on in these schools. Although the new curriculum and teaching methods are to be applied in all schools in the country, it is unclear how this will be enforced. At present, rural and urban private schools do participate in the experimentation phase, and many rural private schools which were already teaching children in Creole, have now adopted the official government curriculum. Some 900 private school teachers were trained in this new curriculum in early 1982, and government policy is to treat rural private schools the same as public schools, providing them with teacher training, textbooks, teacher guides, and supervision. Yet it remains unclear how wide the participation of the private sector is or will be in the future, or how (and if) this participation can be enforced.

CONCLUSION

The process of modernizing primary education and making it more accessible to all Haitian children, especially those in the rural areas, has barely begun. The implementation of the educational reform will last a decade or more. This education reform, enthusiastically and ably prepared by Haitian institutions such as IPN, faces enormous difficulties—it is complex, and after more experimentation and classroom experience, it needs to be better defined; it is costly in terms of qualified human capital, a scarce commodity in the country, and in recurrent costs to continue the support of the innovations in terms of better paid and trained teachers, and learning materials in schools. The educational reform is not equally well-received by all segments of the population and its general implementation will face a political battle. Lastly, with the diffuse lines of responsibility, it is a very difficult undertaking to manage.

Yet, the stakes are high. Education is crucial for the development of Haiti. Haiti, now in the midst of an economic recession, looks towards the expansion of the industrial sector to promote economic growth. Industry will need workers at the skilled-worker and managerial levels. In agriculture, the largest sector, the workers need to be able to understand simple recommendations on cultivation practices and erosion control. Four years of education are positively correlated with increases in agricultural output, although the percentage gain in output in a modern agricultural environment as a result of four years of education is 10% higher than in a traditional one such as Haiti (Lockheed et al., 1980). Still, production increases would be expected if the farming population had this education. Research has also shown positive correlation between the education levels of mothers and the health of their children. The relationship between fertility and education is inverse; mothers with high levels of education have low levels of fertility, those with lower education have high levels of fertility, probably because of the higher survival rate of the former children due to better health (Birdsall and Cochran, 1982). Healthier children in turn will be able to better absorb education. The reform, with its new curriculum taught in Creole, aims at providing Haitian children with better education. The generation receiving this education can be expected to make a better contribution to Haiti's social and economic development.

Table 1: Regional Discrepancies in Enrollments, Total and Rural (ages 6-11)
Source: DEN (Department of National Education)

Department	Rural Representation Index	Gross Enrollment 1978-79 Total	Ratio 1978-79 Rural	Net Enrollment 1978-79 Total	Ratio 1978-79 Rural
Quest	0.726	65.6	37.3	50.8	27.3
Nord	1.193	78.4	55.4	59.3	45.2
Nord-Est	0.886	75.7	55.2	55.9	46.2
Nord-Ouest	1.360	97.8	80.9	71.1	64.5
Artibonite	1.847	69.9	49.1	43.5	30.1
Centre	0.810	73.0	51.6	52.0	39.5
Sud-Est	1.571	58.6	50.1	36.9	31.1
Sud	0.794	67.0	44.5	48.9	33.5
Grand'Anse	0.519	58.6	35.3	43.7	28.0
TOTAL	1.000	68.8	43.7	50.0	32.2

Representation Index: The percentage of school enrollment in any given department divided by the percentage of school age population 6-11 years old in that department.

Table 2: Number of Schools and Classrooms
(1979/1980)

	Schools Total	Rural	Urban	Classrooms Total	Rural	Urban
Public	958	623	335	4,995	2.232	2,763
Private	2,038	1,176	862	7,676	3,327	4,349
Total	2,996	1,799	1,197	12,671	5,559	7,112

**Table 3: Promotion, Repetition and Dropout Rates for 1977/78
Urban and Rural**
(Percentage of Students Enrolled)

	Grade						
	Preschool[4]	1	2	3	4	5	6
Rural							
Promotion Rate	30	56	67	60	66	73	80
Repetition Rate	34	31	27	27	26	21	14
Dropout Rate	36	13	6	13	8	6	5
Urban							
Promotion Rate	—	67	69	68	68	85	84
Repetition Rate	—	19	19	21	21	15	7
Dropout Rate	—	14	12	11	11	(-)3	9

**Table 4: Efficiency of the Education System
1978/79 Cohort**

	Years of Study (1)	Student-Years Invested in Cohort (2)	Number of Graduates (3)	Student-Years per Graduate (4)	Input/ Output Ratio (5)	Student-Years Wasted	
						Number	%
						(6)	
Rural	7	4,058	202	20.1	2.87	2,644	65.1
Urban-Public	6	4,784	314	15.2	2.54	2,900	60.0
Urban-Private	6	4,617	660	7.0	1.16	657	14.2

Note: (4) = Total number of student-years invested, divided by number of
       graduates [(2):(3)].
       (5) = (4):(1).
       (6) = (2) — [(a) (3)].

Table 5: Supervision Structure (1981/1982)

Administrative Supervision Collection of School Statistics		Pedagogical Supervision	
Level	No.	Level	No.
DEN: Primary Education Dept.		IPN	
Department Inspectors	9	Regional Pedagogical Centers	19
Zonal Inspectors	24	With Pedagogical Advisors	100
District Inspectors	59		
Directors	3,000		

—Average 154 teachers
　per inspector

—Average 127 teachers
　per advisor

Table 6: Curriculum for Grades 1-4

	Reading*	Writing*	Math	Environmental Sciences
Grade 1 School Readiness Training (3 months)	X	X	X	X
Grade 2	X	X	X	X
Grade 3	X	X	X	X
Grade 4	X	X	X	X

*Reading and writing would be in Creole; oral French would be introduced in grade 1, written French only from grade 3 on.

Chart 2: Organization of the Department of National Education

I. OLD STRUCTURE

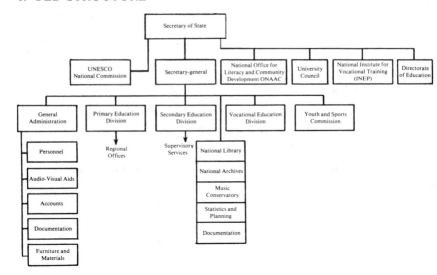

II. NEW STRUCTURE

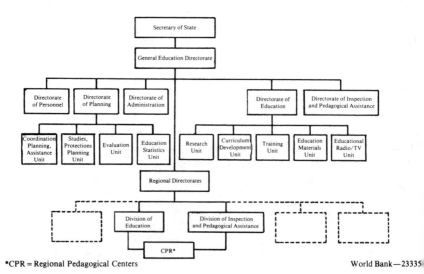

*CPR = Regional Pedagogical Centers

World Bank—23335

NOTES

[1] All statistics are taken from the following publications: Département d'Education Nationale, Département de Planification et Projet PNUD/UNESCO/006:
— Annuaire Statistique 1978-79, No. 2—November 1980
— Annuaire Statistique 1979-80, No. 3—October 1981
— Annuaire Statistique 1980-81, No. 4—November 1982
— Population et Scolarisation en Haïti, Juin 1981
— Evolution des Effectifs dans l'enseignement—Étude No. 1, Mai 1979
— Resultats de l'enquête par sondage sur les écoles de l'enseignement primaire, 1980-81, Decembre 1981
— Resultats de l'enquête sur les écoles privées en milieu Rural Analyse Statistique, Decembre 1980.

[2] Gross enrollment rate: total primary school enrollments divided by the school age population.
Net enrollment rate: number of children enrolled in school in the age bracket divided by the total number of children in that age bracket.

[3] In 1978, the two separate school systems, urban and rural, were officially united. The rural system consisted of seven years of education, starting with a preschool year focussing on school readiness (*inter alia* teaching of rudimentary French). In practice, however, many rural schools still have this preschool year.

[4] For the last decade, educators in international education fora have discussed in depth how much training is required to attain functional literacy. Commonly, a period of four years is accepted as an adequate amount of time. To my knowledge, however, there is no systematic research that really proves that four years is sufficient, because other factors such as number of contact hours, and quality of the training received, would greatly influence the outcome.

[5] An independent advisory body of education professionals from the private and public sector set up to establish guidelines for curriculum development.

[6] The premise of encouraging teachers to use a classroom-responsive and innovative teaching style may be incompatible with the Haitian culture and may be too much to ask from basically uneducated teachers. All teacher training programs (pre-service and in-service) pay lipservice to this ideal, but use a structured approach.

THE WOOD TREE AS A PEASANT CASH-CROP:
AN ANTHROPOLOGICAL STRATEGY FOR
THE DOMESTICATION OF ENERGY

GERALD F. MURRAY

Though differing in emphasis from each other, several attempts to explain rural Haitian poverty, including the field studies of Moral (1961) and the more recent literature searches by Zuvekas (1978) and Lundahl (1979), have concurred in their identification of deforestation and soil erosion as major impediments to economic well-being in rural Haiti.[1] Largely in response to Zuvekas' findings, several planners in the late 70's, aware that large sums of money had been wasted on unsuccessful reforestation and erosion control projects in Haiti, asked whether the root of the failure might not lie in Haitian peasant land tenure insecurity, in an unwillingness on the part of the Haitian peasants to make long-term investments in land in which they felt they had little long-term security.

Though such reluctance would make perfect anthropological and economic sense among a truly landless peasantry, this hypothesis appeared at odds with much existing anthropological research which indicates that Haitian peasants not only consider themselves owners of much of their land, but demonstrate their security quite concretely by investing thousands of hard-earned *gourdes* in the purchase of new plots whenever the opportunity arises (cf. Herskovits, 1971; Métraux, 1951; Underwood, 1964; Murray, 1977). In 1978, and at greater length in 1979 (Murray 1978; 1979), I proposed an alternative anthropological approach to the erosion problem, one that laid the blame for failed reforestation projects not on "Haitian peasant land tenure" or on the conservatism of a frightened peasantry, but rather on several crippling flaws that weakened the very design on which most of these projects had been based. The problem resided neither in the

141

culture nor the psyche of the Haitian peasant, the argument went, but in the behavior of planning and implementing institutions.

This general critique was accompanied by a specific series of alternative recommendations. The conceptual cornerstone was the suggestion to cease promoting the tree among peasants as a sacred, untouchable legacy for future generations (a message which is ignored at any rate) and to begin promoting the planting of fast-growing wood as a *privately owned cash-crop planted by peasants on their own land.* The marketability of wood as a fuel has been evident for decades in Haiti and had been discussed or documented in a series of studies specifically addressed to that issue (Earl 1976; Ewell 1977; Conway 1979; Voltaire 1979). During a prolonged visit to Haiti, the forester Michael Benge (1978) was particularly instrumental in acquainting local planners and implementers with the technical possibilities of fast-growing wood.

My own recommendations as an anthropologist focused principally on the institutional, organizational, and motivational dimensions of the task. I argued that if certain anthropological insights were applied and certain institutional barriers removed, a flow of resources would be activated, and Haitian peasants would plant millions of trees on their own land. These claims were put to the test when an $8 million project, based directly on these recommendations, was prepared by USAID. At various points in the planning process, other research was contracted by this agency on one or another specific questions related to the emerging proposal (Smith 1980; Salinas 1980; Smucker 1981; Murray 1981). Despite heavy objections from several quarters against one or another controversial feature of its design, the Project was finally approved. The field operations began in the Fall of 1981.

The project has now been underway for over two and a half years. In view of the newness of the project and the controversial character of some of its design features, definitive judgments about its success must be deferred to the future. But the unprecedented and unexpectedly rapid planting of over five million project trees by Haitian peasants on their own land has given preliminary validation to several of the basic anthropological hypotheses. This burst of voluntary, unremunerated tree-planting by perhaps ten thousand peasant families all over Haiti renders the project at least worthy of description. It will be the purpose of these pages to provide such a description.

BASIC CONCEPT: THE IDENTIFICATION OF RELEVANT FLAWS

When queried by friends and neighbors as to how he is, a Haitian peasant experiencing particular economic stress at the moment will frequently respond: *A, ou konnen, monche, neg-la bare!* This incisive Creole answer ("Well, to tell you the truth, pal, this guy's blocked.") places the peasant in the same intellectual camp as many contemporary anthropologists. For the description of his own poverty as the *blockage of some flow* that could be occurring but is not indicates that the peasant has given his implicit approval to an entire tradition of anthropological theory and model-building, one that focuses not on static structures but on dynamic flows.

It is here being argued that the well-documented national catastrophe of soil erosion, and the behaviors that will reverse these trends, are best analyzed as a series of flows. More specifically I will propose a model which deals with three interlinked but partially autonomous flow-mediating structures:

1. the environmental structures and channels which directly mediate the flow of *agrarian energy.*
2. the structures linking peasants to the external world and involving them in the *flow of cash.*
3. the community-external institutional structures which, though mandated to convey resources and skills to rural communities, more often than not have siphoned off resources into the pursuit of alien institutional or personal objectives.

This latter point is particularly important. Both planners *and* peasants have expressed their frustration over the manner in which millions of developmental dollars sent to Haiti have been blocked from reaching the rural communities for which they have been earmarked. Some of the blockages have been erected before the front gate, as expatriate donors or implementers, with impeccable legality, structure financial flows in a manner that directs much of its volume back toward their own institution or those of other compatriots. But many other barriers have been erected within Haiti itself, strategically placed in such a fashion that much of the impeded flow is diverted, not back to its overseas fountainhead, but into the local chambers of Haiti's many institutional gatekeepers.[2]

Simultaneous attention to all three flows is therefore essential. An anthropologically informed planning strategy will avoid the common error of placing excessive attention onto "technical" problems—the flows of energy and resources into and out of Haitian peasant fields. Technical planning degenerates into a deceptive and trivial ritual unless equal attention is given to redesigning the institutional channels which the resources must traverse before reaching peasants, and to structuring any technical input in a manner which holds out promise to the peasant of eventual cash flows. If the institutional channels are not clean, the money will be diverted and the peasant will be excluded. If on the other hand the project does reach him but holds out little realistic hope for an eventual cash-flow in his direction, he will nod a courteous thank you, return to what he was doing, and ignore the project.

AGRARIAN ENERGY CIRCUITS AND THE VANISHING TREE

Both planners *and* analysts must choose somewhere to start. I propose that we begin first by looking at the ground level structures.

From the point of view of the hills of Haiti, analysts have identified correctly (though implicitly) two problems. One concerns a material flow which has been occurring and which should be stopped; another concerns a material flow which is *not* occurring and which should be activated. The dysfunctional flow concerns Haiti's most significant and most tragic export. I am referring here, not to coffee, cacao, or anything of the sort. I am talking of the uncounted, irretrievable tons of precious topsoil that each year washes into the Caribbean sea. Though they agree on little else, all serious analysts of Haiti have correctly identified soil erosion as the gaping hole which sabotages all efforts, not merely to make the ship move forward, but even to keep it afloat.

Topsoil is lost primarily in the wake of the removal of the major physical structure which has protected Haitian soil: the tree. Where there is a forest canopy cover water reaches the ground, not in unimpeded torrents, but in softened drips and flows. And where there are arboreal root systems, most topsoil remains safely attached to the hillside even during heavy storms. It is the removal of this protective tree cover which unleashes the destructive downward flow of topsoil.

But the removal of the tree has also provoked the cessation of the second flow referred to above: the one which should be occurring but which is not. Throughout human history adaptive tropical hillside farming systems have maintained themselves through cycles in which the nutrients removed during the cropping stage are restored during a lengthy fallow stage. But the restoration comes principally through the mediation of the tree. The shifting cultivator removes the tree cover, burns off the desiccated vegetal debris (thus covering the plot with a veil of organically rich ash which increases yields during the first cycle), crops the ground for two or three cycles, and moves on to new ground to permit the regeneration of the tired plot. The replacement of humus and nutrients occurs principally during this fallow period. The postharvest stubble from the abandoned plot yields to scrub, which in turn yields to thicker brush, which finally yields to the secondary growth tree. It is principally the tree, with its organically rich foliage and (in the case of some botanical families) its nitrogen fixing root systems, which serves as the major efficient cause of soil restoration.

This provides us with a very important corrective to certain popular criticisms leveled at the peasant. The cutting of trees by the Haitian peasant is not an irresponsible behavior against which he must be educated or coerced. Tropical cultivators have been cutting trees for some 15,000 years of human history. What is problematic is *the elimination of the fallow cycle* which would permit the soil restoring tree to carry out its historically recuperative role (cf. Boserup 1965).

CASH FLOWS

The curtailing or elimination by Haitian peasants of the restorative fallow phase can clearly be attributed on the one hand to demographic stress. Enough land is simply not available to cultivators to permit them or their family members to maintain the 15 or 20 year fallow cycle that would permit natural regeneration of the soil. But demography is only part of the story. Involved in the drama is another factor: the dependence of the Haitian peasant on *steady flows of cash*.

Field research by anthropologists, geographers, and economists has exposed the weaknesses of the traditional stereotype of the "subsistence peasant." Though pop articles may still talk about "subsistence farming" in rural Haiti, it is not at all clear that the Haitian peasants "produce most of what they consume and consume most of what they produce." Even allowing for regional variation, it appears more accurate to say that most Haitian peasants produce largely for a cash market, to which large percentages of each harvest are consigned. Furthermore much of the contents of their cooking pots are similarly purchased from that same cash market throughout much of the year. The model of the self-sufficient peasant is generally inaccurate and constitutes a faulty theoretical base on which to found development projects.

This involvement of the peasant in a cash economy activates three mechanisms which impede the tree-mediated regeneration of the soil.

1. *Intensive cropping independently of food needs.* Where a farming system's goal is to feed its members directly (as was the case in many former tribal systems) there is no incentive to produce substantially more than can be directly consumed. Food storage constraints and food spoilage problems

make systematic overproduction irrational. But where there is a cash market, there is no such built-in ceiling to the intensity with which land will be worked. The pull of additional cash will be much more vivid and compelling than the much vaguer and fainter negative payoffs from degrading soil.

2. *The cash-oriented livestock economy.* As is true of many other peasantries, the Haitian peasant uses livestock as an important element in his cash-generating repertoire. Livestock often serve as a bank. One tactic is for cash profits from food harvests to be invested in animals. Interest to the investment comes in the form of weight increases in the animal purchased and in terms of the offspring of female animals. But livestock must be fed. And the current practice of many peasants is to picket cattle in recently cropped fields. But this in turn profoundly alters the course of the regenerative process. Even if the land is left out of cultivation for a long period, the brush and tree species that would otherwise emerge are destroyed by the livestock. The land is rapidly taken over by grass, the regenerative cycle is broken, and the landscape changes to a barren savanna.[4] This tragic sequence has already led to the removal of uncounted thousands of hectares of Haitian soil from agriculture. That is, in addition to population growth per se, cash-oriented livestock raising can provide a partially autonomous impediment to the reappearance of the soil restoring tree.

3. *The commercialization of wood.* But in addition to these factors, the general growth of the population and the appearance of an urban sector which depends on purchased charcoal for fuel energy has endowed the tree with a rapidly increasing economic value. The ancient practice of ignoring dead or fallen trees has disappeared forever. Even in the 19th century there was a vigorous lumber extraction industry (spearheaded not by the peasants but by lumber exporting companies). This industry continues, especially in pine regions. But more recently the growing charcoal market has triggered off feverish tree cutting behavior among poorer peasant groups who, during much of the year, have no other option for ensuring the continual flow of cash on which the Haitian peasantry as a whole has become so irrevocably dependent.

These observations can be rephrased in the idiom of resource flows. The current agrarian system in Haiti emerges as one in which major cash flow mechanisms operate in a manner which unleashes destructive downward soil flows and which subsequently impede the tree-mediated soil-recuperation flows that characterize tropical horticulture under more benign conditions. And let nobody underestimate the importance of the cash flows to the peasant himself. The peasant's awareness of and concern for this vital cash flow are much stronger and more pressing than his concern about destructive soil flows or about the missing flows of nutrients back to the soil. What is central to the consciousness of the agronomist is present but *tangential* to the daily concerns and maneuvers of the peasant. And sadly, what is primary to the peasant—the need for a short term flow of cash income—is often poorly perceived or even dismissed as "short sightedness" or "inability to delay gratification" by many well-paid technicians presumably hired to help him.

CONCEPTUALIZING A SOLUTION: PROPOSAL FOR A SHOTGUN MARRIAGE

The problem can be seen as partially residing in the operation of incompatible flows. Is there no way of producing a technical "package" which maneuvers both flows into the same direction? I propose that we look carefully at the "demon" which is currently blamed for putting the final touches on the environment of Haiti—the market which currently exists for charcoal and construction materials. It is this market, many would argue, which sabotages forever any hopes of preserving the few remaining trees in Haiti.

I would like to argue that it is precisely this market which can restore tree growth to the hills of Haiti. The demon can be "baptized" and joined in wedlock to the ecological imperatives whose major adversary he has been up till now. With creative programming we can turn the tables on history and utilize the awe-inspiring cash-generating energy present throughout Haitian society in a manner which plants trees in the ground faster than they are being cut down. If this is to be done, it must be the peasant who does it. But he will *not* do it voluntarily or spontaneously *unless* tree planting contributes to the flow of desperately needed cash into his home. I propose that the mechanism for achieving this is the introduction of *cash-oriented agroforestry*.

For any such model to work it would be useful if the following principles were incorporated into planning.

1. New inputs must be capable of activating a flow of organic material back to the soil.
2. New inputs must be simultaneously capable of impeding or at least diminishing the current flow of topsoil down from the hillsides.
3. New inputs, to be adopted by peasants, must simultaneously contribute to or enhance the currently precarious short-term flow of cash on which peasant households depend.

To achieve these goals we can perhaps turn to the wood tree. Not only has the wood tree traditionally held soil on the mountainside and restored organic matter to the soil when local conditions permit an adequate fallow period. Most important, the wood tree and its products—lumber and charcoal especially—are now known by the Haitian peasant to be an effective source of cash.

The task of planning is to *formalize, systematize,* and *improve* what is already a latent process in rural Haiti. Up until now, the integration of the tree into the cash-flow regime of the peasant has been done in a fashion which prevents its simultaneous functioning as a soil-preserving and soil-regenerating mechanism. Creative planning, however, can structure inputs in such a way that the tree can be used simultaneously to serve both sets of general functions, the economic/financial functions of interest to rural households, and the long-term ecological functions of interest to macro-planners.

One specific strategy for achieving this integration in rural Haiti would be the design of a cash-generating peasant agroforestry system. In such a system, the vanishing tree will be reintroduced. Now it will function, not as a spontaneously regenerated piece of vegetation, but as a consciously planted and carefully maintained cultivate. That is, a conceptually simple but structurally significant link will be forged between two behaviors which have hitherto remained independent of each other:

1. The Haitian peasant's interest in cash-cropping.
2. The Haitian peasant's interest in cutting wood for sale.

The technical *and* economic prerequisite now exist which permit these two powerful elements of Haitian peasant behavior to be joined to each other for the first time in Haitian peasant history. It is now technologically possible for fast-growing wood trees to become one more crop which the peasant deliberately plants with the conscious purpose of harvesting that wood. If this is done wood trees would cease being treated as gifts of nature and would become a cultivated *crop.*

If this is achieved, both ecology and economy can be served. The peasant will be in effect protecting and restoring his soil with this new crop, but he will be achieving this as a secondary function subservient to a much more immediate imperative, that of providing cash to feed, clothe, and shelter his family. It is this transformed integrated farming system producing both food and wood that is here being referred to as *cash-cropping agroforestry.*

ORGANIZING THE RESOURCE FLOW

The preceding sections have focused on identifying and articulating the underlying principles of the Haiti Agroforestry Project. The following section will turn to a brief discussion of some of its operational features.

Overall Institutional Arrangements

From the point of view of its major funder, USAID, the Project's most unorthodox and controversial feature is its use of non-governmental implementing channels. An $8 million grant was divided among three "Private Voluntary Organizations." One of these, Operation Double Harvest, was funded principally to provide seedlings, produced in small containers, which could easily be shipped to different Project regions in Haiti. The other two grantees, Pan American Development Foundation (PADF) and CARE, were funded to do outreach activities, to establish the organizational and delivery mechanisms which would interest peasant households in tree planting, and to deliver the seedlings to those communities and households that had agreed to participate. CARE focuses its agroforestry activities in the Northwest corner of Haiti. In contrast, Proje Pyebwa (the Creole name of the office established under the grant to PADF) works throughout the rest of Haiti.

The Choice of Tree Species

The project is based on the fast-growing wood tree. Among the major species used thus far by the Project are Leucaena leucocephala (aka Ipil Ipil); Cassia siamea; Azadirachta indica (aka Neem); Casuarina equisetifolia; and Eucalyptus camaldulensis. For regions of higher altitudes pines (especially Pinus occidentalis) are used. And some slower growing more valuable woods such as mahogany and cedar have also been used.

Not all trees are planted, of course, in every community. The particular combination of trees that will be sent to a particular community depends on the altitude, rainfall, and soil conditions in that particular community.

Some observers have expressed surprise at the Project's choice of the wood tree over the fruit tree. In a country beset by malnutrition, the fruit tree strikes such observers as a better option than the wood tree. Under more careful scrutiny, however, the advantages evaporate.

From the point of view of contribution to rural income, the fruit tree is a risky and questionable option. All the fruit in a region is ripe at the same time; prices consequently plummet. Preservation and storage options are virtually nonexistent for the ordinary peasant community. The presence of hundreds of thousands of mangos rotting on the ground throughout Haiti gives eloquent testimony to the low credibility of the fruit tree as a cash crop. Nutritionally, the oft-mentioned reliance of many Haitian peasant communities on mangoes and other fruit at certain times of the year may be true. But this dependence is a signpost pointing, not to a solution, but to a problem. Five hundred mango trees will provide the ordinary peasant household with neither an adequate homegrown diet nor enough cash to purchase adequate food. In contrast, five hundred wood trees, sequentially harvested by the peasant on a sustained yield micro-rotation, will provide income to permit improvement of what is already a major food acquisition device in rural Haiti: purchase in local markets. Fruit tree seedlings can be provided as a supplement; but the fast-growing wood tree still remains the most promising economic option for generating cash for the peasant and, consequently, for being planted by peasants in large numbers. At the present it appears to be the best foundation on which to build tree planting activities in Haiti.

The Production of Seedlings

One of the most important technical elements of the Project is the use of seedling produced in small containers rather than in the heavier and more commonly used polyurethane bags. The transportation dilemmas created by the latter are enormous—the ordinary pickup truck can carry only 250 seedlings. With the small-container seedlings, a pickup truck can transport up to 20,000 seedlings in one trip. Furthermore, the peasant himself can carry over 500 transplantable seedlings as opposed to five or six seedlings in heavier containers.

During the first two years of the Project, most of the seedlings used by Proje Pyebwa were produced near Port-au-Prince by one of the grantees. The seedlings were shipped by truck to the rural areas. This was a startup strategy to permit rapid takeoff of the Project. At present, however, more than a dozen regional nurseries have been set up. The production of seedlings has thus been decentralized and brought closer to the recipient communities themselves.

Organizing the Flow of Information, Seedlings, and Money

With some exceptions, the staff of Proje Pyebwa does not attempt to organize peasant communities themselves. Rather they link up with local "operational" PVOs who are already involved in development activities in different parts of Haiti.

The most common operational arrangement utilized by the project is a "contract" signed between the Project and the local PVO. The Project agrees to furnish seedlings and technical assistance to the PVO and the peasants whom the PVO assists to enter into the project. In addition, the Project makes available a fund from which the PVO can pay local *animateurs,* village residents who will organize the enrollment of tree-planting peasants, the transmission to these peasants of the various technical options, the actual delivery of the tree, and the periodic survival surveillance during the 12 months after planting.

The standard contract has several components, the first of which is a statement of general principles to which both parties agree to adhere.

1. The tree as a cash crop.
2. The need for fast-growing wood trees.
3. The need to integrate trees with preexisting agricultural patterns.
4. The need for the peasant to plant trees on his own land as a condition of security that he will be the eventual beneficiary of the tree.
5. The agreement to plant a minimum number of trees.
6. The right of the peasant to harvest the trees when they can be of economic use to him.

These general principles are then followed by a specific agreement by the PVO to hire a designated number of animators to plant a designated number of trees on the land of an agreed-upon number of peasants. A further element is a detailed description of the responsibilities of the *animateur* at all phases of the project. This is followed by a specification of the manner in which the *animateurs* will be paid—generally on a "contract" rather than a salary basis, according to the number of peasants for whom the *animateur* is responsible. Finally there is a detailed budget.

To assist the *animateurs* in their task, a series of Creole language data sheets has been designed. Each sheet has a specific function, and one sheet is filled out at each contact between the *animateur* and the peasant tree planter. This type of reasonably tight follow-up is necessary in view of the large numbers of trees and peasants involved in the project. It structures the activities of the *animateurs* in a careful way, provides at least some basis for assessing their performance and calculating their remuneration and, above all, gives at least some systematic managerial information on all subprojects.

Constructing Messages for Haitian Peasants

With the assistance of the collaborating PVO, Project staff will meet with farmers in potential tree-planting communities. Several messages are generally included in the presentation: *"Tree planting need not be for your children or your grandchildren only. You can make money from trees you plant."* The trees provided by the Project grow rapidly. Under proper conditions, they can yield charcoal harvests in four years time. Even conservatively speaking current market conditions are such as to yield $1.50 per tree (gross revenue) if the trees are harvested for charcoal. If the trees are planted at two meter by two meter spacing (to permit two or three seasons of continued food cropping among the trees), a hectare of land can hold 2,500 trees. Assuming replanting of trees that do not survive the transplanting trauma, this means a potential gross revenue of $3,750 from each hectare of land over a four-year period from the trees alone, not counting the additional revenue from the crops which can continue to be planted until shade competition becomes too great, and the revenue from animal grazing once the crops have been removed and the trees are large enough to permit grazing without damage to the trees themselves.

The general response of the peasants to this message has been unexpectedly positive. The negative experiences which many communities have had with some reforestation projects (especially those in which tree planting has been imposed from without) have not sufficed to blind peasants to the economic value of trees. What most surprises the ordinary peasant group to whom this presentation is made is:

1. the large number of widely spaced trees that can fit onto a unit of land;
2. The manner in which cropping can continue for the first two or three seasons and in which livestock grazing can subsequently be reintroduced.

That is, an effort is made to present fast growing trees which can mesh with and enhance rather than compete with the preexisting cropping and grazing patterns on which the Haitian peasants currently depend.

This presentation is made with several caveats. The very rapid growth rate, it is explained, occurs on reasonably good soil. On truly eroded, impoverished soil the growth may be slower. But it is also emphasized that some of the species, if left to grow even longer, will eventually be good for construction, even for sawed boards. The yield per tree, in terms of cash income, is substantially higher when wood is sold for construction purposes rather than as charcoal.

During conversations of this sort the peasants themselves frequently point out that wood can be used for both purposes on the same plot. If trees are planted more closely, charcoal wood can be cut down after only two or three years, leaving more widely spaced trees for larger construction growth. And even the branches of these trees can be used for charcoal, saving the trunk for more valuable lumber production.

To sum up, the presentation to the peasant community takes the form of a dialogue in which members of our project familiarize themselves with the economic and ecological underpinnings of the community, and in which the community becomes acquainted with the options.

"Take a Look for Yourselves."

If there is local interest expressed, representatives of the community will be brought to a nursery using the small container system and to a plot where mature trees stand. Here they can see for themselves two critical patterns:

1. The rapid growth of the trees which we are offering.
2. The ease with which these trees can be transported to the planting site and placed into the soil.

Not every farmer can be brought to a site. In most cases the site visits are organized for those farmers who will serve as the local organizers of the Project for other farmers.

"You Will Be the Owners of Any Trees Planted."

During the preliminary community visit, and during subsequent visits to the nursery and established outplantings, repeated assurances are given that the peasant who accepts and plants these trees is the owner of the trees. The project forfeits all rights in the tree once the peasant accepts it and plants it on his land. This reassurance is of incalculable importance. One of the fears that has undermined the effectiveness of many reforestation activities has been the fear on the part of peasants that the trees planted are not theirs. Even peasants who plant the trees on their own land are more often than not unsure, when questioned, as to who owns the trees. Many will say they belong to *konpanyia*—i.e. "the company," a common and revealing way of referring to organizations such as FAO, USAID, and other project organizers, to distinguish them from *leta,* the State. In other regions peasants have been heard to refer even to trees planted on their own land as *pyebwa leta*—the government's trees. To deal with this problem, peasants are assured—by us and by the local PVO—that they, not the Project, are the owners of the trees.

"As Far As We're Concerned, You Can Cut the Trees When You Want."

Another message that is repeated frequently during initial contacts and site visits is the message that our project, far from considering the tree to be a "sacred" object which must never be touches, views the tree rather as something which *should* be harvested when it is mature. This raises the issue of laws regarding tree cutting.

Most Haitian laws which deal with the tree emphasize prohibitions against cutting trees, or the need to secure permission and/or pay a tax for the privilege of cutting a tree. In general the use of the tree as a source of cash has generally been viewed by authorities and planners as a type of destructive irrationality on the part of peasants. One reforestation program after another has come in with the finger-wagging message that the tree should be seen as a sacred soil-conserving, rain-drawing object which the peasant should plant but never cut. Tree cutting is viewed, not as a legitimate economic behavior, but as a type of economic misbehavior. This has produced a situation in which the peasant's use of the wood tree as an element in his cash-flow regime has been done in an implicitly surreptitious fashion. The peasant is aware of the existence of laws which in one manner or another would tend to restrict his tree-cutting behavior were the laws obeyed. And local forest agents are becoming stricter in forcing would-be tree-cutters to pay the required taxes. Despite the legal impediments, peasants do "regle afè yo"—settle matters—with local authorities and continue to cut trees, sell the wood, and generate cash income.

The Project openly discusses—with PVOs as well as peasants—the Haitian laws concerning the cutting of trees. It is stated clearly and repeated several times that the Project can make peasants the owners of the trees that are planted, but that they must continue to deal with local authorities as they have always done. They need not ask the Project for permission to cut the trees. But neither can the Project free them from the "tax" that local forest vigilantes currently charge, even for wood that a person cuts from his own property.

Despite open discussion of this matter, the Project has yet to encounter a peasant community that hesitates to plant trees because of fear of future government restriction in cutting. The virtually unanimous opinion of peasants consulted on this matter is that a person who plants wood will be able easily to "regle afè-li avèk leta," settle matters with local authorities. The key variable in Haiti is ownership of the tree that is planted on one's property. Once the ownership right is guaranteed, the peasant feels free to plant trees.

To emphasize this ownership the Project goes so far as to insist that if, after a year or so, the peasant changes his mind about the trees, he is perfectly free to pull them out. He will never get more trees from the Project. But he is free to do to the tree whatever he wants. The function of such an unusual message is to remove any fear in the peasant's mind that the Project retains any ownership rights in the tree which the peasant plants on his land.

Explaining the Main Conditions of Entry into the Project

If a given community has at least two dozen or so individuals who are interested in proceeding forward with a local tree-planting subproject, the Project explains to them the conditions of entry. There are only two genuine "conditions."

1. *The farmers must plant a minimum of 500 trees each.* (Even at two by two meter spacing, this is only a fifth of a hectare, as explained above.) This criterion and condition tends to be more startling to those outsiders who somehow "know" that peasants couldn't possibly have land for that many trees than to the peasants themselves, who generally do have within their own holdings, or those of their family, underproductive land which could be intercropped with 500 trees. In fact many peasants request more than 500 trees when the space requirements become clear to them.

2. *The trees must be planted on the land of the farmer himself.* Because the tree is being introduced as a crop, it should be planted on the same type of individually controlled land that other crops are planted on. Project staff scrutinize with skepticism any proposal that comes in requesting assistance for "communally owned woodlots." Requests for "communally owned" inputs generally come from organizers of peasants who are trying to encourage peasants to become more "community minded." But Proje Pyebwa does *not* set out in principle to "improve the community orientation of the peasant." This may or may not occur in different cases. The Project is more concerned, however, with assisting farmers to treat wood as a crop. But for wood to become a genuine crop, it has to be planted as other crops—that is, on land owned and operated by the peasant himself. There are regions of Haiti where peasant *groupman* do in fact have some communally run productive activities. The Project does furnish trees to such groupman, but only where the peasant members of the group are also willing to take trees for their own personal land as well. The Project further ascertains whether a "communal organization" proposal truly corresponds to what the peasants in the region are interested in undertaking, or is rather the "pet project" of some higher-level developmental professional.

Preparing for Delivery of the Seedlings

1. *Site Visits.* For every peasant that has enrolled in the project, a rural animateur visits the plot of ground where the 500 trees will be planted. Information is gathered on the slope and general soil type of the plot, on the previous and current agricultural uses to which the plot has been allocated, ownership status of the plot, and the manner in which the peasant plans to plant the trees.

2. *Technical Instruction.* Efforts are made to instruct farmers not only in the proper techniques for planting and caring for the trees, but also in the different options available to the farmer for integrating the tree into his own preexisting agricultural and livestock regime.

3. *Setting a Date for Delivery.* Based on general rainfall patterns in the region, a tentative delivery date is decided upon, to be confirmed when the rains actually begin falling. Each farmer has to come to the nearest roadside to pick up his consignment of 500 trees on the day appointed.

4. *Packing the Seedlings.* A delivery system has been designed which permits seedlings to be removed from the containers in the nursery and rapidly shipped to the peasants who will plant them. Cardboard carton boxes are prepared and lined with heavy plastic paper. The seedlings are thoroughly watered before packing. Once a box is full, the plastic lining is folded over the top of the seedlings as well and the flaps of the carton are folded in. This system preserves the moisture of the seedlings and permits them to survive several days in the box.

5. *Delivering the Seedlings.* The project foresters are each responsible for a region of the country and are each furnished with four-wheel drive diesel pickup trucks. Each pick-up can transport some 20,000 seedlings—that is, enough to furnish 40 farmers with their consignment of seedlings. Dates and dropoff points will have been prearranged with the farmers.

6. *Following Up on the Trees.* Each plot where 500 trees have been planted is visited at fixed intervals for twelve months after planting. Survival counts are carried out and questions are posed concerning the causes of any tree mortality that has occurred since the previous visit. In addition observations are made concerning the presence of other crops planted among the trees, to observe new patterns of land use emerging among peasant tree planters.

PRELIMINARY PROJECT RESULTS

1. The effectiveness of this approach in stimulating the planting of trees by peasants must be judged as impressive in any quantitative measure. The original goal was the planting of three million trees in four years. The three million trees had already been planted before the Project had reached its second year. As of current writing, the Project is in the middle of its third year and has already planted nearly six million trees. In terms of sheer numbers of trees, then, the results are promising.

2. Numbers of trees planted is by itself a potentially deceptive measure of project output. An anthropologist would in fact reject this output as one more failure if the six million project trees ended up on the property of two or three landowners. Of great importance, therefore, is the fact that the trees of Proje Pyebwa stand on the property of over ten thousand peasant families in hundreds of Haitian villages. The Project has succeeded in stimulating unprecedented peasant interest in tree planting and in structuring resource flows in such a way that the outputs do in fact reach their intended peasant beneficiaries.

3. From an early pattern of collaboration with a limited range of local PVOs, the Project has now entered into collaborative arrangements with

several dozen PVOs, many of them with similar projects in other countries. The replicability of the Project is thus being enhanced.

4. From early dependence on one major source of seedling supply, the Project has encouraged the creation of more than a dozen regional nurseries, managed not by Project staff, but by the PVOs themselves, who will remain working in Haiti long after the Project has terminated.

5. Tree survival rates vary by region, the principal determining factor being the amount of rainfall. In some regions a project will have to plant 120 trees to have 100 alive after two years. In drier regions a Project may have to plant 300 trees to have 100 remain alive. But what is important is that mortality appears to be associated, not with livestock depradation, but with climatic stress. That is, the peasants are not only planting trees; they are also according them the same protection against livestock which they accord to their other crops. This suggests that the central objective of the project is being met: the introduction of wood as one more crop in the agrarian inventory of the Haitian peasant.

6. From initial dependence on one donor the field staff has been able to generate more than a half million dollars in funds and/or technical support from Switzerland, Canada, Belgium, and Ireland. The expatriate composition of the field team has also diversified. In addition to the Americans who formed the original expatriate technical core, the Project has received inputs from individuals born in Canada, Belgium, England, Switzerland, and Iran. The importance of this international diversification is to be measured not only in terms of additional resources to this particular project, but also to the diffusion of an approach to other donors. If Proje Pyebwa were ever to succumb to certain pressures that have menaced it from the outset, these other donors and PVOs will have had the experiences permitting them to continue this approach to tree planting on their own and to replicate it elsewhere.

THE FUTURE OF THE PROJECT

The preceding presentation leaves many unanswered questions in the three domains of planning on which the Project rests; technical planning, micro-economic planning, and institutional planning. Foresters, for example, will be dissatisfied with the low survival rates in some drier areas and insist on the need for better technical control in these areas. In the same technical vein soil conservation technicians will be interested in the development of more sophisticated "packages" in which the tree is more effectively combined with mechanical measures of erosion control. Very little emphasis is given to the erosion control function of the tree in the current modus operandi of the Project.

Anthropologists, in turn, will keep a close eye on the microeconomic impact of the cultivated tree on the overall flow of food and money into the peasant household. Will the tree genuinely be integrated into the agrarian activities of the peasant in a way that does not diminish the food-growing activities of peasant households? And will the increased commercial value created by the tree on formerly unproductive land lead to new land-acquisition dynamics by non-peasant groups? When the trees are harvested and the wood or charcoal sold, what percentage of the profits will go to intermediary truckers rather than to the peasants themselves? To repeat: an anthropologist would find many unanswered questions in the preceding presentation.

But all of these technical and microeconomic questions are *secondary* to what continues to be the major black cloud on the horizon of the Project: the institutional issue. If the flow of trees onto the hillsides is ever interrupted, it will probably be due to the behavior of one or another institution or bureaucracy.

The most hotly debated feature of the Project—from its earliest planning days to present—is the non-governmental nature of its implementation. The funds come principally from expatriate "public sectors." But the implementers are in their entirety private citizens of several donor nations working in collaboration with hundreds of private local Haitian organizers. Had the project gone through the local public sector channels normally entrusted with such funding, there is good reason to doubt whether six *thousand* trees would have been planted in the time that six million trees have been planted using the new channels.

Though some Haitian officials have privately congratulated Project staff and urged them to continue current policy, others have criticized this non-governmental tree planting as being a de facto affront to the sovereign right of Haitian government authorities to control and use donor funds as they see fit. The expatriates who planned the Project, many of them experienced in rural Haiti, were unmoved by these bursts of urban, middle- and upper-class patriotism and were much more impressed during the planning stage with the pleas of peasants all over Haiti to channel the Project *away* from government routes. But the flag-wavers *continue to elicit sympathetic echoes among recently arrived expatriate administrators.* There is still a belief that such projects *should* be run through governments. And a recent evaluation of the Project has suggested that in its next phase it should establish operational links with the Haitian government. This recommendation stems not from operational considerations (the flow of trees would probably stop), but from political and philosophical considerations. And what is most paradoxical is the fact that the "government-to-government" arguments tend to come, not from the current high-level management of the

USAID mission in Haiti, but from younger officers who are philosophically uncomfortable with "development through Private Voluntary Organizations," who have no particular personal involvement with Haitian peasants, and who perhaps have visions of succeeding in Haiti where their predecessors have failed—visions of themselves backstopping a multi-million dollar government-run reforestation project, before moving on to some other country.

Dreams are to be encouraged. But in an institutional portfolio filled with problem-ridden projects and multimillion dollar farces, let would-be repairmen direct their attention towards projects that need remedial attention. It would be tragic if young theoreticians were allowed by their superiors to tamper with one of the few Projects successfully transferring donor resources to Haitian peasants. Freedom from interference by governmental officials or government employees is one of the major design features that has kept the trees flowing in Proje Pyebwa. It requires no degree in Anthropology to know that, "if it ain't broke, you don't try to fix it."

NOTES

[1] The project to be described in these pages is funded principally by USAID/Haiti, though additional grants have been made directly to the field office by the governments of Canada (through the Mission Administered Fund of the Canadian Embassy in Port-au-Prince), Switzerland (through Helvetas, a developmental organization that also operates with private funds), and Belgium (through its support of a volunteer Belgian technician working in the Project).

The first draft of this paper was written while I was Director of the Haiti Agroforestry Project of the Pan American Development Foundation, one of the USAID grantees. The paper has been revised to incorporate more recent information on the Project.

Not present at the Conference were four individuals to whom I owe a special debt of thanks: William Sugrue, who made possible my initial research on reforestation; Michael Benge, the forester who first introduced me to the world of agroforestry and to the "miraculous" Leucaena leucocephala; W. Stacy Rhodes, the Program Officer who pushed through, managed, and defended the interests of the Project at all phases; and Fred Conway, a fellow anthropologist who coordinated the overall Project and shared with me two turbulent years in the "belly of the beast."

[2] There is a widespread and well-founded belief that developmental funds entrusted to Haitian government Ministries may never reach the peasants in any useful form. What is perhaps less well known to many Americans is the fact that most diversion of American development funds away from peasants is done by those American institutions—public and private—that are created or hired to carry out development activities. These matters will be dealt with in a forthcoming publication.

[3] Perhaps the strongest argument for the "non-subsistence" nature of the rural Haitian economy can be found in De Young (1958). But evidence for the cash-orientation of peasant life is also present in Simpson (1940), Métraux (1951), Moral (1961), Schaedel (1962), Murray

(1977), and other descriptive studies of rural life. The bulk of "cash-crops" produced are not export crops, but crops consumed internally in Haiti. For descriptions of the market system through which these crops move, see Mintz (1960), Underwood (1970), Locher (1975), Murray and Alvarez (1975), Girault and LaGra (1975).

⁴ For an analysis of changing Haitian landscape patterns see Palmer (1976). The evolution of landscape in the Dominican Republic had earlier been analyzed by Antonini (1968).

STRATEGIES FOR RURAL DEVELOPMENT IN HAITI: FORMATION, ORGANIZATION, IMPLEMENTATION

ROBERT MAGUIRE

To speak of strategies for rural development in Haiti is to open Pandora's Box. In a country of some six million people, where at least 150 international, multinational, bilateral or non-governmental agencies are working to plan, fund, implement or otherwise promote rural development in one form or another, it is no surprise that one writer has described Haiti as "a veritable gallery of the forms of rural development activities" (Girault 1977:4). The seasoned observer of Haiti, Graham Greene, has recently called Haiti "a country of projects." To this plethora of agencies and activities one must add the many Haitian public and private organizations active in some aspect of rural development.

From the number of agencies and the corresponding external capital investment supporting Haitian "development," one would imagine that great progress is being made in alleviating the human poverty and suffering of the rural Haitian people. But Haiti continues to languish as one of the poorest nations in the New World—indeed, in the world. Statistics portraying Haitian poverty are plentiful. Recently, a report of the U.S. General Accounting Office (GAO) presented an overview of Haiti's poverty, characterizing it as "desperate," "absolute," and "discouraging" (GAO 1982:1). There is no need to repeat the bleak statistics here.

Since the desperate poverty of rural Haiti is juxtaposed against a plethora of activities designed to alleviate or eliminate it, one can conclude that a single successful strategy for rural development in Haiti has not been found. Thus attention must be paid to historical and structural constraints and mitigating factors that have given rise to Haiti's poverty and counteracted rural development efforts. This writer sees the following as most critical:

161

(1) Land tenure insecurity, particularly devastating in a country in which close to 80% of the population are still dependent on production directly from the land;

(2) Constant migration of key human resources;

(3) The general lack of investment in human resources, as evidenced by annual public expenditures on education of roughly $1 U.S. per capita and by the resultant illiterate and ill-informed populace;

(4) The dearth of material or capital investment in the rural areas and the people there as, for example, over 4/5ths of the Haitian budget is invested annually in the capital city and environs, which holds only 20% of the country's population;

(5) a weak and overworked natural resource base;

(6) The isolation of the Haitian masses both from the outside world and from each other;

(7) Unequal access to and control over resources, leading to massive socio-economic disparities within the country and to a situation in which five percent of the population controls more than half of the country's wealth;

(8) The uneven and exploitative social and economic relationships existing in Haiti, which render the social structure a hierarchy dominated and controlled by a few at the expense of the vast majority.

It is not the objective of this paper either to fully explore these constraints and mitigating factors or to present an analysis of various rural development strategies currently being pursued in Haiti to try to overcome them. These points have been explored elsewhere (Maguire 1981). Rather, this book looks at one particular strategy of rural development in Haiti. That approach, which falls under the general rubric of "bottom up" development, is viewed in the context of one small rural community.

Formation, Organization, Implementation

It is late afternoon in a small isolated Haitian settlement, or *habitation,* located at the end of a rutted dirt road barely passable to motorized traffic. In a clearing just off the road sits a group of 25 men. From appearance, they range in age from early twenties to fifties. They are dressed in old, sometimes torn, shirts and pants. Most wear straw hats. Several are carrying machetes. Many are barefoot. They are sitting on small, uncomfortable wooden and straw chairs typical of poor Haitian households. Each participant has carried his chair to the meeting. When several arrive without chairs, a chair is turned sideways to accommodate two. With the obvious exception of two participants and the writer, the men at this meeting are local farmers.

As the meeting progresses from the opening prayer to the discussion of pertinent business, it becomes clear that this group is not an *ad hoc* collection of men. The visible structure of the group and the measured pace of the meeting suggest something quite different. Most of the participants are carrying a small *carnet,* or savings book, which is checked by one man holding a larger ledger on his lap. Another man is balancing a copybook on his knee. He is taking notes of the proceedings. A third man is obviously leading the discussion, though he does not dominate it since most of the men add their thoughts and comments as the meeting progresses. They all listen closely. The two men who are not peasants also listen closely, venturing comments when addressed by members of the group. The shoes, clothes, and watches that these two men wear give away their differing status. One has arrived at the meeting on a motorcycle; the other came by a four wheel drive vehicle. I accompanied the latter. The discussion, which is conducted exclusively in Creole, has become animated.

"Listen, brothers," begins one of the barefoot, machete-carrying participants, "we have made good progress using the benefits we earned from the first loan. It makes sense to me that we apply for another." Many others nod in agreement. One of the men with a watch, he who arrived by motorcycle, is also taking notes. He looks non-commital. The apparent leader of the group addresses this man. "If we decide to apply for the loan, will you help us and present our application?" "But, of course," is the response, "as long as, like the last time, the group can show that it has a good, solid plan for using the money so it can benefit and repay the loan on time." Again, there is silent nodding among the men.

To better understand the proceedings and place the discussion in context, I consult with the second man wearing a watch, the one with whom I arrived. He explains that the name of this group is *Tèt Ansanm* (Heads Together). It was formed in late 1977 as a community group to reflect upon and discuss social and economic conditions of the community and of the area's agricultural producers and to pool resources and try to initiate joint action to change some of those conditions. In 1980, the group received a loan for 6,000 gourdes (5 gourdes = $1.00 US). They used the capital to advance payment to group members for the bulk purchase of their own harvest of beans and corn so that they might better control its sale. Rather than having to flood the market at harvest time and thus receive a deflated price for their goods, the group members were able to store much of the harvest in a small, rented depot, selling it months later when prices had risen from what they were at peak harvest time. With the revenue from the sales, the group was able to repay the loan and realize a surplus of about 1,300 gourdes. Some of the surplus was divided among the members, but most was added, for investment in subsequent income-generating activities, to the group's savings fund, which had been capitalized initially by membership dues and income from the members' purchase of shares in the group.

The capital of the group had now reached 11,025 gourdes. About 85 percent (9,608 gourdes) has been invested in a small shop, or *épicerie,* and the remaining 15 percent in agricultural activities. Specifically, this latter investment has been made in the rental of a *carreau* (2.19 acres) of land for a five-year period. The land, which is in coffee, cacao, banana and pine trees, had been rented by the group only the previous month. The members looked forward to working together on that land and to using the income generated from it among themselves and for reinvestment in the group's income-generating activities.

Today, my companion continues, the group is discussing the merits of applying for a second loan so it can purchase the expected harvest of beans and corn produced by its members, some of whom work land they own—or at least claim to own—and some of whom rent or work on a share basis. As with the previous loan, access to these capital resources will enable the producers to have greater control of their harvest 'beyond the farm gate.''

As I receive this explanation, the discussion becomes more specific. There is general agreement among *Tèt Ansanm* members to apply for the loan. The man who arrived by motorcycle is now responding to a question from the man with the ledger concerning exactly how the group should go about figuring out its application. ''Like before, you must put your heads together and figure out how much you will need based on what you realistically expect your harvest to be and what prices will be. You must see how much the group can invest from its own funds and how much is needed as a loan. You should figure out, according to your costs and your expected sales revenue, how you will pay back the loan and what you expect your profit will be. You should plan how you will use that profit.''

After several questions and clarifications from the group, the discussion is over. The group's president sums up the meeting, adding that the members of *Tèt Ansanm* would work among themselves on gathering the needed information so that the next time the man on the motorcycle visits, which would be in three or four weeks, they would be ready to begin to work with him to draw up the application for the loan.

As the meeting concludes, a member of the group volunteers to thank the two men for attending the meeting and for bringing with them a foreign stranger interested in their group and its work. All stand and join hands in a circle as the meeting closes with the singing by all of a song of inspiration. Having finished the song, the men put on their straw hats, shake hands, and begin to drift away from the clearing, each taking his chair with him, following a footpath in the twilight that would take him to his home.

Four months later, the man who rides the motorcycle presented a loan proposal from *Tèt Ansanm* before a Credit Committee of a local private organization that sponsors programs of leadership training, non-formal adult education, and community development assistance. This man, who is a trained agronomist, is employed by that organization to visit community groups such as *Tèt Ansanm* and offer technical assistance in production and marketing as well as project planning and program implementation. In the above-described instance, once the members of the group collected their basic data and formulated their plan, the visiting agronomist assisted them in drawing up the proposal for the loan. Convinced that *Tèt Ansanm* had identified a workable plan, he then took the proposal for presentation before the Credit Committee, which is composed of an agronomist, an accountant, a priest, a lawyer, an administrator, and a peasant group leader.

The man whom I accompanied to the meeting is the Secretary of that committee. He is also involved in several of the leadership training programs. In addition, he is a trained agronomist, though years of experience in the non-formal adult education programs of the sponsoring organization, of which he is now Assistant Director, have given him a wide perspective in Haitian grassroots rural development. Typically, he would not attend meetings such as *Tèt Ansanm's,* but he had taken time to visit the group with the objective of meeting with one particular group member, the individual who had participated in a special training course in community development problems and techniques, and who had also been the "catalyst" in the formation of the *Tèt Ansanm* group. This person is the local *animateur.*

The Inter-American Foundation (IAF) has been supporting the work of this local, private organization facilitating these development programs since 1973, when it made available its first, small grant for a pilot program in leadership training (Maguire 1981). Subsequently, the IAF provided funding for an expanded program, which includes the credit activities, while other funding agencies came forth to assist in covering recurring programmatic costs. Recently, the IAF has made funding available that will assist the sponsoring organization in augmenting the technical assistance that can be offered by field agronomists to the growing number of community groups like *Tèt Ansanm.*

Tèt Ansanm's proposal, presented by the field agronomist, was once again a request for 6,000 gourdes. This money would be used, according to the plans put forth by the group, for the purchase of 600 *marmites* of beans and 1,275 *marmites* of corn, the estimated harvest for the upcoming 4-month period. (A *marmite* is a unit of measure about the size of a large margarine tin and holds 6 pounds of beans, corn, or rice.) The expected return to the group from the 6,000 gourde investment, subtracting both the close to 900 gourdes the group would invest of its own in the activity and the interest on the loan, and considering current prices, would be about 950 gourdes.

The loan was approved by the committee. It was made in June, 1982 for a period of six months. The first repayment, 3,600 gourdes, would be due at the end of September, while the balance would be payable at the end of December.

*   *   *   *   *

The process of change that took place within this isolated *habitation* leading to the events described above was slow and deliberate. Seven years prior to today, there was simply no organizational framework within the community that could give rise to a *Tèt Ansanm* group. The general rule was rather every man for himself, i.e. *chien mangé chien* (dog eat dog), and a network of speculators, money-lenders, and intermediaries—the *gros nèg* —kept producers precariously dependent on them and isolated from each other. To think, given this reality, of these producers forming a group, successfully pooling resources, receiving outside technical assistance to work through a loan proposal, and actually receiving such a loan would have been ridiculous. The small producers of this community, like their counterparts throughout Haiti, suffered on account of their isolation both from each other and from the lack of resources—human and material— needed to effect any change.

This situation was recognized by the urban-based organization involved in non-formal adult education and leadership training programs. These programs are aimed at assisting "natural" leaders from peasant communities in taking first steps at redressing local issues of isolation and dependency. Having examined past attempts at facilitating rural development by both Haitian and foreign agencies, the leaders of this organization devised strategies to help overcome what they are convinced is a fundamental constraint to rural development in Haiti: the uneven and exploitative social and economic relationships. Agreeing with the concept of Haitian society as a "pecking order" where the peasantry remains at the bottom under those who gather and accumulate wealth, but do not correspondingly reinvest either in the wealth-generating areas or in wealth-generators themselves (Maguire 1981:11), these development activists argue that unless steps are taken to change these relationships, there will be no sustained process of human development in the rural areas. The relationship can change only if the weak can become strong and acquire greater access to needed resources, both human and material. Hence, development is seen as change enabling those at the bottom to improve their relative social and economic standing within the society.

To assist the rural poor in coping more effectively with their situation, a program focusing initially on investment in people, i.e. human development, before moving to investment in things, i.e., material investment has evolved. In rough sequence, its activities follow three steps: formation, organization, implementation. Some understanding of these three steps can be gained by tracing the evolution of the group *Tèt Ansanm.*

Formation

Formation is the first key investment in human resources. Formation is comprised of two elements: the provision of information and of knowledge, with the former being the basic input of facts and the latter providing the framework within which those facts are used, and a process of drawing out, legitimizing, and placing within the framework extant but underutilized information, knowledge, and skills. Hence, in addition to providing new inputs, formation, through the development of critical reflection skills, draws upon what already exists in order to develop and refine human resources needed to achieve local, grassroot development goals.

In 1975, during a fieldwork session for *animateur*-trainees held in a neighboring community, the training organization was able to identify, through contact with local community leaders, an individual residing in the general area from which *Tèt Ansanm* emanates who met the "natural" leader criteria. This individual was invited to participate in a ten-month training course for the formation of community social and economic change catalysts, or *animateurs.* After participation in the course, which presented information on a wide range of community development issues and community organizing techniques and which provided several periods of fieldwork, the *animateur* returned home in August, 1977.

The task facing him was to work with others in the area to develop the formation and organizational framework that would enable people like the present members of *Tèt Ansanm* to break out of their isolation. Since other local residents had participated in occasional discussion sessions led by a mobile team of community development activists attached to the leadership training organization, and ten individuals from the area had participated in a month long consciousness raising development education and formation session held at a nearby adult education center, much groundwork for the *animateur* had, in effect, been done before his return.

Organization

While, in the context of formation, information provides the facts, knowledge provides the framework for the utilization of those facts, and critical reflection provides legitimization and a bridge between old and new, organization provides the structure needed for action. For facts to be discussed and for this discussion to be the basis of some kind of social and economic change, organization is necessary. Further, if actions are to represent the interests of those who typically have been in isolation at the bottom of the pecking order, that organization must have the active participation of those people. The *animateur,* typically a member of this peasant constituency, is not to assume the role of group leader. Rather, his efforts are designed to stimulate, challenge, guide, and advise during the formation of an organization. Decisions to act are made within the evolving group, sparked by his catalytic action.

With his return to the zone in which the *Tèt Ansanm* group is now located, the *animateur* applied his newly acquired organizational skills. Working with interested members of the *habitation,* he encouraged the formation of a group where the members would eventually pool their own resources through membership dues and the purchase of shares in the group. The group would decide upon its own internal structure, maintained by regular meetings and annual elections, and would attempt, by pooling limited resources, to implement some activities designed to achieve social and economic change. These goals would be identified by the group members. This particular group, *Tèt Ansanm,* did not form immediately upon the return of the community catalyst. Rather, a period of formation preceded that step as he encouraged individuals of the community to discuss their problems together and consider the possibility of forming a group, pooling their resources in order to overcome some of these problems. The development of mutual trust among the members of the incipient group, and the appearance, transmission, and understanding of the information and techniques presented by the *animateur* took time. It was important that the pace of the group's growth was comfortable to its members. Frustrations arising from setting unrealistic goals most likely would have led to an early demise of *Tèt Ansanm.*

The group evolved slowly, with members becoming accustomed to discussing their problems together and considering joint actions they might take according to the resources they could garner. By late 1977, an informal group of local residents had begun to meet regularly to discuss characteristics and problems of the area. As the group became regular and the formation process of its members continued, they sought a way to work together on their own to start to improve their social and economic standing. Elections were held and in November, 1978, the informal study group became *Tèt Ansanm.* Its members, then numbering 15, decided as a first step to contribute 5 gourdes each as a beginning of a capital investment fund. Almost immediately, the group rented 1/8 of a *carreau* on an eight-year contract at 40 gourdes a year. Group members would plant a community garden on this land. The first harvest of bananas and corn brought *Tèt Ansanm* a return of 252 gourdes, which was invested in the establishment of a nursery of coffee plants for distribution to members of the community. Hence, the group had become organized, with its members taking joint action to achieve small but significant gains. By November, 1978, when the group was formalized, a major stride had been taken to overcome the isolation plaguing the poor of the community.

The *animateur,* as the formation catalyst, played a key role in helping to break down this isolation. Unfortunately, however, the *animateur* could offer the group only limited human resources. His own training, particularly in technical areas, had been general and, hence, restricted. The training of the group members themselves was also limited. The grave lack of formal education and access to information hindered their ability to identify solutions to problems and to implement activities from within the group. Skills needed for this were simply lacking. In addition, though they could garner among themselves some funds for investment, given the constant impoverishment of these people at the bottom of the pecking order, these material resources were sparse. By mid-1979, it was apparent not only to the *animateur* and the group members but also to the organization offering the training and information that, at least in the case of *Tèt Ansanm,* the time was ripe for a progression to the third step listed above. Further investment—both human and material—to implement the group's envisaged activities was needed.

Implementation

Allocation from outside the rural community of needed resources to assist in the implementation of programs designed to assist those at the bottom achieve social and economic gains is not simply a matter of sending money or materials into the community. Typically, those resources, while earmarked to benefit the poor and disadvantaged, more likely benefit those intermediaries and relatively well-off, the *gros nèg,* within the community who are not at the end of the pecking order. A Haitian proverb popular among peasants such as the *Tèt Ansanm* group members, "The mule works while the horse gets the stripes" (*Bourik travay, choual garlonnin*) testifies to this tendency.

Investment linked with action implementation can counteract the effects of the established hierarchy. As the two initial steps had been taken by the poor within the community, there is some greater assurance that the intended beneficiaries of the investment, i.e. the rural poor, will directly benefit. Yet, given the limited development of the human resources of the impoverished within rural Haitian communities and the subsequent dearth of information, knowledge, and skills available to them, more than money or materials should flow into the community.

In the case of *Tèt Ansanm* and the general programs of the sponsoring organization, the investment of additional human resources came with the presence, in late 1979, of the field agronomist. This individual was able to occasionally visit the group and build on both the general foundation-laying work of the *animateur* and the initial activities carried out by the group. As seen above, the agronomist, as an added human resource, plays a critical role in assisting the group with its project identification and program planning. His work is essentially to attempt to ensure that activities implemented by the group have a firm chance of attaining their intended social and economic change objectives.

The agronomist himself, however, does not bring needed materials or capital to the group; his investment is one of information and knowledge— human resources which, if effectively used by the group, can lead to increments in the group's own material resources through the measured, well-planned implementation of limited economic activities. Again, however, even when the group pools its own resources and builds a savings fund for use in material investment, those resources are so meager that they, alone, are insufficient to allow for the effective implementation of most programs: additional capital investment is important. Hence, the sponsoring organization applied for and received a grant and then established a credit fund to provide a source for this additional resource investment. That fund, capitalized to 405,000 gourdes, is a revolving fund. Interest on loans is collected at three percent (3%). The present limit on loans to groups is 15,000 gourdes, increased from an original ceiling of 6,000 gourdes as needs of borrowers increase proportionally to the scale of their activities. Loans are made only for production and marketing activities.

As we have seen, a group's own resources may be meager, but they can be built up, following the process of formation of a solid organizational structure, to provide a starting point for substantive investment. In December, 1979, through regular saving by its members, added to the revenue generated from initial economic activities, *Tèt Ansanm* reached a level of savings of 5,730 gourdes. The group decided to invest its capital in the rental of a small building where it could establish a small shop, or *èpicerie,* and a warehouse for stocking member's agricultural produce. By making this major move, however, the group tied up its total investment base. Rent was paid, the shop was stocked, and the warehouse was there, but *Tèt Ansanm* had no liquid capital remaining to purchase and store its members' harvest of beans and corn for later resale. External resources filled this gap. Hence, in April, 1980, the group, working with the agronomist, applied for and received its first loan. The framework that had been previously established allowed investment to be managed effectively by those intended to be its beneficiaries. Effective implementation had begun to occur. *Tèt Ansanm* has been able to use both its own resources and the additional human and material resources made available to it through a supporting organization in order to implement its programs and achieve tangible benefits for its members. Real change is taking place within the *habitation* where the group members live; members have realized tangible social and economic gains. They have been able to improve their social and economic status within the community and society by breaking down their isolation and reaching levels of greater access to and control over the resources they need to effect change.

The organization facilitating this process argues that for development to occur and sustain itself at the *habitation* level—and that organization effectively argues that it is on this level that human development programs must focus—there must first be formation and organization. This allows for the effective absorption and use of material resources in the implementation phase of programs designed to achieve social and economic gains by the rural poor. Investment in improving the capability of the human resource base, then, is a necessary first step before subsequent capital investment flows into the community from beyond. A reversal of this process most likely will not lead to changes that benefit those at the bottom by enabling them to improve their relative social and economic standing within the society. Rather, the influx of capital or material investment in a community preceeding the formation and organization steps will more likely lead to greater disparities along the "pecking order" by benefiting the *gros nèg* and exacerbating the impoverishment of those at its bottom.

The strategy of formation, organization, and implementation, while shown as effective in the particular case of *Tèt Ansanm* is, unfortunately, not an easy one to follow. There are limitations. The need for many key inputs, most of all for the existence of an organization that can assist in beginning and sustaining a measured process of change and development through its ability to form, develop, organize, and invest human and material resources, makes this a difficult approach to carry out on a broad scale. In addition, given the lack of corresponding public sector support of these activities, the effectiveness of local, private organizations such as that cited above, is further limited. As one student of rural development strategies has recently written:

> Obviously, local organizations and the internal and external resources they mobilize cannot solve the massive problems of rural poverty

without effective state action and policies conducive to participatory and equitable rural development. However, the evolution and strengthening of these local organizations can help create a future framework in which State political and economic action aimed to satisfy the basic needs of the rural masses can be more effective (Healy 1982:40).

The actions of one, relatively small facilitating organization and of the small community groups with which it works will not be a panacea for Haiti's rural development problems. Yet, the gains made by the members of *Tèt Ansanm* with the help of this organization are impressive in their context. Fortunately, *Tèt Ansanm* is not a unique aberration. Other community groups are making similar progress. At least for some of the Haitian rural poor, tangible social and economic change gives some hope for a fulfilling life and a better future.

NOTE

The information presented in this paper was gathered in the field over the course of five years of work with the Inter-American Foundation in the area of funding local, private, generally community-based development initiatives, in collaboration with a host of Haitian rural development specialists, ranging from community group members to development assistance organizations.

COMMERCE IN THE HAITIAN ECONOMY

CHRISTIAN A. GIRAULT

Abstract

Haiti, with a population of more than five million, is characterized within the Caribbean by the low percentage of population living in urban areas, by the persistence of oppressive social relations, and by economic exploitation and grinding poverty. The analysis of commerce and particularly of marketing systems can furnish interesting clues about the Haitian economic structure and the spatial organization of the country.

Qualitative and quantitative data generated during the seventies by the Instituto Interamericano de Cooperación para la Agricultura and other researchers provide a good picture of current commercial activity.

Paradoxically, the marketing system of food staples has become the backbone of a very weak economy where:

- production and productivity are declining,
- and the first priority is *to feed* a young population affected by severe malnutrition.

In comparison, the traditional marketing systems of export crops (cocoa, coffee, essential oils...) are slowly losing their social and economic importance.

Meanwhile, the growth of imports of energy products (fuel, gas, etc.) and of food products points to a substantial deficit in the balance of trade. These imports are done mainly to the benefit of the urban areas. Rural populations are discriminated both as producers and as consumers. If trends are not reversed, Haiti is heading toward a situation where absolute poverty will be added to traditional dependency.

The Republic of Haiti, with a population of more than five million, is characterized within the Caribbean by the low percentage of population living in urban areas, by the persistence of oppressive social relations, and by economic exploitation and grinding poverty. The analysis of commerce and particularly of marketing systems can furnish interesting clues about the Haitian economic structure and the spatial organization of the country.

The Importance of Commerce in the Haitian Economy

The Haitian economy is fundamentally an open economy, both externally and internally. External trade represents an unusually high proportion of the Gross National Product (GNP), even by Caribbean standards: something between 20 to 25% from year to year. Thus, Haiti is not "isolated" or "apart" from the rest of the world as some would tend to present it. It has been well-integrated historically in the networks of primary commodities as an exporter (e.g. bauxite as a mineral, coffee and cocoa as agricultural commodities) and in the networks of energy products and food products as an importer. As weak as it is, the incipient industrial sector exemplifies through the so-called "assembly factories" a working relationship with enterprises in the United States. It is true that in some cases the process of contracting, whereby components made in the U.S. are assembled in Haiti and shipped back to the U.S., is equivalent to sheer integration and does not allow for commercial initiative.

Contrary to those who argue that Haiti has a "subsistence economy" internally, there is a large degree of "openness" in the peasant economy and of all other economic sectors (handicraft, industrial, services, etc.) which react to the impulse of the market. Monetary exchange—and in the most primitive cases, barter—are basic to the functioning of the Haitian economy. This is true at all levels: the local level, the regional level, and the national level. The peasant selects plant crops which will provide the most *cash* money possible. The rationale behind this choice is not his own food requirements as in a subsistence economy. Nor is it the rate of return on his investment as a rational economic mind would have supposed. It is definitely a market-oriented rationale, constrained by very poor information on the market factors. At the regional level many examples of interchange between mountains and flatlands, between adjacent regions, and across the border with the Dominican Republic can be given. But again there are many constraints due to bad communications, poor roads, no phone links and police controls and exactions. At the national level, market forces are oriented toward Port-au-Prince, which is at the same time the only port of entry of imported goods and the destination of much of internal commerce.

New Evidences on Commerce

The first scholars who looked into commerce were Paul Moral in *L'économie haïtienne* (1959) and Sidney Mintz of Johns Hopkins University, who published several articles during the sixties on the anthropology of market places. Mintz's careful descriptions and interpretations of the marketing processes have rightfully become classics. So has the superb analysis of Moral, who made the first inventory and classification of the public markets.

It is not until the middle of the seventies that new qualitative and quantitative data provide a more precise image of the marketing systems allowing us to draw a comparison between the present situation and the situation twenty years before. Several independent researchers, Alvarez, Murray, Locher, Torres, Girault, and Lowenthal, contributed to this effort. The institution that gave much impulse to these studies is the local branch of the Instituto Interamericano de Cooperación para la Agricultura (IICA), an international institute whose main office is in San Jose, Costa Rica. The IICA conducted from 1973 to 1977 a program of intensive research on marketing under the direction of Jerry La Gra. At one time or another, the researchers mentioned above were involved in the program. Precise surveys were conducted on various agricultural products; the market-places were tallied and described in their totality. The result is a rich series of reports that probably have not been tapped entirely.

The ultimate goal of the program set up by the IICA was to propose reforms in order to provide more efficiency to trading activities. In the first place, the IICA helped with the establishment of the Service National de Commercialisation Agricole (SENACA) within the Ministry of Agriculture. But the work of SENACA is very limited and they have not effectively attacked the main problems regarding marketing. The recommendations made by the IICA were not realized. Thus, we are left only with an interesting diagnosis without a remedy. The coordinator of the IICA studies, Jerry La Gra, recently produced a synthesis of their findings which will be published in 1983 in the *Atlas d'Haïti* (La Gra 1983).

The Three Networks of Commerce

Three networks of commerce can be identified:

1. The network of commodities which deals with the marketing system of agricultural export crops such as coffee, cocoa, and essential oils. It is the oldest and the one which has the strongest roots since it dates back to the time of the colony when Saint-Domingue was basically an export economy with a huge trade surplus. Let us call it *network A*.

2. The network of food products which deals with the marketing system of the peasant crops from the small *jardins* to the rural and urban

consumers. This circuit has necessarily taken importance as the Haitian population has multiplied since the beginning of the century from around 1.3 million people in 1900 to a figure above the 5 million mark today. Let us call it *network B*.

3. The network of manufacturing products which relates to the distribution of products such as imported food, building equipment and furniture, home appliances, luxury items, garments, health products, books, cars, etc. Let us call it *network C*.

The three networks are strictly parallel and meaningful comparisons can be conducted on every aspect of them. In a previous publication, La Gra and I listed the opposite characteristics of network A and network B (Girault & La Gra 1977). One notes also broad themes about the three networks that illuminate the Haitian social fabric.

1. Commerce takes place within a *laissez-faire* environment. That means that the state does not intervene in the marketing system even if its legislation and its institutions permit it to do so. One should not misidentify various interventions by the government or by the family in power as state interventions because these are made for purely self-serving reasons, such as the take-over of business of political competitors or of prosperous foreign intrepreneurs. In the same way, decisions to import food or energy products in times of difficulty are not time-planned by the officials but made according to the personal interest of the Duvalier family for purely political reasons. It is true that such decisions have important consequences on the behavior of trade activities even if often unnoticed by observers, influencing the structure of prices of local food, for example. Nor are Haitian government statistics necessarily reliable.

2. Similarly, the "traditional" sector remains very important in commerce. This means that most of the trading activities operate with a minimum of capital. This is particularly true of network A and network B. Defining the term "traditional" is no easy task as in these activities one can meet different levels of business and different procedures of trades: for example the old import-export houses which function as they were functioning at the beginning of this century and also the street vendors who sell a few tooth-brushes or soaps. The "traditional" sector has expanded greatly in the last decades due to the proliferation of the "informal" trade of very small vendors and service people. The principle remains basically the same: the utilization (and the exploitation) of human energy instead of capital or technology. Informal credit and a rapid circulation of money replace bank loans which are very limited. Thus one observes that very little of the money generated by commerce is reinvested in commerce or related activities (transportation, agroindustry, or the like). On the contrary, merchants and export firms have invested in finance, in housing, or in

industry. Also, the impact of transnational firms has been virtually nil in domestic trade and commerce.

3. In spite of the importance of network B and also of network C (in the urban areas only), network A has molded the social and spatial relations within Haitian society since the time of Revolution. This was the argument in my book on the coffee trade in Haiti (Girault 1981).

One of the themes discussed in this book related to *who* are the agents in the trade in the three networks. Basically in network A, the trade of export products is in the hands of *men*. However, if we consider the nationality or ethnic origin of the merchants at the local level of the *bourgs* (small towns), the main middlemen, called *spéculateurs,* are all Haitian while at the higher level of the coastal towns the export houses have been traditionally in the hands of foreigners (of European descent). In network B, the trade of food products is mainly in the hands of *women,* of whom "the central figure is the Madame Sarah who is a travelling intermediary" (La Gra 1983). In network C a large share of the import business and of the distribution of goods is in the hands of foreigners (of Middle East or European descent). Some members of these foreign merchant families have acquired Haitian citizenship but in their social habits and customs they stay very much separate.

The Trade Deficit and the Imperative of Feeding the People

The current Haitian crisis has been characterized during the last ten years by the slow-down of agricultural production and by a decrease in productivity. Exports of staples have declined. Haiti has become a net importer of sugar instead of an exporter. The explorable surplus of coffee has dwindled considerably; more than 50% of the coffee production is consumed in Haiti. Under these circumstances, the external trade deficit has sky-rocketed, as the imports of energy products (fuel, gas, propane, etc.) and food products increased.

This relatively new situation has had important consequences on the organization of marketing systems. Network A has shrunk in size and in comparative importance. The export shippings have disappeared in all the *bords-de-mer* (coastal merchant towns) of the provinces except Cap-Haitien and the commercial activities have not been replaced there, meaning unemployment, out-migration and utter dereliction for these towns. Exports are now concentrated in Port-au-Prince.

In a situation where the Haitian economy seems to have lost every solid base to promote exchanges abroad, the marketing system of food has become the backbone of this poor nation, and of paramount importance for its survival. It is true that the system functions rather efficiently under harsh constraints (poor transportation, lack of information on prices, ramshackle market buildings and facilities, etc.), a fact which has been underlined by various analysts. But what is the human cost of this efficiency, just to reach a *mean* consumption of 1700 calories per head?

The main factor of change has been the tardy urbanization, particularly in the principal city, Port-au-Prince. Hence the demand of food has been strongly on the rise. Because Port-au-Prince has more than its share of affluent, middle-class and working class population with a higher consuming power, it has become the main market for both locally produced and imported food. It is estimated that Port-au-Prince with 17%-18% of the national population consumes as much as 30% of all the food produced in the country and a larger share of imported food.

Previously (Girault 1977), I have described how the whole marketing system (network B) has adapted to supply this demand. Now practically all the regions of Haiti (even the most remote) have entered this supply system to a greater or a lesser degree. Also, specialized zones of production have tended to emerge, contrary to the traditional multi-cropping systems. To give some of the most relevant examples: the Kenscoff area has specialized in temperate vegetables, the southern part of the Leogâne lowlands has specialized in the production of *clairin,* the oasis of Cabaret and l'Arcahaie have specialized in plantain cropping and the Artibonite lowlands have become the major supplier of rice, the more prestigious cereal of the Haitian diet. About thirty regional markets along the roads have taken on the function of collecting agricultural produce in their respective regions, sending them to Port-au-Prince by truck or, in some cases, by boats. Empirical data show that the importance of these markets both in terms of attendance and in terms of volume of produce traded has increased very much, in comparison with the situation pictured by Mintz and Moral twenty years ago.

In Port-au-Prince the change in size and in quality of the demand for food has materialized in different ways. At the wholesale level, the Croix-des-Bossales district has become a large market which serves the whole metropolitan area especially through the dépôts (warehouses) located there. But the problems are many: the disorganization of the bus terminals, the mix-up in the same site of different functions (wholesale, retail, export trade, shops), the absence of facilities (phones, toilets, etc.) and the serious uncleanliness of the entire district. A project of rehabilitation of the district and of construction of a new building is on the agenda with possible funding by the World Bank (1980). At the retail level, the twenty or so public markets which have been surveyed in the metropolitan area are bustling with activity. A new trend has been the increase of small supermarkets (called *markets* in Creole) which attend the needs of the new segment of the population with a higher standard of living.

CONCLUSION

The growth of the food marketing system toward the capital is in fact the result of a crisis whereby declining production of agricultural produce is combined with urbanization (spurred by migration) in a dialectic relation. It is clear that the only solution in such a situation is the importation of food. This has happened on a large-scale basis. With imports of approximately 240,000 tons of cereals in 1981, it is estimated that food coming from abroad represents already 23% of national consumption. This figure, which has risen very much in recent years, could be much higher if the basic diet needs of the population were respected—thus the tremendous potential for food imports.

Some evidence gathered from scant statistics indicates that the distribution of food imports and other products is heavily skewed toward Port-au-Prince against the provinces and the countryside. This would account for very low food balances in the countryside. In this way country people are disadvantaged both as producers of food that is shipped to Port-au-Prince (instead of being retained for their personal use) and also as consumers as they receive only a low proportion of imported food products.

The picturesque, naive painting of rural market-places and of *marchandes* (selling women) going to the market give only an approximate idea of the pathetic social conditions which lie behind the universal phenomenon of commerce. If trends are not reversed Haiti is heading toward a situation where absolute poverty will be added to traditional dependency.

THE ROOTS OF HAITIAN UNDERDEVELOPMENT

MATS LUNDAHL

Underdevelopment in Haiti

"There can be no fixed and final definition of development, merely suggestions of what development should imply in particular contexts," states the author of a recent survey of changes in development theory during the post-war period (Hettne 1982:7). Yet I am certain that anybody possessing even a superficial knowledge of Haiti will agree that this country is "underdeveloped" in most senses. Haiti is, in fact, the most underdeveloped nation in the Western Hemisphere and belongs to the group of least developed countries in the world.

This can be seen in different ways. In terms of development indicators, Haiti ranks low on virtually all indices related to living standards, life expectancy, distribution of the working population, capitalization, technology, etc. We propose to refer to economic development as "the process whereby the real per capita income of a country increases over a long period of time—subject to the stipulations that the number below an 'absolute poverty line' does not increase, and that the distribution of income does not become more unequal" (Meier 1976:6). This simpler approach focuses on three essential development indicators only and will guide us in the present paper.

Unfortunately, we lack reliable knowledge regarding the development over time of the distribution of income in Haiti.[1] The available figures on the rate of growth of real per capita income and the change in the number of people living in a state of absolute poverty, however, clearly present a picture of stagnation and retrogression, i.e. of increasing rather than decreasing underdevelopment during the last 25 to 50 years. Strictly speaking, no very accurate information is available for the period before 1955, but the existing estimates point in the same direction. Thus, the so-called Tripartite Mission (OAS-ECLA-IBD) which at the beginning of the sixties produced Haiti's first national accounts estimated that the real gross domestic product per capita fell with some .1 percent per annum before 1945 and 1959 (OEA-CEPAL-BID 1962:80). A second, much more recent estimate indicates that economic growth took place only during six years out of 36 between 1921 and 1956 (Vilgrain n.d.:45).

Between 1955 and 1975 Haiti's real GDP increased some 1.7 percent per year (W.B. 1976:6), while at the same time the population growth rate amounted to 1.6 percent (I.H.S. n.d.), leaving the per capita product virtually stagnant.[2] The estimates for the latter half of the seventies differ. A World Bank report points to a real yearly growth rate between 1975 and 1979 in the order of 4.4 percent,[3] but this figure is quite probably an overestimate, one which is due to an over-optimistic view of agricultural performance.[4] The last three years, finally, do not appear to change the overall picture very much: 1979 displayed a decline in real GDP per capita of around 0.3 percent; 1980 showing considerable improvement (plus 5.3 percent); and 1981 being a year with no growth at all in real output, i.e. with a decrease in GDP per capita equal to the rate of population growth (W.B. 1981a:5). In 1979, Haiti's GNP per capita was estimated to U.S. $260, the same level as that of Pakistan, Tanzania and mainland China (W.B. 1981b:134).

All the above figures are admittedly based on different sets of crude assumptions and estimation techniques. Still, they quite probably convey a fairly accurate picture of the long-term trends in the Haitian economy, being by and large confirmed by other types of information (cf. Lundahl 1979). Thus, we may conclude that during the past fifty years or so the real gross domestic product per capita during the most favorable moments has been growing, but only very slightly, with stagnation, and at times even decline being the rule.

The Haitian economy during the past 25 to 50 years has failed to show any visible signs of development. The per capita income has by and large remained stagnant and the number of absolute poor has not been reduced. The task of identifying some of the most important forces that impede economic development from taking place in Haiti, i.e. the forces which keep an increasing number of Haitians in a state of absolute poverty, making the real income of important segments of the population stagnate and fall in the long run, will occupy us during the remainder of the present paper.

Since Haiti's rurality is overwhelming, and urban activities occupy a minority of the labor force, we will concentrate mainly on the basic activity: agriculture placed, however, in a wider setting. The discussion will focus on three areas: population growth and erosion, technological stagnation, and market imperfections. Each one of these areas will be dealt with in turn.

Population Growth and Erosion

The most visible, and in a sense, the most central of the mechanisms which keep the Haitian economy in a state of underdevelopment is the destruction of the basic agricultural resource—the land. When Columbus discovered Haiti in 1492, the island was clad in lush tropical forest vegetation. Today, the visitor flying into the country is met by a highly discomforting sight. A mixture of cultivated plots and severely eroded mountain slopes dominates the picture.

Erosion is not primarily a result of natural factors. The mechanism which has led to the gradual denudation of the hillsides is intimately connected with economic factors. Throughout the history of the country there have been very few economic alternatives to agriculture and, in spite of some spotty growth in the industrial sector, the situation remains essentially the same today.

The economics behind the soil destruction process can be described in the following way.[5] When the population grows, so does the labor force. With nowhere for this labor to go in a constant land area, the man/land ratio must increase in agriculture, i.e. the cultivation techniques become more labor-intensive. Products of a more labor-intensive type are thus substituted for those requiring less labor per hectare. Schematically, this imposes the following temporal sequence on a given plot:

1. forest
2. pasture
3. land-intensive crops
4. labor-intensive crops
5. eroded land

The forest disappears for two reasons. In the first place, in Haiti no energy substitutes for charcoal and firewood exist. As the population grows, so does the demand for wood. Secondly, when the population increases forest areas have to be cleared to allow (directly or indirectly) for an expansion of pastoral and crop land.

In the third step of the sequence, animal husbandry, in which labor requirements are very modest, will be replaced by cultivation of crops that require relatively little labor in relation to land but still more than the keeping of animals. The labor intensity of cultivation depends on the type of crops cultivated. If we assume that population growth is an exogenous factor, the latter will serve to substitute more labor-intensive crops for less labor-intensive ones as long as the relative prices of these products do not change.

This conclusion follows from a simple application of what in the theory of international trade is known as the Rybczynski theorem (1955). This theorem states that in a two-good, two-factor model where one of the two factors grows while the other one remains constant, if there are no advantages or disadvantages of scale in production, at constant relative commodity prices, the output of the commodity using the growing factor intensively must increase while the output of the other commodity falls.[6] For this to occur, some of the static factor has to be transferred into the production of the commodity whose output grows.

In the Haitian context this has important implications. Coffee, for example, is a much less labor-intensive product than food. As the labor force grows, food crops will be substituted for coffee, unless the movement of relative prices goes in the opposite direction and is strong enough to outweigh the Rybczynski effect. This type of process can be expected to operate at any given time on any given plot, which in turn means that there is a strong tendency for a given piece of land to move from stage one to stage four in the sequence outlined above.

Unfortunately, given the topographic characteristics of Haiti and the production technology used in Haitian agriculture, where terracing is seldom employed, the process does not end there. For each step in the sequence, the risk of erosion increases. Trees are better than grass at mobilizing and storing nutrients so as to maintain soil fertility. When grass has taken the place of trees, sheep and goats easily remove the cover. Once cultivation is practiced, the situation deteriorates further, since the ground then has to be laid bare periodically for sowing and planting, more often with labor-intensive crops (annual food crops) than with perennial ones (coffee). This usually takes place when the rains start. The humus layer is then easily washed off the mountainsides, which thereafter become eroded.

The erosion process tends to be cumulative. Erosion means that the land area available for cultivation shrinks. This reinforces the tendency to substitute labor-intensive food crops for land-intensive products like coffee. (This follows immediately from applying the Rybczynski theorem "backwards.") Hence erosion has a tendency to produce more erosion. Once the process is put in motion it feeds itself and gathers ever more strength as long as other factors do not work in the opposite direction.

Here, price movements are of special significance. If the price of export goods (coffee) rises, the substitution process may work in the direction of more of the land-intensive products and less of the labor-intensive ones. But for long periods this has not been the case. Unfavorable price movements in the world market for coffee, together with heavy taxation of this product and an increased demand for food as the population grows, have tended to reinforce rather than counteract the erosion process.[7] The situation may also be further complicated by the fact that it is easier to uproot coffee trees than to replant them. If the relative price of coffee falls, food crops can be substituted and made to yield immediately, whereas if relative prices move in favor of coffee, planting of the latter crop may not take place unless the price trend is both strong and persistent, since a coffee plant does not yield during the first five or six years. A decision to replant coffee means that the peasant must forego the potential earnings from food crops during this period. He may not be in the position to afford such a decision.

Haiti's erosion problem seems to be the worst one in the Western Hemisphere (Lundahl 1982a:7a). It is the single most important problem that the Haitian economy is facing. The Haitian countryside is in a state of severe ecological disequilibrium which, if nothing is done to change the situation, will threaten the survival of Haitian society in a not-too-distant future.

Techniques which would allow for better production of the soil are not lacking. In his book on the natural potential of Haiti, Donner (1980:211) identifies three such sets of measures. The first one is the construction of terraces and contour ditches to prevent the soil from being washed down the hillsides when it rains. Secondly, a number of changes in cultivation practices can be introduced, such as contour plowing or digging which, according to Donner, would half the rate of erosion and reduce the runoff by some 70 percent. These processes should be complemented by composting, manuring, and appropriate crop rotation to increase soil fertility. Finally, a number of living plants could be used to protect the fields from wind and water erosion.

These techniques, however, are seldom used in Haiti. Erosion presents some special obstacles to change. One of these arises from the fact that the erosion process contains important externalities. When the individual peasant cuts down trees he inflicts a loss due to increased erosion not only on the plot where the tree is cut but on all the hillside plots below this one as well. The runoff produced by the tree felling takes its toll all the way down the mountainside. If *all* peasants in an area decide to control erosion using the methods listed above, the probability of success would increase. But as long as there is no guarantee that the entire community will participate, the peasant remains better off, at least in the short run, if he does nothing. Besides, the benefits of erosion control affect the future, while the costs are incurred today, and the peasants are likely to discount the former heavily in relation to the latter. People living in a state of absolute poverty tend to put a much higher weight on the present than on the future when making decisions. What matters first and foremost is survival today.

Nor can the peasants expect much help from government institutions. Erosion is a national, not a local or regional, problem in Haiti. It therefore requires a massive attack guided by agricultural expertise and extension efforts that are largely lacking. Haiti possesses a very detailed legal code restricting the use of soils in mountainous terrain in order to protect the hillsides, but this law is universally ignored. Enforcement is lacking and will in all probability not be forthcoming unless the peasants become motivated to change their agricultural practices in a way which leads to stronger efforts to combat erosion within their own community.[8]

Lack of Technological Change

The assumption that no technological progress takes place in Haitian agriculture is a realistic assumption, because innovations which allow the peasants to make a more profitable use of the available resources have been lacking. Indeed, if a comparison is made between today's cultivation practices and those of the nineteenth century or even the colonial period, the differences are often hardly noticeable. In some cases it is even possible to trace technological retrogression (cf. Lundahl 1979:558-74). The lack of erosion control is but one facet of this complex. In an economy operating under population pressure as heavy as Haiti's, where employment opportunities outside the agricultural sector are severely circumscribed, a change from low-productivity to high-productivity technologies is essential if the long-term standard of living is to be preserved. Still, examples of innovations in rural Haiti are difficult to find.[9] Strong forces exist in the economy which tend to create formidable obstacles to the introduction and spread of technologies capable of generating higher rural incomes. In the present section we will identify some such mechanisms.[10]

In the first place, innovation is physically and technically difficult in agriculture because nature puts narrow limits on the changes that can be implemented. First, it is difficult and costly to change the natural cycle of the agricultural year. The mountainous topography of the country provides a second "physical" constraint. It is not possible, for example, to use plows and draft animals when the slope of the ground becomes too steep.

This type of "physical" explanation tells only a very limited part of the story. Economic factors must be added if we are to gain a fuller understanding of why technological change has turned out to be such a difficult matter in Haiti.

Some innovations that have been successfully adopted in other countries may in Haiti be economically *irrelevant*. Technological change frequently is of the capital-using type, i.e it tends to raise the capital-labor ratio. Investments in old or new forms of capital must be undertaken if productivity is to increase. One can define a certain maximum price of capital, in terms of labor, above which such innovations no longer pay. In Haiti, labor is cheap in terms of capital, i.e. in many instances the relative price of capital exceeds this 'break even' factor price ratio for a given innovation which therefore tends to be rejected. (A good example is furnished by the Green Revolution.)

The factor price problem is compounded by the existence of complementarities and indivisibilities. Often, the innovations are not only capital-using but also require investment in *various* types of capital of a certain *minimum* size, animal-drawn plows, for example. It is not possible to buy one-fourth of a horse.

Indivisibilities assume special importance in the context where, as in Haiti, the peasants are not in the situation where they can finance investments with their own funds but have to borrow the money. In the past, agricultural credit from formal sources was not successful in reaching the majority of the peasant population. Instead, the most common way to obtain a loan has been to approach an informal lender (e.g. a middleman). For various reasons[11] the effective interest rates in these markets are high. This in turn may make investments in indivisibilities unprofitable. In the informal credit market, the type of credit generally available is very limited both in size and in time. To pay high rates of interest on small and short loans is one matter. Interest payments on large sums borrowed for a period of several years are entirely different. Thus, the peasant may find himself trapped in a situation where superior technologies are available but financing the transition to these technologies from the traditional, low-yielding ones is impossible because loans are available only on terms which make the profitability of the transition negative.

One of the most important causes of the high effective interest rates prevailing in Haiti is the strong preference for additions to present income in relation to future income, which is a consequence of poverty already discussed. The high rate of time preference serves to make innovative activity difficult in at least one more way.[12] Activities on a Haitian farm may be divided into two groups: those concerned with the daily operations utilizing traditional technology, i.e. with the direct production of food and cash crops, and those concerned with *changes* in the technology itself. For the latter type of activity to take place at all, the economy must produce a surplus beyond what is required to carry out current production. In rural Haiti *per capita* incomes are probably falling, i.e. the standard of living is deteriorating gradually, which means that innovations do not take place at a pace fast enough to compensate for diminishing returns to labor and for the effects of erosion. In a situation in which *per capita* incomes are falling and where the standard of living is already precariously low, resources may be transferred easily from activities that enhance future productivity to activities designed to yield higher *current* output. Expenditures (e.g. on innovative investments) may be cut to allow a higher consumption. This takes place if the preference for the present is high in relation to the preference for the future, in Haiti. A *Gresham's law of innovations* is at work, whereby current production and consumption tend to drive innovative activities out of the market. This may in the long run be fatal, since it produces a downward cumulative spiral in the economy. The rate of innovation is too low to preclude incomes from falling. The reduction in the standard of living in turn makes for a reduction in the extent of innovative activities, and so the spiral continues downward.

Another important obstacle to innovation is risk. The Haitian peasant is poor and has comparatively few means to protect himself against undesirable consequences. This poses a problem in connection with innovation. We must remember that we are dealing with technological change in agriculture, which essentially means that we do not know whether a particular innovation will be successful or not until it has been tried in the *local* context. Changes that have worked elsewhere under roughly, but not completely similar, conditions may fail in the local setting. It is, however, often difficult to find peasants who are willing to do so, unless the beneficial effects of innovation can be established in the *short* run. In the case of more complex consequences, which operate over a longer period of time, it may not be as easy to get the peasants to adopt change.

The existence of risks may also preclude innovation for a very different reason. An innovation, by increasing the productivity of a farmstead, may attract outsiders who attempt to take over peasant lands, since often the situation with respect to legal titles to land is confused.[13] Tenant farmers and sharecroppers are in the most precarious situation, since all innovations are likely to be capitalized in the value of land which means that either the rent will rise or, if the tenants refuse to pay a higher rent, they may be evicted.

Finally, it should also be mentioned that the quality of the human capital may hamper innovative activities. In some cases the mental and physical energy required to undertake innovations may be lacking. In societies of the Haitian type, where caloric requirements are *on average* not satisfied, the distribution of the caloric intake across the year is probably also uneven. The largest caloric intake takes place during the periods of peak effort, i.e. when harvesting and planting are to be done. Outside these periods, the caloric intake probably falls. This may help to explain, on the one hand, why so much of Haitian agriculture is left to nature during the off-peak season and, on the other, why there is little labor effort, for example in terracing (a highly labor-intensive activity).

A second factor related to the quality of the human capital is the low educational level prevailing among the peasants. The 1971 census showed that illiteracy in rural areas must have been in the neighborhood of 90 percent (Lundahl 1979:478). Thus, peasants are cut off from an important means of learning about potentially beneficial changes that could be implemented on the farm. The search for innovation tends to become less efficient (more time-consuming) and more likely to proceed in the wrong direction. This is true not only for the purely illiterate but also for the majority who have been in contact with primary education, since the curricula of rural schools have not offered much scope for the study of subjects related to agriculture.

In the same way as with erosion control, one might look to the government as the natural initiator of change in rural areas, but this has largely been theoretical. The reality is very different. Until recently, a mere token interest has been taken in agriculture on the part of the representatives of the Haitian state. We will return later to the role played by politics in creating and maintaining underdevelopment in Haiti. Presently it is enough to conclude that such crucial activities as extension service have in the main been insufficient both in quantity and in quality. In general, these activities have been spread far too thinly across the rural population to be of any real use, except for in very special, and sometimes somewhat unexpected, cases (see Palmer 1976:167-72).

Market Imperfections

It is debated to what extent the middlemen operating in the marketing of peasant crops are exploiting the peasants by means of oligopsonistic or oligopolistic collusion (Lundahl 1979: Chapter 4). Since Haiti has an economy in which market considerations are extremely important, exploitation could do considerable damage to the peasant producers. In the present section we will discuss whether this is actually the case. Since food crops and export crops are marketed via different channels, we will divide the discussion into two parts, beginning with the food crops.

The marketing of food crops takes place via a well-developed system of market places, more than 500 with a minimum of 50 sellers and buyers on a normal market day in the mid-seventies (La Gra, Fanfan & Charleston 1975). This network of markets extends across the entire country. The goods produced by the peasants move internally in one direction while products of urban origin which the peasants need but do not produce themselves flow in the other direction. Both types of products are handled by the same intermediaries, the wholesale-dealing *Madanm Sara* and the retailing *revendeuses*.

It has been contended that the internal marketing system is an inefficient one because the movement of goods from producers to consumers takes place at high costs and the intermediaries reap profits in excess of what they could earn in other activities. A consensus, however, appears to be emerging that the system *is* efficient (given some constraints) and that no oligopsonistic or oligopolistic exploitation takes place (Zuvekas 1978: 206-15, and Lundahl 1979: 145-74).

In the first place, although strictly speaking no systematic knowledge is available, whatever evidence there is seems to indicate that the profit margins at all levels of the marketing system are not so high as to qualify as "monopolistic." This is definitely true for the retail level where competition is stiff enough to depress profits to a level where it is no longer appropriate to speak of a profit in the economic sense but rather of an implicit wage for the labor expended in the process of trading. The *Madanm Sara* appear to make somewhat higher gross profits. They also provide a wider range of services than the *revendeuses;* for example, bulking, bulk-breaking, and transport from one market place to another. Thus their net profit level probably is not much higher than that of the latter group. The difference in incomes between these two categories of traders actually lies in the fact that the *volume of operations* of the wholesale dealers is larger.

The second indication of competition derives from relative freedom of entry at different levels. This does not mean that anybody can become a *Madanm Sara*. In the early seventies, something like $60 was the minimum required to begin wholesale trading (Murray & Alvarez 1975: 30, 34). This, however, does not preclude entry when profit levels increase, for there are always enough *revendeuses* around with enough capital to enter wholesale trade at least on a part-time basis in times of supernormal profit levels. This applies to all levels of the system. Increasing profits encourage the entry of new competitors, which in turn brings profits back to the normal level.

The third piece of evidence about competition comes from the relative ease with which a given link in the marketing chain can be skipped by the others. This occurs when the link attempts to increase the price above the competitive level (Lundahl 1979: 158-62).

Fourthly, the establishment of prices takes place in a fashion which very closely resembles what one finds in economics textbooks. Qualities and measurements are seldom uniform. This variance is compensated for by means of haggling procedures which can be taken into account when the price is established. Altogether, this leads to prices which for a given quality and a given measure do not differ noticeably from seller to seller in a given market place.

The final indication of the absence of exploitation comes from the existence of various modes of non-price competition. Most important of these is the *pratik,* the mutual concessions given by sellers and buyers. By establishing *pratik* relationships, the intermediaries make sure that they are able to obtain and dispose of goods in difficult market situations where scarcities or gluts exist. *Pratik* is a means of increasing, not decreasing, the competition, as is the practice of making transactions outside the market places.

To sum up, the marketing system for food crops (and goods sold to the peasants) is a competitive one. The extent of competition is limited mainly by the relative ease or difficulty of transporting goods from one market to another. Given the limitations emanating from the bad road network, the system otherwise functions efficiently. Goods and information regarding prices and quantities travel from market to market in a fairly smooth way. Competition between the intermediaries ensures that the risk of exploitation of the peasants remains low.

The situation of the marketing of export crops is different. The most important export crop, and the only one dealt with presently,[14] is coffee, which is marketed by men mainly outside of the market system handling the food crops. In the most simple case, coffee is sold by the producers to middlemen known as *spéculateurs,* who in turn sell to the exporters located in the ports.

Various researchers have contended that the coffee marketing system is almost as competitive as the marketing of food crops.[15] New material, presented in the recent study by Girault (1981), casts considerable doubt on this proposition. Girault's well-documented research demonstrates that the coffee marketing chain contains a number of imperfections, above all on the exporter level. These permit fixing the price paid to the producers at a level which is lower than the one which would have been established in a competitive market.

The export marketing system has a long tradition in Haiti. After independence, bonds between Haiti and France were broken and traditional outlets for export produce disappeared. It did not take very long, however, for foreign merchants to return to Haiti to compete in the sales of export crops. Haitian legislation explicitly forbade foreigners to engage in retail commerce and limited the localization of foreign companies to port towns.[16] In this way, a pattern was established whereby the export-import houses were concentrated in the hands of foreigners, who over time became Haitian citizens. Domestic trade, on the other hand, especially at the retail level, was dominated by the descendants of the slaves.

During the course of the present century a high degree of specialization, either on exports or on imports, was obtained. It is quite likely that this specialization has created comparative advantages in coffee marketing which have been large enough to make entry of new firms somewhat difficult. Presently, it is calculated that at least $1 million is required to start an export firm (Girault 1981:217). This trend towards increased specialization has continued until fairly recently when a number of the leading coffee houses diversified into activities not related to coffee (Girault 1981:168).

If we limit attention to the most recent 20 to 25 years, the number of exporters has not changed very much. Gates identified 35 exporters in the 1950's (1950:27), whereas Girault (1981:164) lists 27 for 1976-77. The rank of order among the exporters has, however, not remained unchanged. Some have left the scene altogether, while new ones have entered. A certain, possibly declining concentration of sales can be observed. During the 1950's, the first four firms accounted for 54-62 percent of total sales while in the seventies the figure was slightly lower: 52-54 percent (Gates 1959:27; Girault 1981:164).

The coffee exporters are organized in the *Association des Exportateurs de Café* (ASDEC), established in 1960. Earlier it was believed that the efforts of this organization to control coffee marketing were unsuccessful (Lundahl 1979:138), but Girault strongly challenges this view. According to him, ASDEC controls some 89-99 percent of total coffee exports (Girault 1981:219), and every year the association fixes the prices to be paid to the *spéculateurs* and producers. Since 1977 the market has been shared by means of sales quotas in order to minimize the competition between ASDEC members. Thus, according to Girault, ASDEC acts like a collusive oligopsony, lowering the price which the peasants receive for their coffee below the competitive level. This is also borne out by the relatively high profit level that seems to prevail among the exporters (Girault 1981:195).

Girault also argues that the peasants suffer not only from monopsonistic pricing at the exporter level but also from imperfect competition among *spéculateurs*. Here, however, I am not convinced that he has interpreted his evidence correctly. Contrary to what was believed a few years ago, the *spéculateurs* have not been reduced to mere agents for the exporters. His conclusion, however, that no competition takes place among *spéculateurs* may be unwarranted. In the first place, the number of *spéculateurs* per speculation center is not low, 8.5 on average in the entire country. Secondly, no district had less than four centers (Girault 1981:142). Naturally, this information may be misleading, but when we look at *spéculateur* gross profit margins the impression of competition is reinforced. Girault's figures show an average *spéculateur* gross profit of a mere 1.3 percent of the f.o.b. price of coffee (Girault 1981:195). For a *spéculateur* to make a profit, a large volume is required. A *gross* profit of 1.3 percent (not a profit net of all costs) does not seem to indicate a monopoly.

Girault also points to various fraudulent tricks among the *spéculateurs* and to the squeezing of peasants via usurious interest rates. It cannot be denied that such tricks are practiced, but they are also employed by the peasants who in various ways attempt to increase the weight of their product. It is very difficult to know in which direction the bias actually is and how important it is in quantitative terms. If fraudulent practices become too obvious one would expect the *spéculateurs* to lose business.

The usury argument, in turn, is an old one. The problem with it is that nobody (including Girault) has been able to support it with any systematic data. That interest rates are high is not *per se* evidence of usury or exploitation. Unfortunately, so far, no direct investigations of the informal credit markets in rural Haiti have been carried out. Whatever indirect evidence there is (see Lundahl 1979: Chapter 11), however, does not seem to indicate monopoly profits from lending. The number of potential lenders is fairly large, and the lender category is not to be found only among the *spéculateurs*. Furthermore, a difference must be made between high- and low-risk loans. The rate of interest is likely to vary substantially between the two. It can easily be demonstrated, for example, that paying the equivalent of 125 percent on a yearly basis is equivalent to taking a one-month consumption loan by selling and repurchasing an asset which yields 5 percent per year with transaction costs both for selling and repurchasing at 5 percent (Lundahl 1979:516-18). We know far too little about how informal lending takes place in rural areas, but I strongly suspect that the picture is much more complex than what the mere identification of high interest rates with usury would lead us to believe.

Thus, to conclude, the marketing system for food crops gives the impression of being relatively competitive whereas some imperfections are found in the marketing of the most important export crop, coffee. These appear to be concentrated mainly in the exporter stage, where the number of buyers is sufficiently low to allow for organization and sharing of the market on a non-competitive basis, to the detriment of the producers who receive a lower price than they would have otherwise. Among the *spéculateurs,* on the other hand, the degree of competition appears to be far more intense.

When judging the effects of monopsonistic pricing among coffee exporters on peasant welfare we must take into account that the peasants produce not only coffee and that not all the coffee produced is marketed via *spéculateurs* and exporters. Some 40 percent of the total, during the first half of the 1970's, would not be subject to monopsonistic pricing. If either was consumed by the peasants themselves or was sold via the internal market place system (Girault 1981:103). When it comes to the remainder, efforts to increase the degree of monopsonistic exploitation are likely to lead to a change in the composition of peasant output, away from coffee and toward food crops instead, as this measure changes the relative prices of coffee and other crops. Thus, it may be that some of the drop in coffee production, for example, during the 1960's may be the result of the foundation of ASDEC and the subsequent sharing of the coffee market among the exporters.[17] By switching to other crops, the peasants reduce their dependency on a market which is organized to their disadvantage.

Politics and Government

No picture of Haitian underdevelopment is complete without reference to the political dimension. To understand why the country has historically stagnated at a low level of real income, we must examine how the process of politics and government has worked during the 180 years since Haiti obtained its independence.

Haitian politics present a rather degenerate picture. The clue to the degeneration of the nineteenth and twentieth centuries is found in the development of land tenure after Alexander Pétion's first redistribution of land in 1809. This redistribution, the subsequent breakdown of the *grande culture* and the creation of a peasant nation where land was more equally distributed than anywhere else in Latin America (Lundahl 1979: Chapter 6) meant that the most obvious road to wealth in an agricultural society— landownership—was essentially closed to the emerging elite.

Instead, the elite and those seeking elite status turned to politics. No one satisfactory rationale exists for the course of Haitian political history,[18] but the economic or pecuniary interests of the main actors explain many of the essential features of the political process, during both the past and present centuries. After the death of Henry Christophe in 1820, Haiti gradually evolved into a "soft state," i.e. a state characterized by corruption at all levels, one where the working assumption of the politicians was that the spoils of government were identical to the private finances of the politicians. Office was sought mainly for the sake of the spoils and the spoils system was carried to extremes. Since without a sufficient political backing no clique could stay in power, it was necessary to distribute the spoils of office across many different levels of the administration.

This distorted view of politics had very unfortunate consequences for Haitian development. First, it engendered an almost total lack of interest in the welfare of the masses who separated from politics at a very early stage of Haitian history. Once the two main aspirations—freedom and land— had been fulfilled, the masses participated in political life only as agents for the various coup makers and insurgents bidding for power, expressing no political ambitions of their own. The ruling cliques, in turn, never identified with the masses. A gulf separated the majority of Haitians from the elite, one which precluded constructive efforts to improve the lot of the general population. Essentially, this situation continues to this very day (Lundahl 1979: Chapter 7).

A lack of positive action can be traced in all important fields of economic development. Haiti has for a long time been plagued by problems of malnutrition and disease. The nutritional standard appears to be declining, not least in rural areas, and whatever progress has been made in the field of disease eradication has largely resulted from outside finance. The Haitian governments have expressed little interest in confronting this situation (Lundahl 1979: Chapter 9).

Education provides another example. For technological change to spread in the countryside, both basic and some vocational education is desirable, although very little of either exists (Lundahl 1979: Chapter 10). During the nineteenth century virtually no educational advancement was achieved. The illiteracy rate probably ranged close to 100 percent in rural areas when the U.S. occupation forces landed in 1915. During the occupation, the Americans failed in an attempt to restructure rural education along vocation-oriented lines. After 1934, the traditional French-oriented education reasserted itself. The school system remained starved of funds, just as during the pre-occupation period. The 1950 census exhibited dismally high illiteracy rates in rural districts—exceeding 90 percent (Lundahl 1979:472). Efforts were subsequently made to increase adult literacy, but little had been achieved at the beginning of the 1970's, as demonstrated by the 1971 census. Rural illiteracy remained above 90 percent (Lundahl 1979:478).

The educational system does not serve first and foremost as a means for human capital formation, but rather as a filter.[19] The combination of French, poor teachers, and tough exams makes it exceedingly difficult for rural youths to pass the primary cycle. This, in turn, contributes to the peasants' isolation from political life by stifling social advancement and breeding ignorance. In this sense, rural education constitutes a medium of social control.

A third area of government inaction is credit (Lundahl 1979: Chapter 11). As mentioned above, the peasants must seek credit from informal lending sources who often demand high effective interest rates. A few scattered attempts to bypass the speculators were made before the 1950's, but little came of them. Since 1951, a number of credit institutes have been created to supply agricultural credit. These efforts have, however, been sufficient to reach only a miniscule fraction of the peasantry.

Finally, the state has provided very little encouragement of technological change in the countryside (Lundahl 1979:610-16). We have already seen that, in Haiti, technological advance rarely occurs spontaneously. For various reasons, assistance is needed to spread innovations. Scientific and technological knowledge must be adapted to suit local circumstances. Contacts with the outside must be maintained and research needs to be undertaken on specifically Haitian conditions. Finally, the results of research have to be disseminated to the final users—the peasants—via an extension process. Haiti, however, has never possessed any efficient agricultural extension service which could be used by the peasants.

Unfortunately, the net impact of government action in the agricultural field has been negative (at best it has been neutral). The peasants have been severely taxed without receiving any corresponding benefits from government actions (Lundahl 1979: Chapter 7-8). The Haitian tax system continues to rely very heavily on export and import taxes. On the export side, coffee has most often borne the brunt of taxation. Concerning imports, necessities consumed by the masses rather than luxury goods have been taxed. Taxes on income and wealth account for ridiculously small fractions of total government revenues.

On the expenditure side, the large items have been repayment of the foreign debt, which was a heavy burden on the Haitian treasury from 1825 to 1947, the maintenance of oversized military and police forces, and wage and salary payments to all the individuals to whom the governments have owed some kind of "political" debt. Haiti has never been a democratic society; thus it requires huge spending on forces to back a sitting regime. Finally, large wage and salary payments to a civilian administration (whose main services have been political) have always absorbed important sums.

The agricultural sector, in turn, has received much less than it has contributed. In principle, there is no golden rule to tell us that a sector must receive funds in the same proportion as it is taxed. It could well be that development can be accelerated by transferring resources from agriculture into, say, industry by means of taxation. In Haiti, however, it is hardly this type of philosophy that has guided the proceedings. Besides, in a country where such a large share of the population depends on agriculture and the possibilities of decreasing this share are slim in the short and medium run, it would be most sensible to direct funds and projects toward the agricultural sector. Historically, the agricultural sector has received less than 10 percent of government expenditures (Lundahl 1979: Chapter 8), a grossly insufficient sum.

External Factors

The final issue for consideration is the most difficult, value-loaded, and the least systematically investigated: the role of external or foreign interests in creating and maintaining underdevelopment in Haiti. The majority of contributions in this field come from researchers with a Marxist orientation, while comparatively little is available from more "traditionally" inclined social scientists. The method employed has either been fairly straight-forward application of orthodox Marxist principles or, less frequently, the use of more recent ideas borrowed from Latin America's *dependencia* school.

We may begin with the influence of Spanish and French colonialism, where matters are comparatively simple. The demographic catastrophe triggered by the Spanish conquest and the negative effects for the black masses of the introduction of slavery are incontestable. General agreement also exists as to the influence of colonial patterns on the subsequent social structure of Haiti. Of particular interest is the cleavage of Haitian society into a tiny elite group and a large mass, two groups with very little in common. Finally, the fact that Saint-Domingue was a colony during the mercantilist era determined the composition of output. Colonies were kept to benefit the colonial powers, not to develop the new territories for their indigenous (or in this case, imported) inhabitants. Hence, the strong emphasis on export crops and foreign trade—the gains of which were not equally distributed among the black and white inhabitants of the colony.

The first important nineteenth-century event involving foreign interests, the 1825 indemnity and the creation of the double debt to France, is also easily analyzed.[20] The indemnity was forced upon Haiti by the French. Thus, it was an example of direct intervention by a foreign power in Haiti's internal affairs. The payment of the indemnity resulted in at least two negative consequences for the country (Lundahl 1979: Chapter 8). In the first place, Boyer had to impose a tax to meet the first installment. This tax, however, to some extent was evaded. Much more important, the indemnity was at least in part responsible for the attempt to reintroduce large-scale agriculture using forced labor. To pay the indemnity, agricultural production for export had to be increased. At this time, however, due to a lack of labor following the wars of independence, coffee cultivation was in a state of neglect, while sugar imports had practically been wiped out. Lacking adequate capital equipment, the only way to restore exports was to increase the labor intensity on the land. The attempt to put the Haitians back into forced labor failed, but during the time the effort lasted, the impact on those affected was negative.

The 1825 indemnity continued to lay a heavy hand on the Haitian economy for several decades, but it is not correct to contend that it was the main cause of the new foreign loans assumed in 1874, 1875, and 1876, or of the domestic loans floated at the end of the nineteenth century and the beginning of the twentieth. These loans were not the result of neocolonial exploitation, but rather of corrupt domestic politicians mortgaging Haiti's development possibilities in order to fill their own pockets (Lacerte, 1981).

The nineteenth century also witnessed some foreign investment in Haiti. The beginnings, however, were slow. When Haiti most needed capital, after the partial destruction of the productive apparatus during the wars of liberation, no foreigners stepped in. At that point, Haiti found itself isolated and even ostracized—a black nation that had recently thrown off the yoke of slavery, surrounded by a number of French, Spanish and British colonies, as well as the slave-owning South of the United States—all fearing slave rebellions. The Haitian constitutions, which all contained clauses prohibiting foreign ownership of land, also acted as obstacles to foreign investment. In quantitative terms, such investment remained fairly modest in 1915 (Lundahl 1979: Chapter 8).

The question, then, is whether the existing investments were beneficial to the country. Undoubtedly, many were dubious ventures conceived to bring quick profits to the investors on the one hand and kickbacks to corrupt administrations on the other. But were there examples of neocolonial penetration? I am not so sure. As David Nicholls has pointed out, the groups contending for power seldom hesitated to turn to foreign interests when it suited them, i.e. mainly when domestic political or economic advantages could be derived from it (Nicholls 1979:247-48). Thus, we have a situation which resembles the chain of loans during the late nineteenth century. The adverse effects foreign investments may have had must be blamed in large part on the corruption inherent in Haitian domestic politics.

This is also true for the post-occupation period. The scandalous banana concessions of the late 1930's and 1940's, the SHADA cryptostegia venture and a number of dubious projects undertaken during the Magloire and Duvalier administrations offer good examples (Schmidt 1971:41). Such considerations must be taken into account as we attempt to sketch the nature of foreign investment.

A second difficulty when evaluating foreign investment is to determine the precise effects of these investments. Some analysts have unfortunately emphasized the creation of dependency (Joachim 1979; Caprio 1979). Instead, the analysis should point out clearly which of the mechanisms serve to keep a country underdeveloped. It is not satisfactory to hint at "dependency" in a vague, general sense, since the concept itself is not a clearcut one, a fact demonstrated not least by the extensive debate that has taken place within the dependency school itself.[21]

Views differ as to the reason for the American occupation. Marxist interpreters see the arrival of the Marines mainly as a step in the expansion of U.S. imperialism at the turn of the century, with economic forces being an essential factor (Castor 1971). The most authoritative work on the occupation, that of Hans Schmidt, lays emphasis on the political and strategic motives (keeping the Germans out during World War I) (Schmidt

1971). In this context, one may again raise the question of how the intervention was provoked. Was it an act of pure intrusion from the outside, or was the intervention, as David Nicholls indicates (Nicholls 1979: 248), the inevitable outcome of a domestic policy that invited foreign interests and was unable to preserve a minimum of order?

The economic effects of the occupation are complex in turn. Marxists stress the eviction of peasants to prepare the ground for foreign investment, and the resulting exodus of peasants to Cuba and the Dominican Republic.[22] It is difficult to measure the accuracy of this argument. Without doubt, peasants were evicted. Their number, however, remains largely unknown. The sources are difficult to interpret, since many of them were written explicitly to provoke resistance to the occupation both inside and outside the country. Emigration, however, cannot be explained solely by evictions. In Cuba, for example, a strong demand pull was at work to provide for a transfer of Haitians to that country (Lundahl 1982:2).

In reviewing the effects of the occupation, it must not be forgotten that strong efforts were made by the occupation forces to modernize agriculture, reform the educational system,[23] and improve the infrastructure of the country (not the least the roads). Further, an end was put to the recurrent series of coups and counter-coups. All this must be considered when attempting an overall evaluation of the occupation. Hardly anywhere else in the history of Haiti does it become as important as here to establish the counterfactual. What would have occurred if the Americans had not occupied Haiti? Would the old order have been discontinued? Would economic development have proceeded at a faster pace? It is doubtful. The drain on the treasury caused by the high priority given to debt repayment might have been avoided, but quite likely a "political" drain would have been substituted for it.

Even more difficult is to establish the case that dependency or international trade is responsible for Haitian underdevelopment. Of course, a country which participates in the international division of labor always risks becoming sensitive to cyclical fluctuations in the world economy, especially in the economies of its trading partners. That this is the case today as well is demonstrated by the vulnerability of the Haitian assembly industries to what takes place in the U.S. economy. Without question, this sensitivity increases with the concentration of trade to one or a few partners. It is also likely that, in a world with tariffs and other obstacles to trade, a trading partner with a major share in exports and imports uses this fact in negotiations to press for tariff reductions, preferential treatment, and other specific favors.[24] Whether this has detrimental effects is a completely different question.

Implicit in the view that Haiti has in some sense been "exploited" by trade with European powers and the United States is the proposition that the country would have done better without trading. At least, this is the logical consequence of this argument. But would real economic development have proceeded faster in a small island subject to increasing population pressure, with few natural resources, and with a limited domestic market, if coffee had not been sold to the outside world? It is doubtful that autarky would have been superior to trade. This must, at any rate, be demonstrated, not merely assumed.

It is difficult to neatly summarize the impact of external factors on the Haitian economy. To be provocative, too many of the efforts have so far been marred by a methodology which places too much emphasis on forcing the Haitian reality into a system where all the answers are given at the beginning rather than judging each case on its own merits. I can only agree with the conclusion reached by David Nicholls in his study of the color issue:

> Most Marxist writers are hampered in their understanding of the present situation in Haiti ... because they feel a need to force Haitian reality into a Procrustean bed built at the British Museum in the nineteenth century and recently reconstructed in the Bois de Vincennes ... excessive attention is paid to a number of doctrinal and conceptual issues; whether Haiti is *really* feudal or semi-feudal, pre-capitalist or neo-colonial. ... Insufficient attention is paid to studying the concrete social, economic, and political structure of the country. ... The work suffers from a determination to see Haiti in terms of categories which were developed in order to understand a quite different situation (Nicholls 1979:243).

I am not arguing that research along Marxist lines has no role to play in our understanding of Haitian development, only that a more open mind in methodological questions may be beneficial. Eclecticism may be a useful approach. It may be preferable to try different approaches and focus more on pointing out the concrete mechanisms at work in each instance, rather than taking for granted that a certain phenomenon (e.g., trade or investment) always produces the same type of results. There is always a burden of proof on the investigator stating a cause-effect relationship.

Conclusions

By virtually any yardstick, Haiti has an underdeveloped economy. The standard of living is low and falling for larger population segments. Some of the most important reasons for this have been discussed here. The most important activity in Haiti is agriculture, and the central problem of agriculture is erosion. The successive destruction of the soil is a consequence of the transition from less labor-intensive to more labor-intensive crops. The latter leave the vegetation and the bare soil more exposed to wind and rain than the former.

Agricultural production takes place with the aid of technology that has remained more or less constant for more than a century. For various reasons the Haitian peasants are reluctant to change their methods. The high relative price of capital, complementarities, indivisibilities, risks, myopia due to poverty and strong preferences for present income over future, lack of energy, and a low educational level, all contribute to making innovation infrequent.

While the marketing of food crops takes place within a system that appears to be strongly competitive, the most important export crop, coffee, passes through a marketing chain which at the end, among the exporters, displays what appears to be a collusive oligopsony. This leads to a lower price to the producers than that found in a competitive system. To the extent that the peasants shift out of coffee production and into food crops instead, the detrimental effects of price fixing among the exporters can, however, be mitigated.

Unfortunately, the Haitian peasant has not received much help from his various governments in the struggle for a decent standard of living. During the nineteenth century, politics gradually degenerated until the stage was reached where public office was sought mainly because of the opportunities it offered for personal enrichment. This "kleptocratic" view of government was, in turn, translated into a lack of positive action. The most important sector, agriculture, was subjected to heavy taxation and received very little in return. This can be seen in a number of contexts: nutrition and health, education, rural credit, erosion control, and technology, to mention a few. Government expenditures have instead been dominated by foreign debt repayment, military and police, and wages and salaries for the bureaucracy.

The influence of external factors, finally, appears to me as much more uncertain than any of the other four. Without doubt, colonialism had a negative impact on the welfare of the majority of the population. Also, the loans caused by the 1825 indemnity to France constituted a drain on the treasury and a burden for the economy. The later foreign loans, however, can be explained more in terms of domestic politics than in terms of neocolonialism or imperialism. Not very much came out of foreign investment during the pre-occupation period, and many post-occupation projects appear in a strange light as well. Often, the ventures were of a dubious nature, but in the same way as the loans they were frequently a result of invitations from politicians eager for quick gains. The American occupation presents a very mixed record, much more complex than usually admitted by Marxist analysts of the period. International trade, finally, probably has been more favorable to Haiti than would a situation of autarky.

This quick sketch of the roots of Haitian underdevelopment does not aspire to be complete. What the present chapter offers should be interpreted largely along the lines of a starting point for economic research. I doubt that we have reached the "final" or "ultimate" truths regarding the causes of underdevelopment in Haiti. In fact, I am not quite sure we ever will. However, with the wealth of material that has been presented and analyzed by a number of researchers over the past 10-15 years, we are in a much better position today than ever before to initiate a fruitful dialogue from different, and sometimes also diverging, points of view. Advances in the social sciences require communication and a constant exchange of ideas. If the present paper, by its contents or by its omissions, can help initiate such a dialogue, it has more than accomplished its goal.

NOTES

[1] The third and last part of the development criterion—that the degree of inequality in the distribution of income must not increase—presents a much more formidable data problem than the first two parts. The available evidence, basically two surveys taken by the Institut Haïtien de Statistique in 1970 and 1976, yield so widely different pictures that one is forced to conclude that they are not comparable. (See World Bank 1976:8-9 and Table 1.4, Zuvekas 1978:34-37 and World Bank 1981a:6-7.) For the period before the 1970's, hardly any information at all is available. (See Zuvekas 1978:120-46 for a discussion of the evidence.) We thus have to admit that it is not possible to conjecture anything regarding trends in the distribution of income.

[2] If anything, this is an overestimate due to a probable overestimate of the growth of the agricultural sector. (Cf. Lundahl 1979:103-105.)

[3] GDP figures from World Bank 1971a:29, population figures from IHS, n.d.

This has been recognized by the Institut Haïtien de Statistique which has lowered its growth rate figure for the 1970-79 period from 3.8 percent per annum to 2.4 as a consequence of an estimated *decline* of the value of agricultural production in the order of 0.7 percent on average (against plus 2.2 percent in an earlier estimate). (Cf. World Bank 1971a:5.)

[5] Cf. ibid. Chapter 5. Erosion and its consequences are also dealt with in some detail in Zuvekas 1978:188-96 and Donner 1980:192-213.

[6] Even if there are decreasing returns to scale in one or both lines of production, the output of the sector using the growing factor intensively will always increase, and if the difference between the labor intensities is large, as it appears to be in Haiti (cf. Lundahl 1979:235-37), the output of the other sector will fall (Hansson & Lundahl 1982).

[7] For evidence, see Lundahl 1979: Chapter 5.

[8] The USAID and the Pan American Development Foundation are currently involved in an interesting experiment promoting the planting of fast-growing trees *as a crop to be harvested* and to be used e.g. for the making of charcoal. The idea is to recognize that the peasants lack alternative fuels and will cut the trees anyway. By treating the trees not as a perennial cover but as a crop to be harvested, it is hoped that replanting will take place as soon as the crop has been taken; see G. F. Murray's article in this volume.

[9]Cf., however, the cases quoted in Erasmus 1952 and Palmer 1976:167-71.

[10]Cf. Lundahl 1977; 1979, Chapter 12; and forthcoming.

[11]A discussion of the interest rates in the informal credit markets is made in Lundahl 1979, Chaper 11.

[12]Cf. Lundahl, forthcoming, for a more detailed discussion.

[13]Cf., however, Murray 1977, Chapter 7, and 1978, where a good case for the security of peasant holdings is made. The subject is also discussed in Lundahl 1980.

[14]Cf. Zuvekas 1978:117-19, for information on other export crops where the marketing is controlled by the government. The overall tendency has been to offer very low prices to the producers.

[15]Notably Gates 1959; JWK Corporation 1976; and Lundahl 1979:133-45.

[16]The establishment of export trade after 1804 is discussed in Turnier 1955; Joachim 1971, 1979; and Girault 1981, Chapter 8.

[17]Note that monopsonistic pricing in the coffee market thus contributes to increasing the rate of erosion. Cf. the argument presented above.

[18]See e.g. Nicholls (1979), for a different emphasis.

[19]The filter hypothesis is presented e.g. in Arrow (1973) and Stiglitz (1975).

[20]Cf., however, Turnier (1955), Schmidt (1971), Nicholls (1974), and Lacerte (1981). Balch (1927) and Munro (1964) are also of interest in this context.

[21]See the survey of this debate in Blomström and Hettne (1981), Chapter 8.

[22]Cf., e.g., Castor (1971), Chapter 5. Haitian emigration to these two countries is discussed in Lundahl (1982:2) and Lundahl & Vargas (forthcoming).

[23]The reform was very partial, however. Cf. Lundahl (1979), Chapter 10.

[24]Schmidt (1971), p. 33. Details regarding the Franco-Haitian commerce during the nineteenth century are found in Joachim (1972).

FOREIGN ASSISTANCE AND
HAITI'S ECONOMIC DEVELOPMENT

JAMES L. WALKER

Haiti is the poorest country in the Western Hemisphere and one of the poorest in the world. The best data available indicates that average annual *per capita* income in Haiti was $270 in 1980.[1] This makes Haiti the only country in the Western Hemisphere to be included in the United Nations' list of "relatively least developed countries." Yet, even this figure fails to communicate the level of poverty in Haiti. The World Bank estimated that in 1979 more than 80 percent of the population had an average income of under $150. Open unemployment is about 16 percent underemployment is approximately 60 percent of the labor force. Other indices of poverty provide an even more graphic impression of current conditions in Haiti than do income and employment data. With respect to health status, malnutrition is widespread, with the percentage of preschool children rated as "normal" ranging from only 20 to 27 percent in the rural regions. Infant mortality is 115 per thousand of live births. Average life expectancy is only 53 years. Malnutrition and gastro-enteric diseases account for over half of the deaths in the country. The extreme rural poverty and high pressure on

The views expressed herein are the author's and do not necessarily reflect those of USAID/Haiti nor the University of Nevada-Reno. The author gratefully acknowledges the helpful comments provided by Harlan Hogbood, Shirley Pryor, and Mikaele Racine and the efficient clerical support provided by Judith Desmornes.

agricultural land and the lack of development of other sectors have resulted in an acceleration of rural to urban migration, especially to Port-au-Prince. Environmental conditions in many of the urban slums are worse than those in rural areas and, by some indices of poverty, the urban poor are worse off than the rural poor.

In response to Haiti's poverty and developmental problems, the international community launched a broad array of development assistance projects in the early 1970's in cooperation with the Government of Haiti. The purpose of this paper is to review the scale and form that foreign assistance has assumed over the past decade, to assess its impact, and to analyze its future role and the importance of Government of Haiti policy decisions.

Growth of Foreign Assistance in the 1970's

Haiti in the early 1970's was just beginning to emerge from a decade of economic stagnation and political chaos. The decade of the 1960's was characterized by conditions which favored neither institutional development nor fixed capital formation. Haiti during the 1960's was, in many respects, a place apart. Whereas other less developed countries were comparably poor, most received governmental foreign assistance and also managed to attract private foreign investment. Haiti received neither. There was no external cushion to offset the declining value of Haiti's principal export products, including coffee, sugar, and sisal. Haiti was thus isolated from the international community and received almost no development capital and only a limited amount of technical assistance.

Against the background of acute resource poverty, deteriorating physical infrastructure, an inefficient administrative system, and isolation from the world community, Haiti's economic stagnation in the 1960's is hardly remarkable. Real GNP fell between 1962 and 1968. The stagnation coupled with population growth caused real GNP *per capita* (US $ at 1980 prices) to decline over the decade, from $230 in 1960 to $210 in 1970 (OAS 1982:162).

The economic recovery that started in 1968 can be largely attributed to the improved political climate that prevailed during the two years preceeding and the years following the death of President François Duvalier (in 1971) and the succession to the Presidency of his son, Jean-Claude Duvalier. The changed political environment was also responsible for the beginning of a substantial commitment by the international and bilateral donor agencies to increase their assistance to Haiti. New commitments of official development assistance (ODA) increased rapidly from $9 million in 1970 to $106 million in 1973 (Table 1). Commitments then declined, with $65 and $92 million being committed in 1980 and 1981, respectively. During the 1970's, ODA commitments totaled over $536 million. Over the ten year period covered by the Government of Haiti's first two development plans (1972-1981), ODA commitments totaled $676 million.

Actual ODA disbursements (actual expenses) have been considerably lower. Disbursements grew from less than $5 million in 1970 to $84 million in 1980 (Table 2). ODA disbursements for the 1970's decade total $384 million while the figure for the 1972-1981 period is $540 million. The $152 and $136 million differences between commitments and disbursements consist mainly of undisbursed grant obligations and loan authorizations ("pipeline"). Cancelled commitments and estimate errors account for the remainder.[2]

Foreign assistance disbursements have become an increasingly important means of financing the Government of Haiti's development program. Over the period 1972-1981, foreign assistance financed approximately 65 percent of the development program. In 1981, over 73 percent of total development expenditures were financed by foreign assistance loans and grants.

Table 1. Foreign Assistance Commitments* +
($ millions)

	Bilateral	Multilateral	Total
1970	3.4	5.5	8.9
1971	4.6	3.4	8.0
1972	6.9	2.5	9.4
1973	9.4	10.8	20.2
1974	15.8	34.2	50.0
1975	23.1	25.4	48.5
1976	37.5	46.2	83.7
TQ**	11.9	21.0	32.9
1977	52.3	26.4	78.7
1978	50.3	39.1	89.4
1979	45.3	61.1	106.4
1980	54.9	9.8	64.7
1981	61.6	30.7	92.3

*Grant obligations and loan authorizations made by governmental agencies.
**Transition quarter.

+ *U.S. Overseas Loans and Grants,* PPC, Agency for International Development, July 1, 1975-September 30, 1981 and *Congressional Presentations,* Annex III, Agency for International Development, FY73-FY84.

Table 2. Foreign Assistance Disbursements +

	Foreign Assistance Disbursements*	Total Development Expenditures**	Proportion of Development Expenditures Funded by Foreign Assistance
	($ Millions)	($ Millions)	(Percent)
1970	4.6	11.5	40.0
1971	6.5		
1970	4.6	11.5	40.0
1971	6.5	16.2	40.0
1972	8.0	18.6	43.0
1973	9.0	19.5	50.8
1974	14.9	32.6	45.7
1975	36.0	57.7	62.4
1976	62.0	87.5	70.9
1977	79.7	106.9	74.5
1978	82.3	144.0	57.1
1979	80.1	138.4	57.8
1980	84.0	115.6	72.6
1981	83.3	113.6	73.3

*Excludes assistance funded by private organizations.
**The official Govenment Development Budget expenditures are financed by foreign donors, the Public Treasury, and Public Enterprise surpluses.

+ World Bank; Government of Haiti, Ministry of Planning; and USAID/Haiti.

The major multilateral donors have consisted of the Inter-American Development Bank (IDB), World Bank, and the United Nations Development Program (UNDP). The major bilateral donors have been the U.S. Agency for International Development (USAID), Germany, Canada, and France (Table 3). Considerable assistance has also been provided by the World Food Program, Food and Agricultural Organization (FAO), World Health Organization (WHO), UNICEF, the Organization of American States (OAS), Inter-American Institute for Agricultural Cooperation (IICA), Nationalist China, and some 130 private voluntary organizations including CARE, Church World Service, and Catholic Relief Service (Table 4).

Table 3. Foreign Assistance Commitments* +
(\$ Millions)

	Bilateral Total	US	Germany	Canada	France	Other
1970	3.4	1.6	0.2	1.6	—	—
1971	4.6	4.3	0.2	—	—	0.1
1972	6.9	4.9	0.8	—	—	1.2
1973	9.4	7.5	0.3	—	—	1.6
1974	15.8	11.4	0.4	1.1	1.9	1.0
1975	23.1	9.3	0.8	2.5	9.0	1.5
1976	37.5	23.4	2.9	3.5	6.0	1.7
TQ**	11.9	11.9	—	—	—	—
1977	52.3	40.7	3.4	4.7	2.0	1.5
1978	50.3	27.5	9.2	8.3	2.4	2.9
1979	45.3	24.8	7.2	8.0	1.2	4.1
1980	61.6	34.6	7.6	7.6	6.2	3.5

	Multilateral Total	World Bank	IDB	UNDP	Other UN
1970	5.5	—	5.1	0.1	0.3
1971	3.4	—	—	2.5	0.9
1972	2.5	—	1.8	0.7	—
1973	10.8	—	10.0	0.5	0.3
1974	34.2	10.0	22.2	1.6	0.4
1975	24.5	20.0	2.3	2.8	0.4
1976	46.2	5.6	38.8	0.8	1.0
TQ**	21.0	16.0	5.0	—	—
1977	26.4	10.0	15.7	0.7	—
1978	39.1	31.6	5.2	2.3	—
1979	61.1	16.5	38.3	6.3	—
1980	9.8	—	4.1	3.7	2.0
1981	30.7	21.2	9.1	0.4	—
1982	73.2	44.0	17.6	6.5	5.1

*Grant obligations and loan authorizations made by governmental agencies.
**Transition quarter.

+ *U.S. Overseas Loans and Grants,* PPC, Agency for International Development, July 1, 1975-September 30, 1981 and *Congressional Presentations,* Annex III; Agency for International Development, FY73-FY84.

Table 4. External Aid to Haiti, 1977-81 +
($ Millions)

AID AGENCY	1977 Disbursements	1978 Disbursements	1979 Disbursements	1980 Disbursements	1981 Budget**
A. Multilateral					
IDB	20.2	21.4	12.1	14.0	21.7
World Bank	17.6	9.6	7.7	14.7	33.7
UNDP	3.4	3.4	7.3	8.6	11.8
World Food Program	1.6	0.8	2.7	—	3.9
FAO	—	—	—	—	0.3
WHO	1.1	0.7	0.7	2.1	0.3
UNICEF	2.0	1.4	n.a.	0.4	0.5
OAS	0.5	0.3	0.5	—	0.7
IICA	0.1	0.2	1.1	0.8	0.2
International Coffee Organization	0.1	0.1	—	—	—
EEC	—	—	—	0.5	0.2
Latin America Energy Agency	—	—	—	—	0.1
Subtotal	46.5	37.8	32.1	41.0	73.6
B. Bilateral					
USAID*	6.9	9.1	7.0	9.5	12.1
Kreditanstalt	2.6	7.0	6.6	6.1	13.4
CIDA	4.3	4.8	12.4	5.7	9.5
FAC (France)	1.9	3.5	0.8	2.1	3.2
SCCT (France)	2.1	2.4	2.7	2.6	1.8
China	0.5	0.6	0.6	—	0.6
Subtotal	18.4	27.3	30.0	26.0	40.5
C. Private Aid					
CARE	3.6	2.1	0.9	0.8	7.0
Haiti Christian Service	1.9	3.5	2.0	0.6	2.2
Catholic Relief Services	1.9	6.4	1.0	1.5	1.6
Subtotal	7.3	12.0	3.9	2.9	10.8
D. Other External	—	—	—	0.4	6.4
TOTAL	72.2	77.1	65.9	70.4	131.3

*Excluding PL480 Title 1

**Budget figures are not strictly comparable with disbursements

+ Government of Haiti, Ministry of Planning, and World Bank.

The foreign donors provided the lion's share of the funding for the public investment program which has been implemented primarily through Haitian Governmental agencies. Hence, the most appropriate way to obtain an overview of where the assistance has gone is to review the total public development program. The Government's first five-year plan (1972-1976) gave priority to rebuilding the country's infrastructure. The government and international agencies alike believed that the development of roads was a prerequisite to Haitian development. The integration of the economy and the development of the agriculture and tourism sectors were dependent upon the improvement of the road network. Outside of Port-au-Prince and its suburbs there were fewer than 200 kilometers of well-surfaced highways and 100 kilometers of once paved but poorly maintained roads. The latter and almost all other roads were impassable at certain times of the year. Provincial towns were consequently isolated from each other and from Port-au-Prince, and the flow of goods and people was severely restricted.

As a result, construction, rehabilitation, and maintenance of roads received the largest share of public investment and official foreign assistance. The transportation sector absorbed 37 percent of development expenditures during the first planning period (1972-1976) and 29 percent during the second plan (1977-1981) (Table 5). The Southern Road linking Les Cayes at the tip of the southern peninsula to Port-au-Prince (196 kilometers) was completed with IDB financing. The World Bank financed the rebuilding of the Northern Road running from Port-au-Prince to the seaport of Cap Haitian (274 kilometers). The French assisted with the highway linking Jacmel on the southern coast with Léogane (75 kilometers). Secondary road rebuilding received support from the World Bank, IDBN, and USAID. The Government's road maintenance service (SEPRRN) was built with USAID funding into one of the few effective governmental organizations serving the rural hinterland. Transportation investments also included the expansion of the Port-au-Prince harbor. The Government completed the first phase with its own resources. The second phase was financed by IDB.

Increasingly severe power shortages and blackouts in the Port-au-Prince area in the 1960's prompted the Government to invest in the hydro-electric plant at the Péligre Dam during the early 1970's. Additional generating capacity for the capital was provided by diesel plants installed during the second planning period (1977-81) with foreign assistance. Electric power generation capacity was increased in a number of provincial towns.

Telecommunications also received heavy emphasis during the first planning period (10 percent of expenditures). While the builk of the service expansions were in Port-au-Prince, some extension of inter-urban services was made with donor assistance.

Table 5. Sectoral Allocation of Public Investment Expenditures, 1972-81 +

	Plan I (Actual)	Plan II (Actual)
Directly Productive Programs	1972/76	1977/81
Agriculture	9.7	17.3
Mines and quarries	0.5	1.1
Industry and crafts	2.9	5.0
Tourism	0.5	0.3
Subtotal	13.6	23.7
Economic Infrastructure		
Power supply	8.6	15.3
Transportation	37.4	29.2
Communications	10.4	3.8
Subtotal	56.4	48.3
Social Infrastructure		
Water supply and sewerage	4.0	1.2
Urban development/housing	0.3	0.8
Education	5.2	7.6
Health	6.7	7.5
Community development	8.7	8.0
Subtotal	24.9	25.1
Other		
Administration	5.1	2.9
Total (%)	100.0	100.0
Total ($ Millions)	$216.4	$618.7

+ Ministry of Planning and World Bank.

Social infrastructure investments made-up 25 percent of development expenditures over the 1972-81 decade. In view of the growing population in Port-au-Prince, there was a clear need to improve the water supply system. IDB assistance provided for major improvements and expansions of the system managed by Centrale Autonome Métropolitaine d'Eau Potable (CAMEP). The needs were such that even though many dozens of small scale water systems were provided for rural communities, the vast majority of the rural population remained without potable water.

With contributions by public and private aid agencies in the international community, hundreds of schools, dispensaries, and community development centers were built or rehabilitated in rural areas. With USAID support, the *National Service for Endemic Diseases* (SNEM) provided nationwide coverage of malaria control activities and a project designed to extend Governmental health services to 70 percent of rural Haitians was begun.

Supplementary food provisions (U.S. PL 480 Title II, Germany, and World Food Program donations) were directed toward school feeding, food for work projects, maternal child health and disaster relief. The school feeding program was (and remains) the largest. Almost 50 percent of all primary level schools in Haiti participated in the program, and it has been estimated that close to 70 percent of all primary children have received this needed assistance.

Public sector investment in agriculture and other directly productive sectors was low (14 percent) during the first plan period (1972-76). The second plan (1977-81) called for an increased emphasis on agriculture and industry. While actual expenditures in these sectors increased less than planned, almost 24 percent was actually disbursed over the 1977-81 period. The largest increase went to agriculture. Agricultural disbursements as a proportion of total development expenditures went from 10 percent during the first plan to over 17 percent during the second plan. Agricultural projects included institutional development projects with the Ministry of Agriculture (USAID) and the School of Agriculture (Canada), credit and technical assistance to the Agricultural Credit Bureau (USAID) and Institut pour le Développement Agricole et Industriel (IDB), and support for a variety of regional agricultural development organizations, including the Organization for the Development of the Artibonite Valley (IDB, China), Organization for the Development of the North (World Bank, Germany), Haitian Community Organization Coordinating Agency (USAID, CARE, Germany), the southern regional organization DRIPP (Canada), and Gonaïves Plain Development Organization (Germany).

In addition to the sectoral support programs, the foreign community provided considerable support for administrative reforms and institution building actions. To increase public savings and to channel them towards efficient investment, considerable efforts were made to improve financial management and to strengthen government departments and autonomous organizations in charge of planning and implementation of public investment projects. This proved to be an extremely difficult task. A unified Public Treasury account was finally established with the Central Bank of Haiti and progress was made to include in the Government's development budget all planned public development projects. While these were significant achievements, much remained to be done to establish effective governmental planning and implementation of development projects.

In addition, the fiscal reforms experienced difficulty with removing the para-fiscal functions of the Régie du Tabac (the government trading company). Although deprived of its taxing power over 46 products, the Régie du Tabac still charged "commissions" on six products (cement, flour, sugar, vegetable oil, cigarettes and matches), which accounted for 80 percent of its pre-1979 operating income. While these revenues were supposed to be fully turned over to Ministry of Finance control, the reform-mandated transfers were less than complete.

Impact of Foreign Assistance

The large increases in foreign assistance over the last decade were accompanied by economic growth as measured by changes in real gross domestic product (GDP). Haiti's real GDP grew at an average annual rate of 4.3 percent during the 1970's, up from an average annual rate of only 0.2 percent in the previous decade. Although world-wide recession has effectively blocked growth of the Haitian economy since 1981, it is anticipated that with the U.S. recovery the Haitian economy will return to the growth path of the 1970's.

While the full rate of progress achieved by the Haitian economy during the past decade would not have been possible without foreign assistance, it is clear that other factors were very important. Haiti's economic recovery from the stagnation of the 1960's began prior to the foreign assistance build-up. Foreign assistance commitments and expenditures only began to increase in 1970, with the major increases taking place in the 1974-1977 period. The Haitian economic recovery, as measured by changes in real GDP, began in 1968. Private sector investment increased rapidly from 1.7 percent of GDP in 1967 to 10.0 percent of GDP in 1973 (Table 6). The recovery was led by the expansion of small scale export oriented assembly industries, the upswing in tourism, and the growth of the construction industry. Gross exports of light manufactured goods to the U.S. grew from $3.8 million in 1968 to $12.2 million in 1970 and $23 million in 1972. Air tourist arrivals increased dramatically during this same period and

Table 6. Foreign Assistance, Investment, and Real GDP Growth +

| | Foreign Assistance Commitments (% of GDP) | Foreign Assistance Expenditures (% of GDP) | Gross Domestic Investment | | | Real GDP Annual Percentage Changes |
			Public (% of GDP)	Private (% of GDP)	Total (% of GDP)	
1965	NA	*	3.6	2.8	6.4	2.1
1966	1.1	*	3.1	2.6	5.7	-0.6
1967	1.4	*	4.2	1.7	5.9	-2.1
1968	1.0	*	3.0	3.2	6.2	3.1
1969	1.0	*	2.2	4.9	7.1	3.8
1970	2.2	1.1	2.1	8.5	10.6	0.1
1971	1.8	1.5	2.7	7.4	10.1	6.3
1972	2.0	1.7	3.0	8.8	11.8	0.1
1973	3.4	1.6	3.4	10.0	13.4	3.0
1974	7.2	2.1	4.8	9.6	14.4	3.2
1975	6.1	4.5	7.3	6.5	13.8	-1.4
1976	10.2	6.3	8.5	5.2	13.7	8.4
1977	8.6	7.1	9.9	4.2	14.1	1.9
1978	7.7	7.0	10.1	4.8	14.9	4.7
1979	8.3	6.3	8.7	5.4	14.1	3.6
1980	4.5	5.7	8.2	6.9	15.1	5.4
1981	5.8	5.2	7.0	5.9	12.9	-2.1

*Less than one percent of GDP.
+ Clarence Zuvekas, Jr., *Agricultural Development in Haiti.* Agency for International Development, May 1978; and World Bank.

surpassed the historic peaks established in the late 1950's. The growth in construction is illustrated by the increase of value added in construction at annual rates in excess of 20 percent between 1968 and 1973. Furthermore, cement sales rose from 70,000 tons in 1968 to an estimated 130,000 tons in 1970. Almost all of the growth that initially occurred was a result of external demand factors and the improved political environment in Haiti. In the case of the assembly industries, improved demand conditions in the U.S. economy were of key importance. Tourism's growth reflected the buoyancy of the world economy and the more favorable international perception of Haiti. Much of the residential construction activity was financed by remittances from Haitians living abroad. The international jet airport, which opened in 1966 in Port-au-Prince, and the increases in electrical generating capacity in 1971-73 were also of importance to both the assembly industry and the tourist sector.

While the decade's growth may have been initiated by non-foreign aid forces, foreign assistance was critical to the maintenance and acceleration of growth. As foreign assistance increased over the decade, the growth rate of real GDP advanced from 3.8 percent per year during the 1970-75 period to 4.5 percent annually over the second half of the decade (OAS 1982). The growth of foreign assistance largely financed the increases in gross domestic investment, which grew from 10.6 percent of GDP in 1970 to 15.1 percent in 1980 (Table 6). Foreign assistance funding amounted to 70 percent of public investment and 44 percent of total domestic investment over the second half of the decade (Table 6).

The investments made in physical infrastructure (roads, power, water, sewage, and ports) were essential for the continued expansion of manufacturing, tourism, and residential construction. Had the investments not been made in public health measures to control malaria, tourism's growth would have been aborted as malaria rapidly reached epidemic proportions. The high growth rates over the decade of production and earnings in the utilities, construction, transportation, and government sectors were largely due to the foreign donor financed investments (Table 7).

Table 7. Gross Domestic Production and Growth by Sector, 1970-80 +
(in percentage)

	Contribution to GDP		Average Annual Growth Rate
	1970	1980	1970-1980
Agriculture	44.7	32.8	1.1
Mining	2.8	1.3	-1.3
Manufacturing	13.0	16.7	6.9
Utilities	0.1	0.3	14.9
Construction	2.7	4.7	10.2
Wholesale and Retail Trade	16.8	18.9	5.5
Transportation and Communicaton	1.8	3.0	9.5
Financial Services	5.3	5.1	3.8
Government	5.6	8.3	8.4
Other Services	7.6	8.9	5.9
Total GDP	100.0	100.0	4.3

+ *Statistical Bulletin of the OAS,* 1982.

The economic growth that took place over the decade had significant but limited impacts on the welfare of the population. The best available data indicate that real per capita annual income (1980 US $) in Haiti increased from $210 in 1970 to $270 in 1980. In spite of this growth, poverty remains a desperate problem. The World Bank estimated that in 1979 more than 80 percent of the population had an average income of under $150. Conditions of absolute poverty affect more than half of Port-au-Prince's population and virtually all of the rural agricultural population.

While the decade's growth has not touched significant proportions of the rural and urban poor, many of whom are indeed desperate and worse off as a result of natural disasters and economic dislocations, signs of limited but broad based social welfare advances are present. Even though only rudimentary statistical data are available, the evidence as published by the World Bank points to significant advances in health, education, private consumption, and energy consumption (Table 8).

Table 8. Haitian Social Welfare Indicators +

	1960	1980
Life expectancy at birth, years	44	53
Crudes death rate per thousand population	20	14
Infant mortality (0-1 year) per thousand	182	115
Child death (1-4) per thousand	47	18
Population per physician	9230	5940 (1977)
Population per nursing person	4020	2940
Percentage of age group enrolled in primary school	46	62 (1979)
Percentage of age group enrolled in secondary school	4	15 (1979)
Adult literacy (percentage)	15	23 (1977)
Average annual growth of private consumption (percentage)	-1.0 (1960-70)	3.5 (1979-80)
Energy consumption per capita (kilograms of coal equivalent)	36	57 (1978)

+ *World Development Report 1982,* World Bank, 1982.

Furthermore, long-term observers note the increased prevalence of such items as tin roofs, radios, bicycles, watches, shoes, decent clothes, etc. in both urban and rural areas. The signs of severe malnutrition that were so common in the 1960's have decreased. World Bank data suggest that the deterioration in per capita food consumption that occurred during the 1960's was in fact reversed during the 1970's. The per capita supply of calories, as a percentage of requirements, which declined from 91.4 percent in 1960 to 86.8 percent in 1970, increased to 92.1 percent in 1977. Likewise the per capita supply of grams of protein per day decreased from 48.7 to 47.0 in the 1960's, but then increased to 50.1 in 1977. While the food deficit and malnutrition problems that remain are of major proportions, much of what progress was made is directly attributable to the donor food aid, which ranged between $15 and $20 million per year in the second half of the 1970's decade and amounted to approximately 40 percent of food imports.

The reasons for the limited economic gains attributable to the donor-assisted development are varied. First, the resources provided by the international community were relatively small in comparison to the problems. While the total assistance provided over the 1970 decade amounted to $541 million (1980 $ prices) and represented on average 4 percent of GDP, in per capita terms the assistance was approximately $12 per year. The only way that this level of assistance could be expected to make significant impacts on Haitian poverty is through its leverage effects on Haitian resources. Unfortunately, the success of foreign donors leveraging Haitian governmental reforms and resources for broad based development has been limited.

Secondly, the foreign donor encouraged growth was very unbalanced. Development focused largely on the urban-industrial capital, Port-au-Prince. Outside of a few success stories, including the development of self-sufficiency in rice production, agriculture largely stagnated, with a 1.1 percent annual average growth rate. In spite of increased emphasis on agriculture during the second half of the decade and the completion of the major highway projects, agricultural production growth actually fell from 1.28 percent annually over the 1970-75 period to 0.77 percent for the 1975-80 period (OAS 1982). As a result, with a population growth rate of approximately 1.7 percent, per capita food production actually fell 8 percent over the decade. The limited growth in agriculture was largely due to the deteriorating physical resource base (deforestation, soil erosion, siltation of irrigation systems and soil exhaustion), limited capital investments, and the difficulties of introducing modern technology given the population pressures on the land and the low literacy and educational levels of the farmers.[3] Also, the institutional difficulties of delivering agricultural extension services through the Ministry of Agriculture have been a major source of frustration. Had it not been for the capital and technical assistance provided by the foreign donors, it is reasonable to assume that there would have been absolute declines in agricultural production and incomes.

Finally, it should also be noted that the donor financed expansions in investment did not lead to a complementary expansion of private sector investment. As a percent of GDP, private investment actually fell off as donor supported public investment accelerated in the middle of the decade (Table 6). In part this reflects the limited capital requirements of the assembly re-export sector (which expanded rapidly throughout the 1970's) and the excess capacity that resulted from manufacturing sector investments made prior to 1975. However, it also reflects the increasing tendency of the Haitian Government to become directly involved in industrial activities that serve the domestic market. The Government made major investments in a variety of the enterprises, including flour milling, cotton ginning, edible oil refining, public transportation, telecommunications, sugar refining, fishing, etc. Many of these investments have proven to be either unprofitable or only profitable because of monopoly rights provided by the Government. As a result, they have reduced the level of government saving, which is necessary to fund future development, and/or they have blocked private investments. The donors have recently come to see the dangers of this and have urged governmental restraint and disinvestments.

Current Development Plans and Programs: 3rd Five-Year Plan

Preparation of the Government's 1981-86 Five Year Plan facilitated a thorough assessment of Haiti's basic social and economic problems and has provided a framework to articulate policies and programs for the 1980's. The Plan explains past failures by slow productivity growth and inefficiency in agriculture, land erosion, and inequalities of income distribution. As a precondition for future success, in face of these problems, the Plan emphasizes administrative reforms to increase the training and efficiency of civil servants, the development of education and research, and the creation of conditions for the retention of skilled labor.

Three objectives are established in the Plan:

1. Real GDP growth of 4 percent per year, with investment growing at 4.7 percent per year. Within this objective the first priority is to increase agricultural production to counter malnutrition. The second priority is to develop industries oriented toward the local market while encouraging the assembly re-export industries to continue to expand.

2. Job creation, by encouraging the use of labor intensive techniques in agriculture, industry, and rural public works.
3. More balanced distribution of growth between metropolitan Port-au-Prince and the provinces. A greater regionalization of government organization and services is envisaged to achieve a better allocation of resources and to promote local initiative and responsibility.

The sectoral distribution of planned spending reflects an increased emphasis on agriculture. The Plan proposes an absolute and relative increase in agriculture, from an average annual level of 17 percent of total development expenditures during the 1976-81 planning period to a projected level of 20 percent of development expenditures during the 1982-86 period (Table 9). The agricultural sector has been the Achilles' heel of the Haitian economy. Its stagnation has adversely affected growth in other sectors and caused serious imbalances in the country's economic and social development. These imbalances are reflected in the concentration of income in the hands of the urban elite (0.4 percent of the population receive an estimated 44 percent of national income) and by the over-emphasis of government spending on the capital (Port-au-Prince receives some 87 percent of government expenditures but generates only 40 percent of government revenues). Hence, the increased emphasis on agriculture has been welcomed by the foreign donor community and will be encouraged with a high proportion of donor financing (Table 9).

The electric power sector is allocated second highest priority in the Plan, with 18 percent of the development budget. The Plan calls for further increases in generating and distribution capacity in Port-au-Prince, completion of the la Chapelle and Guayamouc I hydroplants, expansion of power in provincial towns, and the beginning of construction of the remaining hydroplants on the Artibonite river. The donors recognize the need to expand electric generating capacity for urban-industrial growth. The problems of limited arable land, small and fragmented holdings, increasing population pressure, limited rural infrastructure, and growing soil erosion are forcing urbanization on an increasing proportion of the population. Hence, urban industrial infrastructure investments, including electric power, will be heavily supported by donor financing.

The proposed investments in the transport sector for the period 1982-86 provide for the continuation of the rehabilitation of secondary roads with World Bank, IDB, and USAID support. The World Bank will also finance the construction of coastal shipping harbors and purchase of some road maintenance equipment.

Table 9. Sectoral Allocation of the Third Development Plan, 1982-86 +

Sector	Total Allocation ($ Millions, Constant 1981 Prices)		To be financed from Domestic Resources (%)	External Resources (%)*
Agriculture	$218.0	20.0	20.0	80.0
Electric Power	197.3	18.1	26.3	73.7
Transportation	171.1	15.7	27.8	72.2
Health	87.2	8.0	12.3	87.7
Education	83.9	7.7	28.7	81.3
Urban development & housing	56.7	5.2	12.4	87.6
Industry and crafts	54.5	5.0	50.8	49.2
Community development	54.5	5.0	8.0	92.0
Communications	50.1	4.6	93.2	4.8
Drinking water/sewerage	42.5	3.9	17.8	82.2
General Government	41.4	3.8	71.4	28.6
Mines and quarries	21.8	2.0	30.7	69.3
Tourism	10.0	1.0	53.8	46.2
Total (%)		100.0	32.5	67.5
Total Expenditure	1089.8			

*Includes PL 480 Title I resources provided by USAID.
+ *Plan Quinquennal de Développement Economique et Social,* 1981-86, Vol. II, and *Budget d'Execution des Programmes et Projets de Développement,* 1981-86, Vol. I, Government of Haiti.

In the health sector, the Plan calls for the expansion of government health services to rural areas, major campaigns against endemic diseases, improvement of nutrition, maternal and child care, and family planning. These development activities are to be primarily funded by the foreign donors. However, the proposed expansion of rural health services raises the difficult question of how the Government can afford the associated increases in recurrent costs. Given the country's poverty, least cost alternatives must be sought that more fully utilize the numerous foreign and indigenous private voluntary organizations and the resources available in the beneficiary communities.

Education in Haiti has traditionally focused on the needs of the urban elite, with only limited opportunities available for the rural and urban poor.

Since 1979, the Government has been implementing a major reform of the educational system. The new strategy places increased emphasis on practical subjects, promoting efficiency and utilization of education to improve productivity and life of both the urban and rural poor. For the 1982-86 Planning period, the reform will focus on primary education. Quantitatively, the objective is to raise the present 42.3 percent (net) primary school rate and to raise the rate of student progression through the system from its current level of 46 percent. The use of Creole in the first cycle of primary education may be instrumental in improving the efficiency of the system. The donors have been instrumental in the development of these reforms and can be expected to provide continuing assistance. Given Haiti's deteriorating natural resource base and the obstacles that illiteracy poses for agricultural and urban industrial development, basic and applied education will increasingly be seen as a priority need for continuing development.

Of the remaining sectors, the foreign donors are projected to supply the bulk of the resources for urban development and housing, community development, and drinking water and sewerage. Overall, the Plan calls for foreign assistance to provide for 67.5 percent of the 1982-86 development program, up to 66 percent in the previous planning period (1977-81). In absolute terms, foreign assistance is projected to increase from a level of $143 million in 1982 to $263 million in 1986 (Table 10). Compared to 1981 foreign assistance disbursements of $83.3 million, these projections of required foreign assistance represent significant increases. When expressed in constant 1981 dollars, total foreign assistance over the 1982-86 planning period ($736 million) is 44 percent greater than total assistance provided over the previous planning period ($511 million). This rate of increase is less than the 114 percent increase in total foreign assistance that was disbursed during the 1977-81 period compared to the 1972-76 period.

Total development expenditures are projected by the Plan to increase from $210 million in 1982 to $392 million in 1986 (Table 10). In constant 1981 dollars, a total of $1.09 billion is projected for all development projects during the 1982-86 period. This represents an increase of approximately 40 percent over total development expenditures during the previous planning period (1977-81). While this level of development spending for the period annually amounts to only $40 per capita, it is probable that only 60-70 percent of the proposed development budget will be actually disbursed. The reasons for this include: limited Haitian Government savings, balance of payment problems, increasing recurrent costs of development projects, misallocations of domestic development resources, inefficient disbursement procedures, and foreign donor concerns with Government of Haiti performance.

Table 10. 1982-86 Public Development Budget +
($ Millions)

	1982	1983	1984	1985	1986	Total
I. Current Prices						
Public Investment	210.0	250.5	290.8	337.4	391.6	1480.3
Domestic Resources	67.0	81.1	94.0	110.6	128.4	481.1
Foreign Assistance Required	143.0	169.4	196.8	226.8	263.2	999.2
II. In Constant 1981 Prices*						
Public Investment	190.9	206.9	218.4	230.5	243.1	1089.8
Domestic Resources	60.9	67.0	70.6	75.6	79.7	353.8
Foreign Assistance Required	130.0	139.9	147.8	154.9	163.4	736.0

*Assumes 10 percent per year price increases.
+ *Plan Quinquennal de Developpement Economique et Social, 1981-86 and Budget d'Execution des Programmes et Projets de Developpement, 1981-86, Vol. I.,* Government of Haiti.

Foreign donors normally require that the beneficiaries make a contribution to the foreign assistance that is provided. The usual minimum counterpart requirement is 25 percent. While this may be waived by some donors in the case of relatively least developed countries (Haiti is so classified), the usual practice is to require counterpart contributions to insure host government support, involvement, and institution building. To generate the funds for its counterpart contribution to donor projects, the Government of Haiti has three potential sources: (1) PL 480 Title I sales, (2) deficit financing, and (3) government savings. Revenues generated from the sale of PL 480 Title I commodities have provided for approximately a third of the Government's counterpart in recent years.

Government deficit financing has also been a significant source for counterpart contributions. Government spending in excess of revenues became very pronounced in 1980 and 1981. Unfortunately, the large deficits financed by Central Bank expansions of credit led to excessive domestic inflation and balance of payments problems. The balance of payments crisis became so severe that the Government was forced to seek financial assistance from the International Monetary Fund (IMF). Along with the $38 million provided for in the August 1982 Stanby Agreement came IMF mandated limitations on government deficit financing. The Government has basically been barred from seeking international commercial financing and domestic financing has been severely limited. Future IMF agreements will most probably limit deficit financing even more. Hence. deficit financing as a source of counterpart funding will be minimal during much of the current five-year planning period.

The remaining source of counterpart financing, government savings, requires that the Government generate a surplus of current revenues over expenditures. Unfortunately, general government expenditures have been in excess of tax and other revenues over the past three years. Although surpluses generated by government owned business enterprises have largely offset the general government deficits, their total or public sector savings has been diminishing and was even negative for 1981. While the IMF mandated fiscal austerity program has had the effect of improving the Government's saving performance, the short-run prospects for large governmental savings are bleak. As a result, the Government has had to cut back on Public Treasury support of the development budget. Most recently, this support has been cut from $37 million budgeted in FY1982 to $24 million in FY1983. With the diminished domestic counterpart funds, the overall development budget has had to be correspondingly reduced. The impact on the actual development program has been considerably more severe than might be implied from the overall budget reductions, since the Government focused most of the cuts on operating and supply expenses in an attempt to save personnel positions. The resultant shortages of fuel, parts, supplies, etc. have blocked productive work on a number of development projects.

While the problem of insufficient counterpart funds has recently acted as a constraint on foreign assistance disbursements, the problem has been compounded by misallocations of scarce domestic financing. If the Government were to allocate its investment resources to those projects which would attract the highest share of donor concessionary financing, there would be sufficient counterpart for expanded donor assistance. Unfortunately, the Government has concentrated significant amounts of its domestic resources on projects in the industrial and communication sectors with little or no donor assistance. Many of these projects have not been supported by the donors because they are uneconomical and/or inconsistent with Haiti's development priorities.

Increasing recurrent costs associated with development projects have also become a major concern to the Government and donors. Given the poverty and difficulties of significantly raising government revenues, many development projects which have high recurrent operating costs (e.g. health, education, agriculture) imply future financial burdens which are in excess of probable levels of government revenues. While solutions to this problem may, in some cases, be found in donor acceptance of recurrent cost obligations and the encouragement of cost sharing by the private sector, the mounting recurrent cost burden will effectively preclude implementation of many otherwise sound development projects.

Inefficient disbursement procedures have been an impediment to implementation of planned development activities. The disbursement process, which involves the Ministries of Planning, Finance, and the Executing Ministry and Agency, has become overly cumbersome and time consuming. As a result, budgeted development funds have not been made fully available to planned project activities. Unless streamlined, disbursement rates will continue to be adversely affected.

A final reason for the expectation that only 60-70 percent of the development budget program will be fulfilled has to do with donor perceptions of the Haitian Government's performance and commitment to development. A history of fiscal mismanagement, investments in uneconomical projects against the advice of the donors, bureaucratic inefficiencies, a personnel system dominated by political patronage, general inability to deliver services in the rural hinterlands, misuse of project funds and supplies, etc. have made many donors resistant to increasing their support of the Government. Furthermore, a continuing preoccupation at the political leadership level of the donor governments and the donor organizations is with the periodic violation of the human rights of Haitian citizens and the reluctance of the Government of Haiti to take significant and measurable steps toward a democratic society. While recent attempts at fiscal, administrative, and human rights reforms have been strongly supported by the donors, many fear that significant progress may be all too short-lived. The Government's long-run commitment to efficient, equitable, and socially accountable government and broad based development needs to be rigorously demonstrated over a period of years if the international community is to significantly change its views about the Government and the appropriate level of support to be provided.

Alternative Future Development Scenarios

Alternative scenarios of Haiti's economic future for the next several decades may be developed using differing assumptions concerning Government of Haiti policies and donor responses. First, assuming a basic continuation of the *status quo* in terms of government economic and social policies and the associated foreign assistance levels, total investment (including private investment) could reasonably be expected to remain in the 13 to 14 percent range. While recovery from the effects of the U.S. recession and balance of payments problems should produce short-run spurts of growth, especially in export-oriented light manufacturing, depressed coffee and cocoa prices and the cessation of bauxite mining suggest that Haiti's 4.3 growth rate of the 1970's may be difficult to achieve in the 1980's and 1990's. Under these assumptions, national income (as measured by real GNP) would probably grow at an annual rate in the range of 3.0 to 3.5 percent. Even if the 3.5 percent rate were used to project where the economy would be in 1990 and 2000, the results are not encouraging. With an expanding population, which is projected by the World Bank to increase at a rate of 2.0 percent per year, the population will be approximately 6 million in 1990 and 7 million in the year 2000. As a result, real per capita GNP (\$ 1980 dollars) would increase from \$270 in 1980 to \$319 in 1990 and \$368 in the year 2000 (Table 11). Haiti would remain among the World Bank's grouping of low-income economies, which includes India, Pakistan, and much of Africa. The stark contrast with neighboring countries' per capita incomes would remain (e.g. Jamaica \$1040, Dominican Republic \$1160, United States \$11,360).

As an alternative scenario, it might be assumed that adverse Government of Haiti social, economic, and/or political policy decisions resulted in a withdrawal of the foreign donor community. A return to the stagnation that occurred in the 1960's could well result. With a real GNP growth rate of only 0.2 percent per year, per capita GNP would decline from \$270 in 1980 to \$230 in 1990 and \$193 in 2000. The consequences in terms of human suffering and social, economic, and political dislocation would be immense.

More optimistically, one could assume that the Government of Haiti seriously committed itself to and implemented a broad array of policy reforms and that the donors responded with a doubling of foreign assistance. The improved political and economic environment could be expected to generate a large return flow of Haitian capital and professionals currently living abroad. Foreign investments could also be expected to expand rapidly. As a result the economy might reasonably be anticipated to grow at double the *status quo* rate, or 7 percent per year.[4] This would generate per capita GNP levels of \$444 in 1990 and \$717 in the year 2000 (Table 11). The impact of this rate of development on the social and economic welfare of the population would be immense. The increased demand for goods and services would significantly improve income levels and employment opportunities for all social and economic classes in Haiti.

The control over which scenario will actually prevail lies largely in the hands of the leadership of the Government of Haiti. For the optimistic scenario to become a reality, the Government would need to commit itself to the following: (1) increased government revenues, (2) Ministry of Finance budget control of all government revenues and expenditures, (3) administrative reform, (4) rationalized private sector policies, and (5) human and political rights reforms.

Table 11. Haiti's Projected Population and GNP Per Capita

Year	Population	GNP Per Capita ($ 1980 prices)		
		Assuming 3.5% GNP Annual Growth Rate	Assuming 0.2% GNP Annual Growth Rate	Assuming 7.0% GNP Annual Growth Rate
1980	5,009,000	$270	$270	$270
1990	5,986,000	319	230	444
2000	7,297,000	368	193	717

1. Increased government revenues are essential to generate the domestic counterpart required by an expanded donor assistance program. The low level of tax revenues (about 9 percent of GDP in 1980 and 1981) and the low effective rates of taxation of the highest income groups (e.g., the richest one percent of the population is estimated to pay only 6.2 percent of their income in taxes), suggests that there is considerable room for increased tax revenues. There should also be room to reduce the excessive tax burdens on the poor (e.g. coffee tax) so as to make the overall tax structure less regressive. While efforts to reform tax rates and administration have recently been initiated with donor assistance (IMF and USAID), full implementation will require increased technical assistance and a high priority commitment on the part of the Government. The pricing of goods and services produced by government owned enterprises (e.g. water and telephones) is also a potential source of increased revenues which should be carefully reviewed and revised.

2. Ministry of Finance budgetary control of all government revenues and expenditures must be fully and rigorously implemented. The complete integration of all revenue sources into the budget, including the Regie du Tabac and other government enterprises, and the centralization of spending authority in the Treasury is essential to the ongoing fiscal reform efforts of the Government. The budget allocations should demonstrate a serious commitment to the development program. This would include enhancing employees' productivity by allocating a higher proportion of the budget to needed non-personnel expenses. Within the development budget, counterpart funds should be allocated to projects which will maximize donor assistance. Finally, the disbursement process should be streamlined to avoid development project delays, etc.

3. Administrative reform is essential if the government bureaucracy is to effectively manage an enlarged development effort. Civil service reforms, including rationalized hiring and performance standards, improved pay scales, and increased training, are critical. Administrative decentralization

and deconcentration of government services are vital to a more balanced development program. The recent passage of administrative reform legislation, including the law creating the administrative structure for regionalization of the government development program, stems from a broadly based recognition of the need for administrative reform and decentralized development.

4. The Government's private sector policies need to be rationalized if the private sector is to realize its full potential for Haiti's development. The Government should promote investment by increasing competitive opportunities in the economy. Monopoly rights, in the form of import restrictions and prohibitions, should be replaced by import tariff rates that diminish over time and thus allow for increasing competition. With competition, whether actual or potential, most government price controls could be eliminated without adversely affecting consumers. The Government should refrain from making future investments in the industrial sector and liquidate past investments where feasible. These government investments, with their associated controls and manipulations of the free market, inhibit private sector investment and expansion.

5. The protection of human rights and measurable steps toward a democratic society are basic preconditions for an improved international image of Haiti. In addition to its importance to donor assistance levels, an improved international image would yield increased tourism and foreign private investment. The potential pay off to the economy and the Government of a long-run commitment to the protection of human rights and socially accountable government is immense.

The donor community should respond to Government initiatives to implement these and other needed reforms with timely infusions of technical and financial assistance increases. Reforms having high short-run political and economic costs may be more rapidly and vigorously implemented if assistance that partially offsets these costs is forthcoming. In addition, the donor community should also consider supporting recurrent operating costs associated with development projects. This is especially true for education, which should receive increased emphasis in the future.

Donors should also consider a more flexible view on domestic counterpart requirements. In addition to counterpart itself, the Government's contribution to the development effort could take the form of implementation of costly reforms, e.g., a coffee tax reduction.

Given the limited resources available to both the donors and the Government, increased emphasis should be placed on the development of viable private sector activities. Many private sector investments in an economy as small as Haiti's depend upon international trade opportunities. A relaxation of import restrictions in the U.S. and other industrial markets could well be the most important policy reform affecting Haiti's prospects for eventual self-sustaining development.

NOTES

[1] Economic and social data on Haiti have a very weak statistical base and hence should be interpreted with caution. The various agencies of the Government of Haiti and the international community often generate data which are not in full agreement with each other. Unless otherwise noted, data reported in this paper are World Bank estimates, which are largely derived from the most reliable Government of Haiti data.

[2] Estimating the amount of foreign assistance is especially difficult because of the proliferation of donor agencies with a variety of accounting systems. The various estimates of foreign assistance for FY 1980 include the estimate by the World Bank of $76.8 million, IMF estimate of $69.0 million net, UNDP estimate of $98.9 million, and USAID/Haiti estimate of $84.0 million.

[3] The sizeable volume of donor provided food aid, which has ranged between $15 and $20 million a year since 1976, might be expected to have had some negative impacts on food production incentives in Haiti. However, this has not been significant because the intense and growing demand for food in Haiti has caused food prices to rise dramatically during the past decade. As a result farmers have made significant shifts into food crops from cash crops.

[4] Growth at an annual rate of 7 percent would be very difficult to achieve. The averages over the 1970's for low income countries and middle income countries were 4.6 and 5.6, respectively. However, a number of countries did achieve rates in this range, including Malawi (6.3), Kenya (6.5), Indonesia (7.6), Egypt (7.4), Thailand (7.2), Ecuador (8.8), Korea (9.5), etc.

OFFSHORE ASSEMBLY IN HAITI

JOSEPH GRUNWALD
LESLIE DELATOUR
KARL VOLTAIRE

Haiti is among the poorest countries of the world. The country with the next lowest income level in the Americas, Honduras, has more than twice Haiti's per capita GNP, which was estimated by the World Bank in 1979 at $260. The Dominican Republic, with whom Haiti shares the island of Hispaniola and which had a population just a few percent higher than Haiti's 5 million in 1979, has earnings of nearly four times as much per person (World Bank 1980).

Manufacturing in Haiti is of recent origin. It is confined primarily to the processing of food, beverages, agricultural materials, and basic items such as shoes, clothing, soap, and cement. National income figures—as well as other statistics—are still rudimentary, but the World Bank estimates the contribution of manufacturing to GDP to have reached 13.3 percent by 1979.[1] Most of the increase took place during the 1970's, after a decade of near stagnation.

The Importance of Assembly Production in Haiti

The growth of assembly industries has been an important element in the recent dynamism of the Haitian economy. Between 1970 and 1980 the value added in Haitian assembly plants increased by over 23 times or at an average annual rate of 37 percent (Table IV-1). Even in real terms, the growth was 22 percent per year (deflated by the implicit import price deflator of the United States). In part, the dramatic upsurge was aided by government incentives and by changes in the political environment.

Assembly activities have benefited from two types of incentives: new production firms are exempt from income taxes for five years and are then subject to partial payments in increasing yearly proportions so that after ten years they must pay the full tax; the other incentive is a franchise granted to assembly firms which exempts them from any tariff duties on imports. The franchise is given indefinitely for production that is entirely exported, covering offshore assembly production. For production of goods sold on the domestic market, the franchise is given on a temporary basis because the firm is expected to use local materials as inputs after the first few years.

Haiti has no free trade zones which cater to export industries. A successful government-run industrial park in Port-au-Prince has emerged as a result of the growth of assembly plants rather than contributing to their emergence.[2]

Thus, unlike other countries, Haiti's assembly production is not an "in-bond" activity in the strict sense. Although assembly production cannot be sold domestically, any firm can get a duty-free import franchise whether it exports or not. More than half of all manufacturing output (including assembly) is exported, and there are many firms that produce both for the home as well as the export market.

With the advent of a new government in the early 1970's, investors' perceptions of political stability improved.[3] The new environment permitted the huge wage gap between Haiti and the United States to become an enormous attraction for offshore production. Many Haitian professionals and entrepreneurs who were abroad during the previous regime returned and established businesses designed to assemble U.S. components.

While there are no exact figures, estimates by the U.S. embassy in Haiti and the World Bank put the number of assembly plants in 1980 at 200, employing roughly 60,000 persons. All of the assembly plants are in Port-au-Prince, Haiti's capital and by far the largest city. Assuming a dependency ratio of 4 to 1, this means that assembly operations supported about one-quarter of the population of Port-au-Prince in 1980.

Haiti's principal assembly activities have concentrated on sporting goods, particularly baseballs, and textiles, including apparel (Table IV-2). Haiti is the world's principal exporter of baseballs and ranks among the top three in offshore assembly of textile products and stuffed toys. During 1969-1972, more than half of Haiti's assembly exports that entered the United States under U.S. tariff items 807.00[4] consisted of baseballs. While still growing in absolute amounts, their importance in the total declined to less than one-quarter during the mid 1970's and less than one fifth in 1981. Clothing and textile products grew much faster, from less than one-quarter during 1969-1972 to well over one-third of U.S. 807.00 imports since 1973. The textile quotas imposed by the United States apparently did not constitute a binding constraint for most of the period, although they may have limited the expansion of particular categories, such as brassieres.[5]

During the mid 1970's stuffed toys and dolls became number three in Haiti's assembly production, but then declined relatively as did most "traditional" products that were important in the beginning. Electrical (and electronic) machinery, equipment and parts have rapidly grown in importance and now constitute over 30 percent of Haiti's assembly exports to the United States, compared to a little over 10 percent in 1970. Equipment for electric circuits alone accounted for more than 10 percent of Haitian assembly exports, making it the third most important assembly product group in 1981 (Table IV-2).

Available data indicate that value added in assembly plants now constitutes about one-quarter of all industrial value added in Haiti compared to less than 6 percent in 1970.[6] Contributing more than half of the country's industrial exports, assembly production now earns almost one-quarter of Haiti's yearly foreign exchange receipts (see World Bank 1978. Vol. 1. paragraph 54).

It is clear that in the case of Haiti, the impact of assembly operations on employment, income, and balance of payments is of major importance. These effects and some more subtle ones will be discussed later in this chapter. At this point, let it be noted that Haiti's weight in the world offshore production system is far greater than its size (in population and income) in the world community. Of the 47 countries in 1980 which imported non-trivial amounts of U.S. components for assembly, Haiti ranked ninth with imports of more than $105 million. It held a similar position among developing countries in respect to value added in the assembly production which was exported to the United States. While its share in Third World offshore operations is still tiny (about one twenty-fifth of Mexico's value added and one sixth of that of Hong Kong) the proportion has been rising and is now 50 percent above what it was during the early 1970's.

CHARACTERISTICS OF ASSEMBLY OPERATIONS IN HAITI

Ownership and Structure

Unlike Mexican offshore production which is done largely through subsidiaries of U.S. companies, Haitian assembly activities rest on Haitian entrepreneurship to a great extent. Almost 40 percent of the firms in the sample are Haitian-owned, one-third are foreign-owned and 30 percent are joint ventures of which one-third have a Haitian majority ownership (I.S. 1980: Table IV-2). Not all the foreign-owned firms are U.S. subsidiaries.

Several are owned by foreign citizens who reside in Haiti and could have been classified as local firms. In the classification used here, local firms are 100 percent owned by Haitian citizens. Most of the Haitian-owned firms concentrate in textile assembly. In electronics and the miscellaneous category joint ventures predominate; in baseballs, foreign companies predominate. About three-quarters of the firms in the sample had local managers (I.S. 1980: 114-15).

It should be noted that several previously wholly-owned Haitian firms, especially in the baseball category, were sold to foreign interests before the sample was taken. The oldest assembly enterprises are Haitian with an average age of 10 years. The youngest are foreign-owned with the average age of 7 years and the age of the joint ventures is in between. No change in the pattern of ownership can be discerned during recent years. Less than one-third of the firms were established during the five years prior to the survey, with a greater number being wholly Haitian-owned than wholly foreign-owned (and joint ownership making up almost one-third of the total).

Most of the companies interviewed do assembly work for U.S. principals.[7] Those that are not wholly owned by the U.S. manufacturer usually work with machinery and equipment supplied by U.S. principals. About three-quarters of the firms in the survey said that the principals usually furnish the machinery and two-thirds said that the principals always do so (I.S. 1980: IV.8). This arrangement, which is a special form of an "arm's length" relationship, reduces the risks faced by both the subcontractor and the principal. The former does not have to venture his own capital and having his customer's machinery is some assurance that the principal will not run away from his contract. The principal, on the other hand, can have his offshore production without having to establish a subsidiary company and making a major investment. The machinery which he lends to his subcontractor is usually second-hand and often fully depreciated and in any case, he can take it back when a contract is completed. That there is Haitian entrepreneurship is demonstrated by the fact that about three-quarters of the local firms reported that they initiated the relationship with the principal (I.S. 1980: Table IV.19). In many cases the Haitian enterprise will have a relationship with more than one principal. The overall average is three U.S. principals per Haitian firm, and it goes up as high as nine for local firms in the electronics sector (I.S. 1980: Table IV.18).

Size of Firms

As might be expected, foreign firms are larger than locally-owned assembly companies. While the labor force is roughly equally distributed among Haitian, U.S., and jointly-owned enterprises, the average number of workers per foreign enterprise is about 480 and for Haitian firms about one-third less.[8] Since some firms have more than one plant, employment per plant is significantly lower than the overall sample average of about 400 workers per firm. The best available estimate is about 300 workers per plant which is much higher than for other manufacturing enterprises in Haiti. About two-thirds of employment in assembly plants is provided by the one-third of enterprises which employ more than 400 workers each. Export oriented assembly firms are therefore the largest employers in the country.

By far the biggest plants, both in terms of employment and square feet, can be found in baseball assembly, followed by electronics, which is only slightly above average, and textiles, somewhat below average. The smallest plants are in the miscellaneous category.

Capital investment in assembly is extremely low. An average figure is difficult to determine because, as already indicated, so many of the local firms receive machinery and equipment from their principal, the value of which could not be included in the survey. Taking only those firms for which the principal never provided machinery, the average capital invested was about $740,000 in 1979. It was nearly three times as high in electronics, but only about one-third in textiles (I.S. 1980: Table IV.6). Capital requirements for most local assembly companies are, of course, much less because the principals furnish most of the machinery and equipment. Capital is therefore not a great restraint for a Haitian who wants to enter the assembly business. Finding a principal in the United States is probably a greater barrier.

Similarly the capital-labor ratio is very low. The approximate average of $1,500 for assembly operations is far lower than the $25,000 found in Haitian import substituting enterprises (I.S. 1980: Table II.7). On the other hand, average capacity utilization of about 75 percent in assembly plants is double the level in industries producing for the domestic market (I.S. 1980: Tables II.7 and IV.9). Foreign firms work at a higher level of capacity than Haitian firms because subsidiaries can be expected to have a regular relationship with their parents.

Wages·

Haiti, like most countries, has minimum wage legislation. No matter how low minimum wage levels might be in developing countries, the temptation is for economists to claim that they are too high, even in very poor countries, as long as there is as vast a pool of underemployed persons as there is in Haiti. That minimum wages are above the opportunity cost of labor in Haiti can be demonstrated by the fact that the daily earnings of persons who work at home under contract to more formal enterprises ("put-out" system) usually are between one-half and one-tenth of the official minimum wage. The most significant aspect of this problem is that, according to Fass, even the public sector practices this kind of dual system, not by subcontracting out but simply by hiring people on a temporary basis and paying them lower daily wages than "regular" permanent employees even if they do the same job (Fass 1977).

It might therefore be claimed that more capital intensive methods are employed in Haiti than would be warranted by the true opportunity cost of labor ("shadow price"), particularly in industries working for the domestic market where, as indicated above, the average capital per worker is over $25,000. On the other side of the coin, however, capital is not particularly subsidized in Haiti unlike the situation in many developing countries. Long-term financing is generally not available, and there are neither special interest rates nor special exchange rates and/or licenses for the import of capital. Moreover, it was indicated that in the export oriented assembly sector the capital-labor ratio is less than one-tenth of the average in the home market oriented industries. As long as there are non-economic factors underlying some private and public policy decisions, certain capital intensive enterprises (such as a steel mill) may be established even if the official minimum wage would drop close to zero.

The wages reported by the enterprises in the survey averaged more than one-quarter above the official minimum wage of $51 per month, if a five-day week is taken as the norm, the usual work week in assembly operations (Table IV-3). Although the implications of the law are not clear, its strict interpretation could result in a legal monthly minimum of $69 per month (including non-working Sunday pay), compared to the average wage in the enterprise sample of $65 per month. Foreign firms pay a little more, local firms somewhat less and, as expected, wages are higher in electronics than in textiles (for details and explanations, see Table IV-3). The labor cost to the employer is 32 percent above the wage in order to cover legal fringe benefits and social security. (See ADIH 1981: Appendix II, p. 94.) If workers work more than 48 hours or at night, they are legally entitled to time and one-half pay. They are also entitled to a paid rest day (ADIH 1981: Table 16). Often, however, the wage laws are not enforced in Haiti and workers receive the regular rate of pay for overtime and do not receive Sunday pay. It should be recalled that most production workers in Haiti (all of them in the underlying sample) are paid on a piece rate basis. The piece rate is determined by dividing the minimum wage by a productivity norm set on the basis of time and motion studies.

In the worker survey, the respondents reported about $10 per month less in the various categories than the figures given by the managers in the enterprise survey. It should be noted that the wages reported by the worker are the take-home pay and therefore will be less than the levels given by the firms. Nevertheless the average monthly wage of $55 reported by the workers was almost 8 percent above the official minimum under the five-day week assumption. This compares to an average monthly wage paid in Port-au-Prince in 1975-76 of $45 in clothing manufacturing and $49 in industries similar to other assembly operations.[9] The workers in the sample who had previous experience reported an average monthly wage of less than $40 in their former job, about 70 percent of the wages they reported in their present job (I.S. 1980: Table V.A.3).

There is no question that their wages put assembly workers in the upper income groups in Haiti. According to a 1976 survey, 70 percent of the households living in Port-au-Prince had incomes of less than $40 per month (Fass 1978). Even allowing for inflation this would be still below the average take-home pay reported by the assembly workers in the present survey.

Given that fact and the existence of the "put-out" system in the subcontracting industry in Haiti, one would expect to find that a majority of the firms would consider the minimum wage too high. The survey did not show this. In reference to worker productivity, only 10% of the managers considered the minimum wage too high, but 73% considered it adequate and 17% considered it too low (I.S. 1980: Table IV.10). In reply to another question in the enterprise survey, more than 80 percent of the respondents said that they would not hire additional workers if the minimum wage were abolished. This included even a majority of those who considered the minimum wage too high.

This does not mean that the minimum wage is irrelevant. It only suggests that the existence of the minimum wage in 1979-80 did not noticeably affect the level of employment. It should be noted that almost 60 percent of the assembly subcontractors in the sample charge their principal a piece rate based on the piece rate paid to the workers plus overhead and a profit markup. The number of jobs created, therefore, is determined to a great extent by the demand for Haitian labor by the principal in the United States. That demand, in turn, largely depends on the gap between U.S. and Haitian wages, productivity differentials, tariffs, taxes, transportation costs, etc. According to the response in the survey, about half of the firms reported that their productivity was about equal to U.S. levels for comparable product lines and activities, while about one-fifth said that it was superior. Available evidence seems to support these results.[10]

As long as the gap in labor costs between the United States and Haiti greatly exceeds transportation costs plus the U.S. tariffs on Haitian value added, there will be an economic incentive for U.S. companies to subcontract the labor intensive parts of their production processes in Haiti. This does not imply that minimum wages, if enforced, can be pushed higher and higher as long as the gap covers the other costs mentioned. First of all, it may cause severe distortions in the Haitian economy, such as major substitutions of capital for labor which have serious implications for a labor abundant, poverty stricken economy. Second, if the gap is not large enough, it may still cover transportation, tariff and other direct costs, yet may not be able to offset the bureaucratic and political risks in Haiti which are still perceived as formidable. Thus assembly business may be lost if wages rise to much higher levels, although they may remain below those of relevant international competitors.

The Labor Force

Haiti is not different from other countries in having a high proportion of women in assembly plants. The 75 percent found in the survey is slightly lower than in Mexico. In Haiti, however, women seem to constitute a much larger share of the labor force than in Mexico and in many other countries.[11] Except for Lesotho, Haiti, with 55 percent of women in the labor force, has the highest labor force participation rate among 55 of the world's developing countries listed by Lundahl (1979). Abject poverty forces most adult women to go to work. It is also reported that women in Port-au-Prince outnumber men by 30 percent (Fass 1978).

Before working in the assembly plants where they were interviewed, more than half of the women held other jobs or were looking for work. Well over 90 percent said that they would remain in the labor force if they were to lose their present jobs. These responses were not substantially different from those given by men (I.S. 1980: Tables V.1 and V.2). The major difference was that almost one-quarter of women workers were going to school before taking the assembly job, compared to half of that proportion for men.

In Haiti, as in other countries, two main reasons are invoked to explain the predominance of women in assembly plants: women, unlike men, possess the manual dexterity needed in assembly operations, and they are more docile and less militant than men. Yet the survey found that men appear more productive than women. (It is, of course, possible that the tasks performed by men and women in the sample were not identical.) Given that workers are paid a piece rate, the wage should reflect output (I.S. 1980: Table V.4). Wages for men averaged nearly ten percent above those for women. Regarding docility, labor militancy is still unknown in Haiti. Indeed more than three-fourths of the workers did not know what a labor union is and in none of the 51 firms in the sample was labor organized. The high proportion of women in the assembly work force in Port-au-Prince is probably due in part to the more abundant supply of female labor there and in part to cultural factors already referred to in the study of Mexico.

Almost three-quarters of the assembly workers were born outside of Port-au-Prince. Yet the assembly industries have not constituted a particularly strong stimulus to migration. Only six percent of the migrant workers listed assembly work as a reason for migration. About one-third came to look for work in general, another third for family reasons and more than one-fifth to go to school (I.S. 1980: Table V.7). At the time of the survey, the migrant worker had been in Port-au-Prince an average of 14 years, long before the assembly industries emerged as a significant force in Haiti's economic development (I.S. 1980: Table V.A.6).

The existence of a large labor pool for assembly work is demonstrated by the selectivity exercised by the firms in their hiring practices. Since minimum wage is above what needs to be paid for unskilled labor in the informal sector, assembly managers give preference to persons with some skills, such as literacy and previous experience. In the face of a literacy rate of only one-quarter of the adult population in Haiti,[12] more than half of the enterprises always require literacy (in electronics it is more than three-quarters) and generally pay a higher wage than those that never require it as an employment condition. Vocational training, surprisingly, was not required by many firms; the highest level is in textiles where only one-quarter of the companies insist on it. Although about half of the firms require prior experience (in textiles it is much higher, in electronics much lower), they do not pay a higher wage than firms that do not require it (I.S. 1980: Tables IV.16 and IV.17).

Whereas few assembly enterprises say that they require vocational training, about half of the workers in the sample reported such training. About one-third of the workers interviewed had previous assembly experience and another five percent worked in non-assembly jobs (I.S. 1980: Table V.1). While neither vocational training nor previous experience seemed to make much difference in workers' earnings (I.S. 1980: Tables V.8 and V.9), education is positively correlated with assembly wages.[13] Nearly 90 percent of the assembly workers reported at least one year of schooling. One-third had some high school and 44 percent completed elementary school (I.S. 1980: Table V.10). These levels are far above those for the country as a whole and also significantly above those for Port-au-Prince where the educational level is much higher than for the rest of the country.[14] Reflecting the differences in wages, the highest educational level was found in electronics and the lowest in baseball assembly.

Compared to Mexico and other countries in which offshort assembly activities take place, the average age of assembly workers is relatively high in Haiti, about 29 years (I.S. 1980: Table V.A.5). It is somewhat lower in electronics and a little higher in the other assembly categories. Age, unexpectedly, tends to be inversely correlated with wages (I.S. 1980: V.17).

This survey result is consistent with another that indicates that seniority of workers in the factories is unrelated to their earnings. This surprising finding appears to say that learning on the job is not rewarded or that there is no learning or that productivity declines with time spent on the job. The latter may be due to boredom with routine tasks or decline in efficiency with age. Given piece rate pay, lower wages would result in either case. It may be too early, however, for any pattern to emerge since the average seniority is just below four years and about half of the workers have been in their present job for less than three years.

Linkages

From the perspective of developing countries, much is made of the apparent weak linkages of offshore assembly activities with the rest of the economy. In Haiti, however, the rudimentary status of overall industrial development combined with the predominance of imported inputs would lead one to believe that intersectoral linkages are weak in general.

Although assembly plants in Haiti are not isolated from the rest of the economy as they are in other places through "in-bond" and free zone restrictions, the output of sophisticated assembled intermediate goods such as computer harnesses, integrated circuits, etc. could hardly serve as inputs for Haitian industries in a "forward linkage." Nor, for that matter, could the output of assembled finished goods such as baseballs, wigs, stuffed toys, and relatively expensive clothing find a ready market in the country.

In respect to backward linkages, however, significant progress has been made. For example, in the assembly production of cassettes, the plastic shells are purchased from a local producer; in baseballs and softballs, the core is now fabricated in Haiti and the glue is supplied locally; some threads are also purchased on the domestic market even though the price/quality relation may not be up to international standards. All these items were previously imported.[15]

Despite the increased use of local materials in baseballs, there was no increase in the share of dutiable value (value added in Haiti) as a percent of total value of U.S. baseball imports from Haiti under U.S. tariff item 807.00. Value added in Haiti averaged around one-third of total assembly value exported to the United States, according to data obtained from the U.S. International Trade Commission. In some product groups there was a noticeable expansion of the Haitian share of assembly export value since the mid-1970's, perhaps indicating a greater use of Haitian materials as well as an increase in local wages and profits (Table IV-4).

If one examines the overall proportion of Haitian value added in total U.S. imports from Haiti over time, one notes a decline until 1974 and then a gradual increase (Table IV-1). Part of this might result from the change in the composition of output. But the early decline appeared to be due to the use of more expensive U.S. components, as U.S. producers become more confident in Haitian assembly capabilities. The subsequent rise in the Haitian value added share can be attributed to the greater attention being given to quality control in Haitian assembly plants, thus increasing the payroll component of value added through the employment of higher paid supervisory and quality control personnel.[16] This is especially true of the assembly of office machines, where the dutiable value (value added in Haiti) rose from 6 percent of total U.S. (807) imports from Haiti in 1973, the first year of production, to 38 percent in 1981; and assemblies of miscellaneous electric products and parts, where the value-added proportion rose from less than 10 percent in the mid-1970's to 31 percent in 1981 (Table IV-4). In nearly all categories more than one-quarter of total export value is added in Haiti (in "gloves" it has been about one-half since 1977, probably because of the increased use of local leather).[17]

The most important indirect linkage of assembly operations to the Haitian economy is through the consumption expenditures of assembly workers. If one uses the U.S. embassy figure of 60,000 workers and the $55 average monthly wage reported by the workers in the survey, a total annual wage bill of almost $40 million results. This is a higher level than the figure that can be derived from the 1980 dutiable value (value added) of $49 million reported by the U.S. ITC. Assuming that about $2 million of value added of assembly output was exported to countries other than the United States and that wages constitute about two-thirds of value added, the assembly payroll in Haiti would amount to $34 million in 1980. If most of this amount is spent on food, shelter, simple clothing, and transportation, items which would have a very low important content, the impact on Haitian economic development would be substantial.[18] Incomes of managers and profits might have a smaller effect since substantial portions would be spent either abroad or on imported luxury items.

In respect to transfer of technology, there is a flow of technical assistance between the foreign principals and the Haitian assembly plants. Well over half of the firms in the survey reported that foreign principals always provide technical assistance and an additional few indicated that they sometimes do (I.S. 1980: Table IV.20). Much of the assistance comes through foreign technicians sent by the principal on a temporary basis. About 60 percent of the assembly firms said that foreign technicians visit on a steady basis and well over one-third reported that they regularly send their own technicians abroad for training (I.S. 1980: Table IV.21 and IV.22). Since the majority of assembly factories are in Haitian hands, new working methods are production techniques can easily be transferred to other sectors of the Haitian economy, particularly because some Haitians simultaneously operate assembly plants as well as other businesses.

Stability

The general perception is that subcontracting is a volatile business and so assembly operations will be rather unstable. Instability in these activities can be due to two main reasons: sensitivity to the external business cycle, particularly in the United States, and the involvement of footloose U.S. industries and fly-by-night enterprises out to make a fast profit and run.

Regarding the first, a look at Table IV-1 shows that Haitian assembly exports to the United States increased by leaps between 1969 and 1980. The only interruption of the monotonic expansion occurred in 1975 when there was a 3 percent decline in total export value after doubling in 1974 over the previous year. This slight break can probably be attributed to the U.S. recession of 1974-75 and was entirely due to a seven percent drop in the value of U.S. components used for assembly. Haiti, however, was not adversely affected; on the contrary, assembly activities generated an over 7 percent rise in the country's value added in 1975. In textiles there was a barely noticeable 1975 hesitation in the steady increase and the only product group where a significant decline can be found is in equipment for electric circuits where the total drop in value added hardly amounted to $250,000.

The assembly firms in Haiti seem to have a sanguine outlook regarding the frailty of their operations. Nearly one-half of them believe that a U.S. recession will not affect them, according to the survey which was taken at the beginning of 1980 when a business downturn abroad threatened. Textile companies are the least optimistic of the assembly firms, and the most optimistic were the firms assembling stuffed toys (I.S. 1980: Table IV.23). Depending on the industry, either a supply side or a demand side explanation is given. In the former, the assumption is that in a business downturn the U.S. principals will have an additional incentive to reduce production costs and therefore will move more operations abroad; in the latter, the assumption is that consumers will shift from expensive to cheaper products (i.e., instead of buying fancy electronic gadgets for children, adults will give them stuffed toys).

In this respect, it is interesting to note that in Haiti light manufactured exports that use local materials appear to have been deeply affected by the U.S. 1974-75 restriction. There was a drop of about one-quarter in these exports between 1974 and 1975 and a further decline in the following year so that 1976 was almost one-third below 1974. All of the decline was due to the collapse of exports of "coated and impregnated textiles," which dropped by more than 80 percent between 1974 and 1975 and never recovered. It is not clear whether this was due to the imposition of import quotas by the United States. Only in 1978 were 1974 export levels reached in nominal terms (in real terms probably not until 1980).[19]

In respect to the argument that footloose industries impart instability, the record shows that only a few offshore assembly products have emerged and disappeared, while most product lines have steadily increased.[20] Because most of Haiti's assembly plants require a small investment, it is surprising that so few industries disappeared. This does not mean that there have been no fly-by-night operators and that subcontractors in Haiti did not get hurt, but one may conclude that this kind of instability appears to have had trivial effects on the Haitian economy.

Furthermore, Haitian assembly operators have learned how to protect themselves against the ups and downs of subcontracting. Almost all of them work with more than one U.S. enterprise and the majority subcontract with more than two principals (I.S. 1980: Table IV.18). Often this will reduce the risk by tending to smooth the fluctuations in the total orders. It will be especially true if the local enterprise assembles several different product lines, each of which may be subject to diverse seasonal and cyclical variations.

The low capital requirements in this business permit the local entrepreneur to diversify his assembly operations so that he can work for U.S. firms in different industrial sectors, either simultaneously or by shifting his work force from one assembly production to another according to the external demand. It was observed in the survey that the low capital-output ratio enables some firms, with only minor modifications in their factories and equipment, to move from baseballs to cassettes or from electronics to textiles, as they lose contracts in one area but find them in another. Thus, it is not the foreign principal who is "footloose" but rather the Haitian firm, by displaying a high mobility between foreign principals and/or production sectors. It is this flexibility, a manifestation of perceptive Haitian entrepreneurship, which has given stability to the growth of the country's assembly activities.

CONCLUSIONS

Assembly production has become an integral part of Haiti's economic activities. It is not a marginal appendix as in some other countries engaged in these operations, but it is a major contributor to Haiti's economic development and the leading edge of the country's industrialization. It has been the most buoyant sector of the Haitian economy for the past decade. The best estimate is that value added in assembly activities now constitute close to a quarter of all income generated in Haiti's manufacturing sector and provides about the same proportion of the country's export earnings (World Bank 1981b and UN ECLA 1981). While the employment it creates, estimated at 60,000 persons in 1980, may appear small in relation to the total labor force of over 2.5 million, it is probably much larger than employment in the rest of the modern manufacturing sector in the country.[21]

The strong linkages of assembly plants to foreign companies do not appear to have introduced extraordinary instability into the Haitian economy. While there is a dependence on foreign orders or contracts, Haitian entrepreneurs have learned to protect themselves against the extremes of this dependency, often by spreading the risk among several foreign firms and assembly products.

Interestingly, the foreign principal, in turn, apparently wants to keep the dependency relationship to a minimum; while prepared to provide machinery and equipment to the Haitian assembly plant, the principal does not provide much financing. Aside from wholly-owned subsidiaries where the financial link is obvious, the foreign principal frequently provides financing only where he had an equity participation; about half of the joint ventures reported borrowing from the U.S. contractor. Only seven percent of the firms interviewed in the survey reported that they were in debt to the principal. Nearly all of the rest borrowed from private banks in Haiti.

It would be difficult to support the assertion that, as in Mexico, assembly activities form an economic enclave in Haiti. First of all, Haiti is at the bottom of the development ladder so that linkages among its economic sectors are weak and it is still far from being an integrated economy. Second, assembly production is concentrated in the economic and population center of the country, metropolitan Port-au-Prince, and not in a remote region far removed from the capital, as in Mexico. There are no laws explicitly restricting assembly plants to a free trade zone or to "in-bond" operations. However, there is a formal legal barrier to selling assembly items produced with imported components on the local market. As of now, assembly firms have no strong incentives to sell at home in view of the weak demand for their products relative to export demand.

The lack of tight integration of offshore assembly operations into the rest of the economy is not too different from the relatively weak linkages of other industries that use imported materials. This is particularly true of many of the new import substituting industries that are very import-intensive in respect to inputs.

The basic problem of national economic integration is one of the levels of economic development. As income levels rise and improved public policy helps ease supply constraints, the various economic sectors, including assembly industries, will be tied more closely together and therefore raise their contribution to the country's economic development.

In the meantime, the linkages of assembly production have not been trivial and compare favorably with those of other economic activities in the country. Not only do the incomes generated by assembly create a significant demand for local goods and services but assembly production has provided a substantial stimulus to the banking, transportation, and communications sectors, as well as catering services. Bank credit to the private sector increased from $13 million in 1970 to $18 million in 1979. According to one source, foreign banks came into Haiti mainly in response to the demand by the assembly industry. (See ADIH 1981: 12.) While some local components, such as materials for baseball cores, leather for shoes and handbags, plastic cases for cassettes, and corrugated carton boxes and other packing materials are used in assembly production, any substantial increase in the use of local inputs in assembly operations must await the elimination of supply problems in other sectors, in particular, agriculture.

Within the context of an underdeveloped economy such as Haiti's, assembly operations help transfer technology to a significant degree. The mere existence of these activities which comprise perhaps half of the country's modern sector, introduces workers to factory discipline, new equipment and working methods. Even an average training period of only two months provides skill levels far above the mean of the Haitian labor force (World Bank 1978: 23). As was shown, there is a considerable interchange of technicians between the Haitian plants and the U.S. principals. And the mere fact that assembly operations and other production activities often are carried on within the same firm, makes an unusual economic and technological isolation of the former highly unlikely.

Barring a deterioration of Haiti's political situation, indications are that the dynamism of offshore assembly will continue. The vast majority of the firms interviewed (84 percent) expected a further growth of subcontracting activities and said that they planned to expand their own operations, despite the fact that some of them were operating below capacity at the time of the survey (probably due to seasonal factors). At least until 1981, the optimism of the managers has been borne out by the facts: value-added generated in-assembly production in Haiti in 1980 was nearly one-quarter higher than in the previous year and growth continued, although at a slower pace in 1981 (Table IV-1).[22]

A Note on the Sample Surveys Used

Much of the analysis in this chapter is based on two surveys conducted under the direction of Leslie Delatour and Karl Voltaire during December 1979 and January 1980 in Port-au-Prince, Haiti. The surveys were based on two questionnaires—one for enterprises, the other for workers in assembly industries—administered by two Haitian contractors chosen for their intimate knowledge of the assembly sector in Haiti and their privileged access to industrialists.

In Haiti the designation "assembly" is also given to firms using local materials for export production. Thus "assembly" activities are divided into firms using local materials and those using imported materials. The former do not concentrate on actual assembly operations but produce a complete product, usually for export, although some of it may be sold on the home market. Those "assembly" firms using local inputs are not as significant as the true offshore assembly industries using imported components, exporting only about $16 million of light manufactures in 1978 compared to $29 million for the latter.[23] They are not considered assembly firms here. The survey was confined to those enterprises assembling, at least in part, imported components. However, some of the firms included in the sample do both exporting and seeling on the domestic market.

The enterprise sample, consisting of 51 firms, some of which had more than one plant, was selected from a list of assembly companies supplied by the Haitian government and the U.S. Embassy in Port-au-Prince. The selection was made at random within four major categories: electronics, textile (including clothing), sporting goods (primarily baseballs and softballs). Half of the "Miscellaneous" category are firms assembling stuffed toys; the others are a firm sorting coupons for U.S. manufacturers who have issued them to the public for supermarket and retail store discounts, a shoe assembly and a wig assembly firm. The absence of formal accounting and managerial information techniques, as well as the aura of secrecy regarding sales and profit figures, limited the amount of hard data that could be extracted. Nevertheless, enough information was obtained to make an examination of the basic features of the industry possible.

The sample of 500 workers was spread among the 51 firms, selecting at random about 10 from each. Only piece rate workers (no foremen or supervisors) were included. The question, although printed in a formal questionnaire, were asked orally, in Creole rather than French, in order to facilitate communications.

Given the absence of precise information about the universe, it is impossible to determine the representativeness of the samples. There are disagreements between the various reports consulted as to how many firms there are in the assembly sector, and as to how many workers they employ. The same used here with 51 firms employing 20,000 workers appears consistent with the figures of the World Bank and the American embassy.

Since these are the first in depth surveys of enterprises and workers taken in Haiti, most of the information obtained cannot be compared with data previously available.

NOTES

This chapter is based on a detailed case study by Leslie Delatour and Karl Voltaire entitled *International Subcontracting Activities in Haiti*. It was prepared especially for the present volume and was submitted to the second "Seminar on North-South Complementary Intra-Industry Trade," sponsored by the United Nations Conference on Trade and Development and The Brookings Institution, and held under the auspices of El Colegio de Mexico in Mexico City, August 18-22, 1980.

Two sample surveys make up the core of the case study. Specific references to it and other parts of the underlying document will be cited here as I.S. with the page and/or table number.

[1] International Bank for Reconstruction and Development (IBRD) 1981: Table 1, p. 1. The United Nations preliminary estimates are 12.3 percent for 1979 and 12.4 percent for 1980. See Comisión Económica Para America Latina (CEPAL) 1981: Table 3. The Inter-American Development Bank 1979:2 estimates manufacturing share in GDP to be between 15-17 percent. Figures of 16-17 percent for the manufacturing contribution to GDP are mentioned in Association des Industries D'Haiti 1981:3.

[2] For details about the role of the public sector in Haiti's assembly activities see I.S. Chapter II, particularly pp. 11-17.

[3] In 1981 a reversal of perception may have started, as a part of Haiti's business community seems to have moved into opposition of its current government.

[4] There have been occasional U.S. imports from Haiti under U.S. tariff item 806.30, which permits the duty-free entry of U.S. components processed abroad. The amounts, however, were very small, usually below $50,000, and therefore constituted a trivial proportion of U.S. imports from Haiti.

[5] Although the overall quota on Haitian textile exports to the United States was lifted in 1979, the new agreement still subjects several items to formal quotas.

[6] Calculated from Table 2.1 and Table IV in IBRD 1981, on the basis of import price deflators given in Council of Economic Advisors, *1981 Economic Report of the President*, Table B-3.

[7] This does not mean that all of the output is shipped to the United States. Some of it may go to U.S. customers in Europe or Canada, at the direction of the U.S. parent company. However, the amounts involved are usually a small proportion of the production that is shipped to the United States.

[8] I.S. 1980: IV.4 and Table IV.5. The size differences between foreign and domestic firms and among assembly sectors is confirmed by the ranking according to square footage of factory space. See I.S. 1980: Tables IV.4 and IV.5.

[9] Calculated with data in Table 2.1 of the World Bank 1979. The table reports total salaries (in gourdes) and number of employees according to registration in the national insurance system (OFATHA).

[10] C. R. Droesch estimates Haitian productivity in subcontracting at 75-80 percent of U.S. levels. See United Nations Industrial Development Organization 1979:16. Richard Bolin, Director of the Flagstaff Institute, supplied the authors with hourly costs in Haiti and put productivity virtually at par with U.S. levels in textile and electronics for the better-trained Haitian workers.

[11] See Fass 1977: 80-81; International Labour Office 1976: 46; and World Bank 1979: 19. The World Bank showed a 53 percent labor force participation rate in 1971. Fass found a 76 percent rate in St. Martin, a slum section of Port-au-Prince.

[12] The adult literacy rate was 23 percent in 1976, the last year for which such data are available. See World Bank 1981.

[13] I.S. 1980: Table V.11; a significant correlation is shown on p. V.15.

[14] Locher (1977: 9) found 54 percent of the slum dwellers he interviewed had some schooling.

[15]This does not mean that all imports in these assembly activities have been replaced by domestic production. Most of the components are still foreign; in the assembly of baseballs for professional games, the core materials and the glue are still being imported.

[16]For example, in electronics the salaries of foremen and supervisors are 32 percent of production worker wages, while the average for the sample survey is 15 percent.

[17]Both in textiles and baseballs, Haitian firms assembled more expensive U.S. components over time, which in the case of baseballs offset the effects of the increasing use of Haitian materials. In textiles, changes in the composition of products may account for the erratic behavior of the value-added share. Brassieres, however, remain the largest single component.

[18]For comparison's sake, it can be noted that the total payroll of Haiti's 16,000 civil servants was about $23 million in 1977. See World Bank 1978: Table 5.6.

[19]I.S. 1980: Tables III.3 and III.5 and Graph C.1; IBRD 1981: Table 1.13; and World Bank 1981b: Table A-4.

[20]The only "rises and falls" were in the following categories (entire products and/or parts) listed in descending order of magnitude: electric tubes, jewelry, recording media, valves, internal combustion engines, and watches. But even at their peak, output of the largest of these did not exceed $1.5 million, with only about $300,000 of value added. In the last two product groups value added in the peak year was $10,000 or less. Information about disappearances at the plant level is not available. (Data from special magnetic tapes supplied by the U.S. ITC.)

[21]Based on data in World Bank 1979: 22.

[22]It should be noted that Haiti's other exports, as well as GNP, declined dramatically in 1981.

[23]The comparison was made with value added in assembly exports (dutiable 807.00 value—Table IV-1) so as not to count the value of U.S. components (total assembly exports were $105 million). See also I.S. 1980: Tables III.5 and III.6.

Table IV-1. Haiti: U.S. Imports from Haiti under Tariff Items 807.00 and 806.30 by Total, Dutiable and Duty Free Components, and Dutiable as Percent of Total 1969-1980

Year	Total Value 807.00 and 806.30 millions of U.S. dollars (1)	Duty Free (Value of U.S. Components) (2)	Dutiable Value Added in Haiti (3)	Dutiable As Percent of Total 3—1 (4)
1969	4.0	2.4	1.6	39.8
1970	6.1	4.0	2.1	34.7
1971	9.1	5.9	3.2	34.9
1972	16.1	11.0	5.1	31.7
1973	28.5	20.3	8.2	28.9
1974	56.5	43.0	13.5	23.9
1975	54.7	40.2	14.5	26.4
1976	78.1	56.6	21.5	27.5
1977	84.3	61.3	23.0	27.3
1978	104.9	76.1	28.7	27.4
1979	133.7	94.5	39.2	29.3
1980	153.8	105.3	48.5	31.5
1981	171.3	117.1	54.2	31.6

Source: Special Magnetic Tapes from U.S. I.T.C. and U.S. I.T.C., *U.S. Tariff Items 807.00 and 806.30-Imports for Consumption,* Various Issues.

Note: U.S. imports from Haiti under 806.30 are negligible (less than $50,000)

Table IV-2. Haiti: Ten Most Important U.S. Imports from Haiti under Tariff Item 807.00 by U.S. ITC Categories as Percent of Total 807.00 Imports from Haiti, Total 807.00 Value and Ranking* 1970, 1978 and 1981

U.S. ITC Product Group	1970			1978			1981	
	% of Total 807.00 Value	Ranking** "Within"	"Between"	% of Total 807.00 Value	Ranking** "Within"	"Between"	% of Total 807.00 Value	Ranking "Within"
Baseballs & Softballs	52.2	1	I	23.3	2	I	18.4	2
Textile Products	24.6	2	VI	37.8	1	III	35.6	1
Equipment for Electric Cir., etc.	1.9	6	IX	2.9	7	IV	10.3	3
T.V. Receivers & Parts	2.9	4	VIII				0.2	
Fur & Leather Products	2.4	5					1.2	
Footwear							1.5	
Office Machines, etc.				5.3	4	XI	0.9	
Toys, Dolls & Models	3.6	3	V	7.2	3	II	4.3	5
Resistors & Parts	1.3	10					1.3	
Electric Motors, Generators, etc.	1.6	8		1.9	9	III	3.1	8
Radio, Phones, etc.							1.5	
Tape Recorders, Players, etc.	1.6	9					0	
Valves & Parts, etc.	1.8	7					0	
Other Miscellaneous Machinery							1.8	9
Capacitors				3.4	6	III	3.9	6
Semiconductors & Parts							1.0	
Misc. Electrical Products & Parts				4.1	5		3.8	7
Luggage, Handbags, etc.							4.8	4
Gloves				1.7	10	III	1.7	10
Games & Other Sporting Goods							0.9	
Other Miscellaneous Articles				2.4	8		1.5	
Total 807.00 Value in Millions of Dollars	6.1			104.9			171.1	

*Negligible amounts were imported from Haiti under tariff item 806.30
**"Within" ranks in arabic numerals the ten most important product groups for Haiti in each year. "Between" ranks in roman numerals selected product groups among all countries, indicating the position Haiti holds among other countries for the particular product group.
Source: Special magnetic tapes from U.S. I.T.C.

Table IV-3. Haiti: Wages Reported in Surveys Compared with Official Minimum Wages

December 1979
(in U.S. dollars

| Sector | Monthly Wages Reported by Firm | Monthly Wages Reported by Workers | —— Minimum Wages Per Month —— | | | | Official Daily Minimum Wage |
			A 22 days/ month	B 24 days/ month	C 26 days/ month	D 30 days/ month	
Textiles	64	54	48	53	57	66	2.20
Electronics	72	59	57	62	68	78	2.60
Baseballs	60	51	53	58	62	72	2.40
Miscellaneous	63	59	51	55	60	69	2.30
Average	65	55	51	55	60	69	2.30

Note: Detailed information of the Haitian minimum wage law could not be obtained. A provision of the law provides for non-working Sunday pay under certain circumstances (after working 28 hours in a 6 day week). Most assembly plants, however, work only a 5 day week. Therefore the monthly minimum wage was calculated on the basis of four assumptions:

  A 5 day week
  B 5 1/2 day week
  C 6 day week
  D 7 day week

Sources: *Int...*, Tables IV-11 and V-4; IBRD, Report No. 3079 HA. Feb. 17, 1981, Table 2.5, corrected by the authors.

Table IV-4. Haiti: Total U.S. 807.00 Imports from Haiti and Dutiable Value as Percent of Total for Selected Products, 1969-1978

	TEXTILES		BASEBALLS		TOYS & DOLLS		OFFICE MACHINES		EQUIPMENT FOR CIRCUITS	
	Total 807 Value	Dutiable % of Total	Total 807 Value	Dutiable % of Total	Total 807 Value	Dutiable % of Total	Total 807 Value	Dutiable % of Total	Total 807 Value	Dutiable % of Total
1969	1.0	46.4	2.0	38.6	0.1	44.2			0.1	25.2
1970	1.5	38.3	3.2	34.7	0.2	37.7			0.1	21.4
1971	1.8	36.2	5.0	36.7	0.3	38.4			0.4	18.2
1972	4.1	35.0	8.0	31.8	0.4	40.0			0.8	17.1
1973	10.1	29.9	9.2	29.7	1.2	33.0	1.7	5.9	1.0	27.0
1974	19.7	25.3	12.4	29.8	2.2	28.9	4.6	4.4	1.9	21.2
1975	19.4	25.2	13.6	31.8	3.0	28.3	3.1	6.9	1.1	25.5
1976	27.1	23.8	16.8	37.6	6.1	31.4	6.3	10.4	2.2	23.6
1977	30.7	24.7	17.4	29.2	7.2	30.3	5.5	13.7	2.3	30.6
1978	39.7	27.6	24.4	25.6	7.6	29.6	5.5	17.6	3.1	25.8
1981	61.0	31.3	31.5	29.9	7.4	33.3	1.5	37.9	17.6	23.1

	CAPACITORS		ELECTRIC MOTORS		GLOVES		MISC. ELECTRICAL PRODUCTS & PARTS		LUGGAGE AND HANDBAGS		OTHER MISC. MACHINERY	
	Total 807 Value	Dutiable % of Total	Total 807 Value	Dutiable % of Total	Total 807 Value	Dutiable % of Total	Total 807 Value	Dutiable % of Total	Total 807 Value	Dutiable % of Total	Total 807 Value	Dutiable % of Total
1969			0.1	10.1								
1970			0.1	13.8	0.1	38.6	0.1					
1971			0.1	13.3	0.1	40.8	0.1	28.6				
1972			0.2	16.4	0.3	38.3	0.3	14.9				
1973			0.2	24.8	1.1	40.9	1.1	10.4				
1974	0.3	24.0	0.5	39.0	1.2	35.7	1.3	7.5				
1975	2.8	21.1	1.3	31.4	1.4	44.3	2.0	9.8				
1976	6.0	23.9	1.8	33.1	1.5	31.4	2.6	11.8				
1977	4.5	27.2	2.0	35.6	1.7	50.0	4.3	13.4				
1978	3.5	20.7	5.3	28.1	2.9	53.2						
1981	6.7	28.3				48.6	6.6	31.0	8.2	37.8	3.0	34.6

Note: The absence of a number signifies zero or less than $50,000, except for the last two products listed where 1969-1978 data were not available.

Source: magnetic tapes from U.S.I.T.C.

PAST AND PRESENT IN HAITIAN POLITICS

DAVID NICHOLLS

"Everyone was amazed," writes an English journalist, "when the succession passed smoothly ... to Duvalier's teenage son" (Stone 1980). The reasons for the amazement will be examined in this paper in an attempt to explain the smooth succession and to consider some recent developments that have been taking place in the politics of Haiti. As archdeacon Paley (1980) has suggested, the explanation for the surprise is to be found in a basic misunderstanding of the Duvalierist phenomenon and in a failure to see it in the context of Haitian history. There are certain enduring features of the Haitian past which must be taken into account in any attempt to explain the rise and progression of Duvalierism.

The first of these features is the complex relationship between class and color, the second is the importance of a *classe intermédiaire,* the third is concerned with the role of the state. They are, of course, related and taken together they provide a basis for understanding and explaining recent events in the black republic.

* * * * *

Color and Class

Elsewhere I have attempted to delineate the relationship between class and color in Haitian history (Nicholls 1978 & 1979). In Haiti, as in other parts of the Caribbean, there is a broad coincidence between these two elements, going back to the system of slavery in colonial days. In general, the blacks are poor and the lighter skinned people are relatively rich. There

253

are, of course, many exceptions but the general assumption is that if you are poor you are likely to be black. Furthermore you are likely, not entirely without justification, to ascribe your poverty to your color. Wealth is acquired by inheritance, by corruption and occasionally by enterprise or hard work. With respect to the first, mulatto children inherit from their mulatto fathers; the second means of acquisition normally demands literacy combined with political or bureaucratic power; the third means is effective only when certain favorable conditions prevail and these are set by individuals and groups who already possess economic or political power.

Throughout the nineteenth century literacy and wealth were largely the preserve of a small elite composed mostly of mulattoes though it included a few black families. Beyond this elite there was, however, a considerable class of peasants with medium-sized holdings. When members of this class managed to achieve high rank in the army, at a national or even at a local level, they were able to challenge the elite for political power. This brought with it the possibility of corruption or patronage and a consequent improvement in the long term prospects for their families. Bitter divisions among the elite provided the opportunity for such moves when rival members of the elite would recruit support among this *classe intermédiaire*.

From colonial times, however, the overwhelming majority of blacks were poor. Attempts by black politicians of the elite or of the *classe intermédiaire* to secure their support were often made on the basis of color. There was certainly, among the masses, a deeply felt antipathy towards the mulattoes, who were frequently identified *tout court* in the popular mind with the elite. Unscrupulous politicians, however, exacerbated the color issue for their own ends and it became one of the factors determining political alignments.

It is important to note that the explicit and public appeal to color loyalties was generally resorted to only by blacks. Mulattoes, like the leaders of the nineteenth century Liberal Party, tended to avoid an open discussion of the color question, preferring to justify their discriminatory actions in terms of "power to the most competent"; this, however, was little more than a thinly disguised appeal to color prejudices. The 1946 election slogan which called for a president who was "an authentic representative of the masses" was, to be sure, also a disguised appeal to black loyalties but *noiriste* politicians were less coy about explicit reference to the color question than were their mulatto counterparts.

Although color loyalties and antipathies have never been the sole factors in determining political alignments, they have rarely been absent from political conflict in Haiti, and have on occasion been predominant. The few situations when color became the most important factor affecting the formation of contending parties have occurred in crises which followed long periods of mulatto dominance. One such crisis was in the years 1844-47, which succeeded twenty-four years of undisguised mulatto rule. The same may be said of the 1946 crisis, which followed a similar period of white (United States) and mulatto domination. No one who has read the political propaganda of the 1946 election campaign can fail to recognize the continued importance of color in the political configurations of Haiti and it is impossible to understand the Duvalierist phenomenon without reference to it. Nevertheless, to ascribe all divisions in Haiti to color factors would be an error only marginally less grave than to treat these factors as trivial. In most conflicts, color is one issue among many and frequently takes second place to economic class, regional loyalty, or personal allegiance in determining the lines of battle.

The Middle Class

In discussing the question of color and class we have inevitably touched on the importance of the middle classes, though mostly in the rural context. The rural *classe intermédiaire* is, as we have noted, composed of peasants with medium-sized holdings; these men are in a position to offer occasional employment, to make loans and to give credit to their poorer neighbors and thereby, to build a whole structure of dependence and patronage. In addition to owning land, many of them also act as *spéculateurs*—agents of coffee exporters—who buy from peasant producers in their region. Although in some areas there are a number of these *spéculateurs* operating, it would be a mistake to think of the situation as being one of perfect competition. Each of them has built up a constituency, based on financial dependence and even on affective ties; the *spéculateur* may be godfather to one of the small proprietor's children; another of his children may be lodging at his house in the local town during school term. The small producer may thus have an obligation, customary as well as financial, to sell to a particular *spéculateur* rather than shop around on the open market for the one who will offer the best price. These middle classes, particularly in the countryside and in the small towns, formed the basis of *cacos* and *piqet* bands of irregulars, who played a vital role in political developments particularly in the period leading up to the United States invasion of 1915.[1]

The latter part of the nineteenth century saw the rise of an urban middle class of some significance. This class was constituted mostly by members of black families who had managed—by luck, hard work, or corruption—to achieve a level of literacy and education which enabled them to become school teachers, clerks, and civil servants, or to save enough money to establish themselves in small businesses. They sometimes joined together with rural blacks or with the urban proletariat in order to remove an unpopular government, replacing it with one more sympathetic to their interests. One of the most significant and enduring consequences of the nineteen years of occupation was a decline in the significance of the countryside and the provincial towns with the centering of power in the capital. The rural *classe intermédiaire* consequently suffered a loss of influence, while its counterpart in the capital became a more crucial political force. With the departure of the U.S. Marines in 1934, the stability of the government of Sténio Vincent depended upon support from some key elements of this class and the collapse of the Lescot regime in January 1946 is largely to be explained by the hostility of the black urban middle class.

The Role of the State

An acquaintance of mine once returned to his home on the outskirts of Port-au-Prince, after a day in the countryside, and could not find his servant. He called and eventually from behind some bushes at the end of the garden the man appeared. On being asked what he had been doing, the man replied "*létat té vini è m'caché*" (literally: the state arrived and I hid). An Army officer had arrived at the house and the man's first thought was that this meant trouble.

When European or North American newspaper reports predicted the downfall of François Duvalier's government on the ground that it had done nothing for the people, they manifested a misunderstanding of Haitian history. On the part of the mass of the people there has never been an expectation that the state will do any good for them. The state comes to confiscate, to tax, to prohibit or to imprison; consequently, the less seen of it the better. When the Haitian proverb says, "*Apré bon dieu cé létat*" (after God comes the state), it is not the goodness or the benevolence of God that people have in mind: it is rather his remoteness, his unpredictability, and his power.

Though the mass of the people have no expectations of welfare from the state, there is, however, a small class which lives from state patronage, or at least whose standard of living depends upon the political policies pursued by governments. They need foreign aid, foreign trade, and foreign investment in order to maintain their privileged position. The class I refer to is, of course, the urban and suburban bourgeoisie. In certain circumstances the fate of a government might depend upon this class—though this was not the case with the government of François Duvalier. I shall, however, return to this point when considering the position of Jean-Claude Duvalier.

*   *   *   *   *

The explanation for the fact that François Duvalier was able, in 1971, to hand over power to his teenaged son is that by this time his regime was fairly stable, being based on support from certain key groups which had a vested interest in a continuance of Duvalierism in some form. Other groups who might have wished for a change were either without significant political power or were so unsure of the outcome that they held on quietly, hoping for better days.

Duvalierist Support

François Duvalier had a profound knowledge of the expectations and fears of the Haitian masses. His study of Haitian history and social structure together with his ethnological research and his practical experience as a country doctor combined with a shrewd and ruthless disposition, making him a formidable politician. He built up a system of support throughout the country, based on the key role which had traditionally been played by the *classe intermédiaire*. Many of the local leaders whose support he secured were *houngans* (voodoo priests) who had considerable influence in the communities where they operated. It is instructive to look at the photographs printed in volume two of the *Oeuvres essentielles* of Duvalier, to see the kind of people who were his supporters in the election campaign of 1956-7 and who continued to back the regime in the years that followed.

The countrywide organization of the Volontaires de la Securite Nationale, the principal *tonton macoute* organization, served not merely as an instrument of terror, but also as a means of recruiting support for the regime. The leaders of the movement came from just that class which had provided the backbone for the *cacos* and *piqet* bands of the pre-occupation period. The *noiriste* rhetoric of the Duvalierist regime appealed to this class rather than to the very poor, and it was through this middle class that the government was able to control the masses. Duvalier recognized their crucial importance and rarely tried to by-pass them; rather he used the structures of power which already existed to extend his control throughout the country.

Whereas in the period prior to 1915 successful revolutions frequently began in the countryside, after the U.S. invasion it was events in that capital that were decisive. Only during the election campaigns of 1946 and 1956-7 was there an apparent reversal of this trend. Once the election was over, however, power reverted to Port-au-Prince. Certain gestures were made by the governments of Estimé and François Duvalier in the direction of a rebirth of rural influence. The latter's electoral strength had been in the countryside and in the provincial towns, with powerful groups in the capital backing his opponents. The huge demonstrations which were organized in Port-au-Prince to support the regime on such anniversaries as October 22 and January 1 were largely composed of rural Haitians transported in trucks to the city by local *macoute* leaders. The significant thing to note here is that while Duvalier's basis of support might have been rural, it was essential to demonstrate this support in the capital where ultimate power lies. The growth of the *tontons macoutes,* many of whose leaders enjoyed a rural power base, is perhaps an aspect of the changing balance between capital and countryside. Nevertheless this change should not be exaggerated and although provincial *macoute* leaders enjoyed considerable local control, their activities were circumscribed by the president and in order to exert influence at the national level it was necessary for them to have connections in the capital. François Duvalier's own rise to presidential office and his continued tenure depended to a great extent upon active endorsement by members of the *classe intermédiaire.* As we shall see, their changing role in the regime of Jean-Claude Duvalier is of considerable importance in understanding recent developments in the country.

The black middle classes, rural and urban, which formed the keystone of François Duvalier's power structure, were not accustomed to receiving many benefits from the state and their loyalty could therefore be purchased at a modest price; they knew that they were unlikely to improve their lot by switching support to opposition groups. Throughout the lean years of 1962-66 when foreign aid was practically cut off and determined attempts were made by the U.S. government, together with the Dominicans, to remove Duvalier from office, these middle class leaders remained faithful to the regime; this was partly through fear and partly in the hope that things would improve. The class which suffered most from international pressure was the elite, which was, generally speaking, already hostile towards the government.

Opposition Forces

During the first years of his regime François Duvalier had systematically reduced the political power of all the major groups and institutions in the country. The Army officers, the Roman Catholic hierarchy, the United States embassy, the business elite, the intellectuals, the trade union leadership, one by one had their wings clipped. By 1966 Duvalier was in a strong enough position to be able to begin an accommodation with each of these former centers of power; it was, however, made quite clear to them that limited freedom to pursue their own ends did not include interference in politics. It was now evident that the president did not seriously intend to eliminate the economic power of the mulatto elite, to reduce the religious role of the Roman Catholic Church, nor to move his country into the Soviet or into the non-aligned block, despite earlier hints to this effect. It appeared to be in the interests of these institutions—elite, Army, church and U.S. embassy—to reach an agreement with Duvalier on the terms which he offered. In the case of the church and the Army this accommodation was facilitated by the changes in leadership which Duvalier had effected, replacing a determined and powerful set of bishops and officers by more docile and compliant figures.

By 1971 the opposition had effectively been eliminated, through murder, imprisonment, or exile and there remained no major group capable of constituting a center of political resistance or revolution. The above-mentioned groups had decided that they could live with Duvalierism and that attempts to improve their position within the parameters of the system were preferable to the confusion which might result from revolution. Thus, when François Duvalier's death occurred in April 1971 they were prepared to support a smooth transfer of power to his son.

The Smooth Succession

The generally held view, based upon newspaper accounts of Haiti, was that the regime of François Duvalier had no popular support and remained in office solely by a system of terror. This led to the confident prediction that the regime would fall on the death of "Papa Doc." In fact, although terror was widely used and was an indispensible requirement for survival, it was not the whole story; as I have indicated Duvalier and his associates had carefully constructed a support structure throughout the country based on the Parti Unité Nationale and on the various *macoute* organizations. Although there was considerable hostility on the part of the masses to a number of the more ruthless *macoute* leaders, this hostility did not seem to be transferred to the President himself. There was the belief that if only he knew what was going on he would take steps to remedy the situation. Constant propaganda, particularly on the radio, led to a widespread acceptance of the government and even to a belief in its benevolence. The paternal image of "Papa Doc"—a figure possessing fearful power yet having a deep love for his people—was developed. At Duvalier's funeral, which I attended, there were numerous scenes of sadness and distress. We may well think that this popular attitude was ill-founded and misplaced but it did exist and is part of the explanation for the survival of the regime.

More important factors in accounting for the transition from father to son were the disablement of the opposition and the belief among important groups that a major disruption of political life in Haiti would be against their interests. This certainly applies to the United States, to the army leadership, to the church hierarchy, and to much of the business community. Jean-Claude succeeded his father, but how far has he managed to maintain the power structure so carefully and ruthlessly constructed throughout the 1960's?

*   *   *   *   *

The Teenaged President

The young Jean-Claude Duvalier faced a number of serious difficulties on assuming office. The system of support which had been built by his father was delicately balanced and needed continual adjustment. In particular there was a tension between the *noiriste* politicians and *macoute* leaders on the one hand and the younger technocrats who had been recruited in more recent years who were less committed to Duvalierist ideology, on the other. In addition to this, there were the pretensions of ambitious businessmen and Army officers to be watched. Relationships within the presidential family complicated the situation; François Duvalier's widow was associated with a number of the old guard of *noiristes,* while one of her daughters was married to a leading Army officer.

To the surprise of foreign observers, the young president—under the tutelage of his mother—managed to hold the regime together and by astute moves to curb dangerous groups, in the Army and elsewhere, he ensured his survival. Although he had obviously learned from his father in this respect, he lacked that intimate knowledge of Haitian social structure and dynamics which had been acquired by Papa Doc over many years. After a few years the President began to take action independently of his mother and put into positions of power a number of individuals, mostly from sections of the elite, whom he had met in his school days. These moves were resented by the old guard of Duvalierists and Jean-Claude gradually lost touch with that important *classe intermédiaire* (upon which his father had relied), especially those from the rural areas. More and more he has sought support from the business community and from the younger technocrats, many of whom come from elite mulatto families. In order to secure foreign aid it is necessary to have people in government who are able to speak the right languages. These men, like Marc Bazin and Henry Bayard, are prepared to co-operate with the President only if they think that it will pay them to do so.

Many of the younger technocrats were unwilling to collaborate with a government which included such notorious characters as Luckner Cambronne and other old guard Duvalierists. They realized that the presence of such figures in positions of power ruined the cosmetic operation designed to convince the international community that Haiti was a country deserving foreign aid and investment. The regime of President Carter in the U.S. was prepared to back the efforts of these technocrats. His interest in human rights, together with a desire to keep Haiti in the "free world," led to considerable pressure being brought on President Jean-Claude Duvalier to liberalize his regime.

The "Liberalization" of Duvalierism

Moderately independent journals, like *Petit Samedi Soir* and *Hebdo Jeune Presse,* began to appear and to make cautious criticisms of the administration, though carefully avoiding any suggestions that the President himself was responsible for any of the problems of Haiti. Popular plays in Creole were performed in the capital, pouring scorn on the administration of the country. Radio commentators, including Jean Dominique and Compere Philo of Radio Haiti Inter, who broadcasted in Creole, voiced outspoken attacks on the more scandalous aspects of government policy. By 1979, Sylvio Claude and Grégoire Eugéne had formed their Christian Democrat parties and a non-Duvalierist had been elected to the legislative assembly. It was an extraordinary sight to behold newspapers and pamphlets, openly critical of the government, being sold on the street. The liberalization of Duvalierism seemed to be in full swing and to be on a course which was irreversible.

The volume of opposition had clearly worried the presidential entourage and by a stroke of good fortune a change of administration in the United States coincided with a realization that unless something was done to clamp down on the opposition, the days of Jean-Claude were numbered. President Reagan's concern for human rights was somewhat less palpable than that of his predecessor and he was unprepared to risk good relations with a neighbor merely on the grounds that the courtesies which the U.S. public had come to expect at home were sometimes dispensed with abroad. Towards the end of November 1980 the clamp-down occurred. Opposition leaders were arrested and others managed to flee to foreign embassies; Radio Haïti was destroyed; journals and news sheets disappeared from the streets.

Migration

Two aspects of the foreign affairs of Haiti are important in assessing prospects for the future. Both of them are the consequence of the economic misery of the mass of the Haitian people, exacerbated by political oppression. The first is the migration of Haitian cane cutters to the Dominican Republic, the second is the relatively recent phenomenon of the "boat people" arriving in the United States. Rural Haitians have for many years migrated to other parts of the Caribbean to seek employment in the cane fields. In the last few years, however, this has become a major feature of the sugar industry in the Dominican Republic. Both the Dominican and the Haitian governments have a financial interest in the system. The Dominican government which owns much of the sugar industry is eager to maintain a supply of cheap labor and pays the Haitian government a fee for each migrant. The cane cutters live in barrack-like buildings reminiscent of the Indian indentured laborers in Trinidad and Guyana up to 1917; church groups, together with humanitarian agencies, have recently protested against the system. Also the presence of these migrants is resented by Dominican workers who see it as undercutting the wage rates of the country. It is possible that the situation will change, as the government party in the Dominican Republic is dependent on financial aid from social democratic parties in West Germany, France, and Scandinavia, who could bring pressure on them to this end. This would cut off a substantial source of revenue for the Haitian government. Nevertheless, the Dominican government, too, has a strong financial interest in maintaining the system as it would be impossible to get Dominicans to cut cane at such low rates of pay.

With respect to the second issue, the U.S. appears to believe that it is in its interest to come to some agreement with the Haitian government to prevent this migration. The cooperation of the Duvalier regime has been sought and U.S. vessels have been patrolling the northern waters off the island of Hispaniola to prevent Haitians from leaving. Both governments have been criticized for this policy. Liberals in the United States have attacked their government, while Haitian nationalists (some of whom had supported the Duvalier regime in the past) have been incensed by this humiliating situation. Although the "boat people" crisis appears temporarily to have strengthened the hand of Duvalier in dealing with Washington, it may well be that a future administration in the White House will think that there is a more satisfactory way of coping with the phenomenon and cease supporting a corrupt and ineffective government.

Recent Developments

Although, as I have already mentioned, François Duvalier had come to some kind of compromise with most of the business elite, the foundation of his power structure remained the black middle classes. In this matter there has been a major change in Duvalierism. The regime of Jean-Claude has come increasingly to depend upon elite support and his wooing of these groups has had the effect of alienating many of the *noiristes*. A number of *macoute* leaders in recent years have voiced disquiet with the way things have been going, and some of them no longer see any probability of future benefits; they are unwilling to stick out their necks very far to preserve a government from which they have little if anything to gain. The marriage of Jean-Claude to Michele Bennett, the daughter of a rich and ruthless mulatto businessman, set the seal on these developments. While it is unlikely that these erstwhile Duvalierist supporters will initiate a revolution, they can now no longer be depended upon to resist a serious attempt to overthrow the government, as they could in the past (Paley 1982).

The elite, upon which the regime now relies heavily, is very much less dependable than the black middle classes. This elite is composed of groups many of which live off the state and whose members expect the government to ensure that their standard of living is maintained. If it fails to do this, they are likely to look around for other presidential possibilities. Up to now the government, thanks largely to U.S. aid, has been able to satisfy the elite, but for how much longer?

François Duvalier used the black *classe intermédiaire* to control the rural masses. The present government, having lost influence among this group, has attempted to appeal, over their heads, to the people themselves. This has been done partly by means of such popular radio stations as Radio Nationale, which has encouraged ordinary Haitians to make known their grudges against the incompetence and corruption of local officials.[2] The move has met with a considerable response, but has had the side effect of further alienating local *macoute* leaders, *chefs de section,* and other rural functionaries. This form of direct populism is likely in the long run to weaken rather than to strengthen the regime.

A key factor in the situation is, of course, the position of the armed forces. Haiti has a long tradition of militarism in politics. Independence was secured by military action and from 1804 to 1913 the head of state was invariably a military officer. One of the avowed objects of the U.S. occupation was to remove the Army from politics but soon after the departure of the Marines in 1934 the military began to reassert its traditional role. In 1946 a triumvirate of Army officers took over the country and after just four years of civilian rule the same junta stepped in to ensure the termination of President Estimé's period in office. For the next six years the country was ruled by an Army officer and in the disburbed period from the fall of Magloire in 1956 to the accession of François Duvalier the Army's role was crucial. By a series of carefully designed moves, the new President dealt effectively with the danger of a military coup. Senior officers were changed frequently, new men—mostly blacks— were promoted to high positions and the various branches of the military and paramilitary apparatus were carefully balanced, with their hierarchies meeting only at presidential level. By 1964, Duvalier could claim, with some justification, "I have removed from the Army its role of arbiter ... of national life."

Today the armed forces number about seven thousand, with half of them composing the police. There are a few hundred in the Navy and Air Force and the remaining men are divided between the Cassernes Dessalines, the Presidential Guard (with roughly 800 each), and the Léopards—a more recently formed brigade, which is somewhat better trained and equipped than the rest of the armed forces—numbering about 600.[3] While it is always possible that Army officers will in the future play an independent role in the political process, there are certain institutional safeguards against their initiating a revolution at the present time. Each branch keeps a check on the others and the *macoutes,* in turn, remain a considerable counter force. A number of recent clashes between *macoutes* and members of the armed forces suggest that relations between them are frequently strained. Though it would be unwise to rule out the possibility of a military coup, it does not at the moment look likely. What is less clear is the role that various branches of the armed forces might play in the event of a serious invasion or a large scale popular movement against the government. The performance of the armed forces in subduing the 1982 "invasion" of the island of La Tortue, by less than a dozen exiles, does not suggest that they are a particularly efficient and reliable buttress!

By shifting the basis of his support, Jean-Claude Duvalier has placed himself in a vulnerable position, particularly with respect to the United States. While the father was able to resist enormous pressure from the Kennedy regime in the early 1960's, it is unlikely that the son could survive such pressure today. With President Reagan in the White House, he is perhaps safe from this quarter and even feels able to ignore U.S. sensibilities, as he did recently in the sacking of Minister of Finance Marc Bazin. Nevertheless with a U.S. president less tolerant of dictatorship, corruption, and torture, foreign aid might be withdrawn and the regime of Baby Doc, with its recently acquired feet of clay, would be likely to totter and fall.

NOTES

[1] See the important works recently published by Turnier (1982) and Gaillard (1973f). For the role of these groups during the occupation see Millet (1978).

[2] I am indebted to Ira Lowenthal for drawing my attention to the significance of this development.

[3] These figures are based on those given in Delince (1979).

OVERVIEW OF HAITIAN FOREIGN POLICY AND RELATIONS: A SCHEMATIC ANALYSIS

PATRICK BELLEGARDE-SMITH

> *Dèyè mòn gen mòn.*
> (Behind the mountain,
> are more mountains.)

Haitian foreign policy is constrained by limitations arising from the nexus of international economic systems and domestic socio-economic conditions interacting in a symbiotic relationship. As with other underdeveloped nations, Haiti is the victim of historical circumstances whose worldwide economic imperatives stem from Western Europe. The anthropologist Ribeiro succinctly summarized the impact of such developments, writing "each people, each human being even was affected and caught up in the European economic system or in the ideals of wealth, power, justice, or health inspired by it" (1971:49).

The weight of external factors and the dynamics of the national class structure, which evolved in response to the former, are so interwoven as to make it difficult to categorize easily the necessary elements accounting for an overview of Haitian foreign policy, diplomatic history, and international relations. Indeed, social fabric and international patterns must be taken into account for an appraisal of Haitian successes and failures in external affairs, and for assessing the future course and potential of that country.

The history of Haitian foreign relations in all of its dimensions—state to state, foreign business sector to state, individual to state, within the framework of a political economy in a worldwide environment—has portents for the well-being of the Haitian body politic; it resembles a weak, insulated organism which is unable to ward off infections. In this sense, one observes a deterioration in the quality of the relationship entertained by Haiti with the world outside its borders, from a position of relative "strength" to the present condition of vassality to Western interests, and particularly to United States interest. In this connection, this essay provides an insider's view, a Haitian perspective so often neglected.

Power Relationships and Haitian Relationships to Powers: The Foundations

Haiti was the first modern state of African origins, the only one to emerge out of slave uprisings. It is one of the few nations to have survived a successful revolution. Haitian political independence in 1803 followed that of the United States by twenty-seven years, preceding Mexican and Colombian independence. Despite that "originality," well-anchored in the historical conditions of the moment, Haiti has generally failed to elicit much scholarly interest abroad, save for a titillating exoticism which led to the image of the country as being an isolated, unique, or extreme case (see Heinle and Heinle 1978; Rotberg 1971).

Saint-Domingue's territory was exiguous, yet there was nothing insignificant about it in the beginning. Almost twenty percent of the French population depended directly or indirectly on trade with the colony (Rotberg 1971:32), a state of affairs which indicated its importance in terms of economic production. Haitian wealth helped maintain the ostentatious living conditions of the French aristocracy and bourgeoisie, as well as the financing of French industrial might, whose development was carefully nurtured through protectionism. This massive transfer of wealth toward France, and away from local investments, is at the basis of Haitian underdevelopment (see Williams 1942:14).

The wealth produced by Haiti was based on the slave labor of Africans and controlled by a Franco-Haitian cadre. The status quo was maintained and enhanced by the web of laws and regulations created by economic, political, social, cultural and religious institutions, and summarized in the plantation system. But the same imperative that later led Latin American *criollo* elites to rebel operated in Haiti (Bellegarde-Smith 1980). The dilemma leading to a rebellion against *le pacte colonial* was revealed in the writings of early white and *affranchi* Haitian thinkers. Paraphrasing an anonymous pamphleteer writing in 1750, the French historian G. Debien (1954:14-17) specified: "[Haiti] buys European goods dearly and sells its own [production] cheaply ... The colonist chafs under metropolitan directives ... The tutelage is too strong, too visible." Such conclusions led to dissatisfaction at the top of the class structure, while the harsh conditions of efficient slavery led to dissatisfaction.

With independence, Haiti defied the international system to which it belonged; the country was ostracized and isolated, although it remained a part of that system. Unfortunately, traditional analyses neglect such perspectives (St. John 1889; Schoelcher 1843). Similarly, the pervasive element of "size" became an obsession with some; in mainstream literature it becomes a negative factor (see Vital 1967; Lewis 1976; Ince 1979).

The Netherlands, the Scandinavian countries, and the United Kingdom engaged early in trade relations with Haiti without necessarily recognizing its existence diplomatically. Despite intensive lobbying by the Haitian government, the United States refrained from diplomatic intercourse with the new state until 1862. An act of Congress prohibited trade between the two states in 1806, 1807, and 1809 (Griggs and Prator 1968). French Foreign Minister Charles Talleyrand wrote to Secretary of State James Madison in July 1805 discouraging the establishment of relations: "The existence of a Negro people in arms, occupying a country it has soiled by the most criminal acts, is a horrible spectacle for all white nations ... There are no reasons ... to grant support to these brigands [terrorists] who have declared themselves the enemies of all governments" (Lubin 1968). Under direct pressures from the United States an invitation for Haiti to attend the 1826 Panama Conference was subsequently withdrawn. Regarding Haiti's role in the conferences, U.S. Senator Benton stated, "I would not go to Panama to determine the rights of Haiti and the Africans in the United States" (Cleven 1968). The impact of the Haitian Revolution was felt in slave uprisings in the United States (Fordham 1975), giving weight to U.S. senatorial concerns. In contrast to such attitudes Haitian contributions to U.S. independence, including participation of about nine hundred Haitians in the battle of Savannah in 1799, and a cause and effect relationship between the Haitian Revolution and the Napoleonic sale of the Louisiana territory in 1803 (Logan 1941:142) went unacknowledged. The racial element nevertheless remained in diplomatic relations, tied as it were to slavery and its rationale—racism (Bellegarde-Smith 1974).

Haitian interventionism, predicated on the French revolutionary concept of universal freedom—we would now say, national liberation within internationalism—extended to South America as well. The "precursor" Francisco Miranda had conferred with Haitian leadership and received advice on guerrilla warfare. Simon Bolivar, later jointed by Commodore Aury at the head of ten Venezuelan ships, disembarked at Les Cayes in 1815. Haiti contributed 4,000 rifles, ammunitions, a printing press on which South American slave emancipation would be printed, as the price for Haitian assistance to their war effort. Haitians joined Bolivar's expeditionary forces and died in the Venezuelan battlefields. An unsuccessful Bolivar returned to Haiti where he spent six months (Verna 1969; Cordova-Bello 1967).

Haiti's impact in the Caribbean basin was strong, although totally non-interventionalist. Article nine of the Constitution of the State of Haiti (1807) stated: "The government of Haiti declares to those powers who have colonies in its neighborhood, its fixed determination to give no disturbance to the government of these colonies. The people of Haiti make no conquests outside their own islands; and they confine themselves to the preservation of their own territory." King Henry I reiterated the tenets of that policy in a letter to Thomas Clarkson, writing "Why then should it suppose that we intend to deviate from the principles which we have always professed? [Why should we] ever seek to upset the regime of the British colonies? Is it because these same colonies have experienced troubles and internal commotions? But these have nothing and can have nothing in common with the cause which we defended for twenty-seven years" (Griggs/Prator 1968:99). The slave-owning European colonial powers, however, were fearful of the spread of the Haitian example in the face of ever so numerous slave revolts. In reaction to the Revolution, the Danish West Indies allowed some mulattoes to become "white" based on "good behavior," in order to forestall an alliance across the color divide as had occurred in Haiti (Lewis 1972:29). Haitian intervention in South America (against a weak Spain) and Haitian non-intervention in the Caribbean (to placate strong England and France) indicated a realistic approach to international relations within the imperative of national security and survival: the creation of friendly independent states while "disarming" world powers by demure behavior.

Eastern Haiti presented a special challenge for national security. The eastern two-thirds had become French territory through the Treaty of Basel (1795) and consequently also declared independent by the Haitians in 1803. However, it remained under French control until reverting to the Spanish Crown in 1814. The substitution of Haitian control of the eastern sector or the establishment of an independent state in demographically weaker Santo Domingo were preferred Haitian choices over continued European (later, American) domination. The Haitians tried both solutions in turn, at first occupying Santo Domingo from 1822 until 1844, later granting diplomatic and military assistance to Dominican insurgents against Spain.

That the "Dominican question" was a centerpiece of Haitian national survival was made clear by President Fabre-Nicolas Geffrard. The occasion was Spanish annexation of Santo Domingo. In April 1861, he stated:

> None will contest that Haiti has a major interest that no foreign power establishes itself in the eastern part. When two people inhabit the same land, their destinies, in relations to foreign initiatives are, of necessity, interdependent. The survival of one is intricately tied to the survival of the other as they are bound to guarantee their mutual security . . . These are the powerful motives why our constitutions have, from our political beginnings, declared continuously that the entire island would form a single state. And it was not an ambitious conquest which

dictated such declaration, but only the profound sentiment for our security, for the founders of our young society were proclaiming at the same time that Haiti forbade itself any enterprise that could upset the domestic regime of neighboring islands (Price-Mars 1953 II: 210-11).

No sooner than the Dominican Republic reclaimed its independence, (*"la Restauración"*), overtures were made by some Dominican factions and the American government for annexation to the United States. The latter was renewing its expansionist mode after the lull of its Civil War. The Haitians were right: annexation of Santo Domingo was not the sole aim of the United States as it negotiated with Denmark and Spain for the acquisition of territories. In a report to the Navy Department, Vice-Admiral Poor wrote from Cap Haitien in 1866:

I then told [the President of Haiti] that the instructions I had received from my government consisted of this: that negotiations were pending between the United States and the Dominican Republic, and that during the negotiations, the government of Washington was determined to use all its power to prevent an intervention [from Haiti] ... The President and the Secretary of State [of Haiti] expressed the hope that the friendly relations that now exist between the Haitian and American governments would not be interrupted. They added that, although they were conscious of their weakness, they knew their rights and would maintain these as well as their dignity, and that one should expect them to be the only judges of the policy to follow" (Price-Mars 1953 II: 256).

Before, during, and after that period, the U.S. made efforts to encroach on Haitian independence, notably in the hope of acquiring the port of Môle Saint-Nicholas (Himelhock 1971). Between 1857 and the turn of the century, U.S. warships intervened nineteen times on behalf of American business interests (see Logan 1941: 397, 457; Schmidt 1971:31). A more permanent occupation lasting nineteen years would follow in 1915.

The above illustration is significant in terms of delineating, out of a same situation, the *force motrice* behind U.S. and Haitian behavior. The latter ought to preserve its independence, a difficult challenge for one of the world's first modern mini-states; the former sought to expand its commerce through the "acquisition" of territory, markets, and resources, the state acting for the private sector. These imperatives were antithetical as were the goals; the issues are unresolved, *despite power discrepancies* in the antagonists

The United States had intervened directly in Cuba, Puerto Rico, Panama (Columbia), the Dominican Republic, the Danish West Indies, Nicaragua. At the same time, the United States had sought to control Haitian customhouses whose collections were virtually the sole source of revenue for the Haitian government. Already by 1818, there were twenty-four foreign merchant houses in Port-au-Prince, while in Cap Haitien alone, as early as 1811, British property was valued at $1.041 million (Lacerte 1981:500). In 1915, U.S. investments in Haiti amounted to $4 million and did not rise markedly as expected during the Occupation. In 1918, German investments in the three republics (Haiti, Cuba, Dominican Republic) amounted to $1 million (Schmidt 1971:246).

The investment figures can be misleading, however. In the absence of countervailing power provided by the indigenous elite, any presence of foreign capital could overwhelm the socio-political system. As illustrated in stringent legal restrictions levied against non-Haitians (see Janvier 1886:52), this would skew the carefully laid plans to nurture the Haitian upper-class as a commercial elite, rather than as a land-owning or industrial elite. At the turn of the century, Levantine and Italian merchants infiltrated the commercial sector as well, under French, U.S., or Haitian citizenship, or a combination thereof. They used an earlier European ploy of marrying Haitian women who, subsequently, would lose their citizenship in retaliation (see Turnier 1955) to circumvent Haitian law. In this light, the major change in the U.S.-imposed Haitian Constitution of 1918 was the lifting of the interdiction of foreign ownership of property, followed by the establishment of the referendum as a manipulative tool to be used against Haitian authorities. That constitution was passed fraudulently under U.S. supervised elections. The French legal expert Renaud (1934:120) wrote: "il y a quelque chose comme une raison d'Etat, qui commande de sauvegarder la terre contre les convoitises de l'étranger. Comme si le laboureur, venu de loin, représentait déjà le conquérant et menacait l'intégrité du territoire."

Virtually all Haitian state revenues came from import-export taxation, as already pointed out. As late as 1915, eighty percent of these customs revenues were pledged to servicing the external debt owed France (Schmidt 1971:43). In fact, what the United States was attempting, in the words of [U.S. Ambassador] Mercer Cook (1940:128): "the true cause of the intervention—the [U.S.] ambition to dominate the economic resources of the little country—soon became apparent," had already been tried with a varying degree of success by France. At gunpoint, President Jean-Pierre Boyer was forced to accept the Ordinance of 1825 by Charles X recognizing Haitian independence in exchange for the payment of 150,000,000 francs indemnity to slave-owners in five installments, and a 50% reduction of import duties in perpetuity of French goods. Citing records of that period Lacerte (1981:502) stated: "when the full implications of what the

Ordinance involved was realized, a wave of antipathy towards the Europeans surfaced in Haiti ... and Haitian writers began to decry their presence as destructive to the nation's economic development." Loans realized in France in 1875, 1896, and 1910 were further attempts by Haiti to fulfill its "international" obligations acquired at gunpoint. Unlike several other Latin American republics, Haiti always met its debt obligations in the hope of averting foreign intervention.

German business interests in Haiti were in the ascendence in the areas of wholesale trade, service, utilities, and finance. By 1900, these interests surpassed those of the French, and German gunboat diplomacy replaced French gunboat diplomacy (see Menos 1898). Furthermore, foreign support for Haitian "revolutionaries" in the interneccine wars was rampant (Davis 1936:155-58).

The period 1890-1915 was also pivotal for the expansion of American economic activities. United States colonial expansion was in full-swing in the Caribbean and the Pacific. By 1910, it controlled sixty percent of the Haitian import market. At the end of the First World War, it had eliminated European competition throughout the independent Caribbean (Manigat 1967). In 1907, recognizing the U.S. danger for Haitian national security, particularly when coupled with internal difficulties, the Haitian social thinker Dantès Bellegarde (1929:3) uttered the warning: "God is too far and the United States is too close."

The United States decision to intervene was made in advance of the date it occurred, plans having been drafted with the date left blank (Rotberg 1971:115). Following a massacre of political prisoners on order from U.S.-backed President Vilbrum Guillaume Sam, the U.S.S. Washington landed its contingent of U.S. Marines. The immediate rationale was given by Admiral Caperton who said he had landed "to protect property and preserve order" (Davis 1967:158), in that order. Later, it would be argued that the invasion was necessary in order to forestall Franco-German financial hegemony. But France and Germany were at war (Balch 1927:20).

The immediate cause for the United States occupation was the disputes between the Haitian government and *Banque Nationale,* and with the National Railroad Company. The National City Bank of New York had acquired twenty percent of the stock of the Haitian bank, and the United States government had been successful in limiting German interest to five percent (Millspaugh 1931:22). The bank was the treasurer of the Haitian government, and under conventions signed in 1910 and 1914, would advance funds monthly rather than hold all receipts until the fiscal year had ended. In a report to Secretary of State William Jennings Bryan, the U.S. envoy to Haiti gave this rendition of the events:

If then, by the end of the fiscal year ... the Bank shall not have renewed the Convention, the [Haitian] government will find it most difficult to operate. The statement that the government, in the absence of a budget convention, will be without income is based upon the fact that under the terms of the Loan contract of 1910, the Bank is designated as the sole treasury of the government, and as such receives all moneys of the government, and further is empowered to hold such moneys intact until the end of the fiscal year ... It is just this condition that the Bank desires, for it is the belief of the Bank that the government when confronted by such a crisis, would be forced to ask the assistance of the United States in adjusting its financial tangle and that American supervision of the customs would result (Balch 1927:15).

The National City Bank impounded all Haitian government revenue in 1914 and, at the Bank's request, the U.S.S. Machias landed a contingent of Marines who seized Haiti's gold reserves for "safekeeping" on December 7 1914, for which little interest was paid and an exorbitant service charge levied (Chatelain 1954:105).

The National Railroad provided yet another reason for the occupation of Haiti in 1915. In 1910 the company had secured a concession to build twenty-one segments of rails linking Haiti's two major cities. The Haitian government guaranteed six percent interest on the cost up to $32,000 a mile Having only built three unconnected segments at the staggering cost of $3.6 million, the government declared that the company had defaulted and hence would not be paid. The concession was to have reverted to the state in 1960 (Millspaugh 1931:21).

The major investor in the National Railroad scheme was the National City Bank of New York. The major advisor on Haitian matters to Secretary of State Bryan was Roger L. Farnham of the National City Bank, and head of the National Railway. According to John H. Allen, Bryan revealed his ignorance of the Caribbean when, after a briefing on Haiti, he is said to have exclaimed: "Dear me, think of it! Niggers speaking French" (Allen 1930:325). Racial bias, resulting partly from the evolution of Euro-American sociological thought, had always been a disturbing element in Haitiano-American relations. It did not, however, obscure the economic and financial, and later, the strategic and ideological factors regulating the relationship between the two countries (see Nicholls 1979; Dash 1981).

Small State and Power Politics: Some Contemporary Issues

The preceding attempted to delineate the context in which Haitian international relations and the formulation of Haitian foreign policy evolved through specific illustrations. Certain fundamental issues that have surfaced *as a result* of the foregoing are now examined. These issues, I contend, cannot be understood until the historical dimension is both elucidated and internalized in one's analysis.

In brief, successive Haitian governments and their opposition had confronted the challenges of the international environment with unified *élan,* whatever the domestic political difficulties of the moment, forging a Haitian diplomatic presence in all possible forums with a great deal of success (Gouraige 1974:14). Diplomats representing Haiti spoke the language of the country to which they were accredited. Haiti had rejoined the European political orthodoxy of the nineteenth century, following the Revolution of 1791-1806 and reintegrating of the international economic system (Bellegarde-Smith 1982). Internal arrangements reflected these externalities through the local power structure that developed and which consolidated itself over time.

Three dissimilarities distinguished Haiti from other Latin American countries: 1) the elite, a pseudo-bourgeois group with aristocratic pretenses, claimed to be a commercial elite involved in import-export trade; 2) an autonomous peasantry in control of small landholdings had developed out of political imperatives in contradistinction with the plantation economy found elsewhere; 3) Haiti was African. In the first instance, one must read increased dependence upon the existing world order in the economic, political, and cultural fields. In the second and third instances, one understands the institutionalization of a "gap" in which "independence" of means and cultural integrity on the part of the peasantry created a shield of resistance to alien modes in all realms, whether they originated from the outside or from within the domestic elite. It must be noted that Haitian political economy until mid-century had given rise to the highest standard of living of any peasant society in Latin America, according to Furtado (Schaedel 1969:14).

It is generally understood that the United States Occupation, 1915-1934, was the "watershed" event in contemporary Haitian history. The Haitians' most careful efforts in avoiding foreign entanglements and most slavish imitation of Western cultural norms had not been sufficient to forestall the disaster (Sinha 1967:11-27).

Following the establishment of American hegemony, which replaced that of France, the United States military control in the early part of this century, the perspective changed. Throughout the history of Haiti the peasantry had rebelled against the central authority. The Cacos and Piquets uprisings, starting in 1843, had continued for the remainder of the century. The landing of U.S. troops and the reinstitution of an old law, the *Corvée* (forced labor disguised as voluntary work), by the Americans created the conditions for a direct challenge to the United States in terms of a massive guerrilla outbreak (Castor 1974). The American response was swift and drastic: the establishment of a constabulary, as elsewhere, and the pacification of the territory through military reprisals, concentration camps, and torture.

The elite was divided. And although a "political" resistance movement formed, as symbolized by *L'Union Patriotique,* and a "cultural" movement arose, in *Indigénisme/Négritude,* there were substantial groups which accepted or excused the American takeover. Millspaugh (1931) wrote: "there were, of course, a few of this class who were prompted by their conception of patriotism to favor American control as necessary for the good of the country. Personal interests of the others were in one way or another furthered by American activities and aims." President Sténio Vincent (1939 I: 278-79), a "nationalist," wrote that "the conditions under which the American government intervened in Haiti, opened an easy path for its altruistic action and its civilizing influence . . . The most intransigent patriots, those who were obstinately refusing to accept the *fait accompli,* came to consider it a necessary evil, albeit temporary, faced with the evidence of the results." The American intervention strengthened the political hold of the light-skinned elite at the time that their power was rapidly disintegrating. The American anthropologist Sidney W. Mintz (Leyburn 1966:xvii) reflected on the U.S. creation of a modern Haitian *gendarmerie:* "[Its founding] turned the army into the major locus of non-electoral, president-making power, and may have ended forever the possibility of an agrarian revolt against the central authority." An authoritarian institution was made more efficient.

An expected outcome of the U.S. policy of pacification was widespread destruction of property and heavy losses of lives in both the civilian population as well as among guerrilla fighters. Of course, the distinction between the two, if it need be established in the first instance, was difficult to establish. Millspaugh (1931:89) had estimated the "bandits" to account for one fifth of the Haitian population. David (1936:224) argued that the killing of civilian bystanders was the price to pay for such military operations. As few as 5,000 Haitians may have been armed with machetes and pre-World War I rifles (Rotberg 1971:122). Clashes between the insurgents and the U.S. Marines and *gendarmerie* occurred daily, until pacification in 1920. Evidence of torture was reported, mostly outside of U.S. government channels (Balch 1927:126-27). Based on population statistics, the Haitian geographer Anglade (1974:33) placed the loss of life at 50,000, while Buell numbered the dead at 9,475 for the concentration camp at Chabert and the Cap Haitien prison alone (Bellegarde 1937:67).

A logical, although not expected, outcome of the U.S. measure was what seems to be a rather massive exodus toward the Dominican Republic and

Cuba (Castor 1974:83-84). The net impact, as they entered the economy as cane cutters on U.S. plantations, was to undercut the cost of labor and heighten anti-Black prejudice in these "white" societies. These Haitian peasants were escaping poverty as much as terror and the uncertainty it brought in its wake (see Lundahl 1982:22-36). Early migrants, following the Revolution (1791-1804), were Haitian planters, white and *affranchis,* fleeing a revolution in a time-honored tradition; such lower-class migration was a somewhat new phenomenon.

If American military operations proved cathartic in peasant emigration, they were by no means the only or perhaps the most essential cause. A parallel movement with far-reaching consequences for the Haitian economy was occurring. The systematic dismantling of French and German financial and economic hegemony in Haiti (and elsewhere in Latin America), was proceeding apace, together with the consolidation of small land parcels in the most productive regions of the country into large American-owned plantations. The Haitian-American Sugar Company (HASCO), the United Fruit Company, and the Haitian-American Development Corporation established a monopoly in their respective fields, sugar, bananas and sisal, helped by the Haitian government which appropriated 120,000 hectares for such use (Pierre-Charles 1973:125). Seven years after the occupation had ended, the *Société haitiano-américaine de développement agricole* (SHADA) received 133,400 hectares of prime land, nearly 22% of the country's cultivated area for the monopoly planting of rubber and the exploitation of timber. This state of affairs has a negative impact upon food production, particularly as other local big businesses were geared toward food production for Jamaica and Puerto Rico (Labelle 1978:60). The immediate impact upon the peasantry, predictably, was scarcity of land and food, leading to a breakdown of the land tenure system; the diversion of members of this class into cheap labor power for the new corporate landowners; and an idle surplus population in urban centers. If production in a previous era had been labelled, somewhat inaccurately, to be at the "subsistence level," the structural changes in the offing could, in no way, assure the well-being of Haitians. If the *Corvée* was seen as the re-establishment of slavery by the peasantry, it was in the final analysis a mere symbol of the dissolution of the highest achievement of the Haitian (slave) Revolution: the conversion from plantation to small private landholdings; the conversion from slave to peasant.

Further dependence was established in the financial arena as well. As early as 1916, U.S. authorities attempted to force a loan on the Haitian government, *contingent* upon a ten-year extension of the Treaty of 1915 that justified the occupation. All budgetary expenditures were threatened with suspension, in a move reminiscent of the National City Bank sponsored crisis a few years earlier. Neither the 1916 nor 1919 efforts for a larger sum of $40 million were successful because of a lack of creditors. Later in 1920, the U.S. applied pressure so that the *Banque Nationale* would have a monopoly on gold transaction and become a wholly-owned subsidiary of the National City Bank. The government's domestic debt was to be transformed into a foreign debt. In 1922, a U.S. loan was finally forced upon Haiti, from the National City Bank which kept a large sum in its coffers for accelerated payment: "In order to redeem more rapidly the debt of 1922, the [U.S.] Financial Advisor [to Haiti] ordered kept in National City Bank coffers a considerable sum upon which it paid Haiti $2 \, ^1/_2 \%$ interest while it had the opportunity to place that sum in the money market for a far higher interest rate. It is in this sense that one of the [U.S.] Financial Advisors [to Haiti], Dr. W. W. Cumberland, could say in 1926 that Haiti 'was lending money to Wall Street" (Bellegarde 1954:284). The accelerated payment of the national debt left precious little for the development of the infrastructure, agriculture and industry. One also notes that the American authorities were also "Haitian state employees" who garnished a salary in a pattern previously established by colonial powers elsewhere. The Haitian economist, Pierre-Charles (1967:140), stated: "A considerable part of the funds of the loan then returned to the National City Bank or to creditors intimately linked to that institution; another part went to satisfy the sempiternal complaints of foreigners, supposed victims of political disturbances. Only $2,411,736.95, the 11% of the nominal value of the loan will find its way into the public treasury. It was no more, no less than a sophisticated financial maneuver from which the National City Bank desired the economic strangulation of the nation. In 1929, U.S. investments amounted to $35.2 million, up from 4 million in 1915" (Pierre-Charles 1967:142). In Cuba at that time, U.S. investments amounted to a billion dollars.

Not so paradoxically, the era of the United States occupation inaugurated a most vibrant period in Haitian diplomacy. Despite the antagonism of the American authorities, the needs of the United States not to appear as a colonial power coincided with those of the Haitian state for widespread diplomatic representation. "Traditional" alliances were reinforced to counterweight the United States, and to re-establish France in its role as paramount power. Men of great personal merit and impressive education were appointed by the President of the Republic, and served at his pleasure. Indeed, internal strife was never allowed to interfere with the quality of the diplomats selected. Haiti participated at all important international forums. It signed the Treaty of Versailles in 1919 as a belligerent power. It was a member of the League of Nations, the Pan-American Union, the United Nations, and the Organization of American States from their inceptions. A strong presence at the Holy See, selected Western European capitals, at the Hague Court, at Pan-African Conferences, among others, insured that Negro representation was assured by this *acte de présence*. The country's diplomats at times had to pay for their expenses out of pocket, since the American Financial Advisor could withhold funds on a whim (Bellegarde-Smith 1977:163). To this *acte de présence* was added *la volonté d'agir,* which under the impact of the American occupation would include strong and sustained contact with prominent African-Americans and their organizations (Bellegarde-Smith 1981b). Like the earlier peasant uprising through which Haiti gained independence, the objective was to recover freedom in applying pressure internationally against the United States.

Following the end of the United States occupation, a complex effect was observed. Whereas French culture had commanded admiration, and the leadership of France was sought in international gatherings as an inoffensive paramount, the United States benefitted only grudgingly from this new situation, at the Pan-American Union and, later, at the United Nations. American racism had unleashed Haitian racial pride to become worldwide Negritude. With it came the realization that the country had been placed firmly in the economic and political orbit of the United States. The amost total domination by the United States of the Haitian economy, longstanding U.S. racial and cultural antagonism had contributed to the malaise which became reflected in the political forces at work within Haiti. The middle-class "revolutions" of 1946 and 1957, whose arguments were based more on color than class, would, as a result, garnish United States assistance (Bellegarde-Smith 1981a:109-127).

But analysis of neo-colonialism awaited the political independence of the Afro-Asian bloc in the 1950's and 1960's to be fully understood. The trend was apparent in the policy statement marked confidential, issued by the Haitian Ministry for External Affairs to its delegation to the Eighth Pan-American Conference (Lima, 1938). It stated in part: "the Haitian delegation will, as much as possible, enter into contact with the American delegation and will not neglect anything which can, in one way or another, affirm more our complete approval of the Good Neighbor Policy of President Roosevelt, a policy which must establish, define and maintain the conditions and the spirit of the mutual aid necessary to all nations on this continent, as much from the political as from the economic and financial standpoint." Between the lines of long-standing Haitian internationalism, was the realization of Haitian powerlessness and the need for accommodation.

A *quid pro quo* was established between the postwar presidents Estimé, Magloire, Duvalier, and Dualier and the U.S. government, particularly on matters of the Cold War for which they would receive economic and military aid and security for the duration of their usefulness to the United States. Haiti would grant its support to the U.S. against Guatemala in 1954, against Cuba in 1961 and 1962, and against the Dominican Republic in 1965. Haiti's was the swing vote at the OAS Eighth meeting of consultation that assured sanctions against Cuba, and once more for the creation of the Peace Force that endorsed the U.S. invasion of the Dominican Republic. Between 1953 and 1961, U.S. assistance to Haiti amounted to $75.4 million. In 1980 alone, all foreign assistance reached $137 million with a 20% increase scheduled for 1981 (Davis 1975:198-218; Stepick 1981:55).

From 1963 until 1972—dates that saw the consolidation of the Cuban Revolution—American-Haitian relations were chaotic. This was due to Haitian domestic tension between two classes vying for control and the resulting political repression. Violations of human rights and corruption in the Post-Castro era were seen as problematic for the image the United States now wished to project. The change from upper to middle-class leadership in 1946 led to some substantial emigration. The flood of refugees was augmented considerably in the late 1950's, in 1963, and more recently in 1972. As elsewhere, there seemed to be some correlation between U.S. aid, American investments, and political repression (Chomsky and Herman 1979). Emigration, when an option, is the likely outcome.

Distinctions have to be established amongst various migratory movements, especially as "class" becomes significant for the receiving countries. There were parallel movements in the elite/middle class as in the peasantry: the latter's political situation in the countryside has not been studied as diligently as the former located in the "Republic of Port-au-Prince." Between 1915 and 1929 as many as 300,000 Haitians immigrated to Cuba, about the same number had migrated to the Dominican Republic (Boswell 1982:18-21). Although the actual numbers in those countries later decreased, the flow was re-established. Presently one out of six Haitians resides abroad. They are at the lowest rung of the socio-economic ladder in the Dominican Republic, the Bahamas, and the United States. Charges of "slavery" have been levelled against employers in these countries (Lemoine 1981). The Cayo Lobos incident where Bahamian authorities attempted to starve marooned Haitians, then forcibly evicted them to Haiti, resulted in worldwide attention to the problem in the fall of 1980. Widespread arrests of dissenters who had protested their government's inaction to this blot on the national honor occurred in Haiti. Evidence shows that refugees, when returned, are considered "political," if they are not so already. An American sociologist (Stepick 1981) argued that the maldistribution of wealth, whereby .8% of the population own 44.8% of the wealth, makes the Haitians both political and economic refugees, since the methods of political control used to maintain the status quo will of necessity be repressive.

The situation found in Haiti's political economy at the turn of the century, augmented and aggravated considerably under U.S. sponsored legislation, financial and economic desiderata, continued explicating contemporary conditions. The Inter-American Foundation stated: "It becomes obvious why changes in the infrastructure—roads, irrigation systems, market—will not benefit peasants if they remain in their present condition of dependency. Indeed, infrastructural change may actually lead to further underdevelopment. Any improvements to the land itself, or in access to the land, may well only pave the way for land-grabbing by the relatively wealthy *under a cloak of legality* and result in peasant disenfranchisement from the land." The italicized words show the symbiotic connection between the political structure and the economic system, and subsequent repression.

Present patterns of Haitian "development," with few intersectoral links, are based on foreign companies taking advantage of the "official" daily minimum wage of $2.64, on massive unemployment (50 to 70%), and the strict control of vestigial labor unions that make conflict in the workplace unlikely. These factors are said to make Haitian workers 20% more productive than Puerto Rican workers and 40% more productive than their American counterparts (Garrity 1981). The value of Haitian manufactured exports to the United States, made mostly of imported components, assembled locally, increased from $3.2 million in 1967 to $38.7 million in 1973, representing about 33% of the country's exports (Garrity 1981:26). These assembly industries, representing about 250 American businesses, account for 45% of salaried jobs, but only 4% of the working population. Profits are understandably high, 30 to 50% on equity, capital invested low (Stepick 1981:55), particularly as one adds other substantial incentives granted by this model of industrialization by invitation," such as relief from income taxes, from custom duties on imports of equipment, machinery, and raw materials, and subsidized industrial sites" (Garrity 1981:28). She adds: "The assembly industries tend to reinforce disintegration of the Haitian economy in both regional and sectoral sense. All the firms are concentrated in Port-au-Prince and even the few infrastructure projects undertaken by the public sector since 1967 have been geared toward supporting these industries" (Garrity 1981:34). In point of fact, while 80 to 90% of the population is rural and about 65% of export revenues come from the countryside, Port-au-Prince accounts for 83% of state expenditures.

Epilogue

The international relations and political economy of Haiti are hopelessly interwoven. As the capacity for *sui-generis* economic transformation under the impact of the international system are lost over time under pressure from the North-American super-power, the state's capacity for independent policy decisions is curtailed accordingly. Traditional analyses, viz. those that have currency in traditional Euro-American power centers, would argue that territorial size, the lack of significant natural resources (presently in demand), a large population, compounded by governmental corruption would define the terms of Haiti's limitations. Under such conditions, the only solutions forthcoming are more of the same: more foreign investments, foreign experts, closer ties with powers with which ties cannot possibly become more obvious. Not wishing to overlook the impact of such factors which confuse cause and effect, these analyses, being ahistorical, usually ignore two primordial elements in the configuration: first, the ways and means by which Haiti's incorporation or integration to a worldwide economic system occurs over time; second, and a corollary to the first, the process of re-adjustment which must occur internally[1] to allow a relatively smooth relationship to exist between an international bourgeoisie and its domestic counterpart, itself the product of international conditioning.

Analyses resting upon an understanding of neo-colonialism and dependency, of which Haiti is a very early prototype, are more adequate. They leave less to the imagination, being more secure in objective reality. Processes by which France benefited enormously in the 18th century are repeated in the 20th for the benefit, not of the United States or its national interest, but of the American private sector. The comments of a junior American diplomat in Port-au-Prince to an American seeking advice rung sincere: "by all means invest, then get out! *We* are losing Haiti." Each segment of the statement would warrant commentary. In order to know what is, one needs to know what was, and how it changes or does not. In other words, the preceding analysis is useful for studying the elements in their dynamic interrelationships. I have tried to provide a succinct background to the partial comprehension of a portion of the Haitian reality, affording the reader a backward glance, *le recul nécessaire* in which to comprehend an otherwise baffling situation.

Decision-making in the foreign policy area cannot overlook power considerations unless it further curtails its own effectiveness. In Haiti, one observes the steady and systematic narrowing of that power from a force for liberation and the rehabilitation of Africa, to a situation of powerlessness. From its inception universal fears of the Haitian example and Haitian actions existed. At the present, derision is found even in Third World circles concerning the rather severe constrictions under which Haiti operates. Haiti was a creator of the Pan-African and Negritude movement, but did not become a part of the non-aligned movement as its history might have suggested. From this standpoint, Haitian power, presence, and prestige will continue to wane as its economic importance and self-sufficiency decrease. If the impetus for, and the definition of, independence is found in the freedom of action of a government to operate within a context of sovereignty, national survival and development, and state security, contemporary international conditions force a redefinition of the very concepts of autonomy and self-determination. Thus the antagonistic literatures on "interdependence" and "dependence" can be explained.

Economic considerations were an integral part of the Monroe Doctrine. Preventing "foreign influences" had meant that within a traditional balance of power, which would accommodate spheres of influence, Western European economic competition would be eliminated in favor of American interests. With the Cold War, however, in its first as well as present stage, preventing foreign influence means to prevent Caribbean states from experimenting with different methods in their quest for socio-economic development through autonomous definitions of self. This could include the re-ordering of norms, aspirations and priorities, away from Western consumption values toward realities attuned to economic potential. How else can one interpret the U.S. multinational media effort to place a *rideau de fear* between peoples and their national interests, instituting a paralyzing timidity?

Men must be caressed or annihilated, for they will revenge themselves for small injuries but cannot do so for great ones. The injury that we do to a man must therefore be such that we need not fear his vengeance.

— Machiavelli

NOTE

[1]The term "internally" being chosen judiciously for its psycho-cultural and sociological dimensions.

THE POLITICIZATION OF
HUMAN RIGHTS IN HAITI

MICHAEL S. HOOPER

Throughout much of its history, Haiti has suffered various forms of authoritarian government, political instability, systematic human rights violations, economic deprivation and instability. The "Duvalier Era" of two successive Presidents-for-Life, now in its 27th year, did not initiate economic dislocation, poverty, starvation and disease, and it is not the first ruling elite in Haiti designated a kleptocracy, a state bureaucracy that pursues policies of malign neglect of the most elemental needs of the Haitian citizenry.

Rather, the uniqueness of the François Duvalier "political revolution" has consisted of adding to this institutionalized misery a violent political repression. Systematic human rights violations committed by the secret police and the Military Police in the Duvalier regime have been complemented by the random, arbitrary terror of an uneducated, undisciplined, and brutal force, the infamous *Tonton Macoutes.* Loyal only to their benefactor, these volunteers are unpaid below the officer ranks and prey on the population in an economic as well as political sense. Through a pattern of executions without trial, torture, arbitrary arrests, prolonged detentions, and other human rights abuses, the rule of law has been all but eliminated. In 1963, the International Commission of Jurists summarized the regime of François Duvalier as follows:

The author thanks Mark M. Murphy for his assistance in the preparation of this chapter.

283

In the world today there are many authoritarian regimes. Many have at least the merit of being based on an ideology, but the tyranny that oppresses Haiti has not even this saving grace. A few men have come to power by force and stayed in power by terror. They seem to have only one aim, to bleed for their own gain, one of the most wretched countries in the world.[1]

Under the regime of François Duvalier human rights violations were virtually institutionalized from 1957 to 1971. Despite the "liberalization" that was proclaimed by his son, "President-for-Life" Jean-Claude Duvalier, the Duvalier system of political persecution based on the military and the *Tonton Macoutes* (officially renamed *Voluntaires de la Securité Nationale* or VSN) has not changed significantly. Though the Haitian government announced reforms in the past, it has not removed institutional impediments to the protection of human rights.

When nineteen-year-old Jean-Claude Duvalier formally succeeded his father in 1971, personal power of the Duvalier family and the Haitian government were indistinguishable; no institutions enjoyed autonomy within this autocracy. The legislature rubber-stamped bills handed down by the President-for-Life, the press was the mouthpiece of the National Palace, and opposition political groups and labor unions were abolished.

There is no evidence that "liberalization" has produced substantial reform. Institutionalized abuse of human rights has continued in a number of areas: the continuing "states of exception" and disregard of the rule of law; large-scale detention, abuse and torture of persons for political reasons without due process protection; repression of opposition parties and trade unions; the absence of freedom of expression or communication due to recently enacted censorship laws.

The Duvaliers have stifled democratic institutions and the Haitian government is permeated by corruption. The U.S. State Department Report on Human Rights practices published in February 1980 reported that

Corruption is traditional at all levels of society, and significant amounts of domestic revenues usable for development continue to be diverted to personal enrichment (USDS 1979:344).

The extent of corruption was corroborated in the 1979 Report of the World Bank which stated that in 1977 almost 40% of government expenditures and revenues were channeled through special checking accounts at the National Bank, making it virtually impossible to determine their source or eventual disposition.[2] Similarly, a 1980 report by the World Council of Churches documents that the Duvaliers received approximately $70 per head for Haitian workers sold to cut cane in the Dominican Republic.[3]

In Haiti, physical abuse and torture are accepted ways of processing political as well as criminal cases. Individuals are often arbitrarily detained without arrest procedures or due process protections. Government security forces have free reign; no system for disciplining them exists. Security forces derive income from extortion and expropriation of property of "opponents of the regime." Other institutionalized abuses of the Haitian Government are: pervasive press censorship; a corruption in government at all levels, where functionaries divert domestic revenues and foreign assistance into personal enrichment; repression of political opposition and labor unions; and, most recently, the government's disruption of the activities of the Haitian League for Human Rights, the principal human rights organization in Haiti. There is also a total absence of any tradition of effective government service to the Haitian citizenry.

The Politicization of the Haitian Economy

In Haiti today there are direct linkages between the extreme poverty and deteriorating economic conditions and the violations of basic civil and political rights. The present political regime of the President-for-Life Jean-Claude Duvalier combines political terror with a longstanding tradition of official corruption, perpetuating Haiti's poverty and under-development and keeping its people in a condition of stark deprivation and terror. The government is formally committed to furthering the economic and social rights of its own citizens through its Constitution and also by its ratification of the Inter-American Convention on Human Rights in 1978. Effective steps to remediate the poverty and economic chaos in Haiti are initially difficult to plan because of the absence of current statistics. Official indifference toward systematic reform is matched by widespread corruption which further destabilizes the economy. Poverty and official corruption are so pervasive that the small circulatory elite that controls the Haitian state may be accurately labeled a kleptocracy.

Once the richest pearl in the French colonial necklace, today Haiti has the poorest economy in the hemisphere. The average annual income is somewhere between $235 and $270, or less than half of the next poorest country in this hemisphere, Bolivia. This annual per capita income qualifies Haiti for the United Nations list of thirty "relatively least developed countries" (R.L.D.C.'s)[4] unique in this hemisphere. According to the U.S.A.I.D. Strategy Statement for 1984, "Even this figure fails to communicate the level of poverty in Haiti, as income distribution is highly skewed, and only the substantial wealth of the small urban elite brings the national per capita income figure above the absolute poverty levels (page 1). This income inequality is dramatic. In 1981, 0.4% of the population received more than 46% of the national income while more than 80% of the people had an average income of less than $100 per year. Ninety percent of the population live below the absolute poverty level of $140 per capita."[5] Approximately seven thousand Haitian families have incomes exceeding $50,000. About three thousand of these live in the Port-au-Prince area and have incomes around $100,000 per year (IHS: 1977). This concentration of wealth and power in the hands of a small elite in the capital results in centralized decision-making that contributes to the underdevelopment of rural areas.

Other indices reflect the extreme poverty in Haiti. Malnutrition is widespread, affecting 3/4 of preschool children in the rural regions. Infant mortality is 130 per thousand nationally, compared to a level of 31 per thousand in the neighboring Dominican Republic. Life expectancy is less than 53 years, compared to 60 years in the Dominican Republic and 69 years in Jamaica. The number of physicians per person is only about one in 11,000, but outside of Port-au-Prince there is only one doctor for every 30,000 rural inhabitants.[6]

Haiti's institutionalized misery is partly the result of a political system which has made no sustained effort to undertake economic improvements. There have been continual reports of government corruption and mismanagement of public funds under both Presidents Duvalier. The income that does return to the public treasury is inadequate to meet the social needs of public education, public health, or agricultural extension services. The rural population is under-served and 99% lack access to safe water.[7]

Foreign aid, allocated to ameliorate social problems, appears to be ineffective. A 1980 report of the Inter-American Commission on Human Rights of the Organization of American States concluded that "it is questionable whether badly needed foreign assistance programs effectively reach their targets."[8] It is difficult to ascertain that funds are expended for social purposes. In 1978 a CRS report estimated half of these public funds are kept in unbudgeted accounts, and these subject to diversion to private hands.[9]

Under the Duvalier regime, a state monopoly controls distribution of necessities such as fish, cotton, and milk products as well as the supply of alcoholic beverages, perfume, dental products, soap, bandages, air conditioning, autos, airplanes, and electrical appliances. In 1977 the monopoly collected an estimated million dollars, only $580,000 of which reached the public treasury. It has been alleged that other state revenues are similarly plundered. This pattern of corruption has a particularly detrimental effect on the country's rural population.

The Militia are encouraged to extort income from their fellow citizens without fear of punishment. This extortion came to the attention of of Amnesty International, who in 1978 reported:

> Widespread repressive and presumably illegal activities by local authorities in Haiti, which often take the form of extortion, are apparently beyond the control of or knowingly tolerated by the Duvalier Government.

Chataigne Dumont, a former *Tonton Macoute,* who now lives in the United States, describes the manner in which these forces operate:

> One of the most common Macoute practices is the extortion of money from shopkeepers. If they are not given what they want, they can without any fear simply lie about the shopkeeper to the Tonton Macoute Commander, saying that the shopkeeper has spoken bad things about the government. The Commander then would put the shopkeeper in prison, and maybe transfer him to Fort Dimanche, the very bad prison in Port-au-Prince....

> Once the Commander, in my presence, ordered a Macoute named Machoutoute to kill a gardener who was the keeper of a coconut grove. The master of the grove was not there at the time, and the Commander wanted the grove for himself, so he ordered the killing of the gardener and gave the coconut grove to a Macoute to keep ... when I left Haiti, this Macoute still maintained the coconut grove for the Macoute Commander.[10]

In its 1979 report on Haiti, the Inter-American Foundation summarized the effect of these practices on the rural areas of Haiti:

> Since renters and sharecroppers have no security on the land they work, investment is discouraged. Instead, they overwork the land to produce a maximum yearly harvest, often at the cost of environmental damage. This lack of security also affects the peasant freehold farms who rarely have clear title. Facing the very real possibility of appropriation of their land by a *gwo neg* ("big shot"), farmers are also discouraged from investing in their land, and encouraged to overwork it. There are substantiated reports of land-grabs, of judges bribed to issue competing land titles, or extortion by locally powerful quasi-governmental arrangements is the most severe debilitating constraint to peasant development in Haiti....

One begins to understand not only why peasants identify justice as one of their needs, but also the extent of the injustice imposed upon them ... Any improvements to the land itself, or in access to the land may well only pave the way for landgrabbing by the relatively wealthy under a cloak of legality and result in peasant disenfranchisement from the land (Zuvekas, 1978a:260).

These descriptions of injustice and lack of legal protection for the rural population illustrate the complex ways economic privation of the rural sector derives from the abuses of the system which Duvalier represents and enforces.

The government's regional allocation of expenditures exacerbated the problem of rural poverty. Eighty-three percent of government expenditures are in Port-au-Prince, the nation's capital, while agricultural expenditures are less than 10% of the annual budget. The revenue structure is regressive, with taxes imposed on basic commodities produced and consumed by peasants and not luxuries. About 30,000 Haitian farmers flee to Port-au-Prince each year. This impoverished peasantry contributes through taxes and foreign exchange earnings, yet few allocations are made for their welfare.

Though official regional income statistics are unavailable, other data reflects uniformity in the distribution of poverty throughout rural Haiti. One consequence of this poverty is widespread malnutrition. *Haiti Nutrition Status Survey* (1978) found that approximately 30% of pre-school-age children in all five regions of Haiti were moderately or severely malnourished.[11]

In spite of constitutional guarantees of employment, unemployment is widespread. Only one of two workers has employment, making the national right-to-work law somewhat illusory (OAS 1979:59). Eighty percent of adult Haitians are underemployed. Workers are paid low salaries and sometimes renounce one day's wage in every seven in order to keep their jobs; they do not have paid vacation, medical or retirement benefits.

Government statements of official policies in these areas of income distribution and employment seem to be so diametrically opposed to reality as to suggest intentional deception. For example, in 1979 the government set a minimum wage for all workers of 11 gourdes a day. However this minimum is equivalent to an annual income of 3,234 gourdes, a sum achieved by less than 5% of the Haitian workers. The government has never explained this discrepancy. The same discrepancy between policy and practice exists with regard to the right of workers to organize. Despite guarantees under the constitution and despite repeated government assurances that they can organize, Duvalier eliminated associations of workers and unions by 1962. The government ignores the conventions of the International Labor Organization, and the right of assembly is restricted. Article 236bis of the Constitution requires the permission of the government for any informal meeting of more than 15 people and legitimate trade unions have been systematically persecuted and eliminated.

The health picture in Haiti almost defies description. Eighty percent of children under six have malaria, and large numbers also suffer from diarrhea, tuberculosis, typhoid, and tetanus. Few have access to doctors, a fact perhaps best reflected in a national life expectancy of approximately forty-two years, one of the lowest in the world.

Educational opportunity in Haiti is highly restricted. Only 15% to 23% of Haitians are literate, mostly city dwellers who have received education in French. In rural areas, there is only one school teacher for every 550 primary school-age children, and only 2% to 4% of all rural children who begin primary school ever finish it. About two-thirds of all schools in Haiti are non-public (usually church-sponsored in rural areas) and there are no public secondary schools of consequence in rural areas. Although the Haitian Constitution establishes a goal of free, mandatory primary school education to reduce illiteracy, recent figures from UNESCO indicate that 85.5% of the population had no schooling in 1971, and that only 4% had ever finished primary school. It is apparent that Haiti's compulsory education laws are of little value because of the lack of schools in the rural areas. The government, however, has not undertaken significant reforms, for the total government expenditure in 1974 (the last official figures available) for education officially equalled only G24,300,000 ($4.8 million), merely 0.7% of Haiti's GNP (UNESCO, 1977:517-28). This expenditure on education is the lowest rate of existing governments, and Haitian illiteracy is the highest in the hemisphere (W.B. 1978:56).

In Haiti, the highly centralized and concentrated system of government leaves little room for organization at the local level. There are few legally recognized organizations at the community level which represent peasant interests. Thus, there is a lack of initiative at that level. Local actions are stymied or repressed, talent and resources drained, and the result is a pervasive sense of fatalism that all decisions are in the hands of the government. Haiti is a classic example of the center/periphery system in which the center develops at the expense of the periphery. Re-investments at the periphery are made only to maintain or extend the immediate profit of the center.

No reforms have been undertaken to improve the distribution of resources in Haiti. There is no agricultural extension service to the rural sector, no agricultural assistance is available, and no land reform has been instituted.

One immediate consequence of these injustices is a mass exodus of professionals and intellectuals, either through exile or fleeing political persecution. The majority of Haitian professionals—doctors, lawyers, engineers, teachers, and public administrators—have immigrated to the U.S., Canada, France, or Africa.

In sum, Haiti is a poor country with limited resources, but the Duvalier government has neglected the nation's salient problems of illiteracy, malnutrition, and disease. It has exacerbated these problems through land seizures, political instability, pervasive corruption that siphons off public funds and foreign assistance, and an unwillingness to allow any necessary independence to international relief organizations. These issues of poverty and corruption relate to the broader problem of the government's violations of internationally-recognized human rights. Thirteen years after Jean-Claude's succession in 1971, the same institutional impediments to progress remain in place.

Violations of Human Rights in Haiti: A Summary 1982-1983

While some critics understandably focus on the inherent limitations of viewing the complexity of a social system through the reference to human rights or civil liberties standards, these norms represent criteria that are useful in judging the degree to which governments fulfill their fundamental responsibilities to their citizens. Two international conventions, the Universal Declaration of Human Rights and the Inter-American Convention on Human Rights, were signed by both the U.S. and Haiti. They define human rights standards in terms of individual liberties which are so fundamental that the state cannot infringe upon them. Haiti has also signed the Covenant on Economic and Social Rights that commits every signatory government to take responsibility for the economic and social welfare of its citizens. The U.S. has not ratified this Convention. Such fundamental rights as rights to free expression, legal procedures, participation in political activities, rights to organize trade unions, and positive rights to employment, housing, and health care are guaranteed under this Covenant.

Recent Background

An evaluation of the measures taken to guarantee human rights in the twelve-month period 1982 to 1983 reveals that the government of Haiti has not yet removed institutional impediments to the protection of rights nor has it remedied disregard for the rule of law. The effects of the government's massive crackdown on journalists, lawyers, and human rights activists in November of 1980 continued to be experienced in this period. During this wave of arrests, independent journalists and politicians were imprisoned, forcibly exiled, or silenced; human rights monitors were forced to disband or to go underground; and an informal and infant trade union movement was crushed.

This was followed in late 1982 and early 1983 by a campaign of intimidation against the Catholic Church. Just before Central American Bishops met in Port-au-Prince and after the announcement of the visit of Pope Paul II, the secret police detained without charge Gerard Duclerville, a young Catholic lay worker. Duclerville was beaten and interrogated twice in the *Casernes Dessalines,* and the Government once announced that he had died. He was finally released after two and a half months in prison, without explanation of his detention, torture, or release. The newly appointed governmental Commission on Human Rights did not investigate this incident or issue a statement of concern during the period of Duclerville's imprisonment.

Recent changes in the government have further undermined prospects for the restoration of the rule of law and of basic human rights protections. On July 13, 1982, a number of key cabinet members, including Finance Minister Marc Bazin, Justice Minister Dantes Colimon, and Agricultural Minister Pierre Sam, were dismissed. This sudden dismissal appeared to be precipitated by their efforts to halt government corruption, to regularize and fiscalize government accounting and banking procedures, and to collect overdue taxes from persons associated with the government. The Finance Minister Bazin, who had served with the World Bank, vowed to end "no-show" government jobs and to eliminate the widespread practice among officials of receiving more than one government salary. Bazin is said to have alienated the government when he cancelled the issue of $3.7 billion in high interest government promissory notes and when he tried to put in accounting procedures at the Central Bank. According to one source, the Central Bank's report for 1981 shows that up to a third of the national budget was diverted for unexplained "extra-budgetary expenses."

The men who replaced Bazin and his associates included several key ministers who support the old order in Haiti. The new Minister of the Interior, Roger Lafontant, was associated with the secret police, the *Service Detectif,* between 1964-1973—years during which some of the most striking human rights abuses occurred. He is currently a member of the National Security Council, which coordiantes the activities of the military and civilian security forces.

In describing his decision to replace Bazin and his colleagues with this new group of ministers, President Duvalier *fils* noted that these changes were made in response to "the requirements of a satisfactory political balance among the governmental team." The President emphasized that "we must see the strict continuity of the revolution in power."

Human Rights Monitors

The current Haitian government is unwilling to tolerate the existence of persons or organizations that advocate the promotion of human rights in Haiti. The government has effectively suppressed the activities of the Haitian League for Human Rights by arresting and beating, exiling or intimidating its members during the last six years. The government also created an official agency in April 1982, the National Commission on Human Rights, to replace private human rights monitors. Like past government human rights offices, however, this office has failed to issue substantive human rights communications and has never undertaken specific public actions as a consequence of violations.

The official disruption of the League's activities does little to enhance the reputation of the regime. Organized in 1977 by law professors and defense attorneys from the private bar, the Haitian League for Human Rights was formed to promote and defend the principles of the Universal Declaration of Human Rights and of the Haitian Constitution. On November 9, 1979, some sixty security force members disrupted its first public meeting. More than fifty of those present were beaten, including the League's president, Gerard Gourgue, and representatives of the French, Canadian, and West German embassies. Subsequently several members of the League were arrested without charge, including League General Secretary Lafontant Joseph. In January 1981, as he was leaving the principal court of Port-au-Prince, Joseph was forcibly abducted and taken to the *Casernes Dessalines,* where he was interrogated and severely beaten. Other League members, including League founding member Joseph Maxi, were forced into exile or hiding. (Previously, Maxi had been urging members of the Port-au-Prince Bar Association to represent prisoners held without charge in the National Penitentiary and the *Casernes Dessalines.*) Government harassment of League members continued in 1982 and 1983, so that at the present time only League president, Maître Gourgue, is able to speak about human rights in public, and then only in a limited fashion. On May 9, 1983, the Haitian secret police seized five persons from their homes without warrant in the middle of the night and imprisoned them in the *Casernes Dessalines.*

These detentions represent the latest in a series of official actions in 1983 against human rights activists and against the Haitian League for Human Rights in particular. The most prominent of those detained was Maître Duplex Jean-Baptiste, a former lower court Judge and the Legal Advisor to the Haitian League for Human Rights. His detention without official explanation or charge silences one of the few Haitian attorneys still willing to represent clients who are unpopular with the regime. These detentions are further evidence of the Haitian government's disregard and failure to respect fundamental procedural protections guaranteed by its own Constitution. Government security forces routinely detain individuals suspected of insufficient loyalty to the regime without charge, explanation, or due process protections. The National Commission on Human Rights has taken no steps to limit abuses such as those endured by Maître Duplex Jean-Baptiste and others. Such inaction fails to confirm the Haitian government's assertion that formation of the Commission reflects "liberalization."

Role of the Security Forces, 1982-1983

Under both Duvalier governments, a network of official and semi-official security forces carried out a campaign of terror against the people of Haiti. The unchallenged authority of these forces has resulted in innumerable violations of human rights.

François Duvalier came to power in 1957 with the support of the armed forces. To secure his position he weakened the Army by disbanding several sections, dismissing successive commanders-in-chief, closing the Military Academy, repeatedly purging the Officer Corps, and reallocating armed forces funds to his personal security forces.

In this way Duvalier established new security forces outside of the army that were, and have remained, intensely loyal. François Duvalier wrote about the most prominent of these forces, the *Tonton Macoutes,* in his memoirs:

This organization has only one soul: Duvalier; recognizes only one chief: Duvalier; fights for only one destiny: Duvalier in power.[12]

Jean-Claude Duvalier repeated these words in July 1972, in describing his own relationship to the militia. Under his command, the security forces continue to operate with civil immunity as an arm of the government— arresting, interrogating, and often abusing innocent Haitian citizens. Although these forces have become more selective and sophisticated, it remains their role to eliminate political opposition.

On September 29, 1979, the twenty-second anniversary of the Duvalier regime, the President warned the militia that it must fight to preserve the Duvalier government, stressing its major role in eliminating unrest and instability in Haiti.

Men and women of the militia, you are the linchpin of my government; the major force on which I can base myself in order to realize the objectives of democracy and to impose respect for law and order and activist discipline.[13]

In his landmark decision vindicating the rights of Haitian refugees who fled to the U.S., in *Haitian Refugee Center v. Civiletti,* Judge King found that:

> The Macoutes are perhaps the single most pervasive influence on Haitian life. The evidence indicated that they are present in every township in Haiti, and that their method of operation touches nearly everyone. Although many are not actually paid, the Macoutes are rewarded for their loyalty to Duvalier. There is continuing credible evidence that the Macoutes have, and exercise, the power to extort money and crops in rural areas (deposition of Edward McKeon, former U.S. Embassy official in Haiti), and to dispossess the lands of peasants (deposition of David Martin, Office of Human Rights and Humanitarian Affairs, State Department). They recruit, and control, through extortion.
>
> Because the Macoutes are an organization created for political purposes, they bring politics to the villages in Haiti. To challenge the extortion by which Macoutes exist is to challenge the underpinnings of the political system. Accordingly, to resist extortion is to become an enemy of the governments.
>
> The rule of the Duvalier Security Forces is important to this case for two reasons. First, it must be understood that virtually any encounter with a member of the security forces is a political encounter. When determining whether someone has been politically persecuted, this must be kept in mind. Second, the security forces will determine whether someone is persecuted on their return; accordingly their understanding of how returnees are to be treated is more important than the public statements of the Duvalier Government.[14]

This judgment reaffirms the findings of a number of human rights organizations that the regimes of Duvalier and his son, Jean-Claude, have succeeded in suppressing opposition through their policy of imprisonment and torture, a policy which has forced thousands into exile. Arbitrary arrest, abduction, prolonged detention, severe mistreatment of prisoners and harassment of ordinary citizens by the government security forces are commonplace. Little value is placed on the Rule of Law. The government has not begun the task of developing institutional structures which would end these basic violations.

Recently, the complex network of official and semi-official Haitian security continued to violate the rule of law by a series of arrests of persons perceived as opponents of the government. In August 1982, approximately 20 persons were arrested and detained in one of Haiti's political prisons. Well-known lawyers, engineers, and economists were among those held incommunicada and naked in isolation cells. Several were said to have been threatened and mistreated, and others prevented from leaving the country.

Then, in March 1983, the government detained at least eight other persons. Security forces forcibly entered their homes and detained them incommunicado. These individuals have yet to be charged, and Haitian authorities have not officially acknowledged their arrest and detention.

On May 9, 1983 five persons "suspected" of being affiliated with either the Haitian League for Human Rights or the Haitian Democratic Party were detained without explanation or charge for over three months.

On October 9, 1983 Sylvio Claude, President of the Haitian Christian Democratic Party and three or four other party members were detained without charge or explanation in the *Casernes Dessalines*. This detention represents the sixth time in less than five years that Claude has been imprisoned. As in past detentions, Mr. Claude was severely beaten on November 14, 1983 in the *Casernes Dessalines* after refusing in the presence of the German Ambassador to Haiti to be forcibly exiled from Haiti. Before this incident Mr. Claude again expressed his intention to participate in the legislative elections of February 12, 1984. Many observers believe that these elections were planned in response to pressure from the U.S. government for improvement in the Haitian governmental human rights performance.

The Haitian government's continued persecution of Mr. Claude is symptomatic of an official intolerance for any opposition political grouping, or of any independent journalism, broadcasting, or trade union organization. The conditions of Mr. Claude's most recent confinement are also illustrative of the standard treatment of prisoners in Haiti's political prisons. Claude was held for most of this period incommunicado, and was denied all visits and any contact with lawyers from the Haitian League for Human Rights. Food provided by his family was withheld from him, and he was forced to live on the meager prison rations of watery corn meal and bread served once a day.

In legislative elections held in Haiti in 1979, Sylvio Claude, then the leader of the unofficial Haitian Christian Democratic Party, was a candidate in the Mirabalais constituency. He ran against Mme. Rosalie Adolph, who, with her husband, headed the *Tonton Macoutes* under François Duvalier. During this time, meetings of Claude's supporters repeatedly were broken up by military police and the *Tonton Macoutes*. Claude's candidacy was declared illegal and he was removed from the ballot. On Thursday, February 22, 1979, Claude was arrested (but not charged formally), brutally interrogated, tortured with electric shocks and beaten senseless in the *Casernes Dessalines* by Lt. Mont Desire and Lt. Julien, both under the command of Colonel Jean Valme, Chief of the Service Detectif. Colonel Albert Pierre also participated.

Following the demand of the Haitian League for Human Rights that Claude either be charged before a judge or released, Claude was initially released, but then was rearrested and forcibly deported to Colombia on May 5, 1979. Claude was allowed to return to Haiti some three weeks later, but again was detained without explanation for several days upon his return.

On August 26, 1981, nearly nine months after the mass arrests of November 1980, the government of Haiti brought 26 persons to trial before Judge Menan Pierre-Louis in the Central Courthouse in Port-au-Prince. Eleven of the defendants were members of the Haitian Christian Democratic Party (PDCH), including Claude. Two others were journalists imprisoned during the mass arrests of November 1980.

On November 28, 1980, the Haitian military police undertook the mass arrest of perceived opponents of the Duvalier government. Within several days, more than 75 persons were detained and imprisoned without explanation or formal charges. All of those arrested were initially held incommunicado and none were allowed access to lawyers or visitors. Following their arrests, these people were first taken to the *Casernes Dessalines* for interrogation. In early December 1980, sixteen of these detainees were forcibly exiled from Haiti without ever having been charged with any crime or given any explanation for their imprisonment or expulsion. These arrests in 1980 virtually silenced all independent journalistic voices, forced human rights advocates underground, crushed an informal and infant trade union movement, and seriously threatened the few lawyers who had been willing to represent clients in politically sensitive cases. Also arrested were Haiti's only opposition political leaders of national reputation: Maître Gregoire Eugene, leader of the Social Christian Party and publisher of the monthly periodical, *Fraternite;* as was Sylvio Claude. Approximately 39 other sympathizers of Claude's Haitian Christian Democratic Party were also arrested, and some were eventually charged and tried in August 1981. A number of those arrested in November 1980 were held for almost two years in the National Penitentiary.

On August 26, 1981, nearly nine months after the mass arrests of November 1980, the government of Haiti brought 26 persons to trial before Judge Menan Pierre-Louis in the Central Courthouse in Port-au-Prince. Eleven of the defendants were members of the Haitian Christian Democratic Party (PDCH), including Claude. Two others were journalists imprisoned during the mass arrests of November 1980.

The trial, which violated a number of procedural rights guaranteed by the Haitian Constitution and international law, lasted for nineteen hours on a single day and night. All of the defendants were convicted on two charges at 5 a.m.; 22 of the defendants were sentenced to fifteen years of hard labor, and the other four sentenced to one year in prison. The Haitian League for Human Rights labeled the verdict a "judicial scandal of unbelievable proportions," charging that no credible evidence had been presented by the government.

On February 26, 1982, the Court of Appeals announced that it had overturned and annulled the lower court's decision due to procedural flaws and a technical sentencing error. The retrial of the remaining twenty-two defendants—whose date was never publicly announced, despite repeated requests from the defense lawyers and international legal organizations—took place on August 27, 1982. It occurred in an atmosphere of armed intimidation, with up to 60 security police armed with rifles and submachine guns in front and inside the court. Many of the family members of the accused were barred from the courtroom, and one of Sylvio Claude's sons was physically thrown out of the court in the presence of an international legal observer. According to members of the Port-au-Prince Bar who attended the trial as observers (but who did not represent any of the parties), the vast majority of the men who packed the large courtroom were security force members or their relatives and friends, all dressed in civilian clothes.

Throughout the trial, the government prosecutor shouted down the defense lawyers and the defendants. The government prosecutor also frequently shouted at the presiding judge, Theophile Jean Françoise, and often appeared to intimidate him. Throughout most of the last five hours of the trial (which ended at 6:50 a.m. on Saturday, the 28th of August) a majority of jurors were asleep, as were the court clerks responsible for transcribing the proceedings. With no mention of prosecutorial misconduct, or a lack of credible evidence against the defendants, all were found guilty as charged and sentenced to the maximum of six years in prison.

On September 22, 1982, President-for-Life Duvalier granted all twenty-two defendants' request for amnesty on the occasion of the 25th anniversary of the "Duvalier era." The defendants have been allowed to return home, but some cannot leave their homes, and all are under constant surveillance.

As noted above, Claude was harassed by the security forces continuously following his presidential pardon and release from prison. He was never allowed to resume any political activities, and was even prevented from sustaining his family economically. In February of 1983, Claude was threatened by security force members so frequently that he chose to flee

Port-au-Prince and go into hiding to protect himself. Security forces apparently tried several times to redetain him, and on October 9, Claude was imprisoned without charge or explanation.

Victims of the regime's oppressive policies include labor leaders, journalists, members of opposition political parties, and lawyers willing to represent clients in politically sensitive cases. Opponents continue to be arrested and detained incommunicado for long periods without formal charges, then either released, exiled, or subjected to show trials. By this pattern of incommunicado detentions and official intimidations, the Haitian government has silenced independent voices.

Official Respect for the Haitian Constitution and Laws

The Haitian government continues to disregard its own Constitution and international law through the operation of state security legislation. This is exemplified by the "Anti-Communist Law of 1969," the annual suspension by the President-for-Life of important articles of the Constitution through enactment of the *Plein Pouvoir,* and through the systematic disregard of the rule of law by Haitian security forces. Plein Pouvoir, the practice of granting full powers to the President-for-Life during the time when the legislature is not sitting, "enables the President to govern by decree for a period of eight months, during which time the people are deprived of constitutional guarantees and the most elemental human rights" (OAS 1982).

The Haitian judicial system continues to violate various procedural rights of defendants guaranteed both by the Constitution and by international law (see preceding description of the trials of members of the Christian Democratic Party in 1981 and 1982).

Political Prisoners

Those detained in Haiti's political prisons face mistreatment and violations of their fundamental due process rights. While international pressure seems to have improved conditions slightly at the National Penitentiary, no changes have been noted in conditions at other prisons. Most of the 22 defendants in the August 1982 trial of political prisoners complained of mistreatment, beatings, or torture during their imprisonment. At least one person was known to have died in Port-au-Prince during 1982.[15] As of January 1, 1984, at least 48 political detainees remain incommunicado, held without charges at the National Penitentiary and the *Casernes Dessalines.* Beatings are a regular part of interrogation and prison discipline. These beatings can be so severe as to constitute torture, as in the case of Gerard Duclerville, the Catholic lay worker, and the case of Sylvio Claude and a number of the persons detained on March 19, 1983.

Political Participation

The Haitian government continues to suppress political activity or opposition. No political parties or independent civic organizations are allowed to operate in Haiti and most independent political leaders are imprisoned or exiled.

Following significant pressure from the United States government the Haitian government announced selected municipal elections for the summer of 1983 and Legislative elections for February 1984. The office of one U.S. Congressman, a member of the Congressional Black Caucus Task Force on Haiti, issued the results of an observer-mission on the day after the municipal elections in Port-au-Prince and the nearby municipalities of Carrefour and Delmas:

> Although newspapers sympathetic to the Haitian regime referred to Sunday's elections as the culmination of a 'decisive moment in the national life' of Haiti, it would be entirely inaccurate to classify them as evidence of any 'democratization' of the political process. For example, as a practical precondition for running for these offices, the candidates had to declare their loyalty to the present government of Haiti headed by President-for-Life, Jean-Claude Duvalier. It was those with the strongest ties to the regime that emerged as the winners on Sunday. For example, Franck Romain and Elder Pageotte Andre, the victors in the Mayoral contests in Port-au-Prince and Delmas, respectively, possess long-standing ties to the Haitian security forces. In fact one of Mr. Pageotte's campaign suggestions was that a municipal police force should be formed out of the National Security Volunteers, the renamed Tonton Macoutes of the François Duvalier Era.

> The actual mechanics of these local elections eliminated any opportunity for a free and open process. Because no identification was required for registration and because no master registration list appeared to be used, voters could easily obtain more than one voter registration card from different registration locations. Color-coded ballots were available directly from the candidates and voters simply showed a registration card and were then allowed to deposit a color-coded ballot in the election urn in full view of security force officials, election bureau members and the candidates' representatives. Other irregularities appeared to occur at many of the polling sites visited. Many people voted more than once. A security force member spontaneously informed the delegation that it was common for people to vote twice.

The delegation saw voters with as many as three voter registration cards. Some form of compensation for voting for a particular candidate, whether in food or in cash, was alleged by many people. . . .

Many youngsters well under the voting age of 18 were seen to deposit ballots by the delegation. Most voters appeared to be impoverished. When questioned about not participating, persons of moderate or substantial means stated that they 'ate well, so there was no need to vote.' It appears that these elections will not result in any meaningful change or improvement for the Haitian people.[16]

In the summer of 1983 the President of the Haitian Christian Democratic Party, Mr. Sylvio Claude, was forced into hiding soon after he announced his party's intention to contest the municipal elections. The Haitian government's refusal to let Mr. Claude participate in these elections was documented in an interview held with a human rights delegation in late June 1983 by the Minister of the Interior, Mr. Roger Lafontant. He informed the delegation that the police were seeking Mr. Claude because he was conspiring to disrupt the municipal elections.

Informed observers believe that Mr. Claude's efforts to secure participation of the Haitian Christian Democratic Party in the Legislative election of February 1984 led to his most severe detention and beating. Similar is the case of Gregorie Eugene, the leader of Haiti's only other independent political party. Eugene, a law professor and publisher, was forcibly exiled from Haiti in late 1980. After he announced his candidacy for one of the legislative seats in Port-au-Prince in the February 1984 elections, Professor Eugene was refused a visa and permission to return to Haiti on five occasions.

Freedom of Communication

The Haitian Constitution guarantees freeedom of the press and individual expression, as does Haiti's obligations under the Inter-American Convention on Human Rights. In practice, however, opposition or independent newspapers, magazines and radio broadcasts are not allowed in Haiti. The only functioning independent journalists and broadcasters were exiled against their will following their detention in November and December 1980.

Freedom of the press is severely curtailed by state security legislation and by a series of press laws which provide for censorship and harsh penalties for those who are deemed to have insulted the Duvalier family, the government, or its allies. In 1982, these open-ended laws were applied to all printed and broadcast media. The Inter-American Press Association severely condemned these official restrictions of press freedom in Haiti at its annual meeting in November 1982.

Trade Union Rights

In the last three years, the Haitian government has systematically eliminated all remaining legitimate trade union activity. The leaders of the major labor organizations have been arrested without charge, forcibly exiled, or forced underground. In December 1983, in order to receive U.S. tariff preferences under President Reagan's CBI (Caribbean Basin Initiative), the regime pledged the freedom of trade unions. It remains to be seen whether this will result in respect for trade union rights.

Conclusion

The successive regimes of Presidents-for-Life Francois and Jean-Claude Duvalier have succeeded in suppressing opposition through their policy of imprisonment and torture, a policy which has forced thousands into exile. Arbitrary arrest, abduction, prolonged detention, severe mistreatment fo prisoners and harassment of ordinary citizens by the government security forces are commonplace. Little value is placed on the Rule of Law. The government has not begun the task of developing institutional structures which would end these basic violations.

Confronted by this stark and intransigent reality, the Organization of american States Commission on Human Rights has concluded:

... no progress has been made in the situation of human rights in Haiti, and there is no evidence that would lead the Inter-American Commission for Human Rights to suppose that there will be any government opening in the near future that will reestablish free democratic life, ideological pluralism or the free exercise of public freedoms.[17]

NOTES

[1] ICJ Bulletin No. 17, 1963.

[2] Memorandum on the Haitian Economy, World Bank, Latin America and the Caribbean Regional Office, May 13, 1981, p. 6.

[3] "Sold Like Cattle, Haitian Workers in the Dominican Republic," World Council of Churches, No. 10, Geneva, November 1980, p. 11. Quoting from "Migrant Workers in the Dominican Republic," Anti-Slavery Society for the Protection of Human Rights, London.

[4] Country Development Strategy Statement, Haiti, F.Y. 1984, January 1982, A.I.D., Washington, D.C.

[5] Memorandum on the Haitian Economy, World Bank, Latin America and Caribbean Regional Office, May 13, 1981, p. 6.

[6] *Op. Cit.,* U.S.A.I.D. Country Development Strategy Statement for Haiti, FY 1984, p. 2.

[7]Unpublished Preliminary Report of the World Bank, 1982.

[8]I.A.C.H.R. Report, December 1979, p. 74.

[9]"Impediments to Economic and Social Development in Haiti," Congressional Research Service, the Library of Congress, Washington, D.C., June 19, 1978.

[10]Affidavit of Chataigne Dumont, Miami, July 1979.

[11]U.S.A.I.D. FY 1984 Haiti Strategy Statement, p. 2.

[12]"Memories D'un Leader Du Tiers Monde," François Duvalier, Hachette, 1969, p. 324.

[13]Affidavit taken July 1979, Miami (identity confidential).

[14]*Haitian Refugee Center v. Civiletti,* 503 F.Supp. 442, (S.D. Fla. 1980), *modified on other grounds,* 676 F.2d 1023 (5th Cir. 1982).

[15]It is not clear whether the death in custody of one of the defendants in the trial for internal security violations from St. Marc was due entirely to natural causes. Three persons associated with the aborted invasion attempt were known to have been killed after capture. According to reliable informants they were killed in the *Casernes Dessalines* in Port-au-Prince.

[16]See Press Releases of Congressman Ed Townes, Democrat, N.Y., issued August 15, 1983.

[17]Organization of American States, Inter-American Commission on Human Rights, OEA/Ser.L/V/II.57, 20, September 1982.

THE TRAINING OF MANAGERIAL ADMINISTRATIVE PERSONNEL IN HAITI

YVES DAUDET
FRANÇOIS BLANC

The question of the training of managerial administrative personnel is on the agenda in Haiti where, for the first time, a reorganization of public offices should take place with the adoption, in 1982, of a statute for civil servants. In a country where, until the present, there have been public agents indeed but no administration in the modern sense of the term, this planned change is of great importance.

As will be seen, the organization of a coherent public administration is closely linked to the problem of the training of personnel that will compose it. For this reason, it is fitting to begin by calling to mind the main features of Haitian public administration.

Administrative Reform Legislation in Haiti

Only a few years ago, a discussion of the problem of educating managerial personnel in Haiti would merely have led to an enumeration of a series of more or less pertinent declarations concerning administrative reform, without any complementary description of concrete initiatives. The problem, however, has been clearly stated since the beginning of the 1960's, when there emerged a clear recognition of the responsibility of governments and administrative agencies for the improvement of socioeconomic conditions in developing countries.

In Haiti, the first serious recognition of this necessity dates from September 1972, when a seminar on public administration was organized at the University of Law and Economics in Port-au-Prince. The close link between training and administrative reform was at the center of the deliberations. The participants underscored the "urgent necessity" of putting into practice an "appropriate training program" for civil servants.

Indeed, it is perhaps surprising to see the question of administrative reform almost entirely reduced to the question of training civil servants. In a country like Haiti, such an approach is most appropriate in view of the priority that must be accorded to overcoming the nearly general incompetence of civil servants. This incompetence can be explained largely by the clientelism that underlies hiring practices in Haiti. Thus, it has been said that the public agent is a "needy citizen without qualification, to whom is accorded the favor of a job" (Mathieu 1980). Under such conditions, the education and training of managerial administrative personnel clearly stands as the first step towards any reorganization of public administration.

For this reason, on November 20, 1973, the National Institute of Administration, Management and Higher International Studies (INAGHEI) was created. It was charged with the training of managerial personnel, both in the public and private sectors. Lastly, the decreee of September 11, 1974 created the Administrative Commission, the composition and attributions of which had been modified several times before it became, at the end of 1982, the National Agency for Administration and Civil Service. At that time a statute on civil service was also adopted (*Le Moniteur* 1982).

Thus, the Republic of Haiti is now provided with the necessary means for the establishment of a genuine public administration. Nevertheless, one should guard against excessive optimism, especially in a country where firmly entrenched attitudes and practices make it difficult to effect radical changes. In the particular case of administrative reform, it is evident that we are faced with deeply rooted privileges, whose elimination is improbable if one can rely only on the effects of a new set of statutes and on the implementation of a new training program, especially in view of the fact that within the latter remain obsolete teaching practices.

The Organization of the Haitian Public Service Administration

In its present state, Haitian public service administration does not fulfil the principal mission with which it ought to be concerned: national development. On the contrary, it remains an administration concerned mainly with administrative functioning, on the basis of a distinction that seems artificial but which stems no doubt from the existence of massive international aid programs. The latter consider themselves responsible for development, while the state, in the name of sovereignty, controls all administrative matters. Of course, the discourse of political and administrative statements never fails to underscore the primary role of government in the area of development. The fact remains, however, that the administrative machinery is not equipped to take charge of the formulation and management of development programs.

The administrative machinery of the State of Haiti is, in fact, characterized by inefficiency and lack of flexibility. Since the 1940's, we have seen a multiplication of agencies without any overall plan. The missions of these agencies have never been clearly defined, so that their responsibilities have been left to the discretions of their directors. The chronic instability in the ministries, resulting from frequent cabinet changes, has only added to the confusion. As may be expected, the heads of the various agencies and services are concerned primarily with their own future, which becomes more uncertain and difficult to control as one rises in the administrative hierarchy. Furthermore, the phenomenon of clientelism serves to amplify the importance of that factor.

Indeed, the recruitment of civil servants is determined by clientelism in 75 percent of the cases; only 20 percent of civil servants are recruited on the basis of educational status, and only five percent on the basis of competitive entrance examinations. For the 28,000 public agents recruited in this manner, no established set of criteria or procedures for promotion or career development existed, nor did any established salary schedules.

The statute voted on October 12, 1982 is comprised of seven titles and 105 articles and aims at a general reorganization of public administration. Among its main features, it adopts the merit system and the principle of statutory (rather than contractual) status of civil servants. A system of evaluation and advancement is provided in order to ensure career development, and a system of sanctions is established.

In the beginning, the project was drafted as a result of a broad consultation with interested parties, who foresaw the possibility for civil servants of recourse before a special organism against administrative actions. This liberal provision was eliminated by the Council of the Secretaries of State.

The adoption of a statute certainly constitutes an important step for the organization of a system of public administration. Of course, the question that now arises is whether and how it will be implemented. A second question also suggests itself: a statute, but for *which* public administration, and for *which* civil servants?

This leads us back to the original problem of education and training, since if a public administration must have an organizational structure, it is no less necessary that it be composed of competent, well-educated people.

The Structure of Higher Education in Haiti

All the weaknesses of the Haitian educational system are well known; it is recognized even by the country's leaders as being "elitist and thus neglectful of individual differences; it serves only a minority that, only too often, abandons its country" (Secretary of State for Education: 1979).

Since the problems and issues of the Haitian primary school system, including the detailed description of the educational reform currently in progress, are treated elsewhere in this volume, we will proceed directly to a discussion of the implementation of specialized university-level training. However, we should like to underscore the fact that the Educational Reform Program, although it makes provisions for the development of technical and professional training, has not yet dealt with secondary-level instruction or higher education. As in other aspects of administrative organization in Haiti, higher education is characterized by a succession of creations without any overall coordination. Except in the field of medicine, the absence of clearly outlined career paths has as a consequence created a mismatch between the training received at the University and subsequent professional activities of graduates (assuming, of course, that they find employment).

This inadequacy explains why a need was felt for an institution charged specifically with the training of civil servants. Such is the main role filled by INAGHEI, although, while indeed it has since its creation become the principal institution for the training of administrative managerial personnel, other establishments within the University also cooperate in this domain.

The University of Haiti is an old one, since the creation of the Schools of Health (March 1808) dates back to the first years of independence. To these schools, King Christophe added a Royal Academy, comprised of a school of medicine, surgery and pharmacy, a school of agriculture, and a school of engineering. Before the U.S. occupation in 1915, Haiti had four major institutions of higher education; these were the schools of medicine, pharmacy and dentistry, law, engineering and agriculture. In 1942, these schools became the faculties, directed by deans. To these were added over the years a school for higher education and faculties of ethnology, natural sciences, dentistry, and social sciences; the Institute of African Studies and Research; the National Institute for Administration, Management and Higher International Studies (INAGHEI); and the Center for Applied Linguistics. The older institutions have undergone several transformations; for instance, a Faculty of Law and Economics and a Department of Developmental Sciences were added to the faculty of ethnology. These various institutions are grouped together within the framework of the University of the State of Haiti, a denomination acquired in 1960, headed by a Rector.

The revision of the 1960 law is presently being considered with the goal of modernizing and coordinating a rather disparate conglomerate within which overlaps are frequent and wasteful expenditures common; at the same time, the poorly structured organization shows serious shortcomings and fails to accommodate all educational and training needs.

Shortcomings of the Haitian System of Higher Education

Thus, before the creation of INAGHEI, which will be discussed later, Haitian administrative personnel received no specific training. Products of the traditional faculties, such as the Faculty of Law, they did not possess the necessary knowledge to perform their professional duties competently. Of course, the granting of scholarships to foreign countries was, and continues to be, helpful in offsetting this deficiency. But the fact remains that the system of foreign scholarships only provides for the adequate training of those who will become high officials, following studies on the American continent or in Europe: for example, in France, at the International Institute of Public Administration which trains each year three or four holders of French government scholarships. Civil servants who were not fortunate enough to have obtained such scholarships are likely to have received inadequate training.

It should be added that the university studies in Haiti in the area of social sciences (which should be studied by future civil servants) suffer from serious deficiencies. These deficiencies are fundamentally the same as those which affect primary and secondary education. In practice, the only thing higher about higher education is its title, to the extent that neither the available means nor the methods used meet minimal university requirements.

In the first place, there is a near total absence of material means. For instance, the libraries are extremely poor. Apart from a few occasional gifts made under the title of international aid, books are quite outdated, collections incomplete, and libraries are not generally operated by qualified personnel. Students find themselves in a position where acquiring the basic or complementary knowledge they need is practically impossible.

In the case of teaching personnel, the same causes have the same effects. They do not have access to the minimum of indispensable equipment and resources for the preparation of their courses. As a consequence, the instructors are frequently far from being up-to-date or, at best, are half-informed. There is frequently a wide gap between the titles of the courses and their contents; this results in serious deficiencies in the training of the students.

One should also note the absence of a full-time instructional staff at the University. Some halfhearted attempts have been made to correct this, notably at the Faculty of Natural Sciences and the Faculty of Agronomy. The experiment has in general been inconclusive and has little chance of spreading to the field of social sciences.

Thus, with the exception of foreign professors on long-term or short-term teaching appointments (several years or several weeks, respectively), no permanence exists within the teaching corps. As Haitian professors are remunerated on an hourly basis, they naturally tend to multiply their courses in diverse public or private institutions in order to earn a decent annual salary. In this manner, they proceed rapidly from one institution to another, long enough only to give a class without having a real possibility of providing support and counseling to the students.

Lastly, as a general rule, the overall organization of studies and the teaching approaches actually used are not those that should exist in a university. The instruction consists nearly exclusively of theoretical lectures whose content is memorized by the students without concern for concrete application or for adaptation to local realities. Students are rarely invited to reflect on concrete cases likely to offer them a practical experience they will need in carrying out future responsibilities.

Lack of structure and of means of research in the social sciences constitutes the last serious shortcoming of the higher educational system. It is true that a degree in law or in economics is given only after the submission of a thesis. The difficulties encountered by students during preparation of the thesis result in the fact that only a minority of those who complete four years of study at the university obtain a degree (*license*). This piece of research accomplished at the cost of considerable difficulties constitutes the only element of the curriculum which presents an opportunity for originality and concrete application of the training received.

The assessment of the present situation of the traditional institutions of higher learning presented above shows that the latter are not capable of efficiently preparing managerial administrative personnel. In this light, the recent creation of more specialized institutions has certainly led to a marked improvement of the system. In particular, the growing development and reputation of INAGHEI merits mention, in view of the fact that attending that institution is today a prerequisite for any administrative agent who hopes to attain a position of responsibility.

The Role and Structure of INAGHEI

INAGHEI was created by the decree of November 20, 1973, as a result of an extension of the role and attributions of the Institute of Higher International Studies, founded by the law of September 31, 1958, with the mission of forming civil servants in the Department of Foreign Affairs. In addition, the social and administrative section which had existed at the University of Law and Economics since the decree of September 29, 1950, became part of the framework of INAGHEI.

The Institute is assisted in its functioning by the cooperation of Canada and of France, which provide in particular teaching staff and documentation. Studies at INAGHEI lead to several possible diplomas: a *license* in business administration which follows a preparatory year (it contains three options: business management, public administration, accounting); a *license* in political science with specialization in international relations; a diploma in accounting and certificates in business management, public administration, and political science.

Each of these diplomas requires a specified total number of courses: 1,350 hours for the *license,* 900 hours for the diploma in accounting and 450 hours for the certificate. The calculation is made in terms of the notion of course credit units, each unit corresponding to one hour of instruction per week. Thus, a course containing 45 hours (three hours per week for one semester) equals three units; 90 credit units are required to receive the *license.* Students are free to determine the organization of their studies, which, after the preparatory year, will last at least three years for the *license* and may not exceed five years for a full-time student. The choice of credit units rests with students who choose, in consultation with their program advisor, the list of courses to take on the basis of, particularly, the logical ordering of the courses relative to one another and the coherence of the overall program of studies.

The acquisition of the subject matter is controlled according to the system of continuous grading and at least three exams are given each semester. The presentation of a thesis is obligatory to obtain a diploma granted by INAGHEI. The program of courses attempts to combine a general education with that of the area of major study.

During the preparatory year, the 495 hours of courses are divided into general education (culturology, comparative civilization, modern and contemporary history, sociology, etc.), in instruction constituting a general introduction to the upper division classes (principles of amdinistration, introduction to law, introduction to economics), and courses in mathematics and statistics.

The grades received in these different subjects determine admission to one or the other of the different majors. Prospective civil servants opt for the *license* program in public administration or in political science (international relations); the other majors are more appropriate for careers in the private sector.

The diploma in public administration consists of a rather coherent program of instruction during which the student must have acquired the necessary knowledge in the relevant fields and of the political, administrative, and social organization of Haiti. Courses involving comparisons with the systems of foreign countries are also included, as are principles of accounting, of budget, of fiscal systems, of administrative science, personnel and project management, economic planning, etc. The *license* in political science (international relations), addressed to those interested in foreign affairs, comprises a program of study based on a comparable balance between general education and specialized courses.

If the stress placed on writing and research (in particular the organization of research seminars and the preparation of a thesis) are taken into account, theoretically, the future civil servant has received from INAGHEI an education very much adapted to the needs of public administration and most particularly to the administration of development programs. On this basis, the future civil servant should be apt to serve in the various areas of public administration.

Added to this educational and training function for full-time students, products of regular school and university curricula, are other programs related to social promotion, adult education, or advanced training. These activities are best subsumed under the category of part-time student status. Courses are offered in the evening and the length of studies is extended over several years in order to enable those actively engaged in private sector professional activities or in the administration to acquire a diploma facilitating their professional advancement.

In the case of adult education, INAGHEI provides a certificate or a diploma in accounting destined specifically for the private sector. Lastly, a program providing for highly individualized choices enables interested persons to enroll in one or several specialized seminars and to deliver to them a certificate of attendance in an advanced training session. The general mission of INAGHEI is thus to recycle administrative cadres in the private and public sectors.

After this description of the various training programs of INAGHEI, it is nonetheless necessary to take into account the conditions under which the training is conducted as well as the rigidity of the Haitian administrative reality described above, for they severely reduce the effective impact of the training program blueprint. However, the instrument for imparting this professional training does exist in the form of the best managed institution of higher education. Thus, the conditions exist in Haiti for producing adequately trained civil servants.

Links between INAGHEI and other institutions reinforce this positive element. In particular, this link is effected through the training function assumed by the Administrative Commission in its role as educational institution.

Extension Courses and On-the-Job Training Programs

Under the term of "integrated projects for educational and advanced training," programs for the training of administrative cadres have been devised within the framework of the administrative reform and with the participation of INAGHEI, which makes available instructors and teaching facilities.

Studies leading to different diplomas have been conceived with the aim of training municipal and prefectoral civil servants. Educational programs in personnel management and in organization and methods have been planned for, as well as specialized seminars, depending on the needs of the reform. This vast project has been put into effect, first of all through the "advanced program of personnel management."

This program's goal was to rectify the many variations from one service to another in hiring conditions, salaries, and the work of civil servants. The managers of the various personnel services were invited to take this course in order to be brought up to date with information on new techniques of management and on modifying the job descriptions of agents to make them compatible with the new functions of the State. The program was open to many people since it was addressed to any manager having at least ten persons under his or her supervision.

The selection criteria for candidates were applied cautiously, however, as the Administrative Commission could not take the risk of having many complaints lodged within the framework of this innovative program. The courses given dealt with the principles of management, of administrative organization, of civil service, and on the ethics of the nature of administrative procedures, around the theme of "the notion of public service," a notion notoriously lacking in Haiti.

From the pedagogical perspective, an active approach is used which emphasizes the participation of the chosen candidates: case-studies, oral reports, discussions, debates, etc. After a control of the candidate's attendance and a discussion of one hour with a jury on a problem of administrative organization or of personnel management, a certificate is issued by INAGHEI.

Another joint endeavor of the Administrative Commission, of INAGHEI, and of the Department of the Interior, focuses on training personnel in the area of local administration. The program lasts four months. Its aim is to awaken the *communes* (local administrative units) from their present state of lethargy and to enable them to serve as relays between the central power and the population. In this way they could effectively contribute to the process of overall development, which is the goal of administrative reform. Adequate training of administrative agents might lead to the formulation on the part of the *communes* of their needs and objectives as well as to an improvement in methods for program control. The civil servants trained by this program will be able to provide local magistrates and local commissions with technical assistance in the carrying out of their duties.

In the implementation of this program, the Administrative Commission is the contracting agency; it provides financing and overall supervision.

INAGHEI, the executor of a project, carries it out according to the general guidelines defined by the Commission. It furnishes classroom space and the teaching staff as well as necessary pedagogical support. It delivers the final diploma. The Department of the Interior, the organism to which the *communes* report administratively, is responsible for the recruitment of participants, for providing transportation, and for paying them allowances. At the end of the training session, it must guarantee that they will receive a remuneration adequate enough to motivate them to remain in the communal administrative service.

The results of the first session, which involved the first group of *communes,* are on the whole positive in spite of problems of initial implementation, coming principally from the Ministry of the Interior. Inadequate provisions also render difficult or uncertain the fulfillment of salary guarantees given to the participants at the beginning of the work training session. The amount of energy and work invested by the participants was considerable, and this program has certainly contributed significantly in creating a feeling of *esprit de corps* which is not without interest. It would thus be desirable that this project be continued.

It is clear that through these two training programs destined for the training of administrative personnel, the Administrative Commission demonstrated its ability to assume the role it set for itself, namely, to take into account all aspects of administrative reform, including those which involve the training of administrative agents. The latter represent a necessary, if not sufficient, condition for the implementation of administrative reform.

Conclusion

Finally, other specialized institutions in Haiti are also responsible for the training of administrative cadres: for example, the National School of Financial Administration—which, however, has ceased to function—and the Customs School. The latter dates back to 1950. From that time on, heads of sections or programs who held university diplomas or who had attended a training program abroad, provided instruction to customs agents. The School plays an important role, particularly in the area of internal promotion. Within the framework of a foreign aid program sponsored by the Federal Republic of Germany, completed in September 1982, the Customs School was reorganized and installed in a new site.

The National School of Financial Administration, for its part, had existed for four years, from 1978 to 1982, when it ceased to function. In fact, this school largely overlapped with institutions such as those described above.

The growth of INAGHEI represents a positive factor for the training of administrative cadres, for this institution is becoming the sole institution responsible for administrative training, or, in any case, the one involved in oen way or another with this area. Indeed, a coherent and rational program in the training of public servants requires that duplication be eliminated, that a single institution have an overview of needs so as to be able to satisfy them, particularly those that deal with national development. The foundations have been laid for a well-structured Haitian public administration, but the success of the operation is in no way guaranteed. Even if adequate instruments exist, it is necessary for them to function and to function over a long period of time. It is well known that on this point there are great uncertainties in Haiti, primarily in view of the political situation of the country.[1]

NOTE

[1]For additional information on the training of administrative cadres in Haiti, the reader may consult the following:

Anonymous, 1979. La réforme administrative en Haïti. Publication de la Commission Administrative. Port-au-Prince: Presses nationales d'Haïti.

Anonymous, 1981. Administrative reform and plans for decentralization in Haiti: problems, progress and prospects. Report submitted to USAID. Port-au-Prince.

Anonymous, 1982. Loi sur l'uniformisation des structures, normes et procédures du 30 septembre 1982. Le Moniteur, October 28, 1982. Port-au-Prince.

Rateau, J. n.d. Intégration de l'administration publique. Document de référence pour un effort de développement régional en Haïti.

DEMOGRAPHIC FACTORS
IN HAITIAN DEVELOPMENT

AARON SEGAL

Haiti experiences the most serious demographic problems in the Western Hemisphere. Despite the lack of reliable demographic information, three major problems are apparent: population growth, extremely rapid rural to urban migration concentrated on the city of Port-au-Prince, and large-scale international migration. These contribute to worsening Haitian poverty through agricultural regression, soil erosion and a loss of scarce, skilled manpower. Recent government efforts to respond to these demographic problems have been uneven and erratic and have had, as of yet, little impact.

Demographic information in Haiti is both scarce and unreliable. Since independence in 1804 only two national censii have been conducted, one in 1950 and one in 1971. A national census planned for the early 1980's would be the first to use Creole as the principal language of inquiry. Previous censii encountered administrative and methodological difficulties because of the use of French in the questionnaires and misunderstandings created by unsupervised translation into Creole. Both the 1950 and 1971 censii were based on a 100-percent urban sample and a 10-percent sample for the rural areas. In both cases there were alleged undercountings in rural areas, especially of persons with no fixed abode. The 1950 and 1971 census data have been reworked to correct some of these problems, but a 5-10 percent margin of error remains (Recensement General 1971).

From 1971-1975 a multi-round demographic survey was conducted, and in 1977 a Haitian Fertility Survey was undertaken as part of the World Fertility Survey (Allman 1982). The Fertility Survey included a nationally representative sample of 3,211 women aged 15-49 years and is the most

315

reliable national demographic study ever conducted in Haiti. Its results have been correlated with detailed micro-surveys of health and population.

Current demographic information is still deficient. The Haitian Institute of Statistics publishes a little information in its quarterly bulletin based on reports from rural police on figures of births and deaths. These are grossly inaccurate, since civil registration is not compulsory and no incentive to register voluntarily is provided. The bulletin does contain useful information on tourism but the figures on visas granted to Haitians going abroad do not include destination or purpose of travel. Estimates of the size and rate of growth of the Haitian population vary considerably, since they must rely on census data, the 1977 survey, and estimates of legally and illegally resident Haitians from other countries. The World Bank Atlas gives the 1979 population at 4.8 million; the U.S. Bureau of the Census puts the 1981 population at 6 million, and demographer James Allman, who has worked extensively in Haiti, places the population in 1980 at "over 5 million" (World Population 1980; Allman 1982). These estimates represent 15-20 percent differences, an enormous margin of error when extrapolating demographic trends. This author offers a working estimate of slightly over 5 million for the population in 1982—a figure to be used with caution.

The reconstruction of Haitian demographic history is an equally difficult task, complicated by huge chronological gaps and disagreements between different observers. For instance, there are sketchy estimates for the Colonial period but almost no demographic data during the entire nineteenth century. Mats Lundahl has estimated the Haitian population growth at 1.2 percent annually from 1824-1922, at 1.9 percent annually from 1922-1950, and at 2 percent a year from 1950 to the present (Lundahl 1977). Lundahl also estimates maximum population density at 25 persons per square kilometer in the 1820's and 174 persons per square kilometer in 1978 (Lundahl 1979). A third national census, aiming at a 100 percent sample, would make a major contribution to Haitian development by providing a solid demographic data base for the first time. Included would be data on emigration, fertility, and mortality.

Figures for population, age, and sex composition for Haiti rely on the 1971 census when slightly over 40 percent of the population were under the age of 14 (World Population 1980). A comparison to other countries with a similar demographic structure suggests that these data are reliable. There is no census or other information on the racial composition of the population except for the estimates of observers that mulattoes number around 5 percent or less and that there are several thousand persons of Syrian and Lebanese origin (Heinl 1978; Nicholls 1979).

Haiti is one of the most densely populated countries in the world and has one of the highest concentrations of population in a single city. The 1979

World Bank Atlas cites density as 448 persons per square mile (174 per square kilometer). Allman estimates rural density in 1980 at over 540 and 390 persons per square kilometer of cultivated and cultivable land respectively (Allman 1982). The arrondissement of Port-au-Prince is the only predominantly urban area in the country.

Rural to urban migration serves to reinforce the primacy of the capital. Between 1950 and 1971 Port-au-Prince grew twice as fast as any other area, attaining by 1980 an estimated population of 850,000, 17 percent of the national population. The capital has ten times the total population of the second largest urban center, Cap Haitien, and accounts for 80 percent of the national budget, 90 percent of foreign trade, the bulk of all government services, and almost all industry.

The dynamics of population growth, fertility, mortality, and emigration are only beginning to be understood in Haiti. Table 1 provides a summary of population statistics from several sources. Fertility and mortality data are based on village-level surveys as well as the few attempts at national estimates. Emigration data is scarce at any level within Haiti and most estimates are derived from census data of receiving countries.

Haiti is, by all standards of income and welfare, the poorest of thirty Caribbean societies. Economically, it ranks among the twenty poorest countries globally although its rate of population growth is well below those of other countries in its low-income bracket. One of the major problems in estimating population growth is the lack of reliable figures on emigration. Allman considers that since 1950, 700,000 Haitians have emigrated, or 14 percent of all Haitians (Allman 1982). This author prefers a lower total net emigration figure since 1950 or approximately 500,000 or 10 percent of the population. Thus, a usable annual population growth figure including net emigration for the 1980's may be two percent. A national census would provide data to correct and to update this estimate.

Early estimates of fertility and infant mortality were impressionistic. The 1970 national nutrition study published figures of 160 deaths annually per 1000 live births, and 26.5 annual deaths per 1000 children in the 1-4 age group (Fougere et al. 1970:25-6). Willem Brand used limited rural studies to estimate infant mortality at 150 to 170 per 1000 live births in 1965 (Brand 1965). Robert Rotberg in 1971 stated that "between 7 and 15 percent of all Haitian children die during the first eight weeks of life from umbilical tetanus; about 50 percent of all children die before they are five years old" (Rotberg 1971).

The 1977 Haitian Fertility Survey is the most complete national study of its kind in Haiti. Its representative sample included 3,211 women aged 15-49, of whom 2,176 were in some form of marital union at least once, and of whom 1,842 were in union at the time of the survey. Total fertility rates

Table 1. Summary of Population Statistics from Several Sources

Date	Source	Total Population (millions)	Crude Birth Rate	Crude Birth Rate	Infant Mortality Total	Infant Mortality Urban	Infant Mortality Rural	Child Mort. 1-4 yrs.	Life Expect. e_0
1971	IHS, Census	4.3	36.5	16.0	147	—	—	45	51
1970-1975	Census and Multiround Surveys			16.0	150	—	—	27	
1975-1976	Projet Integre, at Petit-Goave (rural)				—	—	107	18	52.3
1977	Haiti Fertility Survey	5.0	37.0	14.5	124	197	103		47.5
1978	National Nutrition Survey				—	147	119		

		1971	1980	2000
Urban Population (percent)		20.4%	27.5%	36.8%

Population Density per square kilometer	Overall:	156	180
	Arable land:	490-504	626

Annual Growth Rate: 1.9 to 2.2%

Total Fertility Rate: 5.5 overall; 4.0 (Port-au-Prince);
(1974-76)   6.1 (rural areas)

Age structure: Under 5 : 15.4%
(estimates for 1980)   Under 15: 40.5%

Annual Out-migration: At least 20,000 (0.5%);
                                     possibly more than 40,000

Literacy: 10% to 20%

(numbers of live children per woman) were estimated at 5.5 with 6.1 for the rural areas and 4.0 for Port-au-Prince (Allman 1982). These figures are considerably below those of Berggren and other studies and suggest that, for whatever reasons, Haitian fertility may be declining. The 1977 survey also indicates falling infant mortality rates with estimates for 1975 of 124 deaths per 1000 live births for Haiti, 103 for rural areas, and 197 for Port-au-Prince (Allman 1982). But these mortality figures differ from earlier studies and the higher numbers for the capital suggest that more thorough interviewing was done there.

The Fertility Survey also generated the first national information on desired family size, knowledge and use of contraception, and other fertility determinants such as breastfeeding, conjugal union patterns, and access to family planning (Allman 1982). Several of these factors have combined to significantly reduce Haitian fertility well below the biological maximum of 50 births per annum per 1000 women in the age of fertility. The most important may be age at first conjugal union, which was calculated at 21.6 years in the 1977 survey. This makes Haitian adolescent fertility probably the lowest in Latin America. There are some indications that an increasingly acute shortage of arable land may raise the age of first union. Possession of a minimum of arable land is often a condition for initial union in rural Haiti. Prolonged breastfeeding also serves to lower fertility. The average age at weaning has been calculated at 18 months in rural areas and at 12 months in the cities. Only in Port-au-Prince have a significant number of women stopped breastfeeding completely (Allman 1982). Knowledge and practice of traditional and modern contraception is just beginning to play a role in fertility reduction. The Fertility Survey found that women desired an average total family size of 3.58 children, with no preference for sons.

Other factors serve to reduce fertility. Poor health and nutrition result in frequent miscarriages and stillbirths as does the widespread incidence of venereal disease. Social patterns including the absence of adult males away seeking work and the formation of second households, also contribute to lower fertility rates.

Infant and child mortality rates of Haiti are among the highest in the world. They are caused by malnutrition, intestinal diseases, respiratory diseases including tuberculosis, tetanus, typhoid, measles, and other illnesses. These rates could be dramatically and rapidly lowered with an effective and relatively inexpensive rural health program emphasizing post-natal care (Bordes and Couture 1978).

Haiti has yet to enter the classic demographic transition proceeding in stages from high fertility and infant mortality to lower fertility and mortality. Not even in the capital do the available figures indicate that this demographic transition has begun. Most countries first reduce mortality and then, a generation or more later, witness a drop in fertility. A few, such as China and Cuba, have sought to simultaneously reduce fertility and mortality rates, relying on massive propaganda, major changes in the roles of women, easy access to several contraceptive methods, and powerful peer and social pressure.

Haiti may have to follow its own demographic course. It appears that fertility has been falling in spite of negative economic growth, especially in the rural areas. Ecological pressures may be bringing about fertility reductions even though standards of living are stagnant or falling. The lack of longitudinal data makes this no more than a guess. Can Haitian fertility continue to fall in the absence of economic growth? Certainly the relative equality of Haitian women, their independence, and the land shortage could render increasing misery and lower fertility compatible. The prospects for reducing infant mortality are not good, because of financial, personnel, and infrastructure problems in the government. While the increased probability of children surviving has been an important factor inducing couples elsewhere to have fewer children, this has not yet been the case in Haiti. Thus, the safest prediction is that Haiti's population will continue to grow at around two percent a year less net emigration.

Information on Haiti emigration is derived from data available in the countries of reception, including Canada, the United States, France, and other Caribbean nations. These figures may or may not include legal and illegal aliens, and vary considerably in comparability and coverage (Segal 1975). For the period 1950-1980, the totals have been estimated at as many as 700,000 (Allman 1982) or as few as 500,000 (Segal 1975). These figures indicate that since 1950 between 10 and 12 percent of all Haitians have emigrated, a remarkable proportion for a Caribbean country that has no preferential access to non-Carbbean states as do Puerto Rico, the French Antilles, and the British West Indies (until 1962).

The impact of this massive emigration on Haiti is profound. For example, assuming current live births to be 100,000 per year, net legal and illegal emigration may be 25,000-50,000 persons a year, or 0.4 percent of the population. Emigration lowers Haitian annual population growth from 2 to 1.75-1.5 percent. In addition, emigrant remittances have been conservatively estimated at $35-40 million a year and by other observers as much as $160 million a year (World Bank 1981). Remittances rival domestic savings as a source of investment, and as basic sustenance for hundreds of thousands of Haitians.

Estimating net annual emigration is risky. No more than 25,000 Haitian annually can emigrate legally, due to the U.S. quota of 20,000 persons per country and other difficulties in gaining entry to Canada and France. Depending on the demands of the sugar harvest, 15,000-20,000 Haitian enter the Dominican Republic annually as legal temporary workers. Some stay behind and add to the 10,000 or so Haitians who illegally enter the Dominican Republic every year. During the early 1970's, although legal emigration to the Bahamas was ended, 2,000-3,000 Haitians a year entered illegally. Since the late 1970's the Bahamian government has been repatriating Haitians at a rate probably greater than illegal immigrants (Marshall 1979).

Haitians have used two methods to enter the U.S. illegally. One is to obtain student, tourist, or similar visas and then to remain after their legal period of stay has expired. Firmer controls on the granting of visas may have cut the inflow to about 5,000 person a year. Poorer and less educated Haitians, especially from the semi-arid Northwest coast, have sought to enter through southern Florida on small frail boats. Between 1972 and 1980, 42,000 Haitian "boat people" were apprehended by U.S. authorities while an unknown number slipped through undetected. Prior to 1981 many Haitians were allowed temporary entry, which included the right to seek employment while they awaited immigration hearings. Since 1981, however, the Haitian government has allowed U.S. Coast Guard ships in Haitian waters to intercept and turn back Haitian emigre boats. The latter measure, along with others regarding refugee status, has sharply reduced the numbers of boat people.

The largest group in the Haitian diaspora, consisting of over 300,000, nearly half of which is estimated as illegal, resides in the U.S. Haitians are concentrated in New York City, northern New Jersey, and Miami. The illegals and many of the legals are found in low-income factory and service employment. They and their children are likely to speak Creole as a first language, have little formal education, and encounter many problems of cultural adaptation. While many Haitians in the U.S. send their children to Catholic schools, an estimated 30,000 attend public schools, of which only a few have bilingual programs in Creole (Foster 1982). About 50,000 of the Haitians in the U.S. are well-educated professionals, technicians, and small businessmen who have, with considerable effort, adapted well in the U.S. (Dominguez 1975).

The second largest group of Haitians abroad is in the Dominican Republic, where their numbers have been estimated at around 200,000. This group, unlike that in the U.S., is constituted primarily of adult males. These Haitians have little or no formal education and are found in service jobs and casual labor. Some came as temporary workers to cut cane and then stayed illegally. Others came as border-crossers, smugglers, Haitians married to Dominicans, and even Haitians born in the Dominican Republic but lacking documentation (Merino Hernandez 1973).

The Haitian community in the Bahamas has peaked at about 20,000, legal and illegal (Marshall 1979). Attracted by the Bahamian construction and tourist boom of the 1970's, these are mostly adult male construction and service workers, often from the fishing villages of northwest Haiti. Denied legal status or the chance to reunite their families by the Bahamian government, Haitians are being gradually squeezed out. Some seek to enter the U.S. illegally rather than be repatriated.

Haitians in Canada number about 20,000 and are by contrast a well-educated and highly-skilled community of doctors, nurses, accountants, and technicians (Segal 1975; Henry 1982). They are concentrated in the province of Quebec, largely in Montreal, and have done well taking advantage of their fluency in French and French-style education.

France, Africa, Latin America, French Guyana, and other Caribbean states account for another 8,000-10,000 Haitians, primarily professionals and technicians but also laborers. Some work for international organizations or national governments, especially in Africa. Others are in the professions or in business.

Some observers consider the exodus of skilled and educated Haitians as a "brain-drain." For example, half or more of Haiti's newly trained doctors and nurses have emigrated (Segal 1975). While their emigrant remittances are important they are partly offset by Haitian investment costs in educating and training the country's few skilled persons. However, during the 1970's Haitian economic growth was so slow as to make it extremely difficult to productively absorb many of these persons. Yet needs are such that Haiti can more readily lose doctors than scarce nurses. Thus Haiti has joined the ranks of other Caribbean countries, like Cuba and Jamaica, that export manpower already scarce at home.

How has the Haitian government responded to these demographic problems and what have been the consequences of its policies? The government has deliberately encouraged the rapid urbanization of Port-au-Prince by concentrating administration and infrastructure investment in the capital (Anglade 1981). At present trends, by 1990 the capital will have a population of over one million, nearly 20 percent of the total population. The consequences of uncontrolled single-city growth are evident in the experiences of San Juan, Mexico City and other Third World cities (Cross 1979).

There are ample opportunities to promote several of the secondary cities with public works investment and other incentives. For instance, the World Bank is funding a new wharf at Cap Haitien. Since rural-to-urban migrants are primarily seeking employment, some of the internal migration could be diverted from Port-au-Prince, thus easing both massive strains and demands for fresh capital invested in the city.

The Haitian government exercises only limited influence over emigration. Legal emigrants in the 1970's were taxed $500-1000 a person to obtain the required government documents. The boat people paid $500-2000 a person to private parties. Temporary migrant workers to the Dominican Republic pay an inscription fee and a head tax to the Haitian government. Overseas remittances are taxed in a variety of ways. But the government has not sought to prevent skilled Haitians from leaving and has been unsuccessful to date in negotiating agreements to export workers as cultivators to the Bahamas, France, French Guyana, or Belize.

Haiti is becoming more and more economically dependent on the export of labor and less and less able to control or even to guide this export. Future prospects are dim. The Bahamas is closing its doors to migrant workers. Since 1981 the U.S. has been deporting and turning back the boat people at sea. Canada, faced with high unemployment, has tightened its quota for legal entry. Soon the Haitian government's major preoccupation may be the lack of outlets for exporting labor. Should legal and illegal emigration fall sharply Haiti could experience a fiscal and social crisis.

While there is almost no coherent policy on emigration and urbanization, the government now has explicit and ambitious goals for fertility and mortality. The Department of Health has proposed to provide national access to family planning services by the year 2000, to reduce the crude birth rate by 50 percent, and to lower infant and maternal mortality rates substantially by offering prenatal, delivery, and post-natal services to all women. The Agency for International Development is more cautious, but also optimistic. It expects that "effective use of family planning will increase to at least 20 percent of the population of reproductive age and result in a measurable decline in fertility" (AID 1981).

The history of family planning, population discussions, and the evolution of government policies has been provided in detail elsewhere (Allman 1982; Bordes and Couture 1978; Segal 1975). Essentially a few foreign non-profit organizations and their dedicated Haitian collaborators brought family planning to the country during the 1960's. The government marked time until 1971 when a Division of Family Hygiene was established in the Ministry of Health. Family planning was formally endorsed by 1973 and the requisite external aid sought. During the 1970's and early 1980's family planning services were gradually extended through government and private non-profit programs, with an emphasis on combining maternal and child health and access to contraception. The first systematic research on birth control was also initiated.

This research showed that Haitian women of all educational levels and social classes desired fewer children, with older women often wanting no more children. Over 85 percent of the women surveyed, ever in union, had heard of one or more contraceptive methods. An estimated 25 percent of women currently in union and fecund were using a contraceptive method in 1977, compared to 34,000 using government family planning services. Few abortions were reported while nearly 40 percent of contraceptive users relied on pharmacies and private doctors. However, of the fecund women in union 18 percent were using inefficient methods, 7 percent efficient methods, and 75 percent were not practicing contraception. In spite of impressive gains family planning is not yet having a significant impact on fertility.

Dr. Ary Bordes, the pioneer of Haitian family planning, has consistently urged the need to simultaneously reduce fertility and infant mortality in order to change parental attitudes towards childbearing (Bordes and Couture 1978). His desire to combine family planning and maternal health services has been accepted in principle, but its implementation has been slow. Once assured that the children they bear are likely to survive, parents may be more willing to have fewer children. Children present an economic burden to families in the capital, while in rural Haiti they are an asset. They are sent to work when quite young and later are expected to support their parents. Dr. Bordes pioneered rural clinics, family planning radio programs in Creole, house-to-house experimental contraceptive distribution, and other programs. As Director of the Division of Family Hygiene, he has struggled with cumbersome bureaucracies, staff and equipment shortages, and other problems. The prospect during the 1980's of sustained UN, AID, and other external funding could provide an important impetus for wider adoption of programs he initiated.

Elsewhere it has been easier to reduce infant mortality than fertility. This may not be the case in Haiti. Normally mortality falls when children have shoes or sandals and protection against intestinal diseases through improved nutrition, potable water, minimal sewage disposal, and vaccinations. Reductions in fertility, on the other hand, depend primarily on changes in human behavior brought about by education and employment for women, and changes in the age of marriage and initial childbearing.

Haiti cannot afford to see infant mortality fall while fertility remains constant. Fertility must come down first or both rates must fall together. Otherwise, with emigration outlets closing, Haiti risks a population increase that its strained resources cannot support. Even if present emigration levels continue they serve as outlets limited mostly to adult males. The approach of combining family planning with pre- and post-natal simple rural health services is sound and has been proven in Haiti on a limited scale. During the 1980's Haiti will have to expand control of birth and mortality rates together or else risk environmental havoc.

MIGRATION IN HAITI

ULI LOCHER

The migrations of Haitians have only recently attracted the attention of researchers, planners, and politicians. A few dissertations (Ahlers 1979; Locher 1978) and smaller pieces (Pierre 1975; De Ronceray 1979) are proof of the interest of several Haitians and foreigners in internal migration during the past fifteen years. The subjects of Haitian emigration and emigrants have also been treated in various forms (Glick 1975; Marshall 1979). Yet, the major publications on Haiti since 1965 (e.g., Rubin and Schaedel 1975; Rotberg 1971; Mintz 1975; Lundahl 1979) have all lacked a systematic analysis of migration, even where they have included passing references or short sections on some of its aspects.[1] The plight of the boat people has changed all that. With news of their tragic fate filling every newspaper and journal from *Times* and *Time* to *NACLA* and *Collectif Paroles,* it is unlikely that future accounts of Haiti and its people will omit an analysis of population movements.

Furthermore, it is unlikely that one might research any Haitian topic without constant reference to issues like the entanglement of the Haitian and North American economies, population flows, remittances, etc. Haiti has come to be seen as an integral part of a wider constellation, be it the capitalist world system or the Caribbean Basin with its big brother. Thus, one can no longer write about something "Haitian" in isolated terms. More specifically with regard to this paper, the separation of internal and international migration appears to be artificial in a situation in which they are structurally linked. The treatment of a topic such as urban growth must include an analysis of the stimulants located outside of the country. The study of the causes and effects of migration becomes a cyclical argument about cumulative causation, in Myrdal's fashion.

Few data sources concerning Haitian migration exist and those have often been inadequately exploited. Despite its shortcomings, the 1971 census remains the most important data source as long as the data accumulated by the participants in this conference are not made accessible. The absence of coherent theory is as limiting as the paucity of data. At the present time, little more is available than a collection of theoretical fragments, impressions, and frequently untested hypotheses, grouped around catchwords such as rural exodus, population pressure, and exploitation. A number of these theoretical impressions are listed and their appropriateness is questioned below.

This paper consists of three parts. The first section briefly outlines the three analytical models which seem to underlie most recent discussions of Haitian migration. A subsequent section presents some of the demographic and sociological evidence as it is currently available. Finally, structural determinants and the effects of migration are considered, and some generalizations and projections into the future conclude the paper.

Three Paradigms[2]

The first and perhaps most widely accepted paradigm which attempts to explain migration in Haiti falls under the general heading of *equilibrium*. Equilibrium models come in the form of social and economic variants. Social variants are mainly concerned with modernization while economic variants deal with labor market differences and the flows of human capital resulting from modernization. These models see internal migration as a response to the penetration of modern western values, communication systems, production forms and opportunity structures within a traditional and backward society. Modern sector jobs create hopes and expectations which spread, thanks to telephones, radio, and roads, or simply the *télédjol,* and motivate people to migrate. The modernization of certain sectors, regions, and institutions creates imbalances which render migration advantageous. Ahlers' (1979) human capital analysis fits into this frame as does Todaro's (1969) tested model. While Todaro is not as concerned with modern value structures as were the original modernization theorists (Lerner 1965; Black 1967), his work should nevertheless be seen as an analysis of how the regional imbalances created by unequal modernization induce migration.

While Ahlers' is the most sophisticated analysis falling within this paradigm,[3] several others should not be overlooked. These studies are associated with CHISS (Centre Haitien d'Investigation en Sciences Sociales) and are primarily concerned with the results of migration rather than its structural determinants. They portray the slums of Port-au-Prince and Cap Haitien as harbours for maladapted marginals: maladapted in that they have traditional rural values, inappropriate skills, and insufficient knowledge of the larger city; and marginal in that they are trapped in their disadvantaged condition, outside the modern urban opportunity structure and probably anomic.[4]

One must not confuse the issues with broad generalizations. Ahlers' human capital analysis is a far cry from De Ronceray's Chicago School sociology. Yet, the two approaches share a common concern for migration as a response to regional imbalances. In both cases, the massive migration to the capital city ideally lowers urban incomes and ultimately restores some kind of equilibrium. "Migration decreases the pressure of population in low-growth areas and provides for the labor needs in the growing regions, thus helping restore balance between human and capital resources" (Portes 1978:6).

The *cumulative causation* paradigm is radically different from the equilibrium paradigm. Applied to Haiti by Mats Lundahl, it focuses on "a downward spiral of circular and cumulative causation which slowly depresses the standard of living among peasants" (Lundahl 1979:18). Falling rural incomes and poverty are the cause of migration. This process has accelerated since the 1950's and 1960's and there is no end to it in sight.

Unlike the modernization and Todaro models, the cumulative causation paradigm makes a restoration of equilibrium appear impossible. Human and capital resources flow in the same direction—from the disadvantaged and increasingly impoverished region to the relatively advantaged one, be it Gonaives, Port-au-Prince, or Miami. The paradigm predicts disaster for most of Haiti.

A third paradigm belongs to the *dependency* school of research. Its best application to Haitian migration is contained in an article published by *Collectif Paroles* (Holly et al., 1979). The dependency paradigm stresses the contribution made by peripheral regions to central regions through the transfer of surplus human resources. It also emphasizes the powerlessness of peripheral regions within the periphery. Migration is seen as a tax imposed by the (relatively) rich upon the poor. Various inducements introduced by outsiders and outside forces are seen as causes of migration. While the cumulative causation paradigm does not exclude the operation of such outside forces, they become the only crucial element for the dependency model,[5] sometimes to the point of presenting the process of underdevelopment and its resulting population movements as a single grand conspiracy.

The following presents data selected in order to allow a choice between the paradigms. While data presentation follows those which have been attempted elsewhere (Charles and Fanfan 1981; Locher forthcoming), the conclusions attempt to break new ground.

The Extent of Internal Migration in Haiti

Two results of the 1971 census[6] merit immediate mention. The great majority of the population is stable, with 93.4% residing in their community of birth. This stability, documented in 1971, is primarily a characteristic of rural Haiti. Fully 40% of the urban population are migrants.[7] Thus, migration is a major factor in urban growth. By the year 2000, approximately one half of the Haitian population will be concentrated in the (old) Département de l'Ouest.

Table 1 shows figures for all twenty interdepartmental migration streams and counter-streams. Six of these streams are important in that they involve significantly more than 5,000 persons. The most significant stream moves from the South to the West, representing almost the equivalent of the other nineteen streams combined. Within one generation the South has lost more than 100,000 people to the West; 10% of its 1971 population have moved, primarily to Port-au-Prince.

Two more of the important streams lead to the capital: those from the Artibonite and the North. A third one has the same direction, if not destination; it connects the North to the Artibonite. Finally, numbers five and six in rank are counter-streams linking the West to its neighbors, the South, and the Artibonite. The remaining streams are much less significant, generally linking destinations which are far from the capital city. The insignificance of these streams serves as proof of the dominant role played by the *"République de Port-au-Prince"* in integrating the country.

The department of the West is the big winner in all migratory exchanges documented by the 1971 census. It displays an extremely positive net migration while the department of the South has a correspondingly negative net migration outcome. When the absolute numbers in Table 2 are seen in relation to the 1971 population, the similarity between the North and the North-West becomes visible. Each department succeeds in attracting only 1.5% of its population from other departments while losing approximately 5%. The net loss is 3.5%. Only the Artibonite displays a slightly positive net migration. In this case, an in-migration of 4.1% offsets an out-migration of 4%. The Artibonite serves as a stage for a migration flow from the North to the West. It has received four times more migrants from the North than it has sent there and has relinquished twice the number of migrants to the West as those received from that department.

Since the census is limited to interdepartment migration, movements within smaller administrative units cannot be analyzed here. This probably leads to a serious underestimation of rural-rural migration in comparison to

Table 1. Internal Migration Streams in Haiti, by Number of Migrants

Rank	Origin	Destination	Number of Immigrants
1	South	West	101,998
2	Artibonite	West	21,667
3	North	West	20,911
4	North	Artibonite	16,680
5	West	South	12,846
6	West	Artibonite	10,359
7	North-West	West	5,049
8	Artibonite	North	4,528
9	North-West	Artibonite	2,778
10	West	North	2,237
11	Artibonite	North-West	1,585
12	North-West	North	1,309
13	South	Artibonite	1,303
14	West	North-West	935
15	North	North-West	858
16	South	North	576
17	North	South	379
18	Artibonite	South	257
19	South	North-West	195
20	North-West	South	121

Source: IHS, 1971 Census

urban moves. A clear picture of the latter is available. While the cities of Cap Haitien, Gonaives, Cayes, Jérémie, Saint-Marc, Port-de-Paix and Jacmel all roughtly doubled in size between 1950 and 1971, Port-au-Prince nearly tripled (Locher 1978). This faster growth increased urban primacy, since in 1950 the population of Port-au-Prince was already six times as great as that of Cap Haitien, the second ranking city. Thus, urbanization has meant the growth of metropolitan Port-au-Prince at 6.1% annually, in comparison to 4.1% for all cities and 1.6% for the country as a whole (Ahlers 1979:1).

What role does migration play in this urban growth? In applying the estimation method as described by Davis (1965), one finds that between 1950 and 1971 rural-urban migration accounted for 59% of Haitian urban growth, while natural population increase accounted for only 8%.[8] Migration was the key factor during that period. However, as both the total and the urban populations of Haiti continue to grow, the proportions

**Table 2. In-Migration, Out-Migration, Net Migration and
Urban Population of the Five (Old) Departments**

	Artibonite	North	North-West	West	South
In-Migrants	31,120	8,650	3,573	149,625	13,621
Out-Migrants	28,037	38,846	9,257	26,377	104,072
Net Migration	+3,983	+30,196	—5,684	+123,248	—90,451
% Urban Population	11.8	16.9	12.3	33.2	9.2

Source: IHS, 1971 Census

become reversed. Extrapolating figures for the years 1990 and 2000, the increase in urban population during that decade will be due more to natural population increase (55%) than to migration (38%). Haiti, the least urbanized country of the Western hemisphere, will thus display a trend which Davis found typical of Third World countries and which has moved him to become a prophet and advocate of birth control.

Migrant Characteristics

Two issues related to characteristics have emerged as important: migrant selectivity and economic achievement. Both subjects have been discussed in the literature and have been studied on the basis of data collections other than the census. However, the census provides some important evidence with regard to the selectivity issue.

The socio-economic variables in the 1971 census suffer methodological shortcomings and are better left aside (Dautruche and Margaritis, 1980). The sex variable appears to be more reliable. Table 3 lists migrations according to type with corresponding sex ratios. Rural-urban migration is predominant and is highly selective of women, displaying a sex ratio of only 49.1 men per 100 women. This migration is primarily directed toward Port-au-Prince as previously noted. Urban-urban migration is similarly biased towards the capital city. It is somewhat more balanced with a sex ratio of 66.7. Migrations toward rural areas consist of a majority of men, especially in streams which originate in cities.

Explanations for this pronounced sex selectivity can be found in the occupational opportunity structures characteristic of rural and urban areas. The domestic service, commercial, and light manufacturing sectors in the city offer much more employment to women than to men. Conversely, agricultural work in rural Haiti is mainly carried out by men. However, the above must be qualified immediately, since the estimates of employment and employment opportunities may be off-target due to overt and hidden

Table 3. Sex Ratios for Four Types of Migration

Type of Migration	Number of Immigrants	Sex Ratio
Rural-urban	81,587	49.1
Urban-urban	76,865	66.7
Rural-rural	36,800	103.0
Urban-rural	11,320	121.5

Source: IHS, 1971 Census

unemployment. In addition, the census data conceal seasonal, circular, irregular, cyclical, and other types of moves which have been consistently reported in empirical fieldwork. Employment opportunities appear to be a convincing, however incomplete, explanation of sex selectivity.

Another type of selectivity is socioeconomic and is specifically based on formal education. Rural education levels are generally extremely low. However, individuals with comparatively higher levels are more likely to move to the city. Ahlers' (1979) findings on this point confirm what has been generally found in most countries. However, this should not lead one to view education as a cause of migration. It is more likely that families which are able to afford to send their children to school are also capable of locating and realizing opportunities non-existent in rural areas. Furthermore, as rural Haiti progressively declines, many families find it indispensable to relocate at least some of their members to Port-au-Prince in order to maintain their overall economic status. They send their most promising offspring to the capital.

Such a behavior is rational both for the rural poor and for other strata, such as the elite of the provincial towns. Many of the latter have permanently relocated in Port-au-Prince and abroad. In sum, on an individual or familial level, it is not poverty which causes migration. On the contrary, persons who are relatively better off are selected to become migrants. This tendency does not negate basic cost/benefit considerations. A farmer who has a comparatively sound economic base in Fonds-des-Négres will not sell out, pack up, and move to Port-au-Prince unless his anticipated gains offset his presumed losses and foregone opportunities. However, he might send his children to school in Port-au-Prince. They will probably remain there, setting in motion the process generally discussed under the headings of "chain migration" or "migration networks."

The term "rural exodus" is probably inadequate in describing Haitian rural-urban migration. Not only does the rural population continue to grow, but the term "exodus" implies large-scale movement of a largely non-selective character. These are inappropriate descriptions of Haitian reality. Only a portion of the population increase is transferred to cities and this transfer is highly selective.

Another migrant characteristic which is frequently mentioned in the literature is poverty. The argument is an old one and can be found in policy documents as well as sociological studies. Illiterate rural populations are seen as filling urban slums. The poor are disadvantaged by their lack of urban skills and are therefore condemned to poverty. Migration is viewed as a cause of poverty at both the individual level and that of the city as a whole.

Empirical research does not generally support this hypothesis. When the appropriate control variables are introduced, the difference between migrants and urban natives disappears. Socioeconomic background variables and education explain economic achievement differences, while migrant status as such explains nothing (Locher 1978). To present migration as the cause of urban poverty is not only to disregard the empirical evidence but also to completely reverse the facts. Whatever paradigm one prefers, there is a universal consensus that migration is a response to regional inequalities and is directed toward the wealthier areas. Consideration of the sequence of events is important in that areas of destination are better off before a given individual migrates there. Migration is selective of the young, the educated, and the mobile (who risk fewer foregone opportunities). The migrants studied in Port-au-Prince display these characteristics when compared to appropriate control groups (Locher 1978).

Structural Determinants of Migration

The previous section of this paper dealt with the characteristics of individual migrants. The following argument, however, looks at structural factors, and this shift to a different level of analysis will have implications when terms such as "poverty" or "exodus" are used. There is some reason to think that individual poverty may prevent a person from migrating while structural poverty can be a stimulus or cause of high out-migration rates.

Let us first consider factors located within rural Haiti. A century of increasing population pressure on the land has led to a situation where peasants face the paradoxical condition of simultaneous shortages of both land and labor. *Land shortage* is the result of population increase, land erosion and the passing of ownership from rural to urban individuals and families. It is thus not a problem of insufficient total acreage but more specifically one of an ever decreasing proportion of good land under peasant control. *Labor shortage* also is not a question of sheer numbers but of capable agriculturalists able and willing to work at extremely low income levels. There is solid documentation for at least one region, showing how peasants have adapted to this situation by tying their kin into sharecropping arrangements (Murray 1977). Since such adaptation has not led to increased productivity of Haitian agriculture, it has really not solved more than a social problem—access to land for aspiring peasants—while leaving the structural problem untouched: rural Haiti is less and less able to feed even the rural population, let alone the cities. In this sense we can indeed speak of poverty (at the structural level) as the cause of migration.

It would be erroneous, however, to focus on structural changes in rural Haiti as the sole determinants of migration. There can be no doubt that Port-au-Prince exercises an attraction felt throughout the country. There is more new employment there, the wages are much higher, the starvation less pronounced, general levels of morbidity and mortality lower, and the prospects for economic betterment are higher. Why is this so? The answer is at least partially political. The capital city has been successful in imposing its demands for produce and cheap labor upon the countryside. The mechanisms of direct and indirect taxation as well as the integration of all of rural Haiti into one market system serve to concentrate advantages in the city without distributing benefits to the countryside. This process is cumulative in that every increase of urban dominance further decreases the competitiveness of rural Haiti. Even remote villages have no choice but to hand over their human and capital resources to the city.

Rural development efforts have occasionally tried to change this trend, yet their chances for success are minimal. Even where they have succeeded in raising rural standards of living they have usually stimulated urban growth even more. Most of the operational budget of Development Agencies is usually spent in cities, in the form of salaries, rent, and supplies. Project budgets again contain similar items, augmented by salary supplements to civil servants, vehicles, consultants' fees, and the like. All these expenditures have multiplier effects in the cities, and mostly in Port-au-Prince. Rural development efforts, be they directed at credit schemes, irrigation, road building, education, the production of higher-yield crops, or anything else, are thus frequently factors which create urban employment and increase rural/urban economic inequality. Their indirect effect is increased rural-urban migration (Locher 1981).

Some of the most important determinants of Haitian migration must be found outside of Haiti. During the first decades of this century American companies operating in Cuba recruited in excess of 200,000 Haitian workers, mainly for work on sugar plantations. A similar migration of *braceros* can be observed today to the Dominican Republic, although in this case we observe both less specialization in plantation work and more labor circulation among those who do work for the *ingenios*. But the migrations to the USA, Canada and other rich nations during the most recent decades have probably involved as many Haitians as the Cuban and Dominican destinations combined. The need of advanced economies for (relatively) cheap labor has attracted hundreds of thousands of legal and illegal immigrants. Their remittances have in turn helped to finance the education, urban residences, and frequently also the emigration of other Haitians. Since relatives established in a "better" place become a resource and potential destination for other family members, today's distribution of Haitian-origin population can be conceptualized as a complex web of individual migration networks, spanning rural and urban areas in Haiti as well as foreign destinations. Some researchers have therefore started to conceptualize migration as a "process of network-building" (Portes 1978:43). Networks facilitate the flow of information concerning opportunities, reduce the cost of migration and initial adaptation, and channel benefits in reliable ways. They constitute significant resources and accelerate migration by their very existence.

Today's international division of labor has a direct impact upon the migrations of the Haitian people. Three of the most important elements of this division of labor are the allocation of poorly remunerated work in the advanced countries' non-unionized sectors to immigrant laborers, the relocation of light assembly industrial production to low-income countries, and the use of peasant labor for the production of agricultural export crops. While the latter has not affected Haiti on a very large scale in recent years, the first two clearly have. Responding to the needs of advanced economies, Haiti is supplying labor both in Port-au-Prince and abroad. The migrations of hundreds of thousands of Haitians must be seen in this larger frame of reference. Much of the stimulus for urban growth in Haiti lies outside of the country, as do some of the principal causes of emigration.

What Does the Future Hold?

The principal countries of destination for Haitians going abroad are currently undergoing an economic recession. Due to their rising levels of unemployment they have reduced the numbers of immigrants they are willing to admit. Canada has done this through the usual legal and bureaucratic channels, while the United States has also found it necessary to deploy armed vessels to intercept and discourage illegal immigration. But this is not likely to be more than an interlude. The advanced economies will continue to need immigrant labor for certain types of work and the next economic boom will mean that more immigrants will be permitted to land on the North American shores and airports.

Furthermore, it is unlikely that the advanced economies will stop exporting work. The assembly worker in Haiti, earning less in a week than many North American counterparts earn in an hour, will sustain the competitiveness of employers on the international markets. The expansion of Port-au-Prince's "industrial park" will thus continue further accentuating rural/urban inequality and accelerating migration to the city.

Nevertheless, these trends should not be exaggerated. As drastic change is unlikely to come about, Haiti will for many decades remain predominantly rural. Agriculture will continue to be the backbone of the economy. The "soft state" will not miraculously create strong institutions, nor will it drastically alter relations of production, per capita output, or productivity. Life in rural Haiti will be miserable, although mortality might decline somewhat, leading to further population pressure.

In the absence of drastic political and economic change, migration to the cities, particularly Port-au-Prince, will continue. The primate city offers advantages to decision-makers. It will continue to receive the bulk of investment, foreign aid, industrial expansion, infrastructural development, and other elements which accelerate migration.

Given these circumstances, migration in Haiti must be allowed to continue. There are no rural development policies in sight which could significantly reduce rural-urban migration. On the contrary, the tendency to accelerate migration has resulted from those policies aimed at increased agricultural productivity. Based on past experiences in Haiti and elsewhere one can even question whether a reduction in internal migration is a legitimate goal of development projects. Clearly only those projects which can simultaneously increase rural levels of employment and income have such a demographic potential.

Concerning Haitian emigration, we come to similar conclusions. To reduce or stop it is to fight a symptom, not its cause. If the United States and Canada admit large numbers of immigrants and refugees from other poor countries, then the restrictions directed at Haitians surely must appear discriminatory. On grounds of equity one would therefore have to say that Haitian immigration must be allowed to continue. On grounds of past experience and the continuing needs of advanced economies one can say, it will continue, following the fluctuations of manpower needs in unprotected sectors.

The present migrations of Haitian labor are one expression of how populations adapt, within firmly established networks of exchange, to the changing needs of an internationalized economy. Equilibrium models have a tendency to obscure this, as have traditional demographic push/pull models. The dependency paradigm does more justice to the external determinants of migration but its focus on exploitation is so exclusive that much of the evidence is just left aside.[9] It appears that the cumulative causation paradigm is most appropriate because of its simultaneous focus on a host of internal and external factors. This theoretical approach is also the one which leads to the gloomiest projections for Haiti's future. As long as the same political and economic forces remain at work in Haiti and her powerful neighbors, the transactions between them will remain similar to what we observe today. This means a continuation of the flow of human capital and material benefits from the countryside to the city and from Haiti abroad. The tragedy which we call underdevelopment will continue to be played on its national and international stages. Migration will continue to allow a better life for some individuals while remaining, at the same time, an expression of the misery of the masses.

NOTES

[1] Of those mentioned, Lundahl (1979) comes closest to giving the topic a full treatment. Nevertheless, it was not intended to occupy a central place in his impressive book.

[2] For general presentations of the "emigration and development" problematic see Todaro (1976) and Portes (1978). The latter presents a way of ordering ideas and problems which has influenced this section of the paper.

[3] Ahlers' (1979) work might in some way also fit under the second paradigm. However, his emphasis on regional imbalances, the Todaro model, human capital, the education variable and the "response" character of migration made, we assign it to the first paradigm where the focus is on the restoration of an equilibrium disturbed by unequal modernization.

[4] Some of these studies are included in De Ronceray, 1979. True to the tradition of Rober Park's "Migration and Marginal Man," rural-urban migration here fits into the larger frame of urban pathology. It is the principal cause of what is "wrong with cities: "En dehors des maux strictement physiques, l'urbanisation entraîne tout un cortège de névroses, de suicides, de divorces, de cas de délinquance juvénile. Elle encourage la prostitution, les viols, le meurtres, les attaques à main armée, l'alcoolisme chronique, l'adultère, la fornication l'homosexualité, etc. Les villes du XXe, siècle sont des organismes malades" (De Ronceray 1979:103).

[5] The controversy between Lundahl and Caprio is illustrative but appears to exaggerate differences (Conjonction 1982).

[6] The methodological problems of the 1971 census are discussed in several publications of the "Unité d'Analyse et Recherches Démographiques" at the "Institut Haitien de Statistiqu et d'Informatique" (formerly "Institut Haitiens de Statistique"). The census covered the whole of the urban population as well as a 10% sample of the rural population. It uses the old administrative divisions of five departments and its methodology precludes an analysis b arrondissments and imposes seven restrictions on the analysis of communes. (Dautruche and Margaritis 1980).

[7] Unless specified otherwise, the term migrant in connection with the 1971 census refers to lifetime migration, i.e., to differences between place of birth and place of residence.

[8] The remaining 23% cannot be disaggregated by Davis' (1965) method.

[9] For example: Why is the exploited periphery growing? Why is most of the population stable? Why are economic levels highest precisely where foreign penetration is strongest (both in Haiti and the Dominican Republic)?

THE ROOTS OF HAITIAN MIGRATION

ALEX STEPICK
with Tom Brott, Dan Clapp, Donna Cook, Julie Doan, Jockesta Megie

The thrust of this paper is theoretical, to reorient our approach to understanding and explaining Haitian migration. Academic models of migration have conceived migration flows as the consequence of aggregate individual decisions in response to regional economic inequalities or disequilibria. U.S. policymakers have tended to depict individual migrants as responding to either political or economic motivation. We argue that both the equilibrium model of migration based on individual decisions and the distinction between political and economic factors impoverish our interpretation of Haitian migration. Thus efforts to resolve the underlying problems which cause it are discouraged.

We intend to demonstrate that both are the historical products of free market normative models of industrial societies which have been misapplied as descriptive explanations. By separating politics from economics they shift responsibility for inequalities from broader social and political forces to individual motivations. In short, they provide a sophisticated, but faulty rationalization for "blaming the victim."

Precisely because it is so distant from the ideal free market nation-state, Haiti exemplifies the inadequacies of the distinction between political and economic and equilibrium theories of migration particularly clearly. At the same time, the Haitian political economy provides excellent examples of the mental gymnastics required to maintain the myth of political, as opposed to economic emigration in the face of contradicting empirical evidence. We conclude this paper by presenting some new empirical data on recent Haitian refugees in Miami, which reveal a population more diverse and significantly better off than either the academics' or policymakers' models would lead one to expect.

The Equilibrium Theory of Migration[1]

Individual decisions form the basis of the equilibrium theory of migration. Individuals survey the landscape of wages, costs and benefits associated with various geographic locations just as they evaluate various products available for purchase in the marketplace (Shaw 1975:54). They choose to migrate or remain based on expected utility, prospects of employment, costs of moving, expected lifetime income and availability of information (Rotherberg 1977:186). Migration flows are simply the aggregate of individual decisions. The relative "attraction" or "repulsion" of locations reflects spatial imbalances in the distribution of land, labor, capital, and natural resources (Wood 1982). Labor power moves away from concentrations of labor and toward concentrations of capital. If too much labor moves toward a particular location of concentrated capital, wages decrease, reducing the attractiveness of the location. The migration of capital and labor are then but particular mechanisms of the dynamic equilibrium of a market economy.

A particularly popular and influential variation of the equilibrium model has been modernization theory. The penetration of western values into the traditional, isolated countryside produces new aspirations among the most outward-looking, adventurous risk-takers. According to the model, migration restores equilibrium as the most modern individuals migrate to cities leaving behind the more risk-adverse traditionals (Portes and Walton 1982:26, 27).

The equilibrium model of migration appeals to our intuition about migration. People want jobs, higher wages, and the things money can buy. Certain other aspects of the theory, however, are troubling.[2] Migration has not produced any noticeable equilibrium. To the contrary, we worry to the point of building political campaigns based on its disruptive effects.

Yet, the failure of migration throughout history to produce equilibrium is not usually attributed to the weaknesses of the underlying theory. Rather, theorists and commentators following normative commitments, rather than descriptive evidence, tend to blame such troublesome features as wage rigidity in advanced countries or Third World cities, which artificially maintain high wages and continue to attract more migrants (Lewis in Portes and Walton 1982:26). And, a pssionate commitment to regain control of borders or to keep the Third World cities from splitting at the seams frequently obscures the essential truth that the vast majority have chosen not to migrate.

This approach tends to focus our attention on the response of individuals to social forces, rather than on the forces themselves. It assumes that society is no more than the aggregate sum of individual decisions. The inequalities or disequilibria between regions are conceived as the products of previous individual decisions; that is, as "givens." Forces broader than individual migrants are not conceived as creating and maintaining the inequalities to which migrants respond. Instead, "economic refugees" are depicted as victims of "natural" conditions or forces beyond the immediate analysis of academics and certainly beyond the control or responsibility of politicians and policymakers. The only individuals responsible for the movement of economic migrants, i.e. those responding to regional disequilibria, are the migrants themselves.

Political Versus Economic Refugees

In contrast, political refugees are depicted as involuntary migrants fleeing under coercion by other individuals, social groups, or governments. They are victims of forces which curtail their basic rights. In the most widely accepted definition, a refugee is a person who "owing to a well-founded fear of being persecuted for reasons of race, religion, nationality, membership of a particular social group or political opinion, is outside the country of his nationality and is unable or, owing to such fear, is unwilling to avail himself of the protection of that country" (U.N. 1951).

In the hurried, desperate flight for freedom, the political refugee has no time for the cool calculation of costs and benefits attributed to the economic migrant. Ideal political refugees have not "decided" to move in the same sense as economic migrants and because of that they are not individually responsible to the same degree for their actions. Instead, the agents responsible for the coercion produce the exile. Since the refugees have been forced to move through no fault of their own, have been persecuted, and are subject to further persecution, they deserve the protections of other states, such as outlined in the United Nations Convention and Protocol on the Status of Refugees.

Some have attempted to construct a theoretical underpinning for the political versus economic dichotomy by depicting political as negative rights and economic as positive rights (Shue 1980). Negative rights do not require any government action. To fulfill individuals' negative rights a government need do nothing. It must resist infringing upon individuals' activities. It simply must not harm or harass them, stifle their freedom of speech, or close their churches.

Positive rights, in contrast, can only be fulfilled if a government actively pursues specific courses of action. Social security, income support, food stampts, subsidized medical care, for example, all place far greater demands on the resources of the state and its citizenry, perhaps more demands than are possible to fulfill. The fulfillment of positive or economic rights, therefore, is conceived as secondary and less basic to that of negative or political rights.

Given this distinction, those whose political rights have been violated have suffered more fundamentally than those whose economic rights are left unfulfilled. Since political rights are relatively easy to respect, their violation should be condemned, and affected individuals should be protected. However, according to this distinction, since economic rights are so difficult and in many countries perhaps impossible to fulfill, we should not condemn governments that fail to fulfill them, nor should we offer special protection to those who suffer from that failure.

In the United States, this perspective has assumed a peculiar twist; those fleeing communist governments are welcomed in large numbers, while those fleeing rightist, authoritarian regimes are virtually always turned away. From January 1974 to May 1975 none of the Filipinos or South Koreans who requested asylum were granted it. The State Department also recommended that asylum requests be denied to 16 Greeks who sought political refuge before the fall of the Junta, and to the eight South Vietnamese who asked asylum from the Thieu regime. Yet during this same period, scarcely any requests from Eastern European countries were denied. Between 1975-76, the last year for which data are available, 96% of the applicants fleeing rightist governments were denied refuge in the United States, while 95% of those applicants from communist countries in the same time period were granted sanctuary in the United States (Shue 1980). In the particular case of the thousands of Haitian boat people who have arrived in Florida since 1972 and requested asylum, 18 have been granted asylum, less than 1% of the total (Hooper, personal communication).

In spite of a humanitarian change in the United States refugee law in 1980, which eliminated any legal basis for discriminating in favor of those fleeing communist countries, fully 95% of those whom the United States has admitted as refugees since the change still come from communist countries in Southeast Asia, Eastern Europe, or the Soviet Union.

Implementors of refugee and asylum law apparently remain consistent with the distinction between economic and political persecution by discriminating between totalitarian and authoritarian regimes. Communist countries are totalitarian; they deny freedoms to all—freedom of speech or religion, or the pursuit of one's interests in any fashion. Hence, all individuals fleeing totalitarian governments are *ipso facto* fleeing persecution.

In contrast, since authoritarian countries do, in theory, permit some freedoms, they persecute only individuals who are "politically involved," i.e. participants in organized, institutionalized activities such as political parties. Any other fleeing authoritarian governments can only be fleeing dire economic conditions unless they can specifically document individualized persecution based on political activities. Those who may be attempting to avoid extortion by local officials are not fleeing persecution but personal disputes.

Constructing and Maintaining the Free Market Normative Model

The basis for this discrimination, however, goes beyond United States Cold War foreign policy. It has deeper roots that stretch back to the emerging bourgeoisie of the Middle Ages and their struggles to eliminate the arbitrary intervention of feudal and early nation-states into the affairs of profit-making enterprises. During the early stages of capitalism in Europe, the state relied heavily upon the bourgeoisie to underwrite state costs. Taxes were high, Although the working classes paid a higher proportion of taxes than nobles, church, or bourgeoisie, it was the bourgeoisie that had the political power to wrest concessions from the state (see Tuchman 1978 for extensive examples).

Their stated goal was to cleave politics from economics, or at least to curtail the state's intervention into their own economic affairs. While expressly arguing for a complete separation of politics from economics, the bourgeoisie frequently used political power to solidify their economic advantage. As Adam Smith recognized, market economies tend toward equilibrium only in the ideal world. In the real world, those who have a temporary advantage constantly seek to solidify that advantage through the political system (Smith 1976: Chapter 10, book one). A truly free market economy has remained an ideal type, a normative goal. The more adequate description is one of the state actively participating in the economy.

Ironically, the free market ideology achieved its apogee when the state most actively intervened in the economy. The role of the 19th century state in subsidizing railroads and ports, establishing protective tariffs, providing public education, and even subsidizing immigrant labor far surpassed the interventions of previous nation-states (Wolfe 1977:54).

But even more important for understanding the deficiencies of the positive versus negative rights distinction is the establishment of the independent judiciary system. The independent judiciary provided legal security for private property, a fundamental basis of a free market economy, ensuring equal protection and due process regardless of individuals' ascriptive status. The protection of these rights, however, is unenforceable and meaningless in the absence of a judicial sphere autonomous and immune from political pressures (Balbus 1973). To establish and maintain the judiciary's autonomy and immunity, the nation-state cannot be passive. It must construct a judiciary, a complicated and expensive apparatus. Political rights, therefore, are not necessarily negative rights as envisioned in the negative versus positive rights arguments.

In reality, the judiciary has not always been as autonomous and immune as ideally depicted. For example, the United States Supreme Court first ruled that the Sherman Anti-Trust legislation did not apply to businesses, but that it did apply to unions (Wolfe 1977:54). Formally, the Court was independent; but, in fact, it favored political intervention into economic affairs for some and not for others. Thus, even in the most advanced nation-states the fulfillment of both economic and political rights requires active state intervention.

Our argument is that nation-states have actively intervened in both economic and political affairs and must, therefore, be held at least partially responsible for their citizenry's economic and political welfare. Moreover, the protection of political rights such as freedom of speech also requires active state intervention. One cannot argue that political rights are easier to fulfill or more basic than economic rights. Theoretically the nation-state can be held equally responsible for both. Historically, it has involved itself in providing or failing to provide both.

Post-Keynesian interpretations of the nation-state do tend to recognize the role the state has in fulfilling society's economic functions. Yet, the myth persists that the state's protection of political rights is of a separate order from economic concerns. The normative ideal of a free market economy continues to guide our description and explanation of the relations between economics and politics. States are not held responsible for creating the conditions which impel migration. Migrants are assumed to be responsible for their decision to migrate. According to the myth, political activity occurs only in the context of familiar political institutions such as elections and political parties. Official and quasi-official penetration of the market place is the exception rather than the rule. None of the beliefs has a firm empirical or theoretical basis. It is our contention, to the contrary, that economics is a product of the politics of the nation-state.

Yet, many still try to perpetuate the myth. They may be successful under certain conditions. The myth can be maintained if governments do not: (1) expropriate private wealth or goods; (2) engage in direct appropriation of revenues for personal use; or (3) redirect public projects for the benefit of government officials, family, or friends. If the government fails to heed the first rule, its commitment to the myth is highly questionable. In a free market economy, or any nation-state striving to emulate one, private property must be protected. The protection of private property from state appropriation provided the historical impetus for the construction of the myth separating politics from economics. If a government fails in this protection, economic and political persecution are one and the same, even for those who believe in the myth.

Only slightly less critical to the myth's maintenance is the government's role as a neutral arbiter of different social groups' interests, rather than the promoter of its own or certain of its individuals' fortunes. We have argued that state economic intervention virtually always does benefit some more directly than others. Even such basic common goods as roads and irrigation advantage those who already have the resources to exploit the new opportunities. Nevertheless, a separation of politics and economics is more convincing if state economic intervention claims to advance the common good. On an individual level, civil servants must truly be servants of the national good. They must act without self-interest and be content to live off their official salaries.

Neither governments nor all their officials are so perfect. Corruption is always possible and many claim it is universal. When confronted with the opportunity to expropriate private wealth or goods, government officials cannot resist. Economics then again becomes clearly infected by politics.

Corruption, however, does not *ipso facto* demolish the myth. Since corruption is a near universal, some degree of it must be tolerated and explained away if the myth is to be maintained. Successfully maintaining the myth in the face of corruption depends upon two factors: (1) the proportion of government officials who seek self-interest before common good; and (2) how much self-intent, as compared to common good, influences them. If indeed corruption is the exception rather than the rule and its occasional occurrence shocks the public, the myth is easy to maintain. Moreover, states which readily and effectively punish and castigate corruption can also easily maintain the myth.

The final area is the most subtle, the redirection of public projects for the benefit of other officials, family, or friends. If a particular project happens to benefit the implementor's friends, cries of outrage are seldom as strong as when the implementor benefits directly. Nevertheless, the process politically directs economic gain away from the common toward private good. While still mixing politics and economics, this last is unlikely to endanger the perpetuation of the myth.

The Free Market Model and Haitian Migration

Precisely because Haiti is so distant from the ideal free market economy, it reveals the weak empirical basis of the political versus economic distinction and the insufficiency of such explanations. The United States State and Justice Departments have claimed that the vast majority of Haitian boat people are economic refugees, little different from the thousands of Mexicans flowing across the Rio Grande every year. Haitian advocates, human rights groups, the press, the United States Federal Courts, and even some academics have questioned these assertions, claiming that at least some, if not the majority of Haitians are fleeing legitimate persecution.[3] To this point, neither side has clearly prevailed. The basic questions still remain: What distinguishes Haiti from such countries as Mexico or the Dominican Republic? Why is it so easy to maintain that Mexicans are economic migrants, but so much more difficult to maintain the same for the Haitian boat people? If our argument in the previous section is correct, if nation-states are responsible for their citizenry's economic well-being, why does virtually no one believe Mexican migrants can legitimately claim they are fleeing persecution while opinion is divided on the Haitian boat people?

To maintain the myth, the government above all must appear to protect those rights which the myth claims are negative rights; it must not interfere with individuals' free speech and free association. Haiti, along with numerous other right and left wing regimes, obviously fails this fundamental test. Even in the face of frequent violations of political rights, the myth is likely to be believed if there exists an independent judiciary to enforce and protect political rights. The recent retrial of Sylvio Claude and others has led many to believe that Haiti has no independent judiciary. In spite of the amnesty later granted, it is still safe to say that the state has not invested in the creation of a judicial system which protects all, regardless of ascriptive status or, more particularly, regardless of their relationship to the Presidential Palace. Haiti's opposition leaders have always recognized this and accordingly found it wise to leave the country after defeat. They appear to be classic political refugees and to constitute the first post-Duvalier migration flow. In this, Haiti is not unlike many other societies ruled by a dictator.

The Duvalier inspired diaspora, however, has reached unprecedented proportions and has progressively encompassed all levels of society. The roots of this migration lie more in the state's failure to protect what the myth refers to as economic rights, and what in our analysis is the product of the mixing of politics and economics.

The most controversial and potentially damaging to the political versus economic rights dichotomy are the allegations of expropriation and extortion by the Tonton Macoutes. Some claim that the Macoutes' actions are no more than an historical extension of the traditional, autocratic rule characterizing the countryside (Maingot 1982). Others emphasize the Macoutes' links to the central government and their propensity to prey upon those who have struggled successfully to improve themselves (Maguire 1979). One resolution is to claim that such behavior is not official, but rather personal disputes that coincidentally involve officials. A more scientific approach is to examine the nature of the migrant population. If the Macoutes' actions are an extension of traditional, autocratic behavior, all levels of peasant society are equally likely to migrate. If, however, the Macoutes' actions are directed more at those slightly better off, we might attribute partial responsibility to the government's failure to provide a judicial system protecting rights to private property regardless of ascriptive status.

There is no disputing the existence of corruption in Haiti. Ironically, the sole place where a free market might paradoxically exist in Haiti is within the government. The pure pursuit of self-interest by all government officials is expected and presumed. Corruption is so extensive that officials of some international organizations judge it to be development's greatest impediment and apparent Haitian willingness to allow an audit of their accounts is considered a tremendous step forward. The pervasiveness of corruption has clearly been one of the reasons many observers are willing to blame the Haitian government for creating the economic woes of its refugees. Corruption's effects on migration, however, are actually unclear. Presumably, greater development would follow a decrease in corruption. Greater development does not necessarily imply less migration.

Even without officials directly appropriating revenues for personal use, they would still be likely to direct projects for the benefit of themselves, family, or friends. Maguire (1979) describes a coffee project designed to assist small-holders. The primary beneficiary was the Minister of Agriculture, even though monies were apparently expended as intended. Girault (1981) advances the argument even further. If the project did reach the small-holders, others with even smaller holdings and the landless would be left further behind. Thus, a successful development project can increase local inequalities, creating further migration. In fact, the development literature contains more examples of development increasing, rather than decreasing migration (see Geisse & Hardoy 1972, Cornelius & Trueblood 1975). We are led to the rather curious conclusion that the most isolated regions are the least likely to produce migrants, while those regions most affected by government development efforts should produce the most migrants. On the individual level, we predict that those most directly affected by government intervention are the most likely to migrate. To some degree, these predictions contradict those derived from the political versus economic arguments and the equilibrium theories of migration which tend to predict higher migration from the most backward regions and among the poorest peasants.

Testing these predictions precisely is difficult because the data on Haitian migration are remarkably sparce, especially considering the attention popularly given the subject. Although there has been some serious study of the Haitian community in New York (Glick 1975), we have had virtually no detailed data on the Haitian boat people. Nevertheless, the common perception persists that they are uniformly poor and illiterate peasants fleeing grinding poverty. That perception, however, is usually based on impressionistic or journalistic accounts guided, I suspect, more by the preconceptions of the political versus economic distinction rather than empirical reality. This paper attempts to test the above hypotheses by presenting some recently collected data on Haitians in South Florida.[4]

The data on Haitians in New York loosely confirms our suppositions. The early and middle 1960's migration flow apparently consisted largely of the urban entrepreneurial and skilled labor classes. After eliminating the immediate potential political opponents, Duvalier's repressive tactics focused on those in urban areas who were most vulnerable and had readily accessible wealth.

Our data on Haitians in South Florida also loosely, but not entirely, confirm our predictions. Those Haitians surveyed are not uniformly poor; they are not the least skilled; they are not illiterate; they are not farmers; they are not from the most isolated areas, nor do they all come from the impoverished Northwest region.

Table 1 reveals that virtually equal numbers were born in the Nord-Ouest and Ouest provinces. The political versus economic perspective implies that the vast majority should come from the Nort-Ouest. The urban versus rural comparisons of birth place are even more interesting. The majority, 51.6%, were born in villages; however, 36% were born in medium-size cities and 12.6% were born in Port-au-Prince. If we look at the numbers who were either born in or lived in different size cities, we see an even greater trend towards urban experience. Over 40% of the migrants were either born or have lived in Port-au-Prince; 34.2% were born or lived in a medium-size city and only 25.4% have spent all their lives in villages.

The non-agricultural base of the migrant population is further emphasized in Table 2, Occupation in Haiti. The migrants are largely one generation removed from their peasant roots. Over 61% of the migrants' fathers were engaged in agriculture, but only 4.5% of the migrants themselves. Almost 21% of the migrants' fathers had semi-skilled occupations, but 67.2% of the migrants had semi-skilled occupations. Most frequent were tailors, but there were nearly as many teachers and mechanics. In both generations there were small numbers of unskilled, non-agriculture workers (5% in the fathers' and 4.5% in the migrants'). There was a slightly higher proportion of fathers engaged in business (7.9% versus 4.5%), but the migrants had a higher proportion engaged in skilled work (8.8% versus 5% for the fathers).

The shift away from agriculture is also reflected in the migrants' educational background. While it is frequently claimed that approximately 80% of the Haitian population is illiterate and has virtually no formal schooling, the migrants have an average of 7.6 years of formal schooling. Only 7% have had no schooling; 31.6% between one and six years; 45% some secondary; and 26.1% have had commercial, short courses, or vocational training.

In short, the migrants are more urban experienced, skilled, and educated than common stereotypes or expectations based on the political versus economic dichotomy.

The survey also gathered detailed information on farming practices for those who were farmers in Haiti. The number of farmers was so small, however, that the data must be interpreted with extreme caution: the average number of karos[5] planted was 3.33; owned, 2.6; sharecropped, 5; and leased, 1.4. Over 50% farmed coffee as the primary cash crop; and corn and millet were the principal subsistence crops. For those who were farmers, 25% sold land to finance their migration and 44% mortgaged land. While these data on farmers are very sparse, they do seem to indicate that those who were farmers were probably not the poorest peasants. Moreover, the selling and mortgaging of land to finance their trip to the United States could lead to a further concentration of landholdings in their villages.

We also asked under what conditions each respondent would return to Haiti: 50% indicated they would return if political conditions changed; 71% would return if economic conditions changed. From the perspective of the migrants themselves, political and economic conditions apparently are not mutually exclusive.

These data are still brief and preliminary. They allow only tentative conclusions and leave many unanswered questions. Nevertheless, they do seem to indicate that most of the migrants do not come from the most backward sectors of Haiti's economy. The data do not allow us to say that they have been impelled to migrate directly by the Haitian government's interventions into the economy. That would require far more detailed knowledge. Our examination of the relationship between Haitian politics and economices does lead us, however, to expect more of these types of migrants than the political versus economic dichotomy predicts.

* * * * *

The primary thrust of this paper has been to redirect our attention from the differences between economic and political factors to the integral linkages between them. Migration is not economically *or* politically motivated, rather, it results from the processes of development, the struggles for control of the nation-state, and the nation-state's economic policies. Distinctions between political and economic rights are fundamentally normative distinctions with important roots in the development of free market oriented societies, but they are not empirically reliable. As explanations of migration, they serve more as rationalizations for policies than as accurate guides to prediction or understanding.

This realization possesses difficult and somewhat contradictory policy implications. It tends to confirm that the United States has discriminated against Haitians and in favor of those fleeing communist countries. It also tends to imply that there is no obvious, easy way to distinguish between political and economic refugees. One may not be able to maintain a humanitarian, unbiased refugee law and a Cold War foreign policy which uses refugee policy as one of its tools. Recent United States policy towards Haitians has slighted humanitarianism in favor of foreign policy concerns.

The peculiar political-economic structure of Duvalier's Haiti highlights the inadequacies of the distinction between political and economic interpretations of migration at the same time that it increases the suffering of some citizens and the rate of out-migration. The political intrusions into the economy are frequently more subtle than anti-Duvalierists claim yet more obvious than in most other developing or even developed countries. Direct corruption needs no further comment, but the indirect corruption of using government position to direct resources towards one family, friends, or class is more visible in a small society highly dependent on external aid under the scrutiny of all kinds of international observers.

The causes of Haitian migration are more than those discussed. I have completely ignored environmental and demographic factors. Moreover, forces beyond Haiti's borders largely demand some continuance of the flow. The Dominican sugar harvest (and increasingly its coffee and urban services sectors) cannot exist without Haitian labor. The Bahamas, in spite of its ambivalence and vacillation towards Haitians, is just as dependent upon them for low wage labor; and, I predict that soon Florida agriculture interests will prefer Haitian labor, as some Miami Beach hotels already do. Regardless of events internal to Haiti, these forces will continue to demand Haitian labor.

Migration, moreover, will continue even in the presence of highly hoped-for internal changes in Haiti—increased accountability, decreased corruption, more technocrats, and a genuine commitment to the protection of human rights. Development produces migration, and the migrants in our sample have been exposed to the processes of modernization and development. Political *and* economic persecution is no less a compelling reason to migrate (or to remain) than political *or* economic suffering. This analysis decreases no one's suffering and is likely to be subject to a common criticism directed at academics: it criticizes without providing positive new directions. Perhaps it will increase our own suffering and frustration at finding workable solutions to difficult problems. Our approach, however, should produce more realistic expectations and deeper appreciation for the complexities of migration and development.

NOTES

[1] Wood (1982) provides an incisive critical summary of the equilibrium model of migration.

[2] There are numerous critiques of the equilibrium model of migration. The most recent include Portes and Walton (1982), Wood (1982), and Bach and Schraml (1982).

[3] The literature surrounding this controversy is extensive. For an overview see Stepick (1982a); for a review of the role of the judiciary's involvement, see Stepick (1982b); and for the United States Federal Court's explicit rejection of the U.S. Executive branch's position, see Haitian Refugee Center vs. Civiletti.

[4] The sample consisted of 125 Haitian Entrants enrolled in English as a Second Language classes in Miami. The questionnaire was adapted from Portes'work with Mexican and Cuban immigrants (see Portes 1978, 1979, 1981, and Portes, Clark, and Lopez 1982). Although the data are more extensive, it cannot be claimed that they are representative. The sample is clearly not random and is probably biased towards the middle socioeconomic migrants. The poorest of the poor and the least educated might be somewhat less inclined to enroll in English classes, although there were a few in the sample who had had no schooling in Haiti. Those from the higher socioeconomic classes in Haiti might also be under represented because they are more likely to be non-Entrants.

[5] A "karo" equals 1.3 hectares.

THE CHILD, THE FAMILY, AND THE SCHOOL IN ENGLISH-HAITIAN EDUCATION

CAROLE BEROTTE JOSEPH

The effect of parental involvement on the education of children has always been of interest to educators. Furthermore, it is well-documented that children whose parents participate in school activities perform better in school. The terms parental involvement and parental participation are often tossed around as if everyone understands exactly what they mean. Parental involvement has been defined as the movement of parents toward the school as well as the reciprocal movement of the school toward the home. It therefore includes school visits, attendance at meetings and/or parent-teacher conferences, home visits by the school personnel as well as all other incidental contacts such as telephone calls and employment-related contacts in the schools.

Many studies have examined the relationship between cognitive development and parental involvement. Cognitive development has been compartmentalized by most of them into the following categories: (1) general reasoning, (2) school related knowledge and skills, and (3) knowledge of verbal concepts. While it is true that other factors may be at play, such as the level of the parents' schooling (especially the mother's), the child's age, and the family income, the evidence is quite strong to confirm the fact that children whose parents participate are likely to be in a more favorable position in all three categories of cognitive development. In spite of the fact that most studies concentrated on parental involvement at the early childhood level, several researchers (Rabin 1972; Donachy 1976; Hubbell 1977; Laosa 1980; Irvine 1980) have shown that the fact that parents were in contact with the schools had a significant effect on the children's overall performance.

351

When we look at who is succeeding, it is generally those children who have favorable home and community environments, namely those of the upper and middle classes. Thus, socioeconomic status (SES) plays a definite role in the child's academic performance, pointing to a distinct correlation between the parents' degree of involvement and SES. The researchers cited earlier have shown that the variables comprising SES are very relevant for any ethnic group. In the case of immigrant children of Haitian background these variables inevitably cause concern.

Let us look at some of the traits which characterize the immigration of Haitians to the United States. On the whole, the Caribbean is generally an area which has "one of the world's highest birth-rates and a declining death-rate." The pressures put on the economy of these countries is very great; these population pressures, in addition to others, have caused a rising unemployment rate and food shortages, as well as changing social and political ideologies (London 1981). Haiti, being an integral part of the Caribbean, has also gone through its share of population growth. Thus since the 1970's there has been a steady flow of Haitians entering the United States and therefore an ever-increasing influx of Haitian children entering the American schools. The educational systems most affected by this influx are in New York, Boston, Miami, Philadelphia, Chicago, and Washington D.C. among others.

Education in Haiti is left very much to the schools and the trained professionals. Parental involvement is virtually nonexistent, as the system does not encourage it. The corresponding professionals in the U.S. are ignorant of their students' background, values, and needs and are therefore quick to judge and to label Haitian parents as *non-caring,* since they are neither involved in nor participate in school-related activities. Anyone who is familiar with the Haitian people would know that this evaluation is incorrect. Haitian parents tend to have high aspirations for their children. Most are concerned with the education of their children and would very much like to see their children succeed, whether they themselves are literate or not. This is true whether the Haitian family finds itself living in Haiti or abroad.

Why is there a lack of involvement in the education system? If we examine the reasons why parents of Haitian background do not participate in the schooling of their children, some light can be shed on the problem and the possible solutions. First and foremost is that involvement, as we have defined it, is a new responsibility for most parents. Second, many live in fear of deportation, since they are not legal residents and therefore do not care to circulate freely in public places. Third, many neither understand nor speak English and believe that, since communication will not take place, there is no need to attend school-related functions. This point is compounded by the fact that many parents are illiterate. The establishment of bilingual education programs has somewhat alleviated this particular problem since a few schools are making an effort to send home notices in Creole and also provide interpreters and/or bilingual staff members at large parents' meetings. Fourth, having come from a political system which does not encourage free speech, many parents may feel inhibited and thus also require training on many basic rights issues. They would not, therefore, be the most vocal parents regardless of the setting. Fifth, because of economic pressures associated with migration in general, some simply do not get involved because of a lack of time due to incongruent working schedules. Many parents are forced to hold two jobs since they are most likely to obtain work at very low wages. Finally, of course, there are always the few who may really not care.

Haitian immigration to the U.S. is a rather new phenomenon and the school systems affected by this population have been very slow to respond to the needs of this particular group. I believe that bilingual education, as defined by Title VII of ESEA, would be a viable alternative in educating Haitian children in the U.S. Although a rebirth of bilingual education took place in the U.S. in the late sixties, the emphasis was on meeting the needs of Hispanics, and other ethnic groups were often told that programs could not be established because of the small numbers of children as compared to the Spanish-speaking population.

Haitians were recently identified as a target population in need of similar bilingual educational services. A few New York City school districts established skeletal programs with virtually no pre-planning. One can say that at least an attempt was made to serve this population, but this kind of haphazard planning sets the programs up for failure. Several problems developed primarily because of the unfamiliarity of school officials with the Haitian people and their culture. Problems also surfaced because programs were being planned with no input or involvement from the community. This is serious since this population is culturally and linguistically very different from other Caribbean immigrants. One of the major issues facing bilingual programs for Haitians is the Haitian language policy issue. Given the fact that French has always been known to be the official language of Haiti, U.S. school officials took it upon themselves to establish the policy that bilingual programs serving Haitians would use French and English as the media of instruction. In most instances, this resulted in French foreign language teachers being reassigned to work with Haitian children in many New York school districts.

While French may be the official language of Haiti, in reality most Haitians communicate best in Creole, the national language, in virtually all situations. This initial *faux pas* is the primary cause for the low success rate of bilingual programs for Haitian children in the U.S. This is not to say that many children have not benefitted from such programs but rather to point out that they could have done even better. In addition to the language policy issue with which the New York Board of Education will have to come to grips, several other factors have been responsible for the inefficiency of some bilingual programs. Among them is the fact that in schools where the largest number of Haitian students were enrolled, few professional educators with the requisites to deal with these students were available. That is to say that the number of either Creole or French/English bilingual teachers currently employed is low, a condition compounded by the fact that the licensing exam for bilingual French/English teachers was last given in 1974. A recent bulletin suggests that another exam is planned for 1983.* The total school-age population today in New York City is sufficient for the establishment of many more bilingual programs, but Haitians are very often the victims of misclassification in census reports. Very often they are classified as "Blacks," a category which does not take their language and culture into consideration. Since parents must opt for bilingual classes in New York City, many are never informed regarding such a choice. In addition, the public schools lose many Haitian children to the parochial, primarily Catholic, schools since parents believe that this type of education is better, i.e. more discipline-oriented. This attitude is of course a result of cultural values brought from Haiti dictating that private schools are better than public schools regardless of the curriculum offered by the school. Because of these factors many New York City school districts cannot offer viable bilingual programs for their Haitian population because of a limited number of students. In the last survey done for the Aspira/Lau reports in 1981, it was found that there were significant numbers of Haitians (approximately 1600) attending fourteen of the thirty-two New York City school districts as well as a significant number in eight New York City high schools. This count is conservative, since it does not include the above-mentioned parochial school populations as well as the small number of students who attend other private schools in the greater New York area. Furthermore, this report deals with students who are labeled "LEP," i.e. those who are limited English proficient. Given the fact that the New York City Haitian population is expected to increase steadily, the needs for bilingual programs designed to meet their needs will become greater.

Many of the programs that were established a few years ago still face some of the problems they had at the outset, namely, the lack of Haitian-speaking (Creole/English) professional educators and the lack of materials in Haitian Creole. The latter is partly the reason for the continuance of a totally French curriculum. When Haitian professionals do enter the system they very often are not the best-trained since they taught under very different systems—in Haiti or in some African countries, e.g. the Congo—prior to becoming licensed in New York City; others have had to wait for the five-year residency requirement to elapse in order to apply for U.S. citizenship since many states require that teachers be U.S. citizens. For those simply wanting to be retrained, a limited number of fellowships have been made available through Title VII funds, but the problem with many teacher-training institutions is that few if any professors are qualified to work with graduate students. As a result, many recipients of fellowships from 1975 onward have abandoned their doctoral studies.

If bilingual programs are to be a viable alternative for Haitian children, then any program which purports to serve the community must come to grips with the language policy issue in order to achieve its goals—both in educating children and in communicating with and educating the parents of those children. Furthermore, if attention is to be given to both second language acquisition and to increasing those pedagogical skills necessary to insure academic success, the need to improve the qualifications and to increase the number of professional pedagogical personnel able to participate in Haitian bilingual programs must be addressed. Recognizing the lack of adequate programs and the amount of time necessary to train a sufficient number of qualified professionals to run such programs, attention must also be paid to the mechanisms of support available to students in their respective homes and communities. Given this data base and what we know about immigrant experiences in general (i.e. the adaptation and adjustments needed in order to function in a new urban environment) and the Haitian experience in particular, it is apparent that the Haitians need more training along the lines of new parental responsibilities in order to facilitate the home-school relations. An effective bilingual program would plan to inform parents about the school's expectations of them; the school in turn should make an effort to establish on-going lines of communications with the home. Project HAPTT advocates this kind of reciprocal communication network. In September of 1981 Project HAPTT, a unique project funded by Title VII of ESEA, began operating out of the City College of CUNY's School of Education in New York City.

Project HAPTT (Haitian Parent-Teacher Training) is primarily a program of training for those future educators and community members who intend to work either directly or indirectly with Limited Proficient (LEP) Haitian children in Haitian-Creole/French/English *bilingual programs*. The project, as originally conceived, has two major interrelated components. The main purpose of one is to prepare prospective teachers at the Bachelor's degree level (thus making this the only undergraduate teacher training program in the U.S. specifically geared toward Haitians). The other centers on training for parents of school-age children, hence the acronym HAPTT.

I will concentrate on the parental component here since this is what we are concerned with in the relationship between the child, the family, and the schools in bilingual education. The parent-training component is a comprehensive effort to educate parents regarding their new environment and the new school system that their children attend. This education and training involves informing them of their rights and responsibilities, providing them with the necessary skills so that they can generally become more effective parents given the limitations of their new environment. It is hoped that such training will in turn supply both academic and emotional support in the home and community environments. Support and eventual involvement have been argued in the literature as the necessary ingredients to facilitate adaptation to the new school system and the acquisition of skills, knowledge, and attitudes necessary to insure academic achievement and eventual social mobility. In addition, parents are counseled into returning to school themselves as a positive role-model for their children as well as a way to return to professional or vocational practice in this country (if they have not been able to retrain or obtain necessary licenses etc. needed to practice in some careers here).

However, when one turns to the home and the community in order to identify the necessary mechanisms of support, one is faced with the following issues: parental illiteracy or lack of schooling; cultural differences; linguistic confusion; and poor living conditions. Of course, these problems do not necessarily face every Haitian but represent a conglomeration which must be dealt with in the preparation of an effective parent-training program. Although many Haitian parents were educated in their home country and also have an understanding of the schooling process (it would seem), the knowledge that these parents have is vastly different from the U.S. school system's and much of the support that their children need is consequently unavailable. These processes are therefore alien to the parents and regardless of their level of education, few are proficient speakers and writers of English and are unlikely to be models for the children at home. They therefore cannot guide their children in acquiring English as a second language on which much of the success in school depends.

The vast majority of recent Haitian immigrants, moreover, are from rural areas and have only a few years of formal schooling. Many lack the skills and the level of education needed to work in a competitive commercial-industrial center such as New York City and are forced to accept the lowest-paying jobs. It is important to point out that these people comprise the target population for the parent-training component of the

Project and should be the direct beneficiaries of the services provided by the HAPTT staff.

Because the cultural differences of this immigrant group are compounded by low socioeconomic status (SES) for much of the population, a number of *normal* or usual mechanisms of acculturation and adaptation are blocked for the children as well as the adults in the community. For example, the free intermingling of children with their peers after school (in the absence of adults or without direct adult supervision) is undercut. Since it is believed that those who engage in such activities as playing in the neighborhood streets are prone to develop into troublemakers, strict social restrictions are placed on children, especially girls. Most of the time away from school is therefore spent in the home. While often the home environment is found to be loving, it cannot be described as conducive to learning. In addition, many grandparents live with their families and often care for the children after school. The television often serves as distraction for them, and so interaction with other children is limited. The problems of the home environment as conducive to learning are compounded by health and nutrition problems due to a variety of causes: inadequate housing, lack of information regarding the ways and means to facilitate adaptation to a temperate climate, and so on. On one level these problems might be seen as due to a reduced or nonexistent flow of information, but many free pamphlets and other instruction leaflets covering a wide range of topics are available in local agencies as well as in the schools. However, this population exhibits a very high illiteracy rate and cannot avail themselves of this *solution;* many of the materials are available only in English or Spanish.

Of obvious need are local community agencies which deal directly with Haitians and the problems they face in adapting to life in the United States. Although more and more Haitian professionals (social workers, psychologists, teachers) are pooling their resources to establish such centers, the number of functioning organizations is still minimal. It is easy to see, therefore, the degree to which the population is removed from the American experience and from those avenues which would allow them to partake in the American social and economic life.

Thus far, Project HAPTT has produced a publication, *Lyezon,* geared towards parents. Among other activities are two major conferences planned and executed by HAPTT, several local workshops in communities that requested them, two mini-conferences with the cooperation of a school district and one community center, as well as a host of information leaflets translated and adapted to the needs of the Haitian population. Needless to say, all of this work has been done in Creole. We have found that several people who would ordinarily not get involved in such activities have done so because they are able to relate to HAPTT staff and to consultants. Communication is no barrier since the most effective medium, Creole, is used. A needs assessment was prepared and distributed through 1982 at all HAPTT activities in order to elicit the input of the greater community. Many have been returned (of course by the literate portion of the population—even though much writing was not required) and the topics most often requested coincide more or less with the priority areas identified by the Project staff. A survey to find out how many people receive and read our publications and also measure their effectiveness is now planned. A great deal of work lies ahead, but this unique beginning is certainly a good one and has had a positive impact on the New York Haitian community. HAPTT is in contact with key people in the Boston and Miami areas and hopes to establish more direct exchanges with them, both at the informational level and at the programmatic level.

In sum, if the child, the parent, and the schools are to become partners in the successful educational process of Haitian immigrant children in United States schools, then comprehensive programs involving all three of these constituents must work together in a supportive mode. This can be done only if communication takes place in an open atmosphere and in a language which all parties can effectively understand.

NOTE

Discussion must still take place regarding the establishment of an English/Creole license or a trilingual (French, Creole, English) interview procedure for such a license.

AGENDA FOR THE FUTURE

CHARLES R. FOSTER

At the end of this volume it is evident that no final answers have been found for the basic question of why Haiti, a country that has been independent for 180 years, remains so underdeveloped? Is this condition due to Haiti's loss of socioeconomic autonomy—which some argue still exists in certain sectors—during the European expansionist days of the seventeenth and eighteenth centuries? Or, are the roots of Haiti's underdevelopment indigenous? The lack of interest of the Haitian elites toward rural development, over-population, soil erosion, and the emigration of the more reform-minded Haitians are all factors that have prevented the Haitian economy from taking advantage of adaptation to international economic networks. But, above all, a series of incompetent, dictatorial, and corrupt governments have prevented serious economic planning for the country. Economic decisions, particularly in the last thirty years, have been generally haphazard and unfocused, despite a modest economic development strategy of the government (largely initiated by the World Bank and USAID). The problem is not a lack of plans but a lack of implementation.

If the shape of our future is likely to resemble the shape of our past, it behooves us to encourage systematic interdisciplinary research into the causes and effects of Haiti's underdevelopment; the essays in this volume are expressive of such an attitude and point to the direction in which such research should proceed.

Haiti provides a more difficult challenge for systematic research than almost any other country. A research and documentation center is nonexistent in Haiti; just such a facility could function as a data collection library and as a clearinghouse for local researchers. Like all governmental activities in Haiti, statistics and data which are collected are at the service of the regime. Most data are soft data—there is not even agreement on the population figures of the country—except for a few statistics which are collected for World Bank and USAID purposes. Even these are sometimes contradictory. We have attempted to provide a selection of these in the Appendix, but as one would expect, without a guarantee of validity.

Nor does there exist abroad, in the United States, Canada, or France, a center for research on Haiti. Specialists tend to be associated with Latin American studies programs that are unable to marshall major efforts for the study of Haiti. The only major specialized center—located at Indiana University in Bloomington, Indiana—has focused its meager resources on language issues and instruction in Haitian Creole. Since many of the researchers abroad are exiled Haitians (with an understood bias), the results of their research are often suspect in Haiti. Conversely, the few intellectuals within Haiti are constrained by a lack of freedom. What is needed, in order to alleviate these constraints on research, is a dialogue and exchange of information among the more serious researchers, both at home and in the diaspora. An objective of the meeting at the Wingspread Center in Wisconsin, from which most of the contributions in this book stem, was to increase such an interchange, particularly among thoughtful people working in the private sector.

In the key sector of agricultural development little has been done to deal with the causes of rural development: the anti-peasant bias of the urban elite, the network of speculators, the high cost of credit, tradition-bound education, and inefficient cultivation methods. Symptomatic of the urban elites' scorn for rural culture and institutions is their opposition to the introduction of Creole as the language of instruction in primary schools and their refusal to grant it official status. The papers by Murray and Giraul lead us to ask for studies on the structure of the agricultural elite, including sociological studies on the role of the "middle man." Does this agricultural elite provide support for the regime? And more importantly, what is the class structure of rural society? Furthermore, research is needed on land tenure. What is the role of the small farmer?

As Port-au-Prince grows in size, work needs to be done on a variety of urban topics. How politicized are urban workers and urban youth? Is there more discontent in Port-au-Prince than in the countryside? As a new, younger, black as well as mulatto elite develops, it would be useful to again do a study relating color and class, but focusing on Port-au-Prince. Many of these new rising elites have been educated in the United States. What are the effects of such an education?

The rise of the assembly industries, discussed in the Grunwald chapter, calls for further studies on business, not simply in economic, cost-benefit, but also in sociological terms.

Very little has been written about the role of the Roman Catholic church as well as the increasingly numerous Protestant sects. Does the church provide a substitute for the missing intellectual class?

The paper by David Nicholls on the rise and progression of the ruling Duvalier family calls for an examination of political leadership in Haiti. Given the increasing role of the military in other Third World countries, the lack of research on the military in Haiti points to a fertile area for exploration. What are the origins of the officer class? And what are their goals?

The Bellegarde-Smith paper on Haitian foreign policy points up the need to examine American policy toward Haiti. The public interest in the United States, especially among our Black organizations, in Haitian-American relations is due to a special relationship between Haiti and the United States. In particular, the waves of immigration since 1957 have resulted in a constituency, as in the case of Israel or Mexico, which follows Haitian-American relations with great interest. This is reflected in the special attention the congressional Black Caucus gives to questions of human rights in Haiti and refugee problems.

What is the role of the researcher dealing with Haitian problems? Are they neutral researchers or engaged technical administrators? Frequently those of us who work on Haitian problems fail to examine our own premises and biases. Too often our framework is that of the Western, Social-Democratic value system. Too few of us have a visceral understanding of the current realities of hunger, cruelty, romance, humor, violence, mystery, and Creole. It is precisely the special culture of Haiti, the first Black republic, the daughter of Africa, the stepchild of France, the ward of the Marine Corps, the hermit of the Western Hemisphere, that differentiates Haiti from any other Third World country and makes it essential for both the researcher and the practitioner to understand its history and culture.

In the cultural area, there is a fair amount of research on religion, folklore, and language. Some Haitian institutions, such as the CHISS (Centre haitien d'investigations en sciences sociales), the IPN (Institut pedagogique national), and the CLA (Centre de linguistique appliquée) have undertaken some small-scale empirical projects. Still, many aspects of the relationship between cultural institutions and other domains remain unexplored. The growing role and impact of the media, particularly radio, on the culture and lifestyles of Haitians merit careful analysis. Nor do we have much research on the occupations and attitudes of exile Haitians. In what ways does migration change the values and attitudes of Haitians?

If one examines the large literature on Haiti one is struck by the generally problematic assessment of the possibilities for an ultimate alleviation of the burdens of the Haitian people. Writing fifteen years ago, Robert Rotberg concluded that Haiti was not ready for a democratic form of government. Yet at the same time, he wrote that with abundant outside technical and financial assistance and a "more responsible government" Haiti could "elevate" in one decade the per capita standard of living. But he failed to examine the question of the limits of absorption of foreign aid or make specific recommendations on various types of aid programs. A more recent study, by Brian Weinstein and Aaron Segal, predicts the continuation of the richness and creativity of the Haitian culture and art, while carefully avoiding any economic or political predictions.

Only a few authors, such as UNESCO's Serge Vieux, who urges a serious, broadly conceived, study of administrative realities in Haiti, correctly note that research on Haiti should be constantly geared to an interdisciplinary perspective, calling for cooperation among specialists in different fields. Given the close inter-relationship between economic, social, and political underdevelopment in Haiti, it is evident that research studies must deal at all times with the psychological and sociological foundations of the Haitian milieu. It may well be that the outcome of research will be specific applications, such as practice projects, rather than brilliant treatises. The treatises may have their audience outside Haiti, whereas the well worked-out projects will be useful for Haitians in their own struggle with underdevelopment.

The future of Haiti lies in the hands of Haitians, and in their ability to effectively fight underdevelopment. In this struggle careful and realistic research on the institutions and practices of the past and the present will be a source of guidance to future Haitian administrators as they work on concrete projects and reforms.

REFERENCES

Ahlers, T. 1979. A Microeconomic analysis of rural-urban migration in Haiti. Unpublished Ph.D. dissertation. Fletcher School of Law and Diplomacy.

Allen, J. H. 1930. An inside view of revolutions in Haiti. *Current History* 32:325-329.

Allman, J. 1980. Sexual unions in rural Haiti. *International Journal of Sociology of the Family* 10:15-39.

_____. 1982. Fertility and family planning in Haiti. *Studies in Family Planning* 13:237-245.

Anglade, G. 1974. *L'Espace haitien*. Montréal: Presses de l'Université du Quebec.

_____. 1981. *L'Espace haitien*. Montréal: Éditions des alizés.

Anonymous. 1092. Statut général de la fonction publique (loi du 12 octobre 1982). *Le Moniteur,* 11 novembre. Port-au-Prince.

Antonini, Gustavo. 1968. Processes and patterns of landscape change in the Linea Noroeste, Dominican Republic. Ph.D. dissertation, Columbia University.

Association des Industries d'Haiti (ADIH). 1981. The industrial sector in Haiti: Situation, prospects and policies. Port-au-Prince.

Bach, R. L. and L. A. Schraml. 1982. Migration, crisis, and theoretical conflict. *International Migration Review* XVI:320-341.

Balbus, I. D. 1973. *The dialectics of legal repression*. New York: Russell Sage Foundation.

Balch, E. G. 1927. *Occupied Haiti*. New York: The Writers' Publishing Company.

Bastien, R. 1951. *La Familia Rural Haitiana*. Mexico City: Libra.

_____. 1961. Haitian rural family organization. *Social and Economic Studies* 10:478-510.

_____. 1966. Voudoun and politics in Haiti. Religion and politics in Haiti. *ICR Studies 1.* Washington, D.C.: Institute for Cross Cultural Research.

Bebel-Gisler, D. and L. Hurbon. 1976. *Cultures et pouvoir dans la caraibe: Langue creole, vaudou, sectes religieuses en guadeloupe et en haiti*. Paris: Librairie Editions L'Harmattan.

Beidelman, T. O. 1974. Social theory and the study of Christian missions. *Africa* XLIV:235-249.

Bellegarde, D. 1929. *Pour une Haiti heureuse*. Port-au-Prince: Chéraquit.

_____. 1934. *Un Haitien parle*. Port-au-Prince: Chéraquit.

_____. 1937. *La Résistance haitienne*. Montréal: Beauchemin.

_____. 1954. *Histoire du Peuple Haitien*. Port-au-Prince: Collection du Tricinquantenaire.

Bellegarde-Smith, P. 1974. Haiti: Perspectives of foreign policy: an essay on the international relations of a small state. *Caribbean Quarterly* 20:21-35.

_____. 1977. Expression of a culture in crisis: Dantès Bellegarde in Haitian social thought. Unpublished Ph.D. dissertation, The American University. Washington, D.C.

_____. 1980. Haitian social thought in the nineteenth century: Class formation and westernization. *Caribbean Studies* 20:5-33.

_____. 1981a. Class struggle in contemporary Haitian politics: An interpretative study of the campaign of 1957. *Journal of Caribbean Studies* 2:109-127.

363

Bellegarde-Smith, P. 1981b. Danes Bellegarde and Pan-Africanism. *Phylon* 42:233-244.

_____. 1982. Race, class, ideology: Haitian ideologies for underdevelopment, 1806-1934. AIMS, *Occasional Papers No. 32.*

Benge, Michael. 1978. *Renewable energy and charcoal production.* Port-au-Prince: USAID.

Benoist, J. 1971. *Population structures in the Caribbean area. The ongoing revolution of Latin American populations,* ed. by F. M. Salzano, 221-249. Springfield, IL: Charles Thomas.

Bentolila, A. and L. Ganni. 1981. Langues et problèmes d'éducation en Haiti. *Langages* 61:117-127 (Bilinguisme et diglossie).

Berggren, G.; N. Murthy; and S. J. Williams. 1974. Rural Haitian women; an analysis of fertility rates. *Social Biology* 21:368-378.

Bernabé, J. 1976. Propositions pour un code orthographique. *Espace créole* 1:25-57.

_____. 1978. A propose de lexicographie créole. *Espace créole* 3:87-101.

Bernard, C. 1979. Speech presented on April 23, 1979.

Birdsall, N. and S. Hill Hochrane. 1982. Education and parental decision-making. *Education and development: Issues in the analysis and planning of post-colonial societies,* ed. by L. Anderson and D. M. Windham. Lexington, MA: Lexington Books.

Bordes, A. and A. Couture. 1978. *For the people, for a change.* Boston: Beacon Press.

Boserup, E. 1965. *The conditions of agricutlural growth, the economics of agrarian change under population pressure.* London: Allen Unwin.

Boswell, T. D. 1982. The new Haitian diaspora. *Caribbean Review* 11:18-21.

Bourdieu, P. 1977. L'économie des changements linguistiques. *Langue Française* 34:17-34.

Brand, W. 1965. *Impressions of Haiti.* The Hague: Mouton.

Brown, O. C. 1972. Haitian Vodu in relation to Negritude and Christianity: A study in acculturation and applied anthropology. Unpublished Ph.D. dissertation, Indiana University. Bloomington.

Brutus, E. 1948. *L'instruction publique en Haiti.* Port-au-Prince: Imprimerie de l'Etat.

Burns, D. 1953. Conséquences sociales et politiques du choix d'une orthographe. *Education de base et éducation des adultes* V:87-93.

Caribbean Review. 1982. The Caribbean exodus. XI (1).

Carrié, T. 1889. *A Castle in Spain.* La Ronde.

Charmant, R. 1946. *La Vie incroyable d'Alcius.* Port-au-Prince: Société d'édition et de librairie.

Castor, S. 1974. *La ocupación norteamericana de Haití y sus consecuencias, 1915-1934.* Mexico: Signo Veintiuno.

Charles, E. and M. E. Fanfan. 1981. *Etude de la migration interne. Phase I: Les données démographiques.* Haiti: Institut Haitien de Statistique et d'Informatique (DARD).

Chatelain, J. 1954. *La Banque Nationale.* Port-au-Prince: Collection du Tricinquantenaire.

Chomsky, N. and E. Herman. 1979. *The Washington connection and third world fascism.* Boston: South End Press.

Cleven, Andrew N. 1968. The first Panama mission and the Congress of the United States. *The Journal of Negro History* 13:237-240.

Colat-Jolivière. 1976. Essai de transformation d'un conte. *Espace créole* 1:59-65.

Colloque International de Sociolinguistique. 1981. Montpellier. Unpublished manuscripts.

Comhaire, J. L. 1955. The Haitian Chef de Section. *American Anthropologist* 57:620.

_____. 1956. The Haitian schism: 1804-1860. *Anthropological Quarterly* 29:1-10.

Comhaire-Sylvain, Suzanne. 1952. Land tenure in the Marbial Valley of Haiti. *Acculturation in the Americas,* ed. by Sol Tax. 1804 pp. Chicago: University of Chicago Press.

_____. 1958. Courtship, marriage and *plasaj* at Kenscoff, Haiti. *Social and Economic Studies* 7:210-233.

_____. 1961. The household at Kenscoff, Haiti. *Social and Economic Studies.*

Comisión Económica Para America Latina (CEPAL). 1981. Haiti: Notas para el estudio económico de America Latina, 1980. CEPAL/Mex/1047.

Conjonction. 1982 (No. 152). *Débat autour d'un livre de Mats Lundahl,* pp. 61-97. Haiti: Institut Français d'Haiti.

Conseil National de Developpement et de Planification, *Plan Quinquennal, 1976-1981,* Tomes I, II, III. Republic d'Haiti, Port-au-Prince, 1976.

Conway, Frederick J. 1979. *A study of the fuelwood situation in Haiti.* Port-au-Prince: USAID.

Cook, M. 1940. Dantes Bellegarde. *Phylon* 1:128.

Cordova-Bello, E. 1967. *La independencia de Haití y su influencia in Hispanoamerica.* Caracas.

Cornelius, W. A. and F. M. Trueblood. 1975. Urbanization and inequality: The political economy of urban and rural development in Latin America, volume 5. *Latin American Urban Research.* Beverly Hills: Sage Publications.

Council of Economic Advisors (CEA). 1981. Economic report of the President.

Country Development Strategy Statement. FY 1983-87. Port-au-Prince: Agency for International Development.

Cross, M. 1979. *Urbanization and urban growth in the Caribbean.* London: Cambridge University Press.

Dash, J. 1981. *Literature and ideology in Haiti, 1915-1961.* Totowa, N.J.: Barnes & Noble.

Dautruche, R. and C. Margaritis. 1980. *Aspects methodologiques du recensement de la population et du logement de 1971.* Haiti: IHS (DARD).

David, H. P. 1967 [1936]. *Black democracy: The story of Haiti.* New York: Biblo and Tannen.

Davis, K. 1965. The urbanisation of the human population. *The city in newly developing countries,* ed. by G. Breese. Englewood Cliffs, N.J.: Prentice Hall.

Dejean, Y. 1975. *Dilemme en Haiti.* New York: Les Editions Connaissance d'Haiti.

_____. 1976. Orthographie créole et passage au français. Brooklyn, N.Y.: Les Editions Connaissance d'Haiti.

_____. 1978. Nouveau voyage en diglossie (unpublished paper).

_____. 1981. Comment écrire le créole d'Haiti: Etude des niveaux de structure. Unpublished Ph.D. dissertation, University of Strasbourg.

Delatour, L. and K. Voltaire. 1980. International subcontracting activities in Haiti. Paper presented at the 2nd Seminar on North-South Complementary Intra-Industry Trade, Mexico City.

Delince, K. 1979. *Armée et politique en Haiti.* Paris: L'Harmattan.

Delorme, D. 1870. *Les Théoriciens au Pouvoir I.* Paris.

De Ronceray, H. 1971. Ou va notre système d'éducation. *Conjonction* 117.

_____. 1979. *Sociologie du Fait Haitien.* Montréal: Les Presses de l'Université du Québec.

Derose, R. 1956. *Caractère, culture, vodou.* Port-au-Prince: Imprimerie de l'Etat.

De Young, Maurice. 1958. *Man and Land in the Haitian-Economy.* Gainesville, FL: University of Florida.

Dibien, G. 1954. *Esprit colon et esprit d'autonomie à Saint-Domingue au XVIIIè siècle.* Paris: Larose.

Dominguez, V. 1975. *Neighbors, then strangers: An overview of the problems of Caribbean immigrants to the U.S.* New York: Ford Foundation.

Donner, W. 1980. *Haiti—Naturraumpotential und Entwicklung.* Tübingen, 1980.

Dutcher, N. 1982. The use of first and second languages in primary education: Selected case studies. *World Bank Staff Working Paper* No. 504. Washington, D.C.: World Bank.

Duvalier, F. 1969. *Essential works, Volume I, Elements of a doctrine.* Port-au-Prince: Collection Oeuvres Essentielles, Presses Nationales.

Earl, D. E. 1976. *Reforestation and the fight against erosion: Haiti—Charcoal as a renewable resource.* Rome: FAO.

Erasmus, C. J. 1952. Agricultural changes in Haiti: Patterns of resistance and acceptance. *Human Organization* 2.

Etienne, G. 1976. Le créole du nord d'Haiti. Thèse de doctorat de l'Université de Strasbourg.

Ewel, Jack. 1977. *A report on soil erosion and prospects for land restoration in Haiti.* Port-au-Prince: USAID.

Fanon, F. 1952. *Peau noire masques blancs.* Paris: Seuil.

Fass, S. M. 1977. *Families in Port-au-Prince: A study of the economics of survival.* Washington, D.C.: Office of Urban Development, USAID.

_____. 1978. Port-au-Prince: Awakening to the urban crisis. *Latin American Urban Research,* ed. by W. A. Cornelius and R. B. Kemper, 155-180.

Ferguson, C. 1959. Diglossia. *Word* 15:325-340.

Fishman, J. A. 1967. Bilingualism with and without diglossia? Diglossia with and without bilingualism. *Journal of Social Issues* 23:29-38.

_____. 1971. National languages and languages of wider communication in developing nations. *Language use and social change,* ed. by W. H. Whitley and D. Forde, 27-56. London: Oxford University Press.

Fleischmann, U. 1977. Entrevue avec Frankétienne sur son roman *Dézafi. Dérives* 7:17-25.

_____. 1978. Das Französisch-Kreolische in der Karkbik. Zur Funktion von Sprache im sozialen und geographischen Raum. Berlin: unpublished manuscript.

_____. 1980. Alphabetisierung und Sprachpolitik: der Fall Haiti. *Sprachkontakte,* ed. by R. Werner, 87-120. Tübingen: Gunter Narr.

_____. 1981. Le créole en voie de devenir une langue littéraire. *Littératures et langues dialectales françaises,* ed. by D. Kremer and H. J. Neiderehe, 247-264. Hamburg: Helmut Buske.

_____. 1982. Migration interne et changement d'attitude envers la langue vernaculaire: une enquête en Haiti. *La sociolinguistique dans les pays de langue romane,* ed. by N. Dittmar and B. Schlieben-Lange, 163-183. Tübingen: Gunter Narr.

Fordham, M. 1975. Nineteenth century black thought in the United States: Some influences of the Santo Domingo revolution. *Journal of Black Studies* 6:115-126.

Foster, C. 1982. Personal communication.

Fougere, W.; I. Beghin; and K. King. 1970. *L'alimentation et la nutrition en Haiti.* Paris: Presse Universitaire.

Franketienne. 1975. *Dézafi.* Port-au-Prince: Editions Fardin.

_____. 1978. *Pèlin-tèt: pyès téyat.* Port-au-Prince: Presses Port-au-Princiennes.

Gaillard, R. 1973f. *Les blancs débarquent.* Port-au-Prince: the author. (Five volumes have been published to date.)

Galeano, E. 1973. *Open veins of Latin America: Five centuries of the pillage of a continent.* New York: Monthly Review.

Garrity, M. P. 1981. The assembly industries in Haiti: Causes and effects. *Journal of Caribbean Studies* 2:25-37.

Gates, W. B., Jr. 1959. The Haitian coffee industry (mimeo). Williams College, Williamstown.

Geisse, G. and J. Hardoy. 1972. Regional and urban development policies, volume 2. *Latin American Urban Research.* Beverly Hills, CA: Sage Publications.

General Accounting Office. 1982. *Assistance to Haiti: Barriers, recent program changes, and future options.* Washington, D.C.: Government Printing Office.

General Secretariat. 1982. *Statistical Bulletin of the OAS,* Vol. 4, No. 1-2. Washington, D.C.: Organization of American States.

GEREC (Groupe d'Etudes et de Recherches en Espace Créole). 1976. En guise d'explication sur le conte.... *Espace Créole* 3:66-69.

Gindine, Y. 1974. Images of the American in Haitian literature during the occupation. *Caribbean Studies* 14:37-52.

Girault, C. 1977. Nouveaux aspects du marché des produits agricoles en Haiti. *Actes du XLIIème Congrès International des Américanistes,* volume I, 471-488. Paris.

_____. 1981. *Le commerce du café en Haiti. Habitants, spéculateurs et exportateurs.* Paris: Editions du Centre National de la Recherche Scientifique.

Girault, C. and N. Hua-Burton. 1977. *Trois Experiences de Developpement Rural en Haiti et en Republique Dominicaine.* Bordeaux: Centre des Etudes de Geographie Tropicale.

Girault, C. and J. La Gra. 1975. *Characteristiques structurelles de la commercialisation interne des produits agricoles en Haïti.* Port-au-Prince: IICA.

Girault, C. and J. La Gra. 1977. *Réseaux de commercialisation et approvisionnement urbain en Haiti. Nouvelles recherches sur l'approvisionnement des villes.* Talence: Travaux et documents de Géographie tropicale 28:3-46.

Glick, N. 1975. The formation of Haitian ethnic group. Unpublished Ph.D. dissertation. New York: Columbia University.

Gobard, H. 1974. *L'Aliénation linguistique. Analyse tétraglossique.* Paris: Flammarion.

Gordon, D. 1978. *The French language and national identity.* The Hague: Mouton.

Gouraige, G. 1974. *La diaspora d'haiti et l'afrique.* Ottawa: Editions Naaman.

Griggs, E. L. and C. H. Prator, eds. 1968. *Henry Christophe and Thomas Clarkson: A correspondence.* New York: Greenwood.

Groupe de recherche et d'expérimentation en alphabétisation de la zone de Côtes-de-Fer. 1976. *Document de recherche.* Port-au-Prince: Departement de l'Education Nationale a.o.

Haiti-Analyses et perspectives pour une nouvelle éducation. 1974. Port-au-Prince: UNESCO/BID.

Haiti: Economic memorandum. 1981. Washington, D.C.: World Bank.

Haiti-Mission d'assistance intégrée. 1972. Washington, D.C.: Organization of American States.

The Haiti pilot project, phase one. 1953. Paris: UNESCO.

Haitian Refugee Center v. Civiletti, 503. Supp, F. 442 (S.D. Fla. 1980).

Hansson, G. and M. Lundahl. 1981. The Rybczynski theorem under decreasing returns of scale (mimeo). Department of Economics, Lund.

Healy, K. 1982. Campesino cooperative networking in Bolivia: Initiatives from below. Paper presented at the Latin American Studies Association Meeting, Washington, .D.C

Heinl, R. D. and N. Heinl. 1978. *Written in blood: The story of the Haitian people, 1492-1971.* Boston: Houghton Mifflin.

Henry, F. 1982. Caribbean migration to Canada. *Caribbean Review* XI:38-41.

Hettne, B. 1982. Development theory and the Third World. *SAREC Report,* R2:1982, Stockholm.

Herskovits, M. 1937. *Life in a Haitian valley.* New York: Knopf.

Hicks, Norman. 1980. Economic growth and human resources. *World Bank Staff Working Paper* No. 408. Washington, D.C.: World Bank.

Hibbert, F. 1905. *Séna.* Port-au-Prince: Impr. de l'Abeille.

_____. 1923. *Les Simulacres.* Port-au-Prince: Impr. Chéraquit.

Himelhock, M. 1971. Frederick Douglass and Haiti's Mole St. Nicolas. *The Journal of Negro History* 56:161-180.

Hoffmann, L.-F. 1980. Les Etats-Unis et les Américains dans les lettres haïtiennes. *Etudes littéraires* 13:289-312.

Holly, D. *et al.* 1979. Dossier: L'emigration haitienne, un probleme national. *Collectif Paroles* 2:18-26.

Hyppolite, M. P. 1949. *Les Origines des variations du créole haïtien.* Port-au-Prince: Imprimerie de l'Etat.

_____. 1951. *Contes dramatiques haitiens.* Port-au-Prince: Imprimerie de l'Etat.

HS (Institut Haitien de Statistique). n.d. *Projection de la population totale d'Haiti de 1950-1986* (mimeo). Port-au-Prince: IHS.

ICA (Institut interaméricain des sciences agricoles). 1974. *Commercial activities in rural Haiti: A community-centered approach* (mimeo). Port-au-Prince: IICA. (Analysis and Diagnosis of the Internal Marketing System for Agricultural Produce in Haiti, Document No. 5).

Ince, B. A., ed. 1979. *Contemporary international relations of the Caribbean.* St. Augustine: Trinidad & Tobago.

Innocent, A. 1906. *Mimola.* Port-au-Prince: Editions du bicentenaire.

Institut Haitien de Statistiques. 1977. *Guide Economique de la Republique d'Haiti.* Republique d'Haiti, Port-au-Prince.

Inter-American Development Bank (IDB). 1979. *Opportunities for industrial development in Haiti.*

Inter-American Economic and Social Council. 1972. An analysis of the external technical assistance requirements for the development of Haiti (mimeo). Washington, D.C.: Organization of American States.

_____. 1973. Final proceedings of the CIAP Inter-Agency Advisory Group meeting on Haiti (mimeo). Washington, D.C.: Organization of American States.

_____. 1977a. Acte Final de la Troisième Réunion de la Commission Mixte pour l'Implantation des Programmes de Coopération Externe en Haiti (mimeo). Washington, D.C.: Organization of American States.

_____. 1977b. Document de Travail pour la Troisième Réunion de la Commission Mixte pour l'Implantation des Programmes de Coopération Externe avec Haiti (mimeo). Washington, D.C.: Organization of American States.

_____. 1978. Acte Final de la Quatrième Réunion de la Commission Mixte pour l'Implantation des Programmes de Coopération Externe en Haiti (mimeo). Washington, D.C.: Organization of American States.

International Bank for Reconstruction and Development (IBRD). 1981. *Haiti: Economic memorandum, recent economic, industrial and section developments,* report no. 3079-HA. Washington, D.C.: World Bank.

International Labor Office. 1976. *Haiti—Problemes de Main d'Oeuvre et d'Emploi.* Geneva.

International Monetary Fund. 1980. *Haiti—Recent economic developments.* Washington, D.C., June 12, 1980.

Jacxsens, Peter. 1976. Working paper on external cooperation with Haiti (mimeo). Prepared for the Second Meeting of Joint Commission on Haiti. Washington, D.C.: Organization of American States.

Jan, J. M. 1958. *Collecta,* Vol. III. Port-au-Prince: Imprimerie H. Deschamps.

_____. 1959. *Diocese du cap-haitien: Un siecle d'histoire, 1860-1960.* Port-au-Prince: Imprimerie Henri Deschamps.

Janvier, L. J. 1886. *Les constitutions d'haiti (1801-1885).* 2 volumes. Paris: C. Marpon et E. Flammarion.

Joachim, D. 1971. La bourgeoisie d'affaires en Haiti de l'Independence à l'Occupation américaine. *Nouvelle Optique,* 1.

JWK International Corporation. 1976. Agricultural policy studies in Haiti: coffee (mimeo). Damien: Départment de l'Agriculture, des Resources Naturelles et du Développement Rural.

Labelle, M. 1978. *Idéologie de couleur et classes sociales en Haiti.* Montreal: Presses Universitaires de Montréal.

Lacerte, R. K. 1981. Xenophobia and economic decline: The Haitian case, 1820-1843. *The Americas* 1981:500-515.

Lafont, R. 1982. Stereotypes dans l'enquête sociolinguistique. *La sociolinguistique dans les pays de langue romane,* ed. by N. Dittmar and B. Schlieben-Lange, 233-236. Tübingen: Gunter Narr.

La Gra, J. forthcoming. Notice "Vivres et marches." *Atlas d'Haiti.* Talence: CEGET-C.N.R.S./Université de Bordeaux III.

La Gra, J.; G. Fanfan; W. Charleston. 1975. Les marchés publics d'Haiti (mimeo). Institut Interaméricain des Sciences Agricoles (IISA), Port-au-Prince.

La Gra, J. and I. Lowenthal. 1975. Demographic aspects of the Fond-des-Nègres regional market. Port-au-Prince: unpublished manuscript.

Laguerre, M. 1977. Ticouloute and his kinsfolk: The study of a Haitian extended family. *The extended family in black societies,* ed. by D. B. Shimkin, *et al.,* 407-445. The Hague: Mouton.

Lambert, W. E. and G. R. Tucker. 1972. *Bilingual education of children: The St. Lambert Experiment.* Rowley, MA: Newbury House Publishers.

Larose, S. 1975. The Haitian *lakou*; land, family and ritual. Family and kinship in Middle America and the Caribbean. *Proceedings of the 14th seminar of the Committee on Family Research of the International Sociological Association,* Curaçao, September, 1975, ed. by A. F. Marks and R. A. Romer, 482-512. Curaçao: Institute of Higher Studies.

_____. 1976. *L'exploitation agricole en Haiti. Guide d'étude.* Fonds St. Jacques, Martinique/ Montreal: Université de Montreal.

Lavalin International Inc. 1980. *Projet de développement urbain en Haiti. Etude de factibilité.* Montreal.

Legerman, C. J. 1975. Observations on family and kinship organization in Haiti. *The Haitian potential: Research and resources of Haiti,* ed by V. Rubin and R. P. Schaedel, 17-22. New York: Teachers College Press.

Lefebvre, C. 1971. La sélection des codes linguistiques a la Martinique. Unpublished M.S. THESIS. Montreal: Université de Montréal.

Lemoine, M. 1981. *Sucre Amer: esclaves d'aujourd'hui dans les Caraibes.* Paris: Nouvelle Société des Editions Encre.

Lerner, D. 1958. *The passing of traditional society: Modernizing the Middle East.* New York: Free Press.

Levy, J. J. 1976. *Un village au bout du monde. Modernisation et structure villagoise aux Antilles française.* Montreal: Université de Montréal.

Lewis, G. K. 1972. *The Virgin Islands: A Caribbean Lilliput.* Evanston, IL: Northwestern University Press.

Lewis, V., ed. 1976. *Size, self-determination and international relations: The Caribbean.* Mona, Jamaica: Institute of Social and Economic Research.

Leyburn, J. G. 1966. *The Haitian people.* New Haven: Yale University Press.

Locher, U. 1975. The market systems of Port-au-Prince. *Working papers in Haitian society and culture.* New Haven: Antilles Research Center.

_____. 1977. Rural urban migration and the alleged demise of the extended family: The Haitian case in comparative perspective. Montreal: McGill University, Center for Developing Area Studies Working Paper no. 20.

_____. 1978. The fate of migrants in urban Haiti. Unpublished Ph.D. dissertation. New Haven: Yale University.

_____. 1981. Internal migration and development activities: A summary of problems and policy options. Santo Domingo: IICA (manuscript).

_____. Forthcoming. Migrations. *Atlas d'Haiti.* Bordeaux: INRS.

Lockheed, M. E.; D. T. Jamison; L. J. Lau. 1980. Farmer education and farm efficiency. *Education and Income,* ed. by T. King. World Bank Staff Working Paper No. 402. Washington, D.C.: World Bank.

Loewen, John. 1982. Summary of donor agency project support activities (mimeo). Port-au-Prince: USAID/Haiti.

Lofficial, F. 1979. *Créole/français: une fausse querelle?* Montreal: Collectif Paroles.

Logan, R. W. 1941. *The diplomatic relations of the United States with Haiti, 1776-1891.* Chapel Hill: University of North Carolina Press.

Louis, M. S. 1968. Introduction au problème du plaçage en Haiti. Les Cahiers du CHISS, *Revue Haitienne de Sciences Sociales* 2:36-54.

Lubin, M. 1968. Les Premiers rapports de la nation haitienne avec l'etranger. *Journal of Inter-American Studies* 10:277-305.

Lundahl, M. 1977. Les obstacles au changement technologique dans l'agriculture traditionelle haitienne. *Conjonction* 135.

Lundahl, M. 1979. *Peasants and poverty: a study of Haiti.* London.

_____. 1980. Population pressure and agrarian property rights in Haiti. *Statsventenskaplig Tidskrift,* 5.

_____. 1982a. Peasant strategies for dealing with increasing population pressure: the case of Haiti. *Development strategies and basic needs in Latin America: Challenges for the 1980s,* ed. by C. Brundenius and M. Lundahl. Boulder.

_____. 1982b. A note on Haitian migration to Cuba, 1980-1982. *Cuban Studies,* 12.

_____. Forthcoming. Peasants, government, and technological change in Haitian agriculture. *Public administration and rural development in the Caribbean,* ed. by H. F. Illy. München.

Lundahl, M. and R. Vargas. Forthcoming. Haitian migration to the Dominican Republic. *Man, land, and markets. Essays on the Haitian economy,* ed by M. Lundahl. London.

Magloire, A. 1908. *Etude sur le tempérament haitien.* Port-au-Prince: Imprimerie du Matin.

Maguire, B. 1979. *Bottom-up development in Haiti.* Rosslyn, VA: The Inter-American Foundation.

Maingot, A. P. 1982. Haiti as a sending society: Notes for an understanding of the problems. Unpublished manuscript, Florida International University.

Malval, Marc E. 1967. La Substitution de la prépondérance americaine à la prépondérance francaise en Haiti au début de XX3eme siecle. *Revue d'Histoire Moderne et Contemporaine* 14:321-355.

Manyoni, J. R. 1977. Legitimacy and illegitimacy: Misplaced polarities in Caribbean family studies. *Canadian Review of Sociology and Anthropology* 14:417-427.

Marcelin, F. 1901. *Thémistocle-Epaminondas Labasterre.* Paris: Olendorff.

Marshall, D. 1979. *The Haitian problem, illegal migration to the Bahamas.* Kingston, Jamaica: ISER.

Martinez, G. 1972. Vaudou et politique. *Nouvelle Optique* 6-7:197-200.

Mathelier, G. 1976. Pédagogie et bilinguisme en Haiti. *Revue de la Faculté d'ethnologie d'Haiti* 28.

Mathieu, R. 1980. Aspects of the rights and obligations of public agents. Unpublished proceedings of a colloquium held in October 1980. Port-au-Prince.

Meier, G. M., ed. 1976. *Leading issues in economic development.* New York: Third edition, 1964.

Menos, S. 1898. *L'Affaire Luders.* Port-au-Prince: Verrollot.

Merino Hernandez, F. 1973. *La immigracion Hatiana.* Santo-Domingo: Ediciones sargazo.

Métraux, A. *et al.* 1951. *Making a living in the Marbial Valley (Haiti).* Paris: UNESCO (Occasional Papers in Education).

_____. 1951. L'homme et la terre dans la vallée de Marbial. Port-au-Prince: UNESCO (mimeograph).

_____. 1972. *Voodoo in Haiti.* New York: Schocken Books.

Métraux, R. M. 1951. Kith and kin: A study of Creole social structure in Marbial. Unpublished Ph.D. dissertation. New York: Columbia University.

Millet, K. 1978. *Les paysans haitiens et l'occupation américaine d'Haiti (1915-1930* [sic]). Lasalle, P.Q., Canada: Collectif Paroles.

Millspaugh, A. C. 1931. *Haiti under American control, 1915-1930.* Boston: World Peace Foundation.

Mintz, S. 1960. Peasant markets. *Scientific American* 203:112-118, 120, 122.

_____. 1960. A tentative typology of eight Haitian market-places. *Revista de Ciencias Sociales* 4:15-57.

_____. 1961. Pratik: Haitian personal economic relationships. Proceedings of the 1960 annual Spring meeting of the American Ethnological Society, ed. by V. Garfield, 54-63. Seattle: A.E.S.

_____. 1971. Men, women and trade. *Comparative Studies in Society and History* 13:247-269.

_____. 1971. The Caribbean as a socio-cultural area. *Peoples and cultures of the Caribbean,* ed. by M. Horowitz, 17-46. New York: Natural History Press.

Mintz, S., ed. 1975. *Working papers in Haitian society and culture*. New Haven: Yale University, Antilles Research Program.

Moral, P. 1959. *L'économie haitienne*. Port-au-Prince: Imprimerie de l'Etat.

Morrisseau-Leroy, F. 1954. *Antigone en créole*. Pétion-ville.

Murray, G. F. 1977. The evolution of Haitian peasant land tenure: A case study in agrarian adaptation to population growth. Ph.D. dissertation, Columbia University.

_____. 1978a. *Hillside units, wage labor, and Haitian peasant land tenure: A strategy for the organization of erosion control*. Port-au-Prince: USAID.

_____. 1978b. *Informal subdivisions and land insecurity: An analysis of Haitian peasant land tenure*. Port-au-Prince: USAID.

_____. 1979. *Terraces, trees, and the Haitian peasant: An assessment of 25 years of erosion control in rural Haiti*. Port-au-Prince: USAID.

_____. 1981. *Peasant tree planting in Haiti: A social soundness analysis*. Port-au-Prince: USAID.

Murray, G. F. and M. D. Alvarez. 1973. *The marketing of beans in Haiti: An explanatory study* (mimeo). Port-au-Prince: Institut Interaméricain des Sciences Agricoles (IICA).

Murray, G. F. and M. D. Alvarez. 1975. Haitian bean circuits: Cropping and trading maneuvers among a cash-oriented peasantry. *Working papers in Haitian society and culture*. S. Mintz, ed. New Haven: Antilles Research Center.

Myrdal, G. 1957. *Rich lands and poor*. New York: Harper and Row.

Nicholls, D. 1970. Politics and religion in Haiti. *Canadian Journal of Political Science* III: 399-414.

_____. 1974. Ideology and political protest in Haiti, 1930-46. *Journal of Contemporary History* 9(4):3-26.

_____. 1978. Caste, class and color in Haiti. *Caribbean social relations,* ed. by C. Clarke. Liverpool: University of Liverpool, Centre for Latin American Studies.

_____. 1979. *From Dessalines to Duvalier: Race, colour and national independence in Haiti.* Cambridge: Cambridge University Press.

Nixon, J. 1973. Development Assistance Program Paper for Haiti (mimeo). Port-au-Prince: USAID/Haiti.

OEA-CEPAL-BID, Mission Conjointe OEA-CEPAL-BID en Haiti. 1962. *Rapport général présénte au Gouvernement de la République d'Haiti.* Washington, D.C.: OAS.

Office of Planning and Budgeting, Bureau for Program and Policy Coordination. 1981. *U.S. Overseas Loans and Grants and Assistance from International Organizations.* Washington, D.C.: U.S. Agency for International Development.

Orjala, P. 1970. A dialect survey of Haitian Creole. Unpublished dissertation, Hartford Seminary Foundation.

Paley, W. 1980. Haiti. The Times Literary Supplement, February 29.

_____. 1982. Power shift imperils Haiti's frail stability. *The Guardian,* January 13.

Palmer, E. C. 1976. Land use and landscape change along the Dominican-Haitian border. Unpublished Ph.D. dissertation, University of Florida, Gainesville.

Pfeiffer, J. E. 1977. *The emergence of society.* New York: McGraw Hill.

Pierre-Charles, G. 1967. *L'Economie haitienne et sa voie de développement.* Paris: Maisonneuve et Larose.

_____. 1973. *Radiographie d'une dictature.* Montreal: Nouvelle Optique.

Pierre, Y. F. 1975. Les Liens de parenté ruraux du migrant. Mémoire de Licence, Faculté d'Ethnologie. Port-au-Prince: Université d'Etat.

Portes, A. 1978a. Migration and underdevelopment. *Politics and Society* 8:1-48.

_____. 1978b. Toward a structural analysis of illegal (undocumented) immigration. *International Migration Review* 12:469-484.

_____. 1979. Illegal immigration and the international system: Lessons from recent legal Mexican immigrants to the United States. *Social Problems* 26:425-438.

_____. 1981. International labor migration and national development. Prepared for the Immigration and Refugee Workshop, Winspread, Wisconsin.

Portes, A. and J. Walton. 1982. *Labor, class and the international system.* New York: Academic Press.

Portes, A.; J. Clark; M. M. Lopez. 1982. Six years later, the process of incorporation of Cuban exiles in the United States: 1973-1979. *Cuban Studies* 11 (12) and 12 (1):1-24.

Pompilus, P. 1961. *La Langue française en Haiti.* Paris: Institut des Hautes Etudes de l'Amérique latine.

Population, Health, Nutrition Department. 1980. *Nutrition, basic needs, and growth.* Washington, D.C.: World Bank (restricted distribution).

Pressoir, C.-F. 1947. *Débats sur la créole et le folklore.* Port-au-Prince: Imprimerie de l'Etat.

Price, R. 1971. Studies of Caribbean family organization: problems and prospects. *Dédalo* 14:23-58.

Price-Mars, J. 1928. *Ainsi parla l'Oncle.* Paris: Imprimerie de Compiegne.

———. 1953. La République d'Haiti et la République Dominicaine. Port-au-Prince: Collection du Tricinquantenaire, 2 vols.

Quelques Problèmes relatifs à la réforme de l'education primaire en Haiti. 1982. Centre d'Education Permanente Internationale de l'Université René Descartes. Paris.

Recensement General. 1971. Institut Haitien de Statistique *Bulletin Trimestrial* 1:13-16.

Renaud, R. 1934. *Le Régime foncier en Haiti.* Paris: Leviton et Cie.

Ribeiro, D. 1971. *The Americans and civilization.* New York, Dutton.

Rotberg, R. 1971. *Haiti: The politics of squalor.* Boston: Houghton Mifflin Company.

Rotherberg, J. 1977. On the microeconomics of migration. *Internal migration: A comparative perspective,* ed. by A. Brown and E. Neuberger, 183-205. New York: Academic Press.

Rubenstein, H. 1980. Conjugal behavior and parental role flexibility in an Afro-Caribbean village. *Canadian Review of Sociology and Anthropology* 17:330-337.

Salinas, Paula. 1980. *Feasibility and design issues of a forestry project.* Port-au-Prince: USAID.

Schaedel, Richard. 1962. *An essay on the human resources of Haiti.* Washington, D.C.: Agency for International Development.

Schaedel, R. P. and V. Rubin, eds. 1969. *Research and resources of Haiti.* New York: Teachers College Press.

Schey, P. A. 1980. Black boat people founder on the shoals of United States policy. *Los Angeles Times,* June 29.

Schmidt, H. 1971. *The United States occupation of Haiti, 1915-1934.* New Brunswick: Rutgers University Press.

Schoelcher, V. 1843. *Colonies Etrangéres et Haiti.* Paris: Pagnerre, 2 vols.

Segal, A. 1975. Haiti. *Population policies in the Caribbean,* ed. by A. Segal, 177-215. Lexington, MA: D. C. Heath.

Shaw, P. 1975. *Migration theory and fact: A review and bibliography of current literature.* Philadelphia: Regional Science Research Institute.

Shue, H. 1980. *Basic rights: subsistence, affluence, and U.S. foreign policy.* Princeton, NJ: Princeton University Press.

Silvain, N. 1927. *Revue indigène,* July 1927, p. 5.

Simpson, E. 1942. Sexual and familial institutions in northern Haiti. *American Anthropologist* 44:655-74.

Simpson, George Eaton. 1940. Haitian peasant economy. *Journal of Negro History* 5:489-519.

Sinha, S. P. 1967. *New nations and the law of nations.* Leyden: A. W. Sijthoff.

Smith, A. 1976. *An inquiry into the nature and causes of the wealth of nations.* Oxford: Clarendon Press.

Smith, R. T. 1978. The family and the modern world system: some observations from the Caribbean. *The Journal of Family History* 3:337-360.

Smith, Ronald. 1980. *The potential of charcoal plantations for Haiti.* Port-au-Prince: USAID.

Smucker, Glenn R. 1981. *Trees and charcoal in Haitian peasant economy: A feasibility study of reforestation.* Port-au-Prince: USAID.

Stepick, A. 1982. Haitian refugees in the United States. *Minority rights Group Report* No. 52.

_____. 19 . Haitian boat people: Both economic and political refugees. *Law and Contemporary Problems* 45.

Stone, N. 1980. The many tragedies of Haiti. *The Times Literary Supplement,* February 15.

Swain, M. 1981. Immersion education: applicability for nonvernacular teaching to vernacular speakers. *Studies in second language acquisition* 4:1-17.

Sylvain, J. n.d. Rapport sur quelques manifestations et causes de la decadence à Marbial. Unpublished manuscript.

Terlonge, H. 1940. *Le Temps,* 3 April.

Todaro, M. 1969. A model of labor migration and urban unemployment in less developed countries. *American Economic Review* 59:135-148.

_____. 1976. *International migration in developing countries.* Geneva: International Labor Organization.

Torres, D. 1979. *Production et commercialisation de la racine de vétiver.* Port-au-Prince: Département de l'Agriculture, des Resources Naturelles et du Développement Rural. Service National de Commercialisation Agricole (SENACA).

Tuchman, B. 1978. *A distant mirror: The calamitous 14th century.* New York: Ballantine Books.

Turnier, A. 1955. *Les Etats-Unis et le marché haitien.* Montréal.

_____. 1982. *Avec Mérisier Jeannis.* Port-au-Prince: the author.

UN ECLA. 1981. Economic survey of Latin America 1980, preliminary survey. E/CEPAL/G. 1153.

UNESCO. 1953. The use of vernacular languages in education: Monographs on fundamental education, No. 8. Paris: UNESCO.

United Nations Convention Relating to the Status of Refugees, July 28, 1951, 189 U.N.T.S. 150.

United Nations Industrial Development Organization. 1979. La Soustraitance Internationale en Haiti, project Ha 1-77-801.

Underwood, Frances W. 1964. Land and its manipulation among the Haitian peasantry. *Explorations in Cultural Anthropology,* Ward Goodenough, ed., pp. 469-482. New York: McGraw-Hill.

_____. 1970. The marketing system in peasant Haiti. *Papers in Caribbean Anthropology,* S. Mintz, ed. New Haven: Human Relations Area File.

Valdman, A. 1975. *Certains aspects sociolinguistics des parlers créole français.* Fonds St. Jacques, Martinique/Montreal: Université de Montréal.

_____. 1978. *Le Créole: Structure, status, et origine.* Paris: Klinksieck.

_____. 1982. Educational reform and the instrumentalization of the vernacular in Haiti. *Issues in international bilingual education,* ed. by B. Hartford, A. Valdman, and C. R. Foster, 139-70. New York: Plenum Press.

_____. 1983. The linguistic situation of Haiti, this volume, p. 77.

Verna, P. 1969. *Petion y Bolívar: cuarenta años, (1790-1830) de relaciones haitiano-Venezolanas.* Caracas: Imprenta Nacional.

Vernet, P. 1980. *Techniques d'écriture du créole haitien.* Port-au-Prince: Centre de linguistique appliquée de Port-au-Prince.

Vilgrain, J. n.d. *Les fluctuations cycliques de l'économie haitienne: Etude économétrique* (mimeo). Port-au-Prince: Institut Haitien de Statistique.

Voltaire, Karl. 1979. Charcoal in Haiti. Port-au-Prince: USAID.

Weinstein, B. and A. Segal. 1984. *Haiti: Political failures, cultural successes.* New York: Praeger (Hoover Institution Series: Politics in Latin America).

Williams, E. 1944. *Capitalism and slavery.* New York: Capricorn Books.

Williams, S. J.; N. Murthy; G. Berggren. 1975. Conjugal unions among rural Haitian women. *Journal of Marriage and the Family* 34:1022-1031.

Wolfe, A. 1977. *The limits of legitimacy: Political contradictions of late capitalism.* New York: Free Press.

Wood, C. 1982. Equilibrium and historical-structural perspective on migration. *International Migration Review* XVI:298-319.

World Bank. 1976. *Current economic position and prospects for Haiti.* Washington, D.C.: World Bank.

_____. 1978. *Current economic position and prospects for Haiti,* report no. 2165-HA.

_____. 1979. *Haiti: Urban sector survey,* report no. 2152-HA.

_____. 1980. *World Bank atlas, population, per capital product and growth rates.*

_____. 1981. *Current economic position,* Vol. II.

_____. 1981a. *Haiti: Country data.*

_____. 1981a. *Memorandum on the Haitian economy.* Washington, D.C.: World Bank.

_____. 1981b. *Memorandum on the Haitian economy,* report no. 3444-HA.

_____. 1981b. *World development report 1981.* New York: World Bank.

World Population 1979. 1980. Washington, D.C.: Bureau of the Census.

Zuvekas, C., Jr. 1978. *Agricultural development in Haiti. An assessment of sector problems, policies, and prospects under conditions of severe soil erosion* (mimeo). Washington, D.C.: US/AID.

INDEX